CAN THE SUBALTERN SPEAK ?

CAN THE SUBALTERN

REFLECTIONS ON THE HISTORY OF AN IDEA

SPEAK?

EDITED BY ROSALIND C. MORRIS

COLUMBIA UNIVERSITY PRESS

New York

COLUMBIA UNIVERSITY PRESS
Publishers Since 1893
New York   Chichester, West Sussex

Library of Congress Cataloging-in-Publication Data

Can the subaltern speak? reflections on the history of an idea /
edited by Rosalind C. Morris
p. cm.
Includes bibliographical references and index.
ISBN 978-0-231-14384-4 (cloth: alk. paper) —
ISBN 978-0-231-14385-1 (pbk.: alk. paper) —
ISBN 978-0-231-51285-5 (e-book)
1. Spivak, Gayatri Chakravorty. Can the subaltern speak.
2. Spivak, Gayatri Chakravorty—Criticism and interpretation.
3. Postcolonialism. 4. Feminist theory. I. Morris, Rosalind C.
II. Spivak, Gayatri Chakravorty. Can the subaltern speak. I. Title.

JV51.C28   2010
325'.3—DC22
2009031453

Casebound editions of Columbia University Press books are
printed on permanent and durable acid-free paper.

This book is printed on paper with recycled content.

Printed in the United States of America

c 10 9 8 7 6 5 4 3 2 1
p 10 9 8 7 6 5 4 3 2 1

IN MEMORY OF
Sivani Chakravorty

CONTENTS

ACKNOWLEDGMENTS

This book is indebted to many people. It emerged from a conference bearing the same title as the book, which was generously supported by Columbia University's Office of the Provost, then occupied by Jonathan Cole. That conference was hosted by Columbia's Institute for Research on Women and Gender, whose staff members, Page Jackson and Amalia Zarranz, worked tirelessly to make my ambitions a reality (I was then its director). Many colleagues and intellectual fellow travelers attended the conference, and their questions informed the final versions of many of the essays here as well as the volume as a whole. I am grateful to all of them.

My thanks go to Jennifer Crewe and Susan Pensak at Columbia University Press for their generous editorial labor, and to those other editors who were involved in the journal or book projects that initially published some portions of some of these essays. Michèle Barrett's essay, "Subalterns at War: First World War Colonial Forces and the Politics of the Imperial War Graves Commission," though written for this conference, was first published in *Interventions* 93.3 (2007) and appears by permission of the journal. Parts of Pheng Cheah's essay, "Biopower and the New International Division of Reproductive Labor," first appeared in his book, *Inhuman Conditions: On Cosmopolitanism and Human Rights* (2006) and are reproduced here by permission of Harvard University Press. Gayatri Chakravorty Spivak's essays appeared in Cary Nelson and Lawrence Grossberg, eds., *Marxism and the Interpretation of Cultures* (1988) and *A Critique of Postcolonial Reason: Toward a History of the Vanishing Present* (1999) and are included here with her permission.

REFERENCE TO SPIVAK'S ORIGINAL ESSAY, "Can the Subaltern Speak?" and to the "History" chapter of *A Critique of Postcolonial Reason* in which it is both reprised and revised appear in both parenthetical and footnoted references. To aid the reader, these are accompanied by a second set of references (immediately following the first, but separated by a /) to those texts, as they appear in the present volume.

CAN THE SUBALTERN SPEAK ?

Rosalind C. Morris

INTRODUCTION

Can the Subaltern Speak? Reflections on the History of an Idea began as a conference, hosted by the Institute for Research on Women and Gender, at Columbia University. The title was a seductive simplification, marking the spot where, it was hoped, several debates and discourses might converge in the consciousness of their debt to an extraordinary essay, "Can the Subaltern Speak?" penned by Gayatri Chakravorty Spivak some twenty years previously. We might have subtitled the conference, or this volume, something as infelicitously expansive as Reflections on the history of some ideas about the s/Subject of history, the international division of labor, the contemporary relevance of Marxism, deconstruction, Asia, Europe, gender, and capitalism's worlding of the world. Though the fulsome description would perhaps have provided a better index of the scope and ambition of the original essay, it too would have been a mere placeholder for the many difficult questions that unfold out of Spivak's essay.

The conference was not occasioned by a retirement; it marked no (anticipated) diminution in the pace or output of Spivak's continued writing. Neither of these possibilities occurred to me when organizing the event. It was, rather, prompted by the felt need to respond to the more intellectually ambiguous demand of an institutional anniversary which simultaneously remarked 250 years of Columbia's University's operation and 20 years since women were admitted to Columbia College. It seemed appropriate to turn to Spivak's essay in this context—not out of any misplaced overidentification with third world women on the part of Western academic feminists, but, rather, in an effort to grasp, once again, the full implications of her insistent and uncompromising introduction of the questions of gender and sexual difference into the critique of radical discourse in the universities of the West and in subaltern studies in India and South Asia.

Our project was, I hope and believe, innocent of nostalgia. Few interventions have retained with such tenacity the radicality or the relevance that Spivak's essay continues to possess today. It has been cited, invoked, imitated, summarized, analyzed, and critiqued. It has been revered, reviled, misread, and misappropriated—in its original and its abridged forms, in English and in translation. And it has, of course, been revisited by Spivak herself, in the expansive "History" chapter of *A Critique of Postcolonial Reason: Toward a History of the Vanishing Present.*

One often encounters inadvertent testimonies to the revolutionary quality of the thought contained in "Can the Subaltern Speak?" Occasionally, these run to the comic, though the pathos of the *differend* (the mutual untranslatability of discourse), which appears as a merely lexical matter, also reveals something about the particular difficulty of writing and reading gender into historical analysis. Consider, for example, a recent translation of the title into Russian (within a translation of a more recent essay on terror). In the initial draft the translator rendered in Russian what, when translated back into English, might have read "Can Junior Officers Speak?"[1] The "woman," as Spivak tells us, inevitably "is doubly in shadow."

Problems of translation are less analogues than metonyms for the problems of reading that "Can the Subaltern Speak?" simultaneously performs, thematizes, and theorizes. But if we are stretched to the limits of our intellectual capacity in the act of reading Spivak's writing on reading the silences of history—there are some categorically untenable misreadings that need to be dispatched before anything further can be said. Among them: those that understand the silence of the subaltern as a simple absence in the record—to be supplemented and transcended by the work of information retrieval (Spivak endorses such retrieval, but she understands it to be a matter distinct from the question of theorizing the impossibility of subaltern speech as audible and legible predication); those that discern in the essay a constitutive opposition between practice and theory, variously attributing to Spivak's own intervention an advocacy for one or the other (she emphatically rejects that binarity); those that claim she has rendered the Indian case representative of the third world (she insists on the choice of India as an accident of personal history and as a nonexemplary instance in which, nonetheless, global processes can be seen to generate their effects); and those, in the most egregious misreadings, that discern in the text a nativist apologia for widow burning on the grounds of its authentic ritual status! (it is a position that she herself terms a "parody of the nostalgia for lost origins" [297/269]).

Perhaps the most quoted and misquoted passage from the text, a sentence conceived as such, *as a grammatical form*, is that in which Spivak writes, "White men are saving brown women from brown men." The sentence appears, in the "spirit" of Freud, but, significantly, in answer to two questions. This doubleness of the question follows on the doubly shadowed status of the woman previously mentioned. Spivak writes—and we note the plural: "When confronted with the questions, Can the subaltern speak? And can the subaltern (as woman) speak? we will be doubly open to the dangers run by Freud's discourse." What were those dangers? They were the dangers of a "reaction-formation to an initial and continuing desire to give the hysteric a voice" (296/268).

For Spivak, the same ideological formation informs the desire to give a voice to the hysteric as that which would speak for the subaltern. The one produces the narrative of the "daughter's seduction" to explain a certain silence or muteness of the pathological woman, the other offers the "monolithic 'third world woman'" as the tautological name of a need to be spoken for. In both cases the "masculine-imperialist" ideology can be said to produce the need for a masculine-imperialist rescue mission. This circuitry obstructs the alternative histories that might have been written—not as the disclosures of a final truth, but as the assemblages of utterances and interpretations that might have emerged from a different location, namely, the place of the subaltern woman. These utterances would not, as she herself remarks, have escaped ideology; they would not have been the truth of the women who uttered them. But they would have made visible the unstable claims on truth that the ideology of masculine imperialism offered in its place. The importance of reading the statement *as such* and of thereby reflecting upon the act of reading lies in its displacement of the question of what a subaltern woman really said or wanted to say (and hence what could be said on her behalf) and its consequent emphasis on the question of audibility and legibility. It enables an investigation of what conditions obtrude to mute the speech of the subaltern woman, to render her speech and her speech acts illegible to those who occupy the space produced by patriarchal complicity (whether of imperialism or globalization), namely the state.

Had Spivak conceived of the ideological question only in terms of an earlier Marxism, as one of capitalist imperialism and bourgeois nationalism or international socialism, the question might not have been double. The woman, or more specifically, the subaltern as woman, is a figure in whom the question of ideology—as the production of subjects in whom desire and interest are never entirely symmetrical or mutually reinforcing—splits wide open. This, then, is the incitement to Spivak's explosive historical excavation of two impossible "suicides"—that which resides in the mutilated accounts of something called *sati*, in the process of Britain's abolition of widow sacrifice in India, and that which lurks in the half-remembered tale of a woman, Bhubaneswari Bhaduri, who took her life in 1926, apparently after losing heart in the task of political assassination to which she had promised herself. I say apparently because, in the first version of the essay, Spivak does not finally decide the question of motivations. She reads them, but the text of what happened that day, when a young woman, menstruating, took her own life, remains somewhat oblique for the reader who has not systematically unlearned the suspicions that ideology attaches to almost any young woman's suicide. Perhaps most readers have wondered "Are there other readings?" But if this intractable doubt refuses to leave us, at the end, it is at least partly because the possibility of another reading has been forcefully opened to us by Spivak's text. And we remain transfixed by the enigma of Bhubaneswari.

One concedes that the pyromaniac metaphor may be in bad taste, in this context. Nonetheless, the story of Bhubaneswari flares up at the end of the essay, and nearly overwhelms all that has gone before. It is not that the story stands as an example—to be emulated or repudiated. It is, rather, that the difficulty of comprehending what might have occurred in the act of suicide confronts us, forcing us to go back, to "unlearn" with Spivak the normative ideals of piety and excess with which the third world woman has come to be associated in the interlaced ideological formations of both West and East.

By now, the reading is widely familiar. It commences with a rigorous interrogation of those Western writers who, at the time of Spivak's first writing on subalternity, were endeavoring to produce a radical critique of the (presumptively) Western s/Subject: Gilles Deleuze and Michel Foucault. It is at the point where, in Deleuze's and Foucault's otherwise brilliant claims to have decentered the subject of theory (and of history, in its Hegelian conception), Spivak discerns its secret reconsolidation, precisely through Deleuze's and Foucault's double incapacity to recognize, on the one hand, the nonuniversality of the Western position and, on the other, the constitutive place of gender in the formation of the subject—as the subject of language not only in the grammatical sense but in the sense of having a voice that can access power. The argument on subalternity takes place here, Spivak's text breaking away from its earlier discourse on Western theory (a discourse shaped by the deconstructionist imperative to perform critique from within, reading as unraveling the weave of the dominant text), first through an interrogation of the historical record and then through the insertion of a fragmentary and speculative account of the suicide of Bhubaneswari Bhaduri. A schematic diagram of the argument's concluding movements might run as follows: An imperial tradition that rendered widow sacrifice as the sign of a cultural failure subsequently outlawed it and misidentified it as *sati* (while misspelling it as *suttee*). This imperial tradition legitimated itself as a rule of law and resignified a ritual—a performatively compulsive discourse—as a crime (and not merely as superstition), while discerning in it the evidence of a retrograde patriarchy. Even contemporary commentators realized, however, that the prevalence of *sati* was historically recent and theologically illegitimate.

As Spivak's tentative excavation of the scriptural treatises and philosophical commentaries on *sati* (good wife) and widow sacrifice in Bengal point out, widow sacrifice, when practiced, tended to be most prevalent in those areas where women could inherit their husband's property (in the absence of male heirs). Hence the rite that represented for colonial powers the most transparent evidence of an absolute negation of female agency was awkwardly situated at a place where a woman might, by law, have at least had some economic power (though her assets would have been managed for her). It would be easy to conclude, as Marx had done, in his reading of Henry Sumner Maine, that the ideological justification for widow sacrifice rested in an economic jealousy of her rights to the deceased husband's property. Marx had chastised Maine for an unforgivable naïveté when he had attributed to the Brahman priests a "purely professional dislike to her enjoyment of property."[2] He was even more derisive when Maine attempted to argue, in a manner that reproduces precisely the *logic* of white men saving brown women from brown men (a logic Spivak writes into a sentence that she produces as a homology of Freud's statement), that only the Church had saved women from the deterioration of their status after the fall of the Roman Empire. The prohibition on divorce, Marx noted, could hardly be construed as a protection of the woman's freedom. But, in the schematic notations that filled his *Ethnological Notebooks*, he generally approved of Maine's conclusion that "the ancient . . . rule of the civil law, which *made her tenant for life*, could not *be got rid of*, but it was combated by the modern institution which made it her duty to devote herself to a frightful death."[3]

Spivak confirms the economic analysis, as have many commentators, but she repudiates the simple ideological reading, which would have made the woman a mere victim of false consciousness. Her reading of the *Dharmaśāstra* teaches her and us that *suicide*—a term that she shows does not mean self-knowing self-killing so much as it means the enactment of a recognition of nonidentity—is rarely sanctioned and only for men. Scripture provides no basis for its normativization, especially for women, whose proper duty is seen in that context as a static grieving commemoration of the husband. "Widow sacrifice" is therefore, Spivak insists, a mark of excess. Moreover, this excess is the only form in which something like woman's agency can be apprehended—as a self-negating possibility. The entire ideological formation seems designed to foreclose the possibility of a woman acceding to the position from which she could actually speak—as a political subject.

It would seem that one cannot retrieve anything but the image of excess and the impossibility of full subjectivity from the discourse on *sati*. There is no place for the woman outside her relation to the marriage contract, no agency that is not excess. The story of Bhubaneswari is heartbreakingly fascinating because it expresses, to such an extraordinary degree, an agency ("unemphatic and ad hoc" in Spivak's idiom) that consists in *resisting misreading*. By Spivak's account, the young woman, who decides against committing an act of political violence, kills herself to safeguard the group. At the time, her membership in the struggle for independence was unknown. Bhubaneswari did nothing to reveal this membership, perhaps out of solidarity with her colleagues, but she at least foreclosed the interpretation that would have imagined her death to be an act of shame for an illegitimate pregnancy. Menstruation was proof of that. Her (young) woman's body offered the signs by which she could resist being reduced to the mere effect of the patriarchal discourse—but only from within the same system. This is why Spivak refers to the suicide in terms of a "trace-structure," what she describes in such powerful shorthand in *A Critique of Postcolonial Reason* as "effacement in disclosure" (310). Within that system the "suicide" remains enigmatic, indecipherable, though not completely invisible. So it is with a certain bitterness that Spivak recounts the various interpretations to which Bhubaneswari's death has been subjected—interpretations that tend to presume a romantic crisis, interpretations that even the most astute feminist reader must have allowed herself to ponder, at least momentarily, if only in shame. Unlearning ideology is never an easy task.

One may wonder, without ceding any admiration for Spivak's text, whether the absolute termination of Bhubaneswari's life doesn't provide too literal a form for the problematic of the general muting that occurs at the place where two mutually untranslatable discourses collide. It is perhaps important to recognize that the story was not offered as a model or even as an example; it was offered as a text—a very moving one—to be read. In reading this text, Spivak showed us how and to what extent historical circumstances and ideological structures conspire to efface the possibility of being heard (something related to but not identical to silence) for those who are variously located as the others of imperial masculinity and the state. And she has admitted, as she must, that the middle-class woman seeking political independence is not in the same position as the unemployed subproletariat of the urban slums, the sweatshop worker, or the child prostitute forced into sexual labor by a depleted environment and diminishing agricultural returns. But this may only prove the point that true subalternity remains in shadow.

Why does this matter now? Much has changed since the initial formulation of "Can the Subaltern Speak?" To name only the most obvious of the epochal transformations to which we have all been subject: the demise of state socialism in the Soviet Union; the globalization of capital; the resurgence of masculinist religious ideologies as reaction formations to the desire for liberation from the false (because not realized) secularity of European capital;[4] and the intensification of global ecological crisis, felt most intensely in the rural peripheries of the global South. Sometime between the planning of the conference from which this volume issued and its publication, the United States commenced a war in Afghanistan and Iraq, ostensibly to pursue the perpetrators of the 9/11 attacks in New York City—the scene of the conference. Among the most potent ideological weapons in the war on terror has been the claim that radical Islam, the putative incubator of terror and the ideological center of opposition to the U.S., is relatively oppressive to women. The emancipation of women once again becomes the legitimating discourse for imperial agendas. And Spivak's sentence returns to condense and expose the many acts and statements by which an ideology is operating. Even in the aftermath of the Bush administration's ignominious departure from power and the rise of a new liberal agenda in the United States under President Obama in 2009, the war in and against Afghanistan has been construed as a morally necessary war, one of whose critical motivating factors is the defense of Afghan women against local patriarchy.

In a world where the international division of labor is so often organized to permit the effective exploitation of women and girl children in the urban and rural peripheries (in sweatshops, factories, and brothels), the imperial project is, we must admit, mainly interested in liberating women for labor, which is to say, surplus value extraction. Human rights have often provided the alibi for that process. So we can be as cautious now of the promise for women's salvation being proffered through war and imperial domination as when Britain made the abolition of *suttee* the mask and means of its own imperialism. This does not mean that we cannot want women, and others, everywhere, to be free of the constraints that inhibit their access to and capacity to speak from a position of subjectivity, representation, economic liberty, and political agency. Nor does it imply a relativist defense of the masculinist ideologies that operate everywhere under the cover of "culture."

And it certainly does not mean that the task of progressive politics can be imagined as "giving a voice" to subalterns.

Subalternity is not that which could, if given a ventriloquist, speak the truth of its oppression or disclose the plenitude of its being. The hundreds of shelves of well-intentioned books claiming to speak for or give voice to the subaltern cannot ultimately escape the problem of translation in its full sense. Subalternity is less an identity than what we might call a predicament, but this is true in very odd sense. For, in Spivak's definition, it is the structured place from which the capacity to access power is radically obstructed. To the extent that anyone escapes the muting of subalternity, she ceases being a subaltern. Spivak says this is to be desired. And who could disagree? There is neither authenticity nor virtue in the position of the oppressed. There is simply (or not so simply) oppression. Even so, we are moved to wonder, in this context, what burden this places on memory work in the aftermath of education. What kind of representation becomes available to the one who, having partially escaped the silence of subalternity, is nonetheless possessed by the consciousness of having been obstructed, contained, or simply misread for so much of her life? Is there any alternative to either the positivist euphoria that would claim to have recovered the truth of her past or the conflation of historiography with therapeutic adaptation by which ideology finally makes the silence of subalternity seem normal?

Today in the halls of the academy it is possible to discern a certain displacement of the critique of power and class, and hence of history, by the cultural analysis of memory. If the latter offers itself as an alternative to the positivism of empiricist historiography, and as a critique of the teleologies implicit in so much Marxist theory, it nonetheless tends to surrender utopianism only to embrace nostalgia. Nostalgia, in this sense, is but the inverse of utopianism, a utopianism without futurity. Ironically, this nostalgia often bears a secret valorization and hypostatization of subalternity as an identity—to be recalled, renarrated, reclaimed, and revalidated. We need to resist the narcissism implicit in this gesture—which ultimately demands a whole image as the mirror of ourselves, not merely as the basis for misrecognition (and hence our own subject formation) but also as the alibi for a politics that imagines the project of emancipation to be over. A quick survey of the contemporary social landscape demands the recognition that it is not.

THIS VOLUME DOES NOT PRETEND to account for all of the social-theoretical itineraries enabled by "Can the Subaltern Speak?" nor all those that sought to defend institutional knowledges against its provocations. But it may be helpful to review, in a very schematic manner, the contours of its future history. There are, by now, a few book-length studies of Spivak's work and thought. There are, in addition, numerous volumes in which her theorization of subalternity as gendered muting, and her argument for an ethical kind of reading attentive to the aporetic structure of "knowing" in the encounter with the other, are attended to in individual chapters.[5]

In general, the two most receptive fields to her work have been South Asian history and feminist studies. We might begin, in this effort at a genealogy of future history, with prehistory. In 1986, David Hardiman reported on the second subaltern studies conference in Calcutta for the *Economic and Political Weekly*. There, he remarked, approvingly, Spivak's argument that "the colonial state often viewed the Indian people as an undifferentiated native 'other.' [Spivak's] paper showed this well, revealing how the body became a space of politics."[6] One can hear, in his account, the echo of "Can the Subaltern Speak?" which had already been delivered as a public lecture but not yet published in the Nelson and Grossberg volume. Hardiman continued by attributing to Spivak a rebuke to subaltern studies, in the form of a definition with the force of a not yet realized norm: "'Subaltern Studies' [Spivak asserted] does not deal only with subaltern consciousness and action; it is just as important to see how the subaltern are fixed in their subalternity by the elites."[7] And he remarked her call for the deployment of deconstructionist reading practices in the service of this more reflective project. The acuity of Hardiman's observation can be seen, in retrospect, by assessing the changes in the subaltern studies group and its theory, and in the disciplines adjacent to it, following the essay's publication.

Leela Gandhi revealingly opens her capacious summary of postcolonial theory with Gayatri Spivak, invoking the date of her lecture (1985) rather than the publication of the essay. In this context she notes, despite the range and profundity of the questions emanating from "Can the Subaltern Speak?" that the essay and its provocations solicited more response from postcolonial studies than any other field. To a large degree the rest of her book is devoted to an unfolding of that response—thought it takes her through territory dominated by other postcolonial theorists, from Edward Said and Homi Bhabha to Partha Chatterjee and Dipesh Chakrabarty.[8] Gandhi's book confirms Gyan Prakash's 1994 tracking of the arrival of subaltern studies into the field of South Asian historiography, at least in the United States, as a kind of model for postcolonial criticism (albeit as an "ambivalent practice, perched between traditional historiography and its failures, within the folds of dominant discourse and seeking to articulate its pregnant silence"). This movement beyond the object-determined field of subaltern studies, he suggests, was made possible partly by virtue of the rapprochement between Marxism and poststructuralism that it performed—largely under Spivak's influence.[9]

A case in point would be the work of Dipesh Chakrabarty, whose book, *Provincializing Europe,* provides a useful aperture onto the mechanism of that infiltration, that generalization of the analysis of subalternity beyond the field of subaltern studies. Indeed, *Provincializing Europe* owes much to Spivak's formulation of the subaltern, though it is not heavily citationally dependent on her essay. This debt—which is exclusive of neither the debt owed to others in the collective nor that to the philosophical architect of deconstructionism, Jacques Derrida—saturates the book at a methodological level. That is to say, despite the contingent overlap in their objects of study, it is the epistemological and historiographic implications of Spivak's essay that inform Chakrabarty's disquisition. Consider, for example, his argument that the forms of knowledge production institutionalized in the university have been constitutively incapable of registering the antimodern except as the antecedent to a teleologically inevitable modernity: "the antihistorical, antimodern subject, therefore, cannot speak as 'theory' within the knowledge procedures of the university even when these knowledge procedures acknowledge and 'document' its existence." He continues, "Much like Spivak's subaltern . . . it can only be spoken for and spoken of in the transition narrative, which will always ultimately privilege the modern, (that is, 'Europe')."[10]

The nonexclusivity of Chakrabarty's debt is related to the fact that it is sometimes difficult to discern the relative force of Spivak's interventions when read in relation to the influence of the group's other luminaries, Ranajit Guha and Partha Chatterjee foremost among them. One of the effects of that collective's writings, and its meticulous recuperation of Antonio Gramsci's thought, was the discernment and analysis of subalternity outside South Asia. Florence Mallon's account of subaltern studies' impact upon Latin American studies illuminates the history of this impact, which would be registered most visibly in the publication of the voluminous collection edited by Ileana Rodríguez, *The Latin American Subaltern Studies Reader.*[11] But one sees it elsewhere, with accounts of oppressed communities in places as remote from each other (and as far from the Indian experience of British imperialism) as Algeria and Afghanistan, Uzbekistan and Uruguay, Turkey and Thailand, Mexico and Morocco, Zimbabwe and Zanzibar.

Of course, the crucial marker, and the orienting question, of Spivak's particular intervention within the theorization of subalternity revolves around the question of gender. This is why, as I said earlier, one of the most receptive disciplines to "Can the Subaltern Speak?" beyond South Asian history, was gender studies. As with the uptake of the essay in history outside of South Asian history, the initial impetus was a methodological and philosophical one. To take but one example, Judith Butler opens her landmark text, *Bodies That Matter,* with an epigraph from an interview of Spivak by Ellen Rooney and continues to invoke Spivak's program of reading (a deconstructionism that does not negate the utility of what it deconstructs) as the basis for her own effort to radically rethink the concept of sexual difference.[12] Butler's enormously influential writings—addressed initially to a queer problematic (as seen from within feminism) and increasingly expanding to encompass the subject of politics in general and, finally, the supplementation of politics by ethics—constitute a significant pathway for Spivak's writings' movement out of the regionalist container in which some of her more acerbic Eurocentric critics would like to have kept it.[13] Nonetheless, there have been many others. Indeed, there are few readers in feminist studies that do not remark "Can the Subaltern Speak?" as an episteme-changing text, a landmark in the necessary displacement of second-wave feminism and a still-to-be actualized call for the transformation of disciplinary feminism.

The direction pursued by Butler nonetheless runs along a path that diverges considerably from that traveled by so many other feminist scholars under the influence of a revisionist historiography and a desire for the retrieval of women's experience. One gets a sense of that other direction in Shetty's and Bellamy's response to "Can the Subaltern Speak?" which takes the essay as an incitement to rethink not only historiographical method but the archive per se. Writing in *Diacritics,* they describe their purpose as "demonstrate[ing] just how crucial the concept of an 'archive'—perhaps even a 'postcolonial archive'—is for a more sympathetic understanding of Spivak's now notorious 'silencing' of the subaltern woman." They then continue with the following question, derived from a reading of Spivak's essay: "Can we approach the gendered subaltern more productively if our project is to recover not 'lost voices' but rather lost texts?"[14] If this very significant question tends to invite the reader to fantasize "the text" as the satisfying substitute—an accessible and bound object behind which the speaking subject's disappearance loses its status as problem—it nonetheless offers an alternative to the kind of longing for authenticity that interpretive social science often sought in Spivak's essay.

It is well, in this context, to recall that Spivak's essay entered the American academy at approximately the same time as there occurred, in the interpretive social sciences, a new and powerful drive to discern and articulate something that was variously termed *resistance, unconscious resistance,* and, sometimes, the *agency of the oppressed*.[15] This drive expressed, on the one hand, an intuition of the collapse of Soviet socialism (which, when it occurred, was nonetheless experienced as a crisis for left intellectuals), but, more generally, it expressed an exhaustion with or turning away from more overtly organized oppositional politics and the questions of class consciousness or class formation that had dominated the radical discourse of the previous two decades. It was, of course, the period of Ronald Reagan and Margaret Thatcher and thus of the near defeat of organized labor within both the U.S. and Britain, the dispute with air traffic controllers in the former and coal miners in the latter providing the ground for the state's attack against organized labor on behalf of capital. In this milieu, under the growing influence of a Gramsci revival and spurred by what appeared to many to be a confluence between Gramsci's and Michel Foucault's thought, when alternative forms of political possibility and intellectuals' participation in it were being sought, interpretive social scientists identified forms of practice, habits of being, ethical dispositions, temporalities of laboring, and so forth, which Spivak would term "defective for capitalism," but often read those forms as traces of an agency that, though unconscious (of its interests or bases in the contradictions of economic organization), could nonetheless be read as evidence of something like nonconformism. This is not the place to examine the complexities and contradictions of a theory of agency as unconscious. It must suffice here to note that such analysis sometimes foundered on the incapacity to differentiate between the ontic realm's incommensurability with the conceptuality from within which it is represented,[16] the abrasive but socially mediated presence that interrupts or obtrudes upon rationalism's ambitions,[17] and the intentionalized nonconformity to dominant and/or normative structures that, though more insurgent than oppositional, can be seen to comprise an intuition for critical politics. It was often coupled with statements of good intention and sympathetic if not identificatory sentiment and an avowed aim to "give voice" to the previously silenced "people without history," as Eric Wolf so named them. Nonetheless, Spivak's essay is somewhat incompatible with this latter ambition. It is a willful misreading that permits Donald Moore to claim, though he is not alone, that "Significantly, Scott, Guha, and Spivak share a tendency to locate culture in a textual metaphor that smuggles an originary autonomy into the field of subaltern cultural production" or that all three are guilty of "positing . . . an originary space of authentic insurgency and insurrectionary otherness."[18] Even Paul Rabinow, a usually acute reader of Michel Foucault, for whom the impossibility of analytic objectivity or critical exteriority to the operations of power was an axiom, asserts in a recent essay, "Spivak's plain-tive query about whether the subaltern could ever speak reflected a normative goal of transparency: if only power relations were different, then."[19] It may be that anthropologists, historians, and those interpretive social scientists less trained in the reading practices that guide literary criticism may be more susceptible to this kind of misreading, but misreading it is. At no point does Spivak ever express a normative goal of transparency; her essay and, indeed all her writing, testifies to the impossibility of such transparency, not because representation is always already inadequate to the real that it seeks to inscribe, as some psychoanalytically inflected readings might have it, but because the subaltern (as woman) describes a relation between subject and object status (under imperialism and then globalization) that is not one of silence—to be overcome by representational heroism—but aporia.[20] The one cannot be "brought" into the other.

Thus far, I have indicated an expansion of the sphere of influence for "Can the Subaltern Speak?" over the past two decades, while suggesting that the result of its movement was a set of profound transformations in the disciplines adjacent to subaltern studies, including South Asian history, history of the global South, postcolonial studies, anthropology, and gender studies. Nonetheless, Gandhi's diagnosis of the containment to which the essay has been subject retains a measure of truth; "Can the Subaltern Speak?" has moved less smoothly across those fields of literary critical study (including that dominated by various strands of deconstructionism) that are not also specifically concerned with postcolonial literary production. By the early 1980s Spivak's translation of Derrida's *Of Grammatology* had opened for English-speaking readers a broader aperture through which to receive deconstructionism than had previously existed. At the same time, the status of postcolonial criticism (and critical race theory) within the field of literary criticism was being solidified by the interventions not only of Spivak herself but many others. It nonetheless remained the case that deconstructionism most dominated those spaces of the literary critical establishment where the textual objects of reading could be recognized as cultural artifacts of the same philosophical system to which it turned its critical eye. Spivak has often reminded her audiences of her training as a Europeanist. And one notes that, in that second subaltern studies conference reported on by David Hardiman, she delivered a paper in which she read Brecht's "Threepenny Opera" next to Mahasweta Devi's "Stranadayini." Nonetheless, it is for the reading of Devi more than of Brecht that her intervention is recalled. The isomorphism between the subject and the object of knowledge, which Spivak shows to be an impossibility for the subaltern in "Can the Subaltern Speak?" is nonetheless a demand made upon "minoritized" persons (women, people of color, persons of alterior sexuality) within the often identitarian formation of the U.S. academy—especially, if ironically, in those domains that resist most vociferously the rise of identitarianism. It would be tendentious to adduce here the place of European literary productions in Spivak's analysis of subalternity, but it is not tendentious to note the degree to which deconstructionist (and other) literary criticism in the Anglo-American academy tends to attribute to the third world literary text an irreducible particularity, to withhold from it the capacity to signify the general (a capacity it grants begrudgingly even to the "women's literature" of Charlotte Brontë, Jean Rhys, or Mary Shelley) and to demand, instead, that it signify itself as, precisely, "third world" literature.[21] This gesture constitutes the inverse and displacement of the desire that subalternity be given a voice. The resistance here is not of or by the third world writer and/or her writings, let alone by the subaltern; it is the resistance of dominance to its possible displacement from the exclusive claim on universality.

IT IS NOT MY INTENTION to conclude or to supplant the work of the writers whose various contributions to this volume pursue many of the threads mentioned so briefly here. Rather, I mean to sketch the space within which their analyses might be productively read.

This book is divided into five parts and has as its bookends an introduction and an appendix. Part 1 contains the revised version of "Can the Subaltern Speak?" as it appears in Spivak's *A Critique of Postcolonial Reason*. Readers will discern a vast movement, but also significant continuity, between this "version" of the text, and original essay which appears here as an appendix following Spivak's "Afterword."

The essays in part 2 are concerned to situate and reflect upon the historic, rhetorical, and philosophical aspects of "Can the Subaltern Speak?" Partha Chatterjee's essay, written by an original member of the subaltern studies group and Spivak's constant interlocutor, sets the stage by describing the intellectual milieu into which the essay arrived in India. It then sketches for us the arguments "Can the Subaltern Speak?" made possible within that country's tradition of radical social analysis. Ritu Birla's essay performs a careful reading of the arguments and rhetorical gestures that structure the original essay, while providing us with a sense of how and in what ways its revision for *A Critique of Postcolonial Reason* reflected new emphases and conceptualizations of the problematic of "speaking." Drucilla Cornell's essay then situates Spivak's essay in the broader context of European philosophical modernism and the ethical turn in deconstructionism as part of an effort to understand what "Can the Subaltern Speak?" made possible as a revised approach to the possibilities and pitfalls of human rights discourse.

Part 3 focuses specifically on the problematic of death in the theorization of subalternity, asking not merely about the material deaths of those who are called subaltern in Spivak's writings but also about the constitutive place of death in the (often thwarted) claim to agency that the subaltern makes, if only in the enabling negation of her subalternity. Rajeswari Sunder Rajan's essay brings to bear new reflections on the case of Bhubaneswari Bhaduri and the question of suicide in the analysis of subalternity, asking once again how and what we can know about subalternity on the basis of this particular figure. Reading Spivak against Guha and Bhubanswari against Chandra, Sunder Rajan both questions the ways in which the body is made to speak in these critics' analyses and reiterates Spivak's conclusion that the subaltern cannot speak. Abdul JanMohammed's essay on African American literatures of death in/and slavery revisits Hegelian dialectics and the labor of the negative in the context of what he perceives to be Spivak's demand for a measurement of silence and offers an ethically demanding alternative to the memory industry. By separating out the question of what preconditions structured the production of speech for deceased slaves, from the issue of what kinds of audition can be learned now in the service of "hearing" the fugitive call of slavery's death-bound-subjects, JanMohammed offers the strongest argument in the collection for the project of recuperation, reading deconstructionism as a labor of the negative in a neo-Hegelian mode. Michèle Barrett, similarly plumbing the archive, takes a contrary approach. Her account of the subaltern soldiers in the British military campaign in Mesopotamia does not point in the direction of a re-presentable but occluded presence. Rather, mobilizing Spivak's concept of "erasure in disclosure," she traces the debates surrounding the memorialization of the subaltern solders as the scene of an effacement of Indian and other colonial combatants in British war memorials.

Part 4 offers readings of the contemporary geopolitical scene with reference to the insight and questions that "Can the Subaltern Speak?" posed for an analysis of the international division of labor as well as for the relations between analysis and oppositional politics. Pheng Cheah's essay moves us into the contemporary moment with a reconsideration of Spivak's debate with Foucault on the question of biopower and then exposes the operations of the new international division of labor in the Asian Pacific. To conclude, Jean Franco's essay on women's writing in Latin America reframes the question of silence in terms of secrecy to introduce an agency that might function through strategies of illegibility and dissimulation rather than self-disclosure.

The volume closes with Gayatri Spivak's final reflection on the metamorphoses and interpretive readings to which the essay has been subject and on the questions that emerged in the context of the conference. Bhubaneswari Bhaduri returns there as the haunting figure of a continually misread woman whose impossible story has, in so many ways, accompanied and perhaps even possessed Spivak in her own effort to be accountable to and for history. From her we learn that, though "Can the Subaltern Speak?" answered its own question in the negative, its corollary question, How can we learn to listen? remains radically open.

NOTES

1   Serguei Oushakine, personal communication, 2006.
2   Marx, *The Ethnological Notebooks*, p. 327.
3   Ibid.
4   I am conscious here that the representation of secularity as an unaccomplished project and thus, perhaps, as a potentially accomplishable project within Western post-Enlightenment philosophy and political life runs against the grain of many current pieties—which read secularity as a mere gesture of self-occlusion within Christological or, more specifically, Protestant discourse. I do not share this sentiment. Rather, I see secularity as the structure of organized self-suspension (without self-negation) in any normativity, one that makes possible the hospitable relation to others without the demand for mirroring or for their performance of submission or accession to one's own normativity. There is a degree to which this question of potentiality takes the form of messianicity without messianism, to quote Derrida: an infinitely deferred but nonetheless urgent politics of the "to-come." (See Derrida's *Specters of Marx*.) And I concede that such gestures are generally only approximated in a parenthetical form or, to put matters slightly differently, in the mode of tolerance. Nonetheless, this approximation of an absolute hospitality that has never been fully actualized can be usefully instrumentalized, I believe, and has as its good but failed examples the early moments of anticasteist, creole Buddhism in South Asia prior to the transformation of Buddhism into an imperial "religion" under Asoka; the expansive and mercantile-friendly Islam of Al-Andalus and the port cities of the Mediterranean; and the state-sponsored pluralism of Tito's Yugoslavia. One must emphasize the sense of good *but* failed examples here, while also recognizing that these secularities were neither the function of spontaneous goodwill among strangers nor an absolute relinquishing of privilege on the part of orthodoxy and normativity. These were formations of pragmatic hospitality in which the ideal of secularity was approximated and sometimes violently, enforced. On the politics of toleration, see

Brown, *Regulating Aversion*. On early Buddhism, I am indebted to the scholarship of Romila Thapar. See her *From Lineage to State* and *Asoka and the Decline of the Mauryas*. On Al-Andalus, I rely on the work of my colleague, Gil Anidjar, *Our Place in Al-Andalus*. For insight into the precarious secularity of Yugoslavia, I thank Amila Buturovic.

5   Among the sympathetic book-length accounts are Stephen Morton, *Gayatri Spivak*, and *Gayatri Spivak: Ethics, Subalternity, and the Critique of Postcolonial Reason*; Sanders, *Gayatri Chakravorty Spivak*; and Ray, *Gayatri Chakravorty Spivak*. Robert Young was among the first to devote a laudatory chapter to her. See *White Mythologies*.

6   Hardiman, "'Subaltern Studies' at Crossroads," p. 288.

7   Ibid., p. 289. It should be acknowledged that Hardiman did not approve all of Spivak's interventions, particularly on how to read Indian literary texts.

8   Gandhi, *Postcolonial Theory*, pp. 1–2. The representation of Spivak's work as postcolonial often places it alongside of Said and Bhabha. Thus, for example, Selden's *A Reader's Guide to Contemporary Literary Theory* devotes a chapter to "Postcolonial Theories: Edward Said, Gayatri Chakravorty Spivak, Homi K. Bhabha, Race and Ethnicity." This placement is a source of some awkwardness given that it requires a separation, at least in its thematizations, of Spivak's work from both feminist and poststructuralist theories. In this context it must be noted that Spivak's insistence on gender as a constitutive and not merely additive dimension of social difference marks it as radically distinct from the works of either Bhabha or Said, for whom the question of gender does not really arise as such.

9   Prakash, "Subaltern Studies as Postcolonial Criticism," p. 1488. Nonetheless, not everyone was persuaded by this visibly sutured relationship. For a revealing debate about the possible tensions between deconstruction and Marxism, a tension that Spivak and Prakash, for example, mobilize to great analytic advantage without, at the same time, effacing it, see O'Hanlon and Washbrook, "After Orientalism"; and Prakash's wittily clarion rejoinder, "Can the 'Subaltern' Ride?"

10 Chakrabarty, *Provincializing Europe*, p. 41. Also see Chakrabarty's *Habitations of Modernity*.

11 Mallon, "The Promise and Dilemma of Subaltern Studies"; Rodríguez, *The Latin American Subaltern Studies Reader*.

12 Butler, *Bodies That Matter*.

13 The significant influence of Spivak's work on Butler's writing notwithstanding, a recent, published conversation between them reveals points of both political convergence and dissonance—particularly around their respective readings of Hannah Arendt's political philosophy. See Butler and Spivak, *Who Sings the Nation-State?*

14 Shetty and Bellamy, "Postcolonialism's Archive Fever," p. 25.

15 A good summary of this emergent aspiration is to be found in Rosalind O'Hanlon's "Recovering the Subject," though she would later express suspicion at the possible conjoining of Marxist and poststructuralist analysis (see note 9). Nonetheless,

the locus classicus and, to some extent, inaugural text for this kind of scholarship is Scott's *Weapons of the Weak* and *Domination and the Arts of Resistance*. Other significant works in this field—though somewhat different from Scott's—include Comaroff's *Body of Power*; Boddy's *Wombs and Alien Spirits*; and Abu-Lughod's "The Romance of Resistance." In some important sense, all of them depended on Eric Wolf's recognition that European expansion itself obscured the possibility of accessing the life-worlds of those transformed by it, that it was the origin of a double erasure, and, hence, that the response to European history and its violence would not disclose itself as the mere flip side or mirroring opposition of European power. His *Europe and the People Without History* remains a watershed text.

16 I am thinking here of the distinction made by Theodor Adorno in *Negative Dialectics*.

17 This presence need not be conscious or even "human." Conceptions of landscape that attribute to it a sacral force that ought not, as a result, be subject to extractive technologies would be an example here. But, to speak of the more obvious social forms of this type, we would include systems of reciprocity that mitigate against individual accumulation and, related to it, mandatory rites of giving, forms of expenditure that convert into rank rather than value (potlatch), and collective labor that is organized to maximize social connection rather than the rationality of production, among others.

18 Moore, "Subaltern Struggles and the Politics of Place," p. 252.

19 Rabinow, "Anthropological Observation and Self-Formation," p. 108.

20 Spivak, "Can the Subaltern Speak?" p. 306/280. References to "Can the Subaltern Speak?" appear with the pagination of the original first and the pagination of this volume second.

21 These writers are discussed in Spivak, "Three Women's Texts and a Critique of Imperialism."

PART ONE

TEXT

Gayatri Chakravorty Spivak

CAN THE
SUBALTERN SPEAK?

Women outside of the mode of production narrative mark the points of fadeout in the writing of disciplinary history even as they mime "writing as such," footprints of the trace (of someone? something?—we are obliged mistakenly to ask) that efface as they disclose. If, as Jameson suggests, the mode of production narrative is the final reference, these women are insufficiently represented or representable in that narration. We can docket them, but we cannot grasp them at all. The possibility of possession, of being haunted, is cut by the imposition of the tough reasonableness of capital's mode of exploitation. Or, to tease out Marx rather than follow Jameson, the mode of production narrative is so efficient because it is constructed in terms of the most efficient and abstract coding of value, the economic. Thus, to represent an earlier intuition, the ground-level value-codings that write these women's lives elude us. These codes are measurable only in the (ebb and flow) mode of the total or expanded form, which is "defective" from a rationalist point of view. We pay the price of epistemically fractured transcoding when we explain them as general exemplars of anthropological descriptions.[1]

As a feminist literary critic pulling deconstruction into the service of reading, I am more attentive to these elusive figures, although of course deeply interested in the accounts of women who are in step with the mode of production narrative, as participants/resisters/victims. If indeed the relationship between capitalism and socialism is that of a *pharmakon* (medicine in *différance* with poison), these elusive figures mark moments where neither medicine nor poison quite catches. Indeed, it is only in their death that they enter a narrative *for us*, they become figurable. In the rhythm of their daily living the elusion is familiarly performed or (un)performed, since to elude constatation in the act is not necessarily a performance. I attend to these figures because they continue to impose the highest standards on our techniques of retrieval, even as they judge them, not in our rationalist mode. In fact, since they are outside of our efforts, their judgment is not intended. Following a certain statement of Derrida's, perhaps we should rather say: they are the figures of justice as the experience of the impossible.[2]

[Here] I will focus on a figure who intended to be retrieved, who wrote with her body. It is as if she attempted to "speak" across death, by rendering her body graphematic.[3] In the archives, Rani Gulari emerges only on call, when needed, as coerced agent/instrument/witness for the colonialism of capital. She is the "purer" figure of fadeout. This woman tried to join uncoerced intending (male) agents of anti-colonialism. She was born in Calcutta a hundred years later and understood "nationalism," another efficient coding.[4] Anticipating her production world-historically though not in intent, Gulari had been a letter in the alphabet of the discursive transformation that remotely set in motion the definition of "India" as a modern nation—miraculating site of state-as-intention—a word that could find enunciative completion only as object of "liberation" in order, then, to constitute "identity." The woman in this section tried to be decisive in extremis, yet lost herself in the undecidable womanspace of justice. She "spoke," but women did not, do not, "hear" her. Before I come to her, I will lay out, in a long digression, some of the decisive judgments that I risked, some years ago, in order to attend to her mystery.

Whatever power these meditations may command has been earned by a politically interested refusal to acknowledge the undecidable, to push to the limit the founding presuppositions of my desires, as far as they are within my grasp. This three-stroke formula, applied both to the most resolutely committed and to the most ironic discourse, keeps track of what Althusser so aptly named "philosophies of denegation," and Derrida, before psychoanalysis, "desistance."[5] Calling the place of the investigator into question remains a meaningless piety in many recent critiques of the sovereign subject. Although I attempt to sound the precariousness of my position throughout, I know such gestures can never suffice.

Some of the most radical criticism coming out of the West in the eighties was the result of an interested desire to conserve the subject of the West, or the West as Subject. The theory of pluralized "subject-effects" often provided a cover for this subject of knowledge. Although the history of Europe as Subject was narrativized by the law, political economy, and ideology of the

West, this concealed Subject pretended it had "no geo-political determinations." The much-publicized critique of the sovereign subject thus actually inaugurated a Subject. I will argue for this conclusion by considering a text by two great practitioners of the critique: "Intellectuals and Power: A Conversation between Michel Foucault and Gilles Deleuze."[6] In the event, just as some "third world women's" critique romanticize the united struggle of working-class women, these hegemonic radicals also allow undivided subjectivity to workers' struggles. My example is outside both circuits. I must therefore spend some time with the hegemonic radicals.

I have chosen this friendly exchange between two activist philosophers of history because it undoes the opposition between authoritative theoretical production and the unguarded practice of conversation, enabling one to glimpse the track of ideology. (Like the conference, the interview is a site of betrayal.) Earlier and elsewhere I have considered their theoretical brilliance. This is a chapter of another disciplinary mistake: telling life stories in the name of history.

The participants in this conversation emphasize the most important contributions of French poststructuralist theory: first, that the networks of power/desire/interest are so heterogeneous that their reduction to a coherent narrative is counterproductive—a persistent critique is needed; and second, that intellectuals must attempt to disclose and know the discourse of society's other. Yet the two systematically and surprisingly ignore the question of ideology and their own implication in intellectual and economic history.

Although one of its chief presuppositions is the critique of the sovereign subject, the conversation between Foucault and Deleuze is framed by two monolithic and anonymous subjects-in-revolution: "A Maoist" (*FD* 205) and "the workers' struggle" (*FD* 217). Intellectuals, however, are named and differentiated; moreover, a Chinese Maoism is nowhere operative. Maoism here simply creates an aura of narrative specificity, which would be a harmless rhetorical banality were it not that the innocent appropriation of the proper name "Maoism" for the eccentric phenomenon of French intellectual "Maoism" and subsequent "New Philosophy" symptomatically renders "Asia" transparent.[7]

Deleuze's reference to the workers' struggle is equally problematic; it is obviously a genuflection: "We are unable to touch [power] in any point of its application without finding ourselves confronted by this diffuse mass, so that we are necessarily led . . . to the desire to blow it up completely. Every partial revolutionary attack or defense is linked in this way to the workers' struggle" (*FD* 217). The apparent banality signals a disavowal. The statement ignores the international division of labor, a gesture that often marks post-structuralist political theory. (Today's post-Soviet universalist feminist— "gender and development," United Nation style—dissimulates it; its rôle will come clear later.[8]

The invocation of *the* workers' struggle is baleful in its very innocence; it is incapable of dealing with global capitalism: the subject-production of worker and unemployed within nation-state ideologies in its Center; the increasing subtraction of the working class in the periphery from the realization of surplus value and thus from "humanistic" training in consumerism; and the large-scale presence of paracapitalist labor as well as the heterogeneous structural status of agriculture in the periphery. Ignoring the international division of labor, rendering "Asia" (and on occasion "Africa") transparent (unless the subject is ostensibly the "Third World"); reestablishing the legal subject of socialized capital—these are problems as common to much poststructuralist as to "regular" theory. (The invocation of "woman" is as problematic in the current conjuncture.) Why should such occlusions be sanctioned in precisely those intellectuals who are our best prophets of heterogeneity and the Other?

The link to the workers' struggle is located in the desire to blow up power at any point of its application. It reads too much like a valorization of *any* desire destructive of *any* power. Walter Benjamin comments on Baudelaire's comparable politics by way of quotations from Marx:

> Marx continues in his description of the *conspirateurs de profession* as follows: " . . . They have no other aim but the immediate one of overthrowing the existing government, and they profoundly despise the more theoretical enlightenment of the workers as to their class interests. Thus their anger— not proletarian but plebeian—at the *habits noirs* (black coats), the more or less educated people who represent [*vertreten*] that side of the movement and of whom they can never become entirely independent, as they cannot of the official representatives [*Repräsentanten*] of the party. Baudelaire's political insights do not go fundamentally beyond the insights of these professional conspirators. . . . "He could perhaps have made Flaubert's statement, "Of all of politics I understand only one thing: the revolt," his own.[9]

This, too, is a rewriting of accountable responsibility as narcissism, lower case; perhaps we cannot do otherwise, but one can tend. Or else, why speak of "the gift," at all?[10]

The link to the workers' struggle is located, simply, in desire. This is not the "desire" of *Anti-Oedipus*, which is a deliberate mis-name for a general flow (where the "subject" is a residuum), for which no adequate name can be found: a nominalist catachresis.[11] I have admiration for that bold effort, especially for the ways in which it is linked with that other nominalist catachresis: value. To check psychologism, *Anti-Oedipus* uses the concept-metaphor of machines: Desire does not lack anything; it does not lack its object. It is, rather, the subject that is lacking in desire, or desire that lacks a fixed subject; there is no fixed subject except by repression. Desire and its object are a unity: it is the machine, as a machine of a machine. Desire is machine, the object of desire also a connected machine, so that the product is lifted from the process of producing, and something detaches itself from producing to product and gives a leftover to the vagabond, nomad subject.[12]

One of the canniest moments in deconstruction is its caution, from early days to the latest, that the catachrestic is bound to the "empirical."[13] In the absence of such a practical caution, the philosopher oscillates between theoretical catachresis and practical naive realism as a contradiction that *may* be harmless in a context, where much goodwill may perhaps be taken for granted. As we see daily, such a contradiction between theory and its judgment is dire if "applied" globally.

Thus desire as catachresis in *Anti-Oedipus* does not alter the specificity of the desiring subject (or leftover subject-effect) that attaches to specific instances of "empirical" desire. The subject-effect that surreptitiously emerges is much like the generalized ideological subject of the theorist. This may be the legal subject of socialized capital, neither labor nor management, holding a "strong" passport, using a "strong" or "hard" currency, with supposedly unquestioned access to due process. Again, the lineaments of the UN-style feminist *aparatchik* are almost identical; her struggles against patriarchal measures are altogether admirable in her location; but dire when "applied" globally. In the era of globalizing capital, the catachreses "desire" and "globe"—the global crust as body-without-organs—are contaminated by empirical paleonymy in particular ways. It is a (Euro-U.S.) cut in a (Group of Seven) flow.

Deleuze and Guattari consider the relations between desire, power, and subjectivity on the "empirical" or constituted level in a slightly off-sync mode: against the family, and against colonialism. This renders them incapable of articulating a general or global theory of interests textualized to the conjuncture. In this context, their indifference to ideology (a theory of which is necessary for an understanding of constituted interests within systems of representation) is striking but consistent. Foucault's work cannot work on the subject-constituting register of ideology because of its tenacious commitment to the sub-individual and, at the other end, the great aggregative apparatuses (*dispositifs*). Yet, as this conversational register shows, the empirical subject, the intending subject, the self even, must be constantly assumed in radical calculations. Thus in his influential essay "Ideology and Ideological State Apparatuses (Notes towards An Investigation)," Louis Althusser must inhabit that unavoidable middle ground, and assume a subject even as he uses "a more scientific language" to describe abstract average labor or labor-power: "The reproduction of labour power requires not only a reproduction of its skills, but also at the same time, a reproduction of its submission to the ruling ideology for the workers, and a reproduction of the ability to manipulate the ruling ideology correctly for the agents of exploitation and repression, so that they, too, will provide for the domination of the ruling class 'in and by words' [*par la parole*]."[14]

When Foucault considers the pervasive heterogeneity of power, he does not ignore the immense institutional heterogeneity that Althusser here attempts to schematize. Similarly, in speaking of alliances and systems of signs, the state and war-machines, in *A Thousand Plateaus*, Deleuze and Guattari open up that very field.[15] Foucault cannot, however, admit that a developed theory of ideology *can* recognize its own material production in institutionality, as well as in the "effective instruments for the formation and accumulation of knowledge" (*PK* 102).[16] Because these philosophers seem obliged to reject all arguments naming the concept of ideology as *only* schematic rather than textual, they are equally obliged to produce a mechanically schematic opposition between interest and desire, when their catachreses inevitably bleed into the "empirical" field. Thus they unwittingly align themselves with bourgeois sociologists who fill the place of ideology with a continuistic "unconscious" or a parasubjective "culture" (or Bretton Woods activists who speak of "culture" alone). The mechanical relation between desire and interest is clear in such sentences as: "We never desire against our interests, because interest always follows and finds itself where desire has placed it" (*FD* 215). An undifferentiated desire is the agent, and power slips in to create the effects of desire: "power . . . produces positive effects at the level of desire—and also at the level of knowledge" (*PK* 59).[17]

This parasubjective matrix, cross-hatched with heterogeneity, surreptitiously ushers in the unnamed Subject, at least for those intellectual workers influenced by the new hegemony of pure catachresis. The race for "the last instance" is now between economics and power. Because, by the unacknowledged inevitable empirical contamination of catachreses, desire is tacitly and repeatedly "defined" on an orthodox model, it can be unitarily opposed to "being deceived." Ideology as "false consciousness" (being deceived) has been called into question by Althusser. Even Reich implied notions of collective will rather than a dichotomy of deception and undeceived desire: "We must accept the screams of Reich: no, the masses were not deceived; at a particular moment, they actually desired a fascist regime" (*FD* 215).

These philosophers will not entertain the thought of constitutive contradiction—that is where they admittedly part company from the Left. In the name of desire, they tacitly reintroduce the undivided subject into the discourse of power. On the register of practice, Foucault often seems to conflate "individual" and "subject";[18] and the impact on his own concept-metaphors is perhaps intensified in his followers. Because of the power of the word "power," Foucault admits to using the "metaphor of the point which progressively irradiates its surroundings." Such slips become the rule rather than the exception in less careful hands. And that radiating point, animating an effectively heliocentric discourse, fills the empty place of the agent with the historical sun of theory, the Subject of Europe.[19]

It is not surprising, therefore, that upon the empirical register of resistance-talk, Foucault articulates another corollary of the disavowal of the rôle of ideology in reproducing the social relations of production: an unquestioned valorization of the oppressed as subject, the "object being," as Deleuze admiringly remarks, "to establish conditions where the prisoners themselves would be able to speak." Foucault adds that "the masses know perfectly well, clearly"—once again the thematics of being undeceived—"they know far better than [the intellectual] and they certainly say it very well" (*FD* 206, 207). The ventriloquism of the speaking subaltern is the left intellectual's stock-in-trade.

What happens to the critique of the sovereign subject in these pronouncements? The limits of this representationalist realism are reached with Deleuze: "Reality is what actually happens in a factory, in a school, in barracks, in a prison, in a police station" (*FD* 212). This foreclosing of the necessity of the difficult task of counterhegemonic ideological production has not been salutary. It has helped positivist empiricism—the justifying foundation of advanced capitalist neocolonialism—to define its own arena as "concrete experience," "what actually happens." (As in the case of capitalist colonialism, and *mutatis mutandis*, of exploitation-as-"Development." Evidence is daily produced by computing the national subject of the global South in this unproblematic way. And an alibi for globalization is produced by calling on the testimony of the credit-baited female.) Indeed, the concrete experience that is the guarantor of the political appeal of prisoners, soldiers, and schoolchildren is disclosed through the concrete experience of the intellectual, the one who diagnoses the episteme.[20] Neither Deleuze nor Foucault seems aware that the intellectual within globalizing capital, brandishing concrete experience, can help consolidate the international division of labor by making one model of "concrete experience" *the* model. We are witnessing this in our discipline daily as we see the postcolonial *migrant* become the norm, thus occluding the native once again.[21]

The unrecognized contradiction within a position that valorizes the concrete experience of the oppressed, while being so uncritical about the historical rôle of the intellectual, is maintained by a verbal slippage. Deleuze makes this remarkable pronouncement: "A theory is like a box of tools. Nothing to do with the signifier" (*FD* 208). Considering that the verbalism of the theoretical world and its access to any work defined against it as "practical" is irreducible, such a declaration (referring *only* to an in-house contretemps with hermeneutics), helps *only* the intellectual anxious to prove that intellectual labor is just like manual labor.

It is when signifiers are left to look after themselves that verbal slippages happen. The signifier "representation" is a case in point. In the same dismissive tone that severs theory's link to the signifier, Deleuze declares, "There is no more representation; there's nothing but action"—"action of theory and action of practice which relate to each other as relays and form networks" (*FD* 206–7).

An important point is being made here: the production of theory is also a practice; the opposition between abstract "pure" theory and concrete "applied" practice is too quick and easy.[22] But Deleuze's articulation of the argument is problematic. Two senses of representation are being run together: representation as "speaking for," as in politics, and representation as "re-presentation," as in art or philosophy. Since theory is also only "action," the theoretician does not represent (speak for) the oppressed group. Indeed, the subject is not seen as a representative consciousness (one representing reality adequately). These two senses of representation—within state formation and the law, on the one hand, and in subject-predication, on the other—are related but irreducibly discontinuous. To cover over the discontinuity with an analogy that is presented as a proof reflects again a paradoxical subject-privileging.[23] *Because* "the person who speaks and acts . . . is always a multiplicity," no "theorizing intellectual . . . [or] party or . . . union" can represent "those who act and struggle" (*FD* 206). Are those who act and *struggle* mute, as opposed to those who act and *speak* (*FD* 206)? These immense problems are buried in the differences between the "same" words: consciousness and conscience (both *conscience* in French), representation and re-presentation. The critique of ideological subject-constitution within state formations and systems of political economy can now be effaced, as can the active theoretical practice of the "transformation of consciousness." The banality of leftist intellectuals' lists of self-knowing, politically canny subalterns stands revealed; representing them, the intellectuals represent themselves as transparent.

If such a critique and such a project are not to be given up, the shifting distinctions between representation within the state and political economy, on the one hand, and within the theory of the Subject, on the other, must not be obliterated. Let us consider the play of *vertreten* ("represent" in the first sense) and *darstellen* ("re-present" in the second sense) in a famous passage in *The Eighteenth Brumaire of Louis Bonaparte*, where Marx touches on "class" as a descriptive and transformative concept in a manner somewhat more complex than Althusser's distinction between class instinct and class position would allow. This is important in the context of the argument from the working class both from our two philosophers and "political" third world feminism from the metropolis.

Marx's contention here is that the descriptive definition of a class can be a differential one—its cutting off and difference from all other classes: "in so far as millions of families live under economic conditions of existence that cut off their mode of life, their interest, and their formation from those of the other classes and place them in inimical confrontation [*feindlich gegenüberstellen*], they form a class."[24] There is no such thing as a "class instinct" at work here. In fact, the collectivity of familial existence, which might be considered the arena of "instinct," is discontinuous with, though operated by, the differential isolation of classes. In this context, one far more pertinent to the France of the 1970s than it can be to the international periphery, the formation of a class is *artificial* and economic, and the economic agency or *interest* is impersonal because it is systematic and heterogeneous. This agency or interest is tied to the Hegelian critique of the individual subject, for it marks the subject's empty place in that process without a subject which is history and political economy. Here the capitalist is defined as "the conscious bearer [*Träger*] of the limitless movement of capital."[25] My point is that Marx is not working to create an undivided subject where desire and interest coincide. Class consciousness does not operate toward that goal. Both in the economic area (capitalist) and in the political (world-historical agent), Marx is obliged to construct models of a divided and dislocated subject whose parts are not continuous or coherent with each other. A celebrated passage like the description of capital as the Faustian monster brings this home vividly.[26]

The following passage, continuing the quotation from *The Eighteenth Brumaire*, is also working on the structural principle of a dispersed and dislocated class subject: the (absent collective) consciousness of the small peasant proprietor class finds its "bearer" in a "representative" who appears to work in another's interest. "Representative" here does not derive from *"darstellen"*; this sharpens the contrast Foucault and Deleuze slide over, the contrast, say, between a proxy and a portrait. There is, of course, a relationship between them, one that has received political and ideological exacerbation in the European tradition at least since the poet and the sophist, the actor and the orator, have both been seen as harmful. In the guise of a post-Marxist description of the scene of power, we thus encounter a much older debate: between representation or rhetoric as tropology and as persuasion. *Darstellen* belongs to the first constellation, *vertreten*—with stronger suggestions of substitution—to the second. Again, they are related, but running them together, especially in order to say that beyond both is where oppressed subjects speak, act, and know *for themselves*, leads to an essentialist, utopian politics that can, when transferred to single-issue gender rather than class, give unquestioning support to the financialization of the globe, which ruthlessly constructs a general will in the credit-baited rural woman even as it "format"s her through UN Plans of Action so that she can be "developed." Beyond this concatenation, transparent as rhetoric in the service of "truth" has always made itself out to be, is the much-invoked oppressed subject (as Woman), speaking, acting, and knowing that gender in development is best for her. It is in the shadow of this unfortunate marionette that the history of the unheeded subaltern must unfold.

Here is Marx's passage, using *vertreten* where the English uses "represent," discussing a social "subject" whose consciousness is dislocated and incoherent with its *Vertretung* (as much a substitution as a representation). The small peasant proprietors

> cannot represent themselves; they must be represented. Their representative must appear simultaneously as their master, as an authority over them, as unrestricted governmental power that protects them from the other classes and sends them rain and sunshine from above. The political influence [in the place of the class interest, since there is no unified class subject] of the small peasant proprietors therefore finds its last expression [the implication of a chain of substitutions—*Vertretungen*—is strong here] in the executive force [*Exekutivegewalt*—less personal in German; Derrida translates *Gewalt* as violence in another context in "Force of Law"] subordinating society to itself.[27]

Such a model of social incoherence—necessary gaps between the source of "influence" (in this case the small peasant proprietors), the "representative" (Louis Napoleon), and the historical-political phenomenon (executive control)—imply a critique of the subject as *individual* agent but a critique even of the subjectivity of a *collective* agency. The necessarily dislocated machine of history moves because "the identity of the *interests*" of these proprietors "fails to produce a feeling of community, national links, or a political organization." The event of representation as *Vertretung* (in the constellation of rhetoric-as-persuasion) behaves like a *Darstellung* (or rhetoric-as-trope), taking its place in the gap between the formation of a (descriptive) class and the nonformation of a (transformative) class: "In so far as millions of families live under economic conditions of existence that separate their mode of life . . . *they form a class*. In so far as . . . the identity of their interests fails to produce a feeling of community . . . *they do not form a class*." The complicity of *vertreten* and *darstellen*, their identity-in-difference as the place of practice—since this complicity is precisely what Marxists must expose, as Marx does in *The Eighteenth Brumaire* —can only be appreciated if they are not conflated by a sleight of word.

It would be merely tendentious to argue that this textualizes Marx too much, making him inaccessible to the common "man," who, a victim of common sense, is so deeply placed in a heritage of positivism that Marx's irreducible emphasis on the work of the negative, on the necessity for defetishizing the concrete, is persistently wrested from him by the strongest adversary, "the historical tradition" in the air.[28] I have been trying to point out that the uncommon "man," the contemporary philosopher of practice, and the uncommon woman, the metropolitan enthusiast of "third world resistance," sometimes exhibit the same positivism.

The gravity of the problem is apparent if one agrees that the development of a transformative class "consciousness" from a descriptive class "position" is not in Marx a task engaging the ground level of consciousness. Class consciousness remains with the feeling of community that belongs to national links and political organizations, not with that other feeling of community whose structural model is the family. Although *not* identified with nature, the family here is constellated with what Marx calls "natural exchange," which is, philosophically speaking, a "placeholder" for use value.[29] "Natural exchange" is contrasted to "intercourse with society," where the word "intercourse" (*Verkehr*) is Marx's usual word for "commerce." This "intercourse" thus holds the place of the exchange leading to the production of surplus value, and it is in the area of this intercourse that the feeling of community leading to class agency must be developed. Full class agency (if there were such a thing) is not an ideological transformation of consciousness on the ground level, a desiring identity of the agents and their interest—the identity whose absence troubles Foucault and Deleuze. It is a contestatory *replacement* as well as an *appropriation* (a *supplementation*) of something that is "artificial" to begin with—"economic conditions of existence that separate their mode of life." Marx's formulations show a cautious respect for the nascent critique of individual and collective subjective agency. The projects of class consciousness and of the transformation of consciousness are discontinuous issues for him. Today's analogue would be "transnational literacy" as opposed to the mobilizing potential of unexamined cultural-ism.[30] Conversely, contemporary invocations of "libidinal economy" and desire as the determining interest, combined with the practical politics of the oppressed (under socialized capital) "speaking for themselves," restore the category of the sovereign subject within the theory that seems most to question it.

No doubt the exclusion of the family, albeit a family belonging to a specific class formation, is part of the masculine frame within which Marxism marks its birth.[31] Historically as well as in today's global political economy, the family's rôle in patriarchal social relations is so heterogeneous and contested that merely replacing the family in this problematic is not going to break the frame. Nor does the solution lie in the positivist inclusion of a monolithic collectivity of "women" in the list of the oppressed whose unfractured subjectivity allows them to speak for themselves against an equally monolithic "same system."

In the context of the development of a strategic, artificial, and second-level "consciousness," Marx uses the concept of the patronymic, always keeping within the broader concept of representation as *Vertretung*: The small peasant proprietors "are therefore incapable of making their class interest valid in their proper name [*im eigenen Namen*], whether through a parliament or through a convention." The absence of the nonfamilial artificial collective proper name is supplied by the only proper name "historical tradition" can offer—the patronymic itself—the Name of the Father (in a not dissimilar spirit Jean Rhys had denied that name to her fictional [Rochester] character): "Historical tradition produced the French peasants' belief that a miracle would occur, that a man *named* Napoleon would restore all their glory. And an individual turned up"—the untranslatable *es fand sich* (there found itself an individual?) demolishes all questions of agency or the agent's connection with his interest—"who gave himself out to be that man" (this pretense is, by contrast, his only proper agency) "because he carried [*trägt*—the word used for the capitalist's relationship to capital] the Napoleonic Code, which commands" that "inquiry into paternity is forbidden." While Marx here seems to be working within a patriarchal metaphorics, one should note the textual subtlety of the passage. It is the Law of the Father (the Napoleonic Code) that paradoxically prohibits the search for the natural father. Thus, it is according to a strict observance of the historical

Law of the Father that the formed yet unformed class's faith in the natural father is gainsaid.

I have dwelt so long on this passage in Marx because it spells out the inner dynamics of *Vertretung*, or representation in the political context. Representation in the economic context is *Darstellung*, the philosophical concept of representation as staging or, indeed, signification, which relates to the divided subject in an indirect way. The most obvious passage is well known: "In the exchange relationship [*Austauschverhältnis*] of commodities their exchange-value appeared to us totally independent of their use value. But if we subtract their use-value from the product of labour, we obtain their value, as it was just determined [*bestimmt*]. The common element which represents itself [*sich darstellt*] in the exchange relation, or the exchange value of the commodity, is thus its value."[32]

According to Marx, under capitalism, value, as produced in necessary and surplus labor, is computed as the representation/sign of objectified labor (which is rigorously distinguished from human activity). Conversely, in the absence of a theory of exploitation as the extraction (production), appropriation, and realization of (surplus) value *as representation of labor power*, capitalist exploitation must be seen as a variety of domination (the mechanics of power as such). "The thrust of Marxism," Deleuze suggests, "was to determine the problem [that power is more diffuse than the structure of exploitation and state formation] essentially in terms of interests (power is held by a ruling class defined by its interests)" (*FD* 214).

One cannot object to this minimalist summary of Marx's project, just as one cannot ignore that, in parts of the *Anti-Oedipus*, Deleuze and Guattari build their case on a brilliant if "poetic" grasp of Marx's *theory* of the money form. Yet we might consolidate our critique in the following way: the relationship between global capitalism (exploitation in economics) and nation-state alliances (domination in geopolitics) is so macrological that it cannot account for the micrological texture of power.[33] Sub-individual micrologies cannot grasp the "empirical" field. To move toward such an accounting one must move toward theories of ideology—of subject formations that micrologically and often erratically operate the interests that congeal the micrologies and are congealed in macrologies. Such theories cannot afford to overlook that this line *is* erratic, and that the category of representation in its *two* senses is crucial. They must note how the staging of the world in representation—its scene of writing, its *Darstellung*—dissimulates the choice of and need for "heroes," paternal proxies, agents of power—*Vertretung*.

My view is that radical practice should attend to this double session of representations rather than reintroduce the individual subject through totalizing concepts of power and desire. It is also my view that, in keeping the area of class practice on a second level of abstraction, Marx was in effect keeping open the (Kantian and) Hegelian critique of the individual subject as agent.[34] This view does not oblige me to ignore that, by implicitly defining the family and the mother tongue as the ground level where culture and convention seem nature's own way of organizing "her" own subversion, Marx himself rehearses an ancient subterfuge.[35] In the context of poststructuralist claims to critical practice, however, Marx seems more recuperable than the clandestine restoration of subjective essentialism.

The reduction of Marx to a benevolent but dated figure most often serves the interest of launching a new theory of interpretation. In the Foucault-Deleuze conversation, the issue seems to be that there is no representation, no signifier (Is it to be presumed that the signifier has already been dispatched? There is, then, no sign-structure operating experience, and thus might one lay semiotics to rest?); theory is a relay of practice (thus laying problems of theoretical practice to rest) and the oppressed can know and speak for themselves. This reintroduces the constitutive subject on at least two levels: the Subject of desire and power as an irreducible methodological presupposition; and the self-proximate, if not self-identical, subject of the oppressed. Further, the intellectuals, who are neither of these S/subjects, become transparent in the relay race, for they merely report on the non-represented subject and analyze (without analyzing) the workings of (the unnamed Subject irreducibly presupposed by) power and desire. The produced "transparency" marks the place of "interest"; it is maintained by vehement denegation: "Now this rôle of referee, judge and universal witness is one which I *absolutely refuse* to adopt." One responsibility of the critic might be to read and write so that the impossibility of such interested individualistic refusals of the institutional privileges of power bestowed on the subject is taken seriously. The refusal of sign-system blocks the way to a developed theory of ideology in the "empirical." Here, too, the peculiar tone of denegation is heard. To Jacques-Alain Miller's suggestion that "the institution is itself discursive," Foucault responds, "Yes, if you like, but it doesn't much matter for my notion of the apparatus to be able to say that this is discursive and that isn't ... given that my problem isn't a linguistic one" (*PK* 198). Why this conflation of language and discourse from the master of discourse analysis?

Edward W. Said's critique of power in Foucault as a captivating and mystifying category that allows him "to obliterate the rôle of classes, the rôle of economics, the rôle of insurgency and rebellion," is pertinent here, although the importance of the name of "power" in the sub-individual is not to be ignored.[36] I add to Said's analysis the notion of the surreptitious subject of power and desire marked by the transparency of the intellectual.

This S/subject, curiously sewn together into a transparency by denegations, belongs to the exploiters' side of the international division of labor. It is impossible for contemporary French intellectuals to imagine the kind of Power and Desire that would inhabit the unnamed subject of the Other of Europe. It is not only that everything they read, critical or uncritical, is caught within the debate of the production of that Other, supporting or critiquing the constitution of the Subject as Europe. It is also that, in the constitution of that Other of Europe, great care was taken to obliterate the textual ingredients with which such a subject could cathect, could occupy (invest?) its itinerary—not only by ideological and scientific production, but also by the institution of the law. However reductionistic an economic analysis might seem, the French intellectuals forget at their peril that this entire overdetermined enterprise was in the interest of a dynamic economic situation requiring that interests, motives (desires), and power (of knowledge) be ruthlessly dislocated. To invoke that dislocation now as a radical discovery that should make us diagnose the economic (conditions of existence that separate out "classes" descriptively) as a piece of dated analytic machinery may well be to continue the work of that dislocation and unwittingly to help in securing "a new balance of hegemonic relations."[37] In the face of the possibility that the intellectual is complicit in the persistent constitution of the Other as the Self's shadow, a possibility of political practice for the intellectual would be to put the economic "under erasure," to see the economic factor as irreducible as it reinscribes the social text, even as it is erased, however imperfectly, when it claims to be the final determinant or the transcendental signified.[38]

Until very recently, the clearest available example of such epistemic violence was the remotely orchestrated, far-flung, and heterogeneous project to constitute the colonial subject as Other. This project is also the asymmetrical obliteration of the trace of that Other in its precarious Subject-ivity. It is well known that Foucault locates one case of epistemic violence, a complete overhaul of the episteme, in the redefinition of madness at the end of the European eighteenth century.[39] But what if that particular redefinition was only a part of the narrative of history in Europe as well as in the colonies? What if the two projects of epistemic overhaul worked as dislocated and unacknowledged parts of a vast two-handed engine? Perhaps it is no more than to ask that the subtext of the palimpsestic narrative of imperialism be recognized as "subjugated knowledge," "a whole set of knowledges that have been disqualified as inadequate to their task or insufficiently elaborated: naive knowledges, located low down on the hierarchy, beneath the required level of cognition or scientificity" (*PK* 82).

This is not to describe "the way things really were" or to privilege the narrative of history as imperialism as the best version of history.[40] It is, rather to continue the account of how *one* explanation and narrative of reality was established as the normative one. A comparable account in the case(s) of Central and Eastern Europe is soon to be launched. To elaborate on this, let us consider for the moment and briefly the underpinnings of the British codification of Hindu Law.

Once again, I am not a South Asianist. I turn to Indian material because I have some accident-of-birth facility there.

Here, then, is a schematic summary of the epistemic violence of the codification of Hindu Law. If it clarifies the notion of epistemic violence, my final discussion of widow-sacrifice may gain added significance.

At the end of the eighteenth century, Hindu Law, insofar as it can be described as a unitary system, operated in terms of four texts that "staged" a four-part episteme defined by the subject's use of memory: *sruti* (the heard), *smriti* (the remembered), *sāstra* (the calculus), and *vyavahāra* (the performance).[41] The origins of what had been heard and what was remembered were not necessarily continuous or identical. Every invocation of *sruti* technically recited (or reopened) the event of originary "hearing" or revelation. The second two texts—the learned and the performed—were seen as dialectically continuous. Legal theorists and practitioners were not in any given case certain if this structure described the body of law or four ways of settling a dispute. The legitimation, through a binary vision, of the polymorphous structure of legal performance, "internally" noncoherent and open at both ends, is the narrative of codification I offer as an example of epistemic violence.

Consider the often-quoted programmatic lines from Macaulay's infamous "Minute on Indian Education" (1835):

> We must at present do our best to form a class who may be interpreters between us and the millions whom we govern; a class of persons, Indian in blood and colour, but English in taste, in opinions, in morals, and in intellect. To that class we may leave it to refine the vernacular dialects of the country, to enrich those dialects with terms of science borrowed from the Western nomenclature, and to render them by degrees fit vehicles for conveying knowledge to the great mass of the population.[42]

The education of colonial subjects complements their production in law. One effect of establishing a version of the British system was the development of an uneasy separation between disciplinary formation in Sanskrit studies and the native, now alternative, tradition of Sanskrit "high culture."

Elsewhere, I have suggested that within the former, the cultural explanations generated by authoritative scholars matched the epistemic violence of the legal project.

Those authorities would be *the very best* of the sources for the nonspecialist French intellectual's entry into the civilization of the Other.[43] I am, however, not referring to intellectuals and scholars of colonial production, like Shastri, when I say that the Other as Subject is inaccessible to Foucault and Deleuze. I am thinking of the general nonspecialist, nonacademic population across the class spectrum, for whom the episteme operates its silent programming function. Without considering the map of exploitation, on what grid of "oppression" would they place this motley crew?

Let us now move to consider the margins (one can just as well say the silent, silenced center) of the circuit marked out by this epistemic violence, men and women among the illiterate peasantry, Aboriginals, and the lowest strata of the urban subproletariat. According to Foucault and Deleuze (in the First World, under the standardization and regimentation of socialized capital, though they do not seem to recognize this) and mutatis mutandis the metropolitan "third world feminist" only interested in resistance within capital logic, the oppressed, if given the chance (the problem of representation cannot be bypassed here), and on the way to solidarity through alliance politics (a Marxist thematic is at work here) *can speak and know their conditions.* We must now confront the following question: On the other side of the international division of labor from socialized capital, inside *and* outside the circuit of the epistemic violence of imperialist law and education supplementing an earlier economic text, *can the subaltern speak?*

ANTONIO GRAMSCI'S WORK on the "subaltern classes" extends the class-position/class-consciousness argument isolated in *The Eighteenth Brumaire.* Perhaps because Gramsci criticizes the vanguardistic position of the Leninist intellectual, he is concerned with the intellectual's rôle in the subaltern's cultural and political movement into the hegemony. This movement must be made to determine the production of history as narrative (of truth). In texts such as *The Southern Question,* Gramsci considers the movement of historical-political economy in Italy within what can be seen as an allegory of reading taken from or prefiguring an international division of labor.[44] Yet an account of the phased development of the subaltern is thrown out of joint when his cultural macrology is operated, however remotely, by the epistemic interference with legal and disciplinary definitions accompanying the imperialist project. When I move, at the end of this essay, to the question of woman as subaltern, I will suggest that the possibility of collectivity itself is persistently foreclosed through the manipulation of female agency.

The first part of my proposition—that the phased development of the subaltern is complicated by the imperialist project—is confronted by the "Subaltern Studies" group. They *must* ask, Can the subaltern speak? Here we are within Foucault's own discipline of history and with people who acknowledge his influence. Their project is to rethink Indian colonial historiography from the perspective of the discontinuous chain of peasant insurgencies during the colonial occupation. This is indeed the problem of "the permission to narrate" discussed by Said.[45] As Ranajit Guha, the founding editor of the collective, argues,

> The historiography of Indian nationalism has for a long time been dominated by elitism—colonialist elitism and bourgeois-nationalist elitism . . . shar[ing] the prejudice that the making of the Indian nation and the development of the consciousness—nationalism—which confirmed this process were exclusively or predominantly elite achievements. In the colonialist and neo-colonialist historiographies these achievements are credited to British colonial rulers, administrators, policies, institutions, and culture; in the nationalist and neo-nationalist writings—to Indian elite personalities, institutions, activities and ideas.[46]

Certain members of the Indian elite are of course native informants for first-world intellectuals interested in the voice of the Other. But one must nevertheless insist that the colonized subaltern *subject* is irretrievably heterogeneous.

Against the indigenous elite we may set what Guha calls "the *politics* of the people," both outside ("this was an *autonomous* domain, for it neither originated from elite politics nor did its existence depend on the latter") and inside ("it continued to operate vigorously in spite of [colonialism], adjusting itself to the conditions prevailing under the Raj and in many respects developing entirely new strains in both form and content") the circuit of colonial production.[47] I cannot entirely endorse this insistence on determinate vigor and full autonomy, for practical historiographic exigencies will not allow such endorsements to privilege subaltern consciousness. Against the possible charge that his approach is essentialist, Guha constructs a definition of the people (the place of that essence) that can be only an identity-in-differential. He proposes a dynamic stratification grid describing colonial social production at large. Even the third group on the list, the buffer group, as it were, between the people and the great macro-structural dominant groups, is itself defined as a place of in-betweenness. The classification falls into: "dominant foreign groups," and "dominant indigenous groups at the all-India and at the regional and local levels" representing the elite; and "[t] he social groups and elements included in [the terms "people" and "subaltern classes"] represent[ing] *the demographic difference between the total Indian population and all those whom we have described as the "elite."*[48]

"The task of research" projected here is "to investigate, identify and measure the *specific* nature and degree of the *deviation* of [the] elements [constituting item 3] from the ideal and situate it historically." "Investigate, identify, and measure the specific": a program could hardly be more essentialist and taxonomic. Yet a curious methodological imperative is at work. I have argued that, in the Foucault-Deleuze conversation, a postrepresentationalist vocabulary hides an essentialist agenda. In subaltern studies, because of the violence of imperialist epistemic, social, and disciplinary inscription, a project understood in essentialist terms must traffic in a radical textual practice of differences. The object of the group's investigation, in this case not even of the people as such but of the floating buffer zone of the regional elite—is a *deviation* from an *ideal*—the people or subaltern—which is itself defined as a difference from the elite. It is toward this structure that the research is oriented, a predicament rather different from the self-diagnosed transparency of the first-world radical intellectual. What taxonomy can fix such a space? Whether or not they themselves perceive it—in fact Guha sees his definition of "the people" within the master-slave dialectic—their text articulates the difficult task of rewriting its own conditions of impossibility as the conditions of its possibility. "At the regional and local levels [the dominant indigenous groups] . . . if belonging to social strata hierarchically inferior to those of the dominant all-Indian groups *acted in the interests of the latter and not in conformity to interests corresponding truly to their own social being.*[49] When these writers speak, in their essentializing language, of a gap between interest and action in the intermediate group, their conclusions are closer to Marx than to the self-conscious naivete of Deleuze's pronouncement on the issue. Guha, like Marx, speaks of interest in terms of the social rather than the libidinal being. The Name-of-the-Father imagery in *The Eighteenth Brumaire* can help to emphasize that, on the level of class or group action, "true correspondence to own being" is as artificial or social as the patronymic.

It is to this intermediate group that the second woman in this chapter belongs. The pattern of domination is here determined mainly by gender rather than class. The subordinated gender following the dominant within the challenge of nationalism while remaining caught within gender oppression is not an unknown story.

For the (gender-unspecified) "true" subaltern group, whose identity is its difference, there is no unrepresentable subaltern subject that can know and speak itself; the intellectual's solution is not to abstain from representation. The problem is that the subject's itinerary has not been left traced so as to offer an object of seduction to the representing intellectual. In the slightly dated language of the Indian group, the question becomes, How can we touch the consciousness of the people, even as we investigate their politics? With what voice-consciousness can the subaltern speak?

My question about how to earn the "secret encounter" with the contemporary hill women of Sirmur is a practical version of this. The woman of whom I will speak in this section was not a "true" subaltern, but a metropolitan middle-class girl. Further, the effort she made to write or speak her body was in the accents of accountable reason, the instrument of self-conscious responsibility. Still her Speech Act was refused. She was made to unspeak herself posthumously, by other women. In an earlier version of this chapter, I had summarized this historical indifference and its results as: the subaltern cannot speak.

The critique by Ajit K. Chaudhury, a West Bengali Marxist, of Guha's search for the subaltern consciousness can be taken as representative of a moment of the production process that includes the subaltern.[50] Chaudhury's perception that the Marxist view of the transformation of consciousness involves the knowledge of social relations seems, in principle, astute. Yet the heritage of the positivist ideology that has appropriated orthodox Marxism obliges him to add this rider: "This is not to belittle the importance of understanding peasants' consciousness or workers' consciousness *in its pure form*. This enriches our knowledge of the peasant and the worker and, possibly, throws light on how a particular mode takes on different forms in different regions, *which is considered a problem of second order importance in classical Marxism*."[51]

This variety of "internationalist Marxism," which believes in a pure, retrievable form of consciousness only to dismiss it, thus closing off what in Marx remain moments of productive bafflement, can at once be the occasion for Foucault's and Deleuze's rejection of Marxism *and* the source of the critical motivation of the Subaltern Studies groups. All three are united in the assumption that there *is* a pure form of consciousness. On the French scene, there is a shuffling of signifiers: "the unconscious" or "the subject-in-oppression" clandestinely fills the space of "the pure form of consciousness." In orthodox "internationalist" intellectual Marxism, whether in the First World or the Third, the pure form of consciousness remains, paradoxically, a material effect, and therefore a second-order problem. This often earns it the reputation of racism and sexism. In the Subaltern Studies group it needs development according to the unacknowledged terms of its own articulation.

Within the effaced itinerary of the subaltern subject, the track of sexual difference is doubly effaced.[52] The question is not of female participation in insurgency, or the ground rules of the sexual division of labor, for both of which there is "evidence." It is, rather, that, both as object of colonialist historiography and as subject of insurgency, the ideological construction of gender keeps the male dominant. If, in the contest of colonial production, the subaltern has no history and cannot speak, the subaltern as female is even more deeply in shadow.

. . . The regulative psychobiography of widow self-immolation will be pertinent in both cases. . . . Let us remind ourselves of the gradual emergence of the new subaltern in the New World Order.

The contemporary international division of labor is a displacement of the divided field of nineteenth-century territorial imperialism. Put in the abstractions of capital logic, in the wake of industrial capitalism and mercantile conquest, a group of countries, generally first-world, were in the position of investing capital; another group, generally third-world, provided the field for investment, both through the subordinate indigenous capitalists and through their ill-protected and shifting labor force. In the interest of maintaining the circulation and growth of industrial capital (and of the concomitant task of administration within nineteenth-century territorial imperialism), transportation, law, and standardized education systems were developed—even as local industries were destroyed or restructured, land distribution was rearranged, and raw material was transferred to the colonizing country. With so-called decolonization, the growth of multinational capital, and the relief of the administrative charge, "development" did not now involve wholesale state-level legislation and establishing education *systems* in a comparable way. This impedes the growth of consumerism in the former colonies. With modern telecommunications and the emergence of advanced capitalist economies at the two edges of Asia, maintaining the international division of labor serves to keep the supply of cheap labor in the periphery. The implosion of the Soviet Union in 1989 has smoothed a way to the financialization of the globe. Already in the mid-seventies, the newly electronified stock exchanges added to the growth of telecommunication, which allowed global capitalism to emerge through export-based subcontracting and postfordism. "Under this strategy, manufacturers based in developed countries subcontract the most labor intensive stages of production, for example, sewing or assembly, to the Third World nations where labor is cheap. Once assembled, the multinational re-imports the goods—under generous tariff exemptions—to the developed country *instead of selling them to the local market.*" Here the link to training in consumerism is almost snapped. "While global recession has markedly slowed trade and investment worldwide since 1979, international subcontracting has boomed.... In these cases, multinationals are freer to resist militant workers, revolutionary upheavals, and even economic downturns."[53]

Human labor is not, of course, intrinsically "cheap" or "expensive." An absence of labor laws (or a discriminatory enforcement of them), a totalitarian state (often entailed by development and modernization in the periphery), and minimal subsistence requirements on the part of the worker will ensure "cheapness." To keep this crucial item intact, the urban proletariat in what is now called the "developing" nations must not be systematically trained in the ideology of consumerism (parading as the philosophy of a classless society) that, against all odds, prepares the ground for resistance through the coalition politics Foucault mentions (*FD* 216). This separation from the ideology of consumerism is increasingly exacerbated by the proliferating phenomena of international subcontracting.

In the post-Soviet world, the Bretton Woods organizations, together with the United Nations, are beginning to legislate for a monstrous North/South global state, which is coming into being micrologically as the trade-controlled colonial state.... If Macaulay had spoken of a class of persons, Indian in blood and colour, but English in taste, in opinions, in morals, and in intellect; and Marx of the capitalist as *Faust's* "mechanical man," there is now an impersonal "Economic Citizen," site of authority and legitimation, lodged in finance capital markets and transnational companies.[54] And if under postfordism and international subcontracting, unorganized or permanently casual female labor was already becoming the mainstay of world trade, in contemporary globalization, the mechanism of "aid" is supported by the poorest women of the South, who form the base of what I have elsewhere called globe-girdling struggles (ecology, resistance to "population *control*"), where the boundary between global and local becomes indeterminate. This is the ground of the emergence of the new subaltern—rather different from the nationalist example we will consider later. To confront this group is not only to represent (*vertreten*) them globally in the absence of infrastructural support, but also to learn to represent (*darstellen*) ourselves. This argument would take us into a critique of a disciplinary anthropology and the relationship between elementary pedagogy and disciplinary formation. It would also question the implicit demand, made by intellectuals who choose the "naturally articulate" subject of oppression, that such a subject come through a history that is a foreshortened mode-of-production narrative.

Not surprisingly, some members of *indigenous dominant* groups in the "developing" countries, members of the local bourgeoisie, find the language of alliance politics attractive. Identifying with forms of resistance plausible in advanced capitalist countries is often of a piece with that elitist bent of bourgeois historiography described by Ranajit Guha.

Belief in the plausibility of global alliance politics is increasingly prevalent among women of dominant social groups interested in "international feminism" in the "developing" nations as well as among well-placed Southern diasporics in the North. At the other end of the scale, those most separated from any possibility of an alliance among "women, prisoners, conscripted soldiers, hospital patients, and homosexuals" (*FD* 216) are the females of the urban subproletariat. In their case, the denial and withholding of consumerism and the structure of exploitation is compounded by patriarchal social relations.

That Deleuze and Foucault ignored both the epistemic violence of imperialism and the international division of labor would matter less if they did not, in closing, touch on third-world issues. In France it is impossible to ignore the problem of their *tiers monde*, the inhabitants of the erstwhile French African colonies. Deleuze limits his consideration of the Third World to these old local and regional indigenous elite who are, ideally, subaltern. In this context, references to the maintenance of the surplus army of labor fall into reverse-ethnic sentimentality. Since he is speaking of the heritage of nineteenth-century territorial imperialism, his reference is to the nation-state rather than the globalizing center:

> French capitalism needs greatly a floating signifier of unemployment. In this perspective, we begin to see the unity of the forms of repression: restrictions on immigration, once it is acknowledged that the most difficult and thankless jobs go to immigrant workers; repression in the factories, because the French must reacquire the "taste" for increasingly harder work; the struggle against youth and the repression of the educational system. (*FD* 211–12)

This is certainly an acceptable analysis. Yet it shows again that the Third World can enter the resistance program of an alliance politics directed against a *"unified* repression" only when it is confined to the third-world groups that are directly accessible to the First World.[55] This benevolent first-world appropriation and reinscription of the Third World as an Other is the founding characteristic of much third-worldism in the U.S. human sciences today.

Foucault continues the critique of Marxism by invoking geographical discontinuity. The real mark of "geographical (geopolitcal) discontinuity" is the international division of labor. But Foucault uses the term to distinguish between exploitation (extraction and appropriation of surplus value; read, the field of Marxist analysis) and domination ("power" studies) and to suggest the latter's greater potential for resistance based on alliance politics. He cannot acknowledge that such a monist and unified access to a conception of "power" (methodologically presupposing a Subject-of-power) is made possible by a certain stage in exploitation, for his vision of geographical discontinuity is geopolitically specific to the First World:

> This geographical discontinuity of which you speak might mean perhaps the following: as soon as we struggle against *exploitation*, the proletariat not only leads the struggle but also defines its targets, its methods, its places and its instruments; and to ally oneself with the proletariat is to consolidate with its positions, its ideology, it is to take up again the motives for their combat. This means total immersion [in the Marxist project]. But if it is against *power* that one struggles, then all those who acknowledge it as intolerable can begin the struggle wherever they find themselves and in terms of their own activity (or passivity). In engaging in this struggle that is *their own*, whose objectives they clearly understand and whose methods they can determine, they enter into the revolutionary process. As allies of the proletariat, to be sure, because power is exercised the way it is in order to maintain capitalist exploitation. They genuinely serve the cause of the proletariat by fighting in those places where they find themselves oppressed. Women, prisoners, conscripted soldiers, hospital patients, and homosexuals have now begun a specific struggle against the particular form of power, the constraints and controls, that are exercised over them. (*FD* 216)

This is an admirable program of localized resistance. Where possible, this model of resistance is not an alternative to, but can complement, macrological struggles along "Marxist" lines. Yet if its situation is universalized, it accommodates unacknowledged privileging of the subject. Without a theory of ideology, it can lead to a dangerous utopianism. And, if confined to migrant struggles in Northern countries, it can work against global social justice.

The topographical reinscription of imperialism never specifically informed Foucault's presuppositions. Notice the omission of the fact, in the following passage, that the new mechanism of power in the seventeenth and eighteenth centuries (the extraction of surplus value without extra-economic coercion is its marxist description) is secured *by means of* territorial imperialism—the Earth and its products—"elsewhere." The representation of sovereignty is crucial in these theaters: "In the seventeenth and eighteenth centuries, we have the production of an important phenomenon, the emergence, or rather the invention, of a new mechanism of power possessed of highly specific procedural techniques . . . which is also, I believe, absolutely incompatible with the relations of sovereignty. This new mechanism of power is more dependent upon bodies and what they do than the Earth and its products" (*PK* 104).

Sometimes it seems as if the very brilliance of Foucault's analysis of the centuries of European imperialism produces a miniature version of that heterogeneous phenomenon: management of space—but by doctors; development of administrations—but in asylums; considerations of the periphery—but in terms of the insane, prisoners, and children. The clinic, the asylum, the prison, the university—all seem to be screen-allegories that foreclose a reading of the broader narratives of imperialism. (One could open a similar discussion of the ferocious motif of "deterritorialization" in Deleuze and Guattari.) "One can perfectly well not talk about something because one doesn't know about it," Foucault might murmur (*PK* 66). Yet we have already spoken of the sanctioned ignorance that every critic of imperialism must chart.

By CONTRAST, the early Derrida seemed aware of ethnocentrism in the production of knowledge.[56] (We have seen this in his comments on Kant . . . . Like "empirical investigation, . . . tak[ing] shelter in the field of grammatological knowledge" obliges "operat[ing] through 'examples,'" *OG* 75.)

The examples Derrida lays out—to show the limits of grammatology as a positive science—come from the appropriate ideological self-justification of an imperialist project. In the European seventeenth century, he writes, there were three kinds of "prejudices" operating in histories of writing which constituted a "symptom of the crisis of European consciousness" (*OG* 75): the "theological prejudice," the "Chinese prejudice," and the "hieroglyphist prejudice." The first can be indexed as: God wrote a primordial or natural script: Hebrew or Greek. The second: Chinese is a perfect *blueprint* for philosophical writing, but it is only a blueprint. True philosophical writing is "independen[t] with regard to history" (OG 79) and will sublate Chinese into an easy-to-learn script that will supersede actual Chinese. The third: that the Egyptian script is too sublime to be deciphered.

The first prejudice preserves the "actuality" of Hebrew or Greek; the last two ("rational" and "mystical," respectively) collude to support the first, where the center of the logos is seen as the Judaeo-Christian God (the appropriation of the Hellenic Other through assimilation is an earlier story)—a "prejudice" still sustained in efforts to give the cartography of the Judaeo-Christian myth the status of geopolitcal history:

> The concept of Chinese writing thus functioned as a sort of *European hallucination.* . . . This functioning obeyed a rigorous necessity. . . . It was not disturbed by the knowledge of Chinese script . . . which was then available. . . . A *"hieroglyphist prejudice"* had produced the same effect of *interested blindness.* Far from proceeding . . . from ethnocentric scorn, the occultation takes the form of an hyperbolical admiration. We have not finished demonstrating the necessity of this pattern. Our century is not free from it; each time that ethnocentrism is precipitately and ostentatiously reversed, some effort silently hides behind all the spectacular effects to *consolidate an inside* and to draw from it some domestic benefit. (*OG* 80; Derrida italicizes only "hieroglyphist prejudice")

This pattern operates the culturalist excuse for Development encountered, e.g., in John Rawls's *Political Liberalism,* as it does all unexamined metropolitan hybridism.[57]

Derrida closes the chapter by showing again that the project of grammatology is obliged to develop *within* the discourse of presence. It is not just a critique of presence but an awareness of the itinerary of the discourse of presence in one's *own* critique, a vigilance precisely against too great a claim for transparency. The word "writing" as the name of the object and model of grammatology is a practice "only within the *historical* closure, that is to say within the limits of science and philosophy" (*OG* 93).

Derrida calls the ethnocentrism of the European science of writing in the late seventeenth and early eighteenth centuries a symptom of the general crisis of European consciousness. It is, of course, part of a larger symptom, or perhaps the crisis itself, the slow turn from feudalism to capitalism via the first waves of capitalist imperialism. The itinerary of recognition through assimilation of the Other can be more interestingly traced, it seems to me, in the imperialist constitution of the colonial subject and the foreclosure of the figure of the "native informant."

CAN THE SUBALTERN SPEAK? What might the elite do to watch out for the continuing construction of the subaltern? The question of "woman" seems most problematic in this context. Confronted by the ferocious standardizing benevolence of most U.S. and Western European human-scientific radicalism (recognition by assimilation) today, and the exclusion of the margins of even the center-periphery articulation (the "true and differential subaltern"), the analogue of class-consciousness rather than race-consciousness in this area seems historically, disciplinarily, and practically forbidden by Right and Left alike.

In so fraught a field, it is not easy to ask the question of the subaltern woman as subject; it is thus all the more necessary to remind pragmatic radicals that such a question is not an idealist red herring. Though all feminist or antisexist projects cannot be reduced to this one, to ignore it is an unacknowledged political gesture that has a long history and collaborates with a masculist radicalism that operates by strategic exclusions, equating "nationalist" and "people" (as counterproductive as the equation of "feminist" and "woman").

If I ask myself, How is it possible to want to die by fire to mourn a husband ritually, I am asking the question of the (gendered) subaltern woman as subject, not, as my friend Jonathan Culler somewhat tendentiously suggests, trying to "produce difference by differing" or to "appeal . . . to a sexual identity defined as essential and privileg[ing] experiences associated with that identity."[58] Culler is here a part of that mainstream project of Western feminism which both continues and displaces the battle over the right to individualism between women and men in situations of upward class mobility. One suspects that the debate between U.S. feminism and European "theory" (as theory is generally represented by women from the United States or Britain) occupies a significant corner of that very terrain. I am generally sympathetic with the call to make U.S. feminism more "theoretical." It seems, however, that the problem of the muted subject of the subaltern woman, though not solved by an "essentialist" search for lost origins, cannot be served by the call for more theory in Anglo-America either.

That call is often given in the name of a critique of "positivism," which is seen here as identical with "essentialism." Yet Hegel, the modern inaugurator of "the work of the negative," was not a stranger to the notion of essences. For Marx, the curious persistence of essentialism within the dialectic was a profound and productive problem. Thus, the stringent binary opposition between positivism/essentialism (read, U.S.) and "theory" (read, French or Franco-German via Anglo-American) may be spurious. Apart from repressing the ambiguous complicity between essentialism and critiques of positivism (acknowledged by Derrida in "Of Grammatology as a Positive Science"), it also errs by implying that positivism is not a theory. This move allows the emergence of a proper name, a positive essence, Theory. And once again, the position of the investigator remains unquestioned. If and when this territorial debate turns toward the Third World, no change in the question of method is to be discerned. This debate cannot take into account that, in the case of the woman as subaltern, rather few ingredients for the constitution of the itinerary of the trace of a sexed subject (rather than an anthropological object) can be gathered to locate the possibility of dissemination.

Yet I remain generally sympathetic to aligning feminism with the critique of positivism and the defetishization of the concrete. I am also far from averse to learning from the work of Western theorists, though I have learned to insist on marking their positionality as investigating subjects. Given these conditions, and as a literary critic, I tactically confronted the immense problem of the consciousness of the woman as subaltern. I reinvented the problem in a sentence and transformed it into the object of a simple semiosis. What can such a transformation mean?

This gesture of transformation marks the fact that knowledge of the other subject is theoretically impossible. Empirical work in the discipline constantly performs this transformation tacitly. It is a transformation from a first-second person performance to the constatation in the third person. It is, in other words, at once a gesture of control and an acknowledgement of limits. Freud provides a homology for such positional hazards.

Sarah Kofman has suggested that the deep ambiguity of Freud's use of women as a scapegoat may be read as a reaction-formation to an initial and continuing desire to give the hysteric a voice, to transform her into the *subject* of hysteria.[59] The masculine-imperialist ideological formation that shaped that desire into "the daughter's seduction" is part of the same formation that constructs the monolithic "third-world woman." No contemporary metropolitan investigator is not influenced by that formation. Part of our "unlearning" project is to articulate our participation in that formation—by *measuring* silences, if necessary—into the *object* of investigation. Thus, when confronted with the questions, Can the subaltern speak? and Can the subaltern (as woman) speak?, our efforts to give the subaltern a voice in history will be doubly open to the dangers run by Freud's discourse. It is in acknowledgment of these dangers rather than as solution to a problem that I put together the sentence "White men are saving brown women from brown men," a sentence that runs like a red thread through today's "gender and development." My impulse is not unlike the one to be encountered in Freud's investigation of the sentence "A child is being beaten."[60]

The use of Freud here does not imply an isomorphic analogy between subject-formation and the behavior of social collectives, a frequent practice, often accompanied by a reference to Reich, in the conversation between Deleuze and Foucault. I am, in other words, not suggesting that "White men are saving brown women from brown men" is a sentence indicating a *collective* fantasy symptomatic of a *collective* itinerary of sadomasochistic repression in a *collective* imperialist enterprise. There is a satisfying symmetry in such an allegory, but I would rather invite the reader to consider it a problem in "wild psychoanalysis" than a clinching solution.[61] Just as Freud's insistence on making the woman the scapegoat in "A child is being beaten" and elsewhere discloses his political interests, however imperfectly, so my insistence on imperialist subject-production as the occasion for this sentence discloses a politics that I cannot step around.

Further, I am attempting to borrow the general methodological aura of Freud's strategy toward the sentence he constructed *as a sentence* out of the many similar substantive accounts his patients gave him. This does not mean I will offer a case of transference-in-analysis as an isomorphic model for the transaction between reader and text (here the constructed sentence). As I repeat in this chapter, the analogy between transference and literary criticism or historiography is no more than a productive catachresis. To say that the subject is a text does not authorize the converse pronouncement: that the verbal text is a subject.

I am fascinated, rather, by how Freud predicates a *history* of repression that produces the final sentence. It is a history with a double origin, one hidden in the amnesia of the infant, the other lodged in our archaic past, assuming by implication a preoriginary space where human and animal were not yet differentiated.[62] We are driven to impose a homology of this Freudian strategy on the Marxist narrative to explain the ideological dissimulation of imperialist political economy and outline a history of repression that produces a sentence like the one I have sketched: "White men are saving brown women from brown men"—giving honorary whiteness to the colonial subject on precisely this issue. This history also has a double origin, one hidden in the maneuverings behind the British abolition of widow sacrifice in 1829,[63] the other lodged in the classical and Vedic past of "Hindu" India, the *Ṛg-Veda* and the *Dharmaśāstra*. An undifferentiated transcendental preoriginary space can only too easily be predicated for this other history.

The sentence I have constructed is one among many displacements describing the relationship between brown and white men (sometimes brown and white women worked in).[64] It takes its place among some sentences of "hyperbolic admiration" or of pious guilt that Derrida speaks of in connection with the "hieroglyphist prejudice." The relationship between the imperialist subject and the subject of imperialism is at least ambiguous.

The Hindu widow ascends the pyre of the dead husband and immolates herself upon it. This is widow sacrifice. (The conventional transcription of the Sanskrit word for the widow would be *sati*. The early colonial British transcribed it *suttee*.) The rite was not practiced universally and was not caste- or class-fixed. The abolition of this rite by the British has been generally understood as a case of "White men saving brown women from brown men." White women—from the nineteenth-century British Missionary Registers to Mary Daly—have not produced an alternative understanding. Against this is the Indian nativist statement, a parody of the nostalgia for lost origins: "The women wanted to die," still being advanced . . . [65]

The two sentences go a long way to legitimize each other. One never encounters the testimony of the women's voice consciousness. Such a testimony would not be ideology-transcendent or "fully" subjective, of course, but it would constitute the ingredients for producing a countersentence. As one goes down the grotesquely mistranscribed names of these women, the sacrificed widows, in the police reports included in the records of the East India Company, one cannot put together a "voice." The most one can sense is the immense heterogeneity breaking through even such a skeletal and ignorant account (castes, for example, are regularly described as tribes). Faced with the dialectically interlocking sentences that are constructible as "White men are saving brown women from brown men" and "The women wanted to die," the metropolitan feminist migrant (removed from the actual theater of decolonization) asks the question of simple semiosis—What does this signify?—and begins to plot a history.

As I have suggested elsewhere, to mark the moment when not only a civil but a good society is born out of domestic confusion, singular events that break the letter of the law to institute its spirit are often invoked. The protection of women by men often provides such an event. If we remember that the British boasted of their absolute equity toward and noninterference with native custom/law, an invocation of this sanctioned transgression of the letter for the sake of the spirit may be read in J. D. M. Derrett's remark: "The very first legislation upon Hindu Law was carried through without the assent of a single Hindu." The legislation is not named here. The next sentence, where the measure is named, is equally interesting if one considers the implications of the survival of a colonially established "good" society after decolonization: "The recurrence of *sati* in independent India is probably an obscurantist revival which cannot long survive even in a very backward part of the country."[66]

Whether this observation is correct or not, what interests me is that the protection of woman (today the "third-world woman") becomes a signifier for the establishment of a *good* society (now a good planet) which must, at such inaugurative moments, transgress mere legality, or equity of legal policy. In this particular case, the process also allowed the redefinition as a crime of what had been tolerated, known, or adulated as ritual. In other words, this one item in Hindu law jumped the frontier between the private and the public domain.

Although Foucault's *historical narrative*, focusing solely on Western Europe, sees merely a tolerance for the criminal antedating the development of criminology in the late eighteenth century (*PK* 41), his *theoretical description* of the "episteme" is pertinent here: "The *episteme* is the 'apparatus' which makes possible the separation not of the true from the false, but of what may not be characterized as scientific" (*PK* 197)—ritual as opposed to crime, the one fixed by superstition, the other by legal science.[67]

The leap of *suttee* from private to public has a clear but complex relationship with the changeover from a mercantile and commercial to a territorial and administrative British presence; it can be followed in correspondence among the police stations, the lower and higher courts, the courts of directors, the prince regent's court, and the like.[68] (It is interesting to note that, from the point of view of the native "colonial subject," also emergent from the "feudalism-capitalism" transition—necessarily askew because "colonial"—*sati* is a signifier with the reverse social charge: "Groups rendered psychologically marginal by their exposure to Western impact . . . had come under pressure to demonstrate, to others as well as to themselves, their ritual purity and allegiance to traditional high culture. To many of them *sati* became an important proof of their conformity to older norms at a time when these norms had become shaky within.")[69]

If the mercantile-territorial/feudal-capitalist transitions provide a first historical origin for my sentence—"white men are saving brown women from brown men"—that origin is evidently lost in the more general history of humankind as work, its origin placed by Marx in the material exchange or "metabolism" between the human being and Nature, the story of capitalist expansion, the slow freeing of labor power as commodity, the narrative of the modes of production, the transition from feudalism via mercantilism to capitalism.[70] As my first chapter has argued, even the precarious normativity of this narrative is sustained by the putatively changeless stopgap of the "Asiatic" mode of production, which steps in to sustain it whenever it might become apparent that the story of capital logic is the story of the West, that only imperialism can aggressively insist upon the universality of the mode of production narrative, that to ignore or invade the subaltern today is, willy-nilly, to continue the imperialist project; in the name of modernization, in the interest of globalization. The origin of my sentence is thus lost in the shuffle between other, more powerful discourses. Given that the abolition of *sati* was in itself admirable, is it still possible to wonder if a perception of the origin of my sentence might contain interventionist possibilities?

I will later place the mobilizing of woman into *Sati* with the place of the epic instance of "heroism"—suicide in the name of "nation"; "martyrdom"—suicide in the name of "God"; and other species of self-"sacrifice." These are transcendental figurations of the (agent of the) gift of time. The feminist project is not simply to stage the woman as victim; but to ask: why does "husband" become an appropriate name for *radical* alterity? Why is "to be" equal to "to be wife?" This may even lead to such questions as the contemporary equation of "to be" with "to be gainfully employed."[71] Let us stop this line of questioning, for it will no longer allow the general reader to keep *sati* contained within the particularisms of "cultural difference"—that allowed imperialism to give itself yet another legitimation in its "civilizing mission," today recoded, it bears repetition, as the more tolerable phrase "gender and development," the copula "and" (with its concealed charge of supplementation) replacing the more transparent earlier phrase "woman in development."[72]

Imperialism's (or globalization's) image as the establisher of the good society is marked by the espousal of the woman as *object* of protection from her own kind. How should one examine this dissimulation of patriarchal strategy, which apparently grants the woman free choice as *subject*? In other words, how does one make the move from "Britain" to "Hinduism"? Even the attempt shows that, like "Development," "Imperialism" is not identical with chromatism, or mere prejudice against people of color. To approach this question, I will touch briefly on the *Dharmaśāstra* and the *Rg-Veda*. Although two vastly different kinds of texts, they can represent "the archaic origin" in my homology from Freud. My readings are an interested and inexpert examination, by a female expatriate, of the fabrication of repression, a constructed counternarrative of woman's consciousness, thus woman's being, thus woman's being good, thus the good woman's desire, thus woman's desire. Paradoxically, these same moves allow us to witness the unfixed place of woman as a signifier in the inscription of the social individual. Thus "woman" is caught between the interested "normalization" of capital and the regressive "envy" of the colonized male.[73] The "enlightened" colonial subject moves toward the former, without asking the less "practical" question of psychobiography. *Sati* returns—once again grasped as victimage versus cultural heroism—in the rift of the failure of decolonization. It is the somewhat fanatical Melanie Klein who has given this writer the confidence to suggest that to ignore the rôle of violence in the development of conscience is to court the repetition of suicide as accountability.[74]

What is it to ask the question of psychobiography? I should need much greater learning to be a real player here. But it is part of the tragic narrative of the atrophy of classical learning that the scholar cannot ask the radical questions.[75]

The two moments in the *Dharmaśāstra* that I am interested in are the discourse on sanctioned suicides and the nature of the rites for the dead.[76] Framed in these two discourses, the self-immolation of widows seems an exception to the rule. The general scriptural doctrine is that suicide is reprehensible. Room is made, however, for certain forms of suicide which, as formulaic performance, lose the phenomenal identity of being suicide. The first category of sanctioned suicides arises out of *tattvajnāna*, or the knowledge of right principles. Here the knowing subject comprehends the insubstantiality or mere phenomenality (which may be the same thing as nonphenomenality) of its identity. At a certain point in time, *tat tva* was interpreted as "that you," but even without that, *tattva* is thatness or quiddity. Thus, this enlightened self truly knows the "that"-ness of its identity. Its demolition of that identity is not *ātmaghāta* (a killing of the self). The paradox of knowing the limits of knowledge is that the strongest assertion of agency, to negate the possibility of agency, cannot be an example of itself. Curiously enough, the self-*sacrifice* of gods is sanctioned by natural ecology, useful for the working of the economy of Nature and the Universe, rather than by self-knowledge. In this *logically* anterior stage, inhabited by gods rather than human beings, of this particular chain of displacements, suicide and sacrifice (*ātmaghāta* and *ātmadāna*) seem as little distinct as an "interior" (self-knowledge) and an "exterior" (ecology) sanction.

This philosophical space, however, does not accommodate the self-immolating woman. For her we look where room is made to sanction suicides that cannot claim truth-knowledge as a state that is, at any rate, easily verifiable and belongs in the area of *sruti* (what was heard) rather than *smriti* (what is remembered). This third exception to the general rule about suicide annuls the phenomenal identity or irrationality of self-immolation if performed in certain places rather than in a certain state of enlightenment. Thus we move from an interior sanction (truth-knowledge) to an exterior one (place of pilgrimage). It is possible for a woman to perform *this* type of (non)suicide.[77]

Yet even this is not the *proper* place for the woman to annul the proper name of suicide through the destruction of her proper self. For her alone is sanctioned self-immolation on a dead spouse's pyre. (The few male examples cited in Hindu antiquity of self-immolation on another's pyre, being proofs of enthusiasm and devotion to a master or superior, reveal the structure of domination within the rite.)

This suicide that is not suicide may be read as a simulacrum of both truth-knowledge and piety of place. If the former, it is as if the knowledge *in a subject* of its own insubstantiality and mere phenomenality is dramatized so that the dead husband becomes the exteriorized example and place of the extinguished subject and the widow becomes the (non)agent who "acts it out": the logical consequence of placing agency in alterity: transforming ethics into an institutional calculus which supposedly codes the absent agent's intention. If the latter, it is as if the metonym for all sacred places is now that burning bed of wood, constructed by elaborate ritual, where the woman's subject, legally displaced from herself, is being consumed. It is in terms of this profound ideology of the displaced place of the female subject that the paradox of free choice comes into play. For the male subject, it is the felicity of the suicide, a felicity that will annul rather than establish its status as such, that is noted. For the female subject, a sanctioned self-immolation, even as it takes away the effect of "fall" (*pātaka*) attached to an unsanctioned suicide, brings praise for the act of choice on another register. By the inexorable ideological production of the sexed subject, such a death can be understood by the female subject as an *exceptional* signifier of her own desire, exceeding the general rule for a widow's conduct.

In certain periods and areas this exceptional rule became the general rule in a class-specific way. Ashis Nandy relates its marked prevalence in eighteenth- and early nineteenth-century Bengal to factors ranging from population control to communal misogyny.[78] Certainly its prevalence there in the previous centuries was because in Bengal, unlike elsewhere in India, widows could inherit property. Thus, what the British see as poor victimized women going to the slaughter is in fact an ideological battleground. As P. V. Kane, the great historian of the *Dharmaśāstra*, has correctly observed: "In Bengal, [the fact that] the widow of a sonless member even in a joint Hindu family is entitled to practically the same rights over joint family property which her deceased husband would have had . . . must have frequently induced the surviving members to get rid of the widow by appealing at a most distressing hour to her devotion to and love for her husband" (*HD* II.2, 635).

Yet benevolent and enlightened males were and are sympathetic with the "courage" of the woman's free choice in the matter. They thus often accept the production of the sexed subaltern subject: "Modern India does not justify the practice of *sati*, but it is a warped mentality that rebukes modern Indians for expressing admiration and reverence for the cool and unfaltering courage of Indian women in becoming *satis* or performing the *jauhar* for cherishing their ideals of womanly conduct" (*HD* II.2, 636).

This patriarchal admiration is consonant with the logic of the practice. By contrast, the relationship between British benevolence and that logic is in fact "a case of conflict . . . that cannot be equitably resolved for lack of a rule of judgment applicable to both arguments. One side's legitimacy does not imply the other's lack of legitimacy."[79] Historically, legitimacy was of course established by virtue of abstract institutional power. Who in nineteenth-century India could have waited for the women's time here?

> In the differend, something "asks" to be put into phrases, and suffers from the wrong of not being able to be put into phrases right away. This is when the human beings who thought they could use language as an instrument of communication learn through the feeling of pain which accompanies silence (and of pleasure which accompanies the invention of a new idiom), that they are summoned by language, not to augment to their profit the quantity of information communicable through existing idioms, but to recognize that what remains to be phrased exceeds what they can presently phrase, and that they must be allowed to institute idioms which do not yet exist.[80]

It is of course unthinkable that such an allowance could ever be made or seized for or through the agency of nonbourgeois women in British India, as it is unthinkable in globalization in the name of feminism today. In the event, as the discourse of what the reformers perceived as heathen ritual or superstition was recoded as crime, one diagnosis of female free will was substituted for another. In the last movement of this chapter we will bear witness to what may have been an effort to institute an idiomatic moment in the scripting of the reproductive body. It was not read or heard; it remained in the space of the differend.

It must be remembered that the self-immolation of widows was not *invariable* ritual prescription. If, however, the widow does decide thus to exceed the letter of ritual, to turn back is a transgression for which a particular type of penance is prescribed.[81] With the local British police officer supervising the immolation, to be dissuaded after a decision was, by contrast, a mark of real free choice, a choice of freedom. The ambiguity of the position of the indigenous colonial elite is disclosed in the nationalistic romanticization of the purity, strength, and love of these self-sacrificing women. The two set pieces are Rabindranath Tagore's paean to the "self-renouncing paternal grandmothers of Bengal," and Ananda Coomaraswamy's eulogy of *suttee* as "this last proof of the perfect unity of body and soul."[82]

Obviously I am not advocating the killing of widows. I am suggesting that, within the two contending versions of freedom, the constitution of the female subject in *life* is the place of the differend. In the case of widow self-immolation, ritual is not being redefined as patriarchy but as *crime*.[83] The gravity of *sati* was that it was ideologically cathected as "reward," just as the gravity of imperialism was that it was ideologically cathected as "social mission." Between patriarchy and Development, this is the subaltern woman's situation today. Thompson's understanding of *sati* as "punishment" is thus far off the mark:

> It may seem unjust and illogical that the Moguls, who freely impaled and flayed alive, or nationals of Europe, whose countries had such ferocious penal codes and had known, scarcely a century before suttee began to shock the English conscience, orgies of witch-burning and religious persecution, should have felt as they did about suttee. But the differences seemed to them this—the victims of their cruelties were tortured by a law which considered them offenders, whereas the victims of suttee were punished for no offense but the physical weakness which had placed them at man's mercy. The rite seemed to prove a depravity and arrogance such as no other human offense had brought to light.[84]

No. As in the case of war, martyrdom, "terrorism"—self-sacrifice in general—the "felicitous" *sati* may have (been imagined to have) thought she was exceeding and transcending the ethical. That is its danger. Not all soldiers die unwillingly. And there are female suicide bombers.

All through the mid- and late-eighteenth century, in the spirit of the codification of the law, the British in India collaborated and consulted with learned Brahmans to judge whether *suttee* was legal by their homogenized version of Hindu law. *Sati* was still contained within the interested use of cultural relativism. The collaboration was often idiosyncratic, as in the case of the significance of being dissuaded. Sometimes, as in the general Sastric prohibition against the immolation of widows with small children, the British collaboration seems confused.[85] In the beginning of the nineteenth century, the British authorities, and especially the British in England, repeatedly suggested that collaboration made it appear as if the British condoned this practice. When the law was finally written, the history of the long period of collaboration was effaced, and the language celebrated the noble Hindu who was against the bad Hindu, the latter given to savage atrocities:

> The practice of Suttee . . . is revolting to the feeling of human nature. . . . In many instances, acts of atrocity have been perpetrated, which have been shocking to the Hindoos themselves. . . . Actuated by these considerations of the Governor-General in Council, without intending to depart from one of the first and most important principles of the system of British Govern-

ment in India that all classes of the people be secure in the observance of their religious usages, so long as that system can be adhered to without violation of the paramount dictates of justice and humanity, has deemed it right to establish the following rules. . . . (*HD* 11.2, 624–25)

(Topically, it is a celebration of Safie over the Monster in *Frankenstein*.)

That this was an alternative ideology of the graded sanctioning of varieties of suicide as exception, rather than its inscription as "sin," was of course not understood. *Sati* could not, of course, be read with Christian female martyrdom, with the defunct husband standing in for the transcendental One; or with war, with the husband standing in for sovereign or state, for whose sake an intoxicating ideology of self-sacrifice can be mobilized. It had to be categorized with murder, infanticide, and the lethal exposure of the very old. The agency was always male; the woman was always the victim. The dubious place of the free will of the constituted sexed subject as female was successfully effaced. There is no itinerary we can retrace here. Since the other sanctioned suicides did not involve the scene of this constitution, they entered neither the ideological battleground at the archaic origin—the tradition of the *Dharmaśāstra*—nor the scene of the reinscription of ritual as crime—the British abolition. The only related transformation was Mahatma Gandhi's reinscription of the notion of *satyāgraha*, or hunger strike, as resistance. But this is not the place to discuss the details of that sea change. I would merely invite the reader to compare the auras of widow sacrifice and Gandhian resistance. The root in the first part of *satyāgraha* and *sati* are the same.

Since the beginning of the Puranic era (the earliest Puranas date from the 4th century B.C.), learned Brahmans debated the doctrinal appropriateness of *sati* as of sanctioned suicides in sacred places in general. (This debate still continues in an academic way.) Sometimes the caste provenance of the practice was in question. The general law for widows, that they should observe *brahmacarya*, was, however, hardly ever debated. It is not enough to translate *brahmacarya* as "celibacy." It should be recognized that, of the four ages of being in Hindu (or Brahmanical) *regulative* psychobiography, *brahmacarya* is the social practice anterior to the kinship inscription of marriage. The man—widower or husband—graduates through *vānaprastha* (forest life) into the mature celibacy and renunciation of *samnyāsa* (laying aside).[86] The woman as wife is indispensable for *gārhasthya*, or householdership, and may accompany her husband into forest life. She has no access (according to Brahmanical sanction) to the final celibacy of asceticism, or *samnyāsa*. The woman as widow, by the general law of sacred doctrine, must regress to an anteriority transformed into stasis. The institutional evils attendant upon this law are well known; I am considering its asymmetrical effect on the ideological formation of the sexed subject. It is thus of much greater significance that there was no debate on this nonexceptional fate of widows—either among Hindus or between Hindus and British—than that the *exceptional* prescription of self-immolation was actively contested.[87] Here the possibility of recovering a (sexually) subaltern subject is once again lost and overdetermined.

This legally programmed asymmetry in the status of the subject, which effectively defines the woman as object of *one* husband, obviously operates in the interest of the legally symmetrical subject-status of the male. The self-immolation of the widow thereby becomes the extreme case of the general law rather than an exception to it. It is not surprising, then, to read of heavenly rewards for the *sati*, where the quality of being the object of a unique possessor is emphasized by way of rivalry with other females, those ecstatic heavenly dancers, paragons of female beauty and male pleasure who sing her praise: "In heaven she, being solely devoted to her husband, and praised by groups of *apsarās* [heavenly dancers], sports with her husband as long as fourteen Indras rule" (*HD* II.2, 631).

The profound irony in locating the woman's free will in self-immolation is once again revealed in a verse accompanying the earlier passage: "As long as the woman [as wife: *stri*] does not burn herself in fire on the death of her husband, she is never released [*mucyate*] from her female body [*strisarir* —i.e., in the cycle of births]." Even as it operates the most subtle general release from individual agency, the sanctioned suicide peculiar to woman draws its ideological strength by *identifying* individual agency with the supraindividual: kill yourself on your husband's pyre now, and you may kill your female body in the entire cycle of birth.

In a further twist of the paradox, this emphasis on free will establishes the peculiar misfortune of holding a female body. The word for the self that is actually burned is the standard word for spirit in the noblest impersonal sense (*ātman*), while the verb "release," through the root of salvation in the noblest sense (*muc > moksa*) is in the passive, and the word for that which is annulled in the cycle of birth is the everyday word for the body. The ideological message writes itself in the benevolent twentieth-century male historian's admiration: "The Jauhar [group self-immolation of aristocratic Rajput war-widows or imminent war-widows] practiced by the Rajput ladies of Chitor and other places for saving themselves from unspeakable atrocities at the hands of the victorious Moslems are too well known to need any lengthy notice" (*HD* II.2, 629).[88]

Although *jauhar* is not, strictly speaking, an act of *sati*, and although I do not wish to speak for the sanctioned sexual violence of conquering male armies, "Moslem" or otherwise, female self-immolation in the face of it is a legitimation of rape as "natural" and works, in the long run, in the interest of unique genital possession of the female. The group rape perpetrated by the conquerors is a metonymic celebration of territorial acquisition. Just as the general law for widows was unquestioned, so this act of female hero-ism persists among the patriotic tales told to children, thus operating on the crudest level of ideological reproduction. It has also played a tremendous rôle, precisely as an overdetermined signifier, in acting out Hindu commu-nalism. (The Internet produced spurious statistics on Hindu "genocide" in Bangladesh.)[89] Simultaneously, the broader question of the constitution of the sexed subject is hidden by foregrounding the visible violence of *sati*. The task of recovering a (sexually) subaltern subject is lost in an institu-tional textuality at the archaic origin.

As I mentioned above, when the status of the legal subject as property-holder could be temporarily bestowed on the *female* relict, the self-immola-tion of widows was stringently enforced. Raghunandana, the late fifteenth-/ sixteenth-century legalist whose interpretations are supposed to lend the greatest authority to such enforcement, takes as his text a curious passage from the *Rg-Veda*, the most ancient of the Hindu sacred texts, the first of the *Srutis*. In doing so, he is following a centuries-old tradition commemorating a peculiar and transparent misreading at the very place of sanction. Here is the verse outlining certain steps within the rites for the dead. Even at a simple reading it is clear that it is "not addressed to widows at all, but to ladies of the deceased man's household whose husbands were living." Why then was it taken as authoritative? This, the unemphatic transposition of the dead for the living husband, is a different order of mystery at the ar-chaic origin from the ones we have been discussing: "Let these whose hus-bands are worthy and are living enter the house, tearless, healthy, and well adorned" (*HD* II.2, 634).

But this crucial transposition is not the only mistake here. The authority is lodged in a disputed passage and an alternate reading. In the second line, here translated "Let these wives first step into the house," the word for first is *agré*. Some have read it as *agné*, "O fire." As Kane makes clear, however, "even without this change Aparārka and others rely for the practice of *Sati* on this verse" (*HD* IV.2, 199). Here is another screen around one origin of the history of the subaltern female subject. Is it a historical oneirocritique that one should perform on a statement such as: "Therefore it must be admitted that either the MSS are corrupt or Raghunandana committed an innocent slip" (*HD* II.2, 634)? It should be mentioned that the rest of the poem is ei-ther about that general law of *brahmacarya*-in-stasis for widows, to which *sati* is an exception, or about *niyōga*—"appointing a brother or any near kins-man to raise up issue to a deceased husband by marrying his widow."[90]

If P. V. Kane is the authority on the history of the *Dharmaśāstra*, Mulla's *Principles of Hindu Law* is the practical guide. It is part of the historical text of what Freud calls "kettle logic" that we are unraveling here, that Mulla's textbook adduces, just as definitively, that the *Rg-Vedic* verse under consideration was proof that "remarriage of widows and divorce are recognized in some of the old texts."[91]

One cannot help but wonder about the rôle of the word *yoni*. In context, with the localizing adverb *agré* (in front), the word means "dwelling-place." But that does not efface its primary sense of "genital" (not yet perhaps specifically *female* genital). How can we take as the authority for the choice of a widow's self-immolation a passage celebrating the entry of adorned wives into a dwelling place invoked on this occasion by its *yoni*-name, so that the extracontextual icon is almost one of entry into civic production or birth? Paradoxically, the imagic relationship of vagina and fire lends a kind of strength to the authority-claim.[92] This paradox is strengthened by Raghunandana's modification of the verse so as to read, "Let them first ascend the *fluid* abode [or origin, with, of course, the *yoni*-name—*ā rohantu jalayōnimagné*], O fire [or of fire]." Why should one accept that this "probably mean[s] 'may fire be to them as cool as water'" (*HD* II.2, 634)? The fluid genital of fire, a corrupt phrasing, might figure a sexual indeterminacy providing a simulacrum for the intellectual indeterminacy of *tattvajnāna* (truth-knowledge). . . . These speculations are certainly no more absurd than the ones I have cited. Scriptural sanction, in other words, is a gesture of evidence, rather than rational textual support.

I have written above of a constructed counternarrative of woman's consciousness, thus woman's being, thus woman's being good, thus the good woman's desire, thus woman's desire. This slippage can be seen in the fracture inscribed in the very word *sati*, the feminine form of *sat*. *Sat* transcends any gender-specific notion of masculinity and moves up not only into human but spiritual universality. It is the present participle of the verb "to be" and as such means not only being but the True, the Good, the Right. In the sacred texts it is essence, universal spirit. Even as a prefix it indicates appropriate, felicitous, fit. It is noble enough to have entered the most privileged discourse of modern Western philosophy: Heidegger's meditation on Being.[93] *Sati*, the feminine of this word, simply means "good wife."

In fact, *sati* or *suttee* as the proper name of the rite of widow self-immolation commemorates a grammatical error on the part of the British, quite as the nomenclature "American Indian" commemorates a factual error on the part of Columbus. The word in the various Indian languages is "the burning of the *sati*" or the good wife, who thus escapes the regressive stasis of the widow in *brahmacarya*. This exemplifies the race-class-gender overdeterminations of the situation. It can perhaps be caught even when it is flattened out: white men, seeking to save brown women from brown men, imposed upon those women a greater ideological construction by absolutely identifying, *within discursive practice*, good-wifehood and self-immolation on the husband's pyre by an ignorant (but sanctioned) synecdoche. On the other side of thus constituting the *object*, the abolition (or removal) of which will provide the occasion for establishing a good, as distinguished from merely civil, society, is the Hindu manipulation of female *subject*-constitution which I have tried to discuss.

(I have already mentioned Edward Thompson's *Suttee*, published in 1928. I cannot do justice here to this perfect specimen of the justification of imperialism as a civilizing mission. Nowhere in his book, written by someone who avowedly "loved India," is there any questioning of the "beneficial ruthlessness" of the British in India as motivated by territorial expansionism or management of industrial capital.[94] The problem with his book is, indeed, a problem of representation, the construction of a continuous and homogeneous "India" in terms of heads of state and British administrators, from the perspective of "a man of good sense" who would be the transparent voice of reasonable humanity. "India" can then be represented, in the other sense, by its imperial masters. My reason for referring to *suttee* here is Thompson's finessing of the word *sati* as "faithful" in the very first sentence of his book, an inaccurate translation that is nonetheless an English permit for the insertion of the female subject into twentieth-century discourse.[95] After such a taming of the subject, Thompson can write, under the heading "The Psychology of the '*Sati*'," "I had intended to try to examine this; but the truth is, it has ceased to puzzle me.")[96]

Between patriarchy and imperialism, subject-constitution and object-formation, the figure of the woman disappears, not into a pristine nothingness, but into a violent shuttling which is the displaced figuration of the "third-world woman" caught between tradition and modernization, culturalism and development. These considerations would revise every detail of judgments that seem valid for a history of sexuality in the West: "Such would be the property of repression, that which distinguishes it from the prohibitions maintained by simple penal law: repression functions well as a sentence to disappear, but also as an injunction to silence, affirmation of non-existence; and consequently states that of all this there is nothing to say, to see, to know."[97] The case of *suttee* as exemplum of the woman-in-imperialism would challenge and deconstruct this opposition between subject (law) and object-of-knowledge (repression) and mark the place of "disappearance" with something other than silence and nonexistence, a violent aporia between subject and object status.[98]

Sati as a woman's proper name is in fairly widespread use in India today. Naming a female infant "a good wife" has its own proleptic irony, and the irony is all the greater because this sense of the common noun is not the primary operator in the proper name.[99] Behind the naming of the infant is *the* Sati of Hindu mythology, Durga in her manifestation as a good wife.[100] In part of the story, Sati—she is already called that—arrives at her father's court uninvited, in the absence, even, of an invitation for her divine husband Siva. Her father starts to abuse Siva and Sati dies in pain. Siva arrives in a fury and dances over the universe with Sati's corpse on his shoulder. Visnu dismembers her body and bits are strewn over the earth. Around each such relic bit is a great place of pilgrimage.

Figures like the goddess Athena—"father's daughters self-professedly uncontaminated by the womb"—are useful for establishing women's ideological self-debasement, which is to be distinguished from a deconstructive attitude toward the essentialist subject. The story of the mythic Sati, reversing every narrateme of the rite, performs a similar function: the living husband avenges the wife's death, a transaction between great male gods fulfills the destruction of the female body and thus inscribes the earth as sacred geography. To see this as proof of the feminism of classical Hinduism or of Indian culture as goddess-centered and therefore feminist is as ideologically contaminated by nativism or reverse ethnocentrism as it was imperialist to erase the image of the luminous fighting Mother Durga and invest the proper noun Sati with no significance other than the ritual burning of the helpless widow as sacrificial offering who can then be saved. May the empowering voice of so-called superstition (Durga) not be a better starting point for transformation than the belittling or punitive befriending of the white mythology of "reasonableness" (British police)? The interested do-gooding of corporate philanthropy keeps the question worth asking.[101]

If the oppressed under postmodern capital have no necessarily unmediated access to "correct" resistance, can the ideology of *sati*, coming from the history of the periphery, be sublated into any model of interventionist practice? Since this essay operates on the notion that all such clear-cut nostalgias for lost origins are suspect, especially as grounds for counterhegemonic ideological production, I must proceed by way of an example.[102]

A YOUNG WOMAN of sixteen or seventeen, Bhubaneswari Bhaduri, hanged herself in her father's modest apartment in North Calcutta in 1926. The suicide was a puzzle since, as Bhubaneswari was menstruating at the time, it was clearly not a case of illicit pregnancy. Nearly a decade later, it was discovered, in a letter she had left for her elder sister, that she was a member of one of the many groups involved in the armed struggle for Indian independence. She had been entrusted with a political assassination. Unable to confront the task and yet aware of the practical need for trust, she killed herself.

Bhubaneswari had known that her death would be diagnosed as the outcome of illegitimate passion. She had therefore waited for the onset of menstruation. While waiting, Bhubaneswari, the *brahmacārini* who was no doubt looking forward to good wifehood, perhaps rewrote the social text of *sati*-suicide in an interventionist way. (One tentative explanation of her inexplicable act had been a possible melancholia brought on by her father's death and her brother-in-law's repeated taunts that she was too old to be not-yet-a-wife.) She generalized the sanctioned motive for female suicide by taking immense trouble to displace (not merely deny), in the physiological inscription of her body, its imprisonment within legitimate passion by a single male. In the immediate context, her act became absurd, a case of delirium rather than sanity. The displacing gesture—waiting for menstruation—is at first a reversal of the interdict against a menstruating widow's right to immolate herself; the unclean widow must wait, publicly, until the cleansing bath of the fourth day, when she is no longer menstruating, in order to claim her dubious privilege.

In this reading, Bhubaneswari Bhaduri's suicide is an unemphatic, ad hoc, subaltern rewriting of the social text of *sati*-suicide as much as the hegemonic account of the blazing, fighting, familial Durga. The emergent dissenting possibilities of that hegemonic account of the fighting mother are well documented and popularly well remembered through the discourse of the male leaders and participants in the Independence movement. The subaltern as female cannot be heard or read.

I know of Bhubaneswari's life and death through family connections. Before investigating them more thoroughly, I asked a Bengali woman, a philosopher and Sanskritist whose early intellectual production is almost identical to mine, to start the process. Two responses: (a) Why, when her two sisters, Saileswari and Raseswari, led such full and wonderful lives, are you interested in the hapless Bhubaneswari? (b) I asked her nieces. It appears that it was a case of illicit love.

I was so unnerved by this failure of communication that, in the first version of this text, I wrote, in the accents of passionate lament: the subaltern cannot speak! It was an inadvisable remark.

IN THE INTERVENING YEARS between the publication of the original essay and this revision, I have profited greatly from the many published responses to it. I will refer to two of them here: "Can the Subaltern Vote?" and "Silencing Sycorax."[103]

As I have been insisting, Bhubaneswari Bhaduri was not a "true" subaltern. She was a woman of the middle class, with access, however clandestine, to the bourgeois movement for Independence. . . . Part of what I seem to have argued in this [essay] is that woman's interception of the claim to subalternity can be staked out across strict lines of definition by virtue of their muting by heterogeneous circumstances. Rani Gulari [discussed earlier in *A Critique of Postcolonial Reason*] cannot speak to us because indigenous patriarchal "history" would only keep a record of her funeral and colonial history only needed her as an incidental instrument. Bhubaneswari attempted to "speak" by turning her body into a text of woman/writing. The immediate passion of my declaration, "the subaltern cannot speak," came from the despair that, in her own family, among women, in no more than fifty years, her attempt had failed. I am not laying the blame for the muting on the *colonial* authorities here, as Busia seems to think: "Gayatri Spivak's 'Can the Subaltern Speak?'—section IV of which is a compelling explication of this role of disappearing in the case of Indian women in British legal history."[104]

I am pointing, rather, at her silencing by her own more emancipated granddaughters: a new mainstream. To this can be added two newer groups: one, the liberal multiculturalist metropolitan academy, Susan Barton's greatgranddaughters; as follows:

As I have been saying all along, I think it is important to acknowledge our complicity in the muting, in order precisely to be more effective in the long run. Our work cannot succeed if we always have a scapegoat. The postcolonial migrant investigator is touched by the colonial social formations. Busia strikes a positive note for further work when she points out that, after all, I am able to read Bhubaneswari's case, and therefore she *has* spoken in some way. Busia is right, of course. All speaking, even seemingly the most immediate, entails a distanced decipherment by another, which is, at best, an interception. That is what speaking is.

I acknowledge this theoretical point, and also acknowledge the practical importance, for oneself and others, of being upbeat about future work. Yet the moot decipherment by another in an academic institution (willy-nilly a knowledge-production factory) many years later must not be too quickly identified with the "speaking" of the subaltern. It is not a mere tautology to say that the colonial or postcolonial subaltern is defined as the being on the other side of difference, or an epistemic fracture, even from other groupings among the colonized. What is at stake when we insist that the subaltern speaks?

In "Can the Subaltern Vote?" the three authors apply the question of stakes to "political speaking." This seems to me to be a fruitful way of extending my reading of subaltern speech into a collective arena. Access to "citizenship" (civil society) by becoming a voter (in the nation) is indeed the symbolic circuit of the mobilizing of subalternity into hegemony. This terrain, ever negotiating between national liberation and globalization, allows for examining the casting of the vote itself as a performative convention given as constative "speech" of the subaltern subject. It is part of my current concerns to see how this set is manipulated to legitimize globalization; but it is beyond the scope of this essay. Here let us remain confined to the field of academic prose, and advance three points:

1 Simply by being postcolonial or the member of an ethnic minority, we are not "subaltern." That word is reserved for the sheer heterogeneity of decolonized space.

2 When a line of communication is established between a member of subaltern groups and the circuits of citizenship or institutionality, the subaltern has been inserted into the long road to hegemony. Unless we want to be romantic purists or primitivists about "preserving subalternity"—a contradiction in terms—this is absolutely to be desired. (It goes without saying that museumized or curricularized access to ethnic origin—another battle that must be fought—is not identical with preserving subalternity.) Remembering this allows us to take pride in our work without making missionary claims.

3 This trace-structure (effacement in disclosure) surfaces as the tragic emotions of the political activist, springing not out of superficial utopianism, but out of the depths of what Bimal Krishna Matilal has called "moral love." Mahasweta Devi, herself an indefatigable activist, documents this emotion with exquisite care in "Pterodactyl, Puran Sahay, and Pirtha."

And finally, the third group: Bhubaneswari's elder sister's eldest daughter's eldest daughter's eldest daughter is a new U.S. immigrant and was recently promoted to an executive position in a U.S.-based transnational. She will be helpful in the emerging South Asian market precisely because she is a well-placed Southern diasporic.

> For Europe, the time when the new capitalism *definitely* superseded the old can be established with fair precision: it was the beginning of the twentieth century. . . . [With t]he boom at the end of the nineteenth century and the crisis of 1900–03 . . . [c]artels become one of the foundations of the whole of economic life. Capitalism has been transformed into imperialism.[105]

Today's program of global financialization carries on that relay. Bhubaneswari had fought for national liberation. Her great-grandniece works for the New Empire. This too is a historical silencing of the subaltern. When the news of this young woman's promotion was broadcast in the family amidst general jubilation I could not help remarking to the eldest surviving female member: "Bhubaneswari"—her nickname had been Talu—"hanged herself in vain," but not too loudly. Is it any wonder that this young woman is a staunch multiculturalist, believes in natural childbirth, and wears only cotton?

NOTES

This iteration of the essay, "Can the Subaltern Speak," appears as the closing section of a chapter entitled "History" in Gayatri Spivak's *A Critique of Postcolonial Reason: Toward a History of the Vanishing Present* (Cambridge: Harvard University Press, 1999), pp. 244–311. The text appears unchanged except where specific reference has been made to earlier sections of the chapter, the most substantive of which concern the account of the Rani Gulari of Sirmur.

1   Therefore, the UN must first rationalize "woman" before they can develop her. Yet, the Rani of Sirmur and Bhubaneswari Bhaduri (*vide infra*), indeed Lily Moya and Rigoberta Menchú (see Shula Marks, *Not Either an Experimental Doll* [Bloomington: Indiana Univ, Press, 1987]; and *I, Rigoberta Menchú: An Indian Woman in Guatemala*, tr. Ann Wright [London: Verso, 1984], will be instructive if they remain singular and secretive (for "secret," see *IM* xxv). They must exceed the system to come to us, in the mode of the literary. Capital remains the accessible abstract in general—the matheme still contaminated by the human. Psycho-cultural *systems*—regulative psychobiographies, psychoanalysis included—tend toward it. In search of the discursive abstractions that are the condition and effect of the concrete singular, Foucault was smart to choose the rarefied rather than the "thick" (for documentation, see Spivak, "More on Power/Knowledge," *Outside*, pp. 25–51). But we must also attend to Menchú, reading her too against the grain of her necessarily identity-political idiom, borrowing from a much older collective tactic against colonial conquest: "Of course, I'd need a lot of time to tell you about all my people because it's not easy to understand just like that. And I think I've given some idea of that in my account. Nevertheless, I'm still keeping my Indian identity a secret. I'm still keeping secret what I think no-one should know. Not even anthropologists or intellectuals, no matter how many books they have, can find out all our secrets" (p. 247). That text is not in books, and the secret keeps us, not the other way around.

2   Since this writing, the textualist study of history has taken on a life of its own. For the U.S. literary critic, the pages of the journal *Representations* would yield the richest harvest. Other prominent texts are Carlo Ginzburg, *Myths, Emblems, Clues*, tr. John and Anne C. Tedeschi (London: Hutchinson, 1990); Martin Jay,

Force Fields: Between Intellectual History and Cultural Critique (New York: Routledge, 1993). Peter de Bolla gives an account of poststructuralist history in "Disfiguring History," *Diacritics* 16 (Winter 1986): 49–58. The list could go on. Joan Wallach Scott has productively unpacked LaCapra's transferential analogy by "historiciz[ing] both sides of [the relationship between the power of the historian's analytic frame and the events that are the object of his or her study] by denying the fixity and transcendence of anything that appears to operate as a foundation…" ("Experience," in Judith Butler and Joan W. Scott, eds., *Feminists Theorize the Political* [New York: Routledge, 1992], p. 37). Scott's model can get "responsibility" going—asymmetrically. But with the Rani the asymmetry is so great that "responsibility" cannot catch. On the cusp of colonialism, she is pre-emergent for colonial discourse. In the pre-colonial dominant "Hindu" discourse she is absent except as a corpse by way of a funerary list. Indeed that dominant discourse goes underground by her living, precisely as (wife and mother) woman. There is no possibility of provincializing Europe here, as Dipesh Chakrabarty would have it, no possibility of catching at semes, as Jay Smith would like (Chakrabarty, "Postcoloniality and the Artifice of History: Who Speaks for 'Indian' Pasts?" *Representations* 37 [Winter 1992]: 1–26; Smith, "No More Language Games: Words, Beliefs, and the Political Culture of Early Modern France," *American Historical Review* 102.5 [Dec 1997]: 1416). What emerges on the figure of the Rani is interpretation as such; any genealogy of that history can see her as no more than an insubstantial languaged instrument. She is as unverifiable as literature, and yet she is written in, indeed permits the writing of, history as coloniality—so that the postcolonial can come to see his "historical self-location" as a problem (Vivek Dhareshwar, "'Our Time': History, Sovereignty, Politics," *Economic and Political Weekly*, 11 Feb. 1995, pp. 317–324).

3 For the argument that all Speech Acts are graphematic, see Derrida, "Signature Event Context," *Margins*, pp. 307–330.

4 Understood and exceeded, keeping her secret, as we shall see in the rest of this chapter, in spite of the most tremendous effort to "speak." Benedict Anderson (*Imagined Communities: Reflections on the Origin and Spread of Nationalism* [London: Verso, 1983]) and Partha Chatterjee (*Nationalist Thought and the Colonial World: A Derivative Discourse* [London: Zed, 1986] and *The Nation and Its Fragments: Colonial and Postcolonial Histories* [Princeton: Princeton University Press, 1993]), together offer us an exhaustive gloss on the mechanics of this coding but, as Homi K. Bhabha points out in "DissemiNation" (*Nation and Narration* [New York: Routledge, 1990], pp. 291–322) with reference to Anderson in particular, accounts of coding cannot account for excess or "incommensurability." Bhabha's argument relates specifically to the unresolvability of the minority; mine, here, as Irigaray's in "The Necessity for Sexuate Rights" (Margaret Whitford, ed. *The Irigaray Reader* [Cambridge: Blackwell, 1991], pp. 204–211) to the excess of the "sexuate" (see Spivak, "Who Claims Sexuality in the New World Order?" forthcoming in a collection edited by Elizabeth Grosz and Pheng Cheah). It is in

the excess of the sexuate, forever escaping formalization . . . that Bhubaneswari speaks, keeps her secret, and is silenced. The rest of the text circles around this enigma, by way of the psychocultural *system of Sati*.

5   Louis Althusser, *Lenin and Philosophy and Other Essays*, tr. Ben Brewster (New York: Monthly Review Press, 1971), p. 66. Derrida, "Desistance," in Philippe Lacoue-Labarthe, *Typography: Mimesis, Philosophy, Politics* tr. Christopher Fynsk (Cambridge: Harvard Univ. Press, 1989), pp. 1–42.

6   Michel Foucault, *Language, Counter-Memory, Practice: Selected Essays and Interviews*, trans. Donald Bouchard and Sherry Simon (Ithaca: Cornell University Press, 1977), pp. 205–217 (hereafter cited as *FD*). I have modified the English version of this, as of other English translations, where faithfulness to the original seemed to demand it. It is important to note that the greatest "influence" of Western European intellectuals upon U.S. professors and students happens through collections of essays rather than long books in translation. And, in those collections, it is understandably the more topical pieces that gain a greater currency. (Derrida's "Structure, Sign and Play in the Discourse of the Human Sciences," in Richard Macksey and Eugenio Donato, eds., *The Structuralist Controversy: The Languages of Criticism and the Sciences of Man* [Baltimore: Johns Hopkins Univ. Press, 1972], is a case in point.) From the perspective of theoretical production and ideological reproduction, therefore, the converstion under consideration has not necessarily been superseded. In my own meagre production, interviews, the least considered genre, have proved embarrassingly popular. It goes without saying that one does not produce a Samuel P. Huntington (*The Clash of Civilizations and the Remaking of World Order* [New York: Simon and Schuster, 1996]) to counter this. More about Huntington later.

7   There is an implicit reference here to the post-1968 wave of Maoism in France. See Michel Foucault, "On Popular Justice: A Discussion with Maoists," *Power/ Knowledge: Selected Interviews and Other Writings 1972–77*, tr. Colin Gordon *et al.* (New York: Pantheon, 1980), p. 134 (hereafter *PK*). Explication of the reference strengthens my point by laying bare the mechanics of appropriation. The status of China in this discussion is exemplary. If Foucault persistently clears himself by saying "I know nothing about China," his interlocutors show toward China what Derrida calls the "Chinese prejudice."

8   This is part of a much broader symptom, as Eric Wolf discusses in *Europe and the People Without History* (Berkeley: University of California Press, 1982).

9   Walter Benjamin, *Charles Baudelaire: A Lyric Poet in the Era of High Capitalism*, tr. Harry Zohn (London: Verso, 1983), p. 12. It is interesting that Foucault finds in Baudelaire the typecase of modernity (Foucault, "What Is Enlightenment," in Paul Rabinow, ed., *The Foucault Reader* [New York: Pantheon, 1984], pp. 39–42).

10 "Even if the gift were never anything but a simulacrum, one must still *render an account* of the possibility of this simulacrum. And one must also render an account of the desire to render an account. This cannot be done against or without the *principle of reason (principium reddendae rationis)*, even if the latter finds there its limit as well as its resource" (Derrida, *Given Time*, p. 31).

11 Deleuze and Guattari, *Anti-Oedipus*, p. 40–41 and *passim*.

12 Ibid., p. 26.

13 "What is writing? How can it be identified? What certitude of essence must guide the empirical investigation? . . . Without venturing up to the perilous necessity of the question or the arche-question 'what is,' let us take shelter in the field of grammatological knowledge" (*OG* 75). In "Desistance," Derrida points out that the critical is always contaminated by the dogmatic and thus makes Kant's distinction "speculative." In *Glas* philosophemes are typographically mimed, rather than "acted out" in intended behavior, as in the conversation we are discussing.

14 Althusser, *Lenin and Philosophy*, pp. 132–133; translation modified.

15 Deleuze and Guattari, *A Thousand Plateaus: Capitalism and Schizophrenia*, tr. Brian Massumi (Minneapolis: Univ. of Minnesota Press, 1987), pp. 351–423.

16 On this see also Stuart Hall, "The Problem of Ideology—Marxism without Guarantees," in Betty Matthews, ed., *Marx: A Hundred Years On* (London: Lawrence and Wishart, 1983), pp. 57–84.

17 For a more appreciative interpretation that attempts to bypass this risk, though never, of course, fully, see Spivak, "More on Power/Knowledge."

18 For one example among many see *PK* 98.

19 It is not surprising, then, that Foucault's work, early and late, is supported by too simple a notion of repression. Here the antagonist is Freud, not Marx. "I have the impression that [the notion of repression] is wholly inadequate to the analysis of the mechanisms and effects of power that it is so pervasively used to characterize today" (*PK* 92). The delicacy and subtlety of Freud's suggestion—that under repression the phenomenal identity of affects is indeterminate because an unpleasure can be desired as pleasure, thus radically reinscribing the relationship between desire and "interest"—seems quite deflated here. For an elaboration of this notion of repression, see *OG* 88,333–34 and Derrida, *Limited inc. abc* (Evanston: Northwestern Univ. Press, 1988), p. 74–75. Again, the problem is the refusal to take on board the level of the constituted subject—in the name of uncontaminated catachreses.

20 Althusser's version of this particular situation may be too schematic, but it nevertheless seems more careful in its program than the argument under study. "Class *instinct*," Althusser writes, "is subjective and spontaneous. Class *position* is objective and rational. To arrive at proletarian class positions, the class instinct of proletarians only needs to be *educated*, the class instinct of the petty bourgeoisie, *and hence of intellectuals*, has, on the contrary, to be *revolutionized*" (*Lenin and Philosophy*, p. 13). It is the effortful double bind, the always already crossed aporia, of this careful program that may be one reading of Derrida's current insistence upon justice as an experience of the impossible, upon decisions being always categorically insufficient to their supposed premises (see Appendix).

21 "Is the repetition really useful here?" my anonymous reader asks. I cite one among a hundred random examples: a conference on "Disciplinary and Interdisciplinary: Negotiating the Margin" at Columbia University on 7 November 1997. The entire conference turned on amity among various minorities in the United

States (read New York) as the end of radical feminism, an end that seemed altogether salutary in the face of the vicious identitarian conflict raging under the surface. A strengthened multicultural U.S. subject, the newest face of postcoloniality, still does nothing for globality and may do harm. The point remains worth repeating, alas.

22 Foucault's subsequent explanation (*PK* 145) of this Deleuzian statement comes closer to Derrida's notion that theory cannot be an exhaustive taxonomy and is always normed by practice.

23 Cf. the suprisingly uncritical notions of representation entertained in *PK* 141, 188. My remarks concluding this paragraph, criticizing intellectuals' representations of subaltern groups, should be rigorously distinguished from a coalition politics that takes into account its framing within socialized capital and unites people not because they are oppressed but because they are exploited. This model works best within a parliamentary democracy, where representation is not only not banished but elaborately staged.

24 Marx, *Surveys from Exile*, p. 239.

25 Marx, *Capital* 1:254.

26 Ibid., p. 302.

27 This is a highly ironic passage in Marx, written in the context of the fraudulent "representation" by Louis Napoleon and the regular suppression of the "revolutionary peasants" by bourgeois interests (*Surveys*, p. 239). Many hasty readers think Marx is advancing this as his own opinion about all peasantry!

28 See the excellent short definition and discussion of common sense in Errol Lawrence, "Just Plain Common Sense: The 'Roots' of Racism," in Hazel V. Carby, et al., *The Empire Strikes Back: Race and Racism in 70s Britain* (London: Hutchinson, 1982), p. 48. The Gramscian notions of "common sense" and "good sense" are extensively discussed in Marcia Landy, *Film, Politics, and Gramsci* (Minneapolis: Univ. of Minnesota Press, 1994), pp. 73–98.

29 "Use value" in Marx can be shown to be a "theoretical fiction"—as much of a potential oxymoron as "natural exchange." I have attempted to develop this in "Scattered Speculations on the Question of Value," in *In Other Worlds*, pp. 154–175.

30 Developed in Spivak, "Teaching for the Times," in Bhikhu Parekh and Jan Nederveen Pieterse, eds., *The Decolonization of the Imagination* (London: Zed, 1995), pp. 177–202; "Diasporas Old & New: Women in a Transnational World," in *Textual Practice* 10.2 (1996): 245–269; and, with specific reference to India, in Biju Mathews *et. al.*, "Vasudhaiva Kutumbakam: The Hindu in the World," unpublished MS.

31 Derrida's "Linguistic Circle of Geneva" (in *Margins*), especially pp. 143–144, can provide a method for assessing the irreducible place of the family in Marx's morphology of class formation.

32 Marx, *Capital* 1:128. This is common sense. Marx then goes beyond this to show that value means abstraction in both use and exchange. To develop that reading is beside the point here.

33 The situation has changed in the New World Order. Let us call the World Bank/ IMF/World Trade Organization "the economic;" and the United Nations "the political." The relationship between them is being negotiated in the name of gender ("the cultural"), which is, perhaps, micrology as such.

34 I am aware that the relationship between Marxism and neo-Kantianism is a politically fraught one. I do not myself see how a continuous line can be established between Marx's own texts and the Kantian ethical moment. It does seem to me, however, that Marx's questioning of the individual as agent of history should be read in the context of the breaking up of the individual subject inaugurated by Kant's critique of Descartes.

35 Marx, *Grundrisse*, pp. 162–163.

36 Edward W. Said, *The World, the Text, the Critic* (Cambridge: Harvard Univ. Press, 1983), p. 243.

37 Carby, *Empire*, p. 34.

38 This argument is developed further in Spivak, "Scattered Speculations." Once again, the *Anti-Oedipus* did not ignore the economic text, although the treatment was perhaps too allegorical. In this respect, the move from schizo- to rhyzo-analysis in *A Thousand Plateaus* was not, perhaps, salutary.

39 See Foucault, *Madness and Civilization: A History of Insanity in the Age of Reason*, tr. Richard Howard (New York: Pantheon, 1965), pp. 251, 262, 269.

40 Although I consider Fredric Jameson's *Political Unconscious: Narrative as a Socially Symbolic Act* (Ithaca: Cornell Univ. Press, 1981) to be a text of great critical weight, or perhaps *because* I do so, I would like my program here to be distinguished from one of restoring the relics of a privileged narrative: "It is in detecting the traces of that uninterrupted narrative, in restoring to the surface of the text the repressed and buried reality of this fundamental history, that the doctrine of a political unconscious finds its function and its necessity" (p. 20).

41 For a detailed account of a this transformation in the case of temple dancers, see Kunal Parker's forthcoming work.

42 Thomas Babington Macaulay, *Speeches by Lord Macaulay: With His Minute on Indian Education*, ed. G. M. Young (Oxford: Oxford Univ. Press, AMS Edition, 1979), p. 359.

43 I have discussed this issue in greater detail with reference to Julia Kristeva's *About Chinese Women*, tr. Anita Barrows (London: Marion Boyars, 1977), in "French Feminism in an International Frame," *In Other Worlds*, pp. 136–141.

44 Antonio Gramsci, *The Southern Question*, tr. Pasquale Verdicchio (West Lafayette, IN: Bordighera, 1995). As usual, I am using "allegory of reading" in the sense suggested by Paul de Man.

45 Edward W. Said, "Permission to Narrate," *London Review of Books* (16 Feb. 1984).

46 Guha, *Subaltern Studies* (Delhi: Oxford Univ. Press, 1982), 1:1.

47 *Ibid.*, p. 4.

48 *Ibid.*, p. 8. The usefulness of this tightly defined term was largely lost when *Selected Subaltern Studies* was launched in the United States under Spivak's initia-

tive (New York: Oxford Univ. Press, 1988). A new selection with a new introduction by Amartya Kumar Sen is about to appear from Duke Univ. Press. In the now generalized usage, it is precisely this notion of the subaltern inhabiting a space of difference that is lost, e.g., in statements such as the following: "The subaltern is force-fed into appropriating the master's culture" (Emily Apter, "French Colonial Studies and Postcolonial Theory," *Sub-Stance* 76/77, vol. 24, nos. 1–2 [1995]: 178); or worse still, Jameson's curious definition of subalternity as "the experience of inferiority" ("Marx's Purloined Letter," *New Left Review*, no. 209 [1994]: 95).

49 Guha, *Subaltern Studies*, 1:1.

50 Since then, in the disciplinary fallout after the serious electoral and terrorist augmentation of Hindu nationalism in India, more alarming charges have been leveled at the group. See Aijaz Ahmad, *In Theory: Classes, Nations, Literatures* (New York: Verso, 1992), pp. 68, 194, 207–211; and Sumit Sarkar, "The Fascism of the Sangh Parivar," *Economic and Political Weekly* 30 Jan. 1993, pp. 163–167.

51 Ajit K. Chaudhury, "New Wave Social Science," *Frontier* 16–24 (28 Jan. 1984), p. 10 (italics are mine).

52 I do not believe that the recent trend of romanticizing anything written by the Aboriginal or outcaste ("dalit" = oppressed) intellectual has lifted the effacement.

53 "Contracting Poverty," *Multinational Monitor* 4, no. 8 (Aug. 1983): 8. This report was contributed by John Cavanagh and Joy Hackel, who work on the International Corporations Project at the Institute for Policy Studies (italics are mine).

54 Saskia Sassen, "On Economic Citizenship," in Losing Control?: Sovereignty in An Age of Globalization (New York: Columbia Univ. Press, 1996), pp. 31–58.

55 The mechanics of the invention of the Third World as signifier are susceptible to the type of analysis directed at the constitution of race as a signifier in Carby, *Empire*. In the contemprary conjuncture, in response to the augmentation of Eurocentric migration as the demographic fallout of postcoloniality, neocolonialism, end of the Soviet Union, and global financialization, the South (the Third World of yore, with shifting bits of the old Second World thrown in) is being reinvented as the South-in-the-North. Even so brilliant a book as Etienne Balibar and Immanuel Wallerstein, *Race, Nation, Class: Ambiguous Identities*, tr. Chris Turner (New York: Verso, 1991) starts from this invention as unquestioned premise.

56 Subsequently, as I indicate at length elsewhere (*Outside*, pp. 113–115; "Ghostwriting," pp. 69–71, 82), his work in these areas has speculated with the tendencies of computing migrancy or displacement as origin; in the figure of the absolute *arrivant*, of the marrano, and, most recently, in his seminars, hospitality. He would figure the indigenous subaltern, from the perspective of the metropolitan hybrid, as a correlative of cultural conservatism, topological archaism, ontopological nostalgia (*Specters*, p. 82). Here, too, he speculates with already existing tendencies. Just as pedigreed Marxists have been told, by Derrida among others, that Marx must be read in Marx's way, *as if* the reader were haunted by Marx's ghost; so might one deconstruct deconstruction (as Klein Freuded Freud): do not accuse, do not excuse, make it "your own," turn it around and use—with no guarantees—except that this formula too will become useless tomorrow—or in

the moment of its saying: "each time that ethnocentrism is precipitately and ostentatiously reversed, some effort silently hides behind all the spectacular effects to consolidate an inside and to draw from it some domestic benefit."

57 John Rawls, *Political Liberalism* (New York: Columbia Univ. Press, 1993).

58 Jonathan Culler, *On Deconstruction: Theory and Criticism after Structuralism* (Ithaca: Cornell Univ. Press, 1982), p. 48.

59 Sarah Kofman, *The Enigma of Woman : Woman in Freud's Writings*, tr. Catherine Porter (Ithaca: Cornell Univ. Press, 1985).

60 Freud, "'A Child Is Being Beaten': A Contribution to the Study of the Origin of Sexual Perversion," *SE* 17. For a list of ways in which Western criticism constructs "third world woman," see Chandra Talpade Mohanty, "Under Western Eyes: Feminist Scholarship and Colonial Discourses," in Mohanty et al., eds., *Third World Women and the Politics of Feminism* (Bloomington: Indiana Univ. Press, 1991), pp. 51–80.

61 Freud, "'Wild' Psycho-Analysis," *SE* 11. A good deal of psychoanalytic social critique would fit this description.

62 Freud, "'A Child Is Being Beaten,'" p. 188.

63 For a brilliant account of how the "reality" of widow-sacrificing was constituted or "textualized" during the colonial period, see Lata Mani, "Contentious Traditions: the Debate on *Sati* in Colonial India," in *Recasting Women: Essays in Colonial History* (Delhi: Kāli for Women, 1989), pp. 88–126. I profited from discussion with Dr. Mani at the inception of this project. Here I present some of my differences from her position. The "printing mistake in the Bengali translation"(p. 109) that she cites is not the same as the mistake I discuss, which is in the ancient Sanskrit. It is of course altogether interesting, that there should be all these errancies in the justification of the practice. A regulative psychobiography is not identical with "textual hegemony" (p. 96). I agree with Mani that the latter mode of explanation cannot take "regional variations" into account. A regulative psychobiography is another mode of "textualist oppression" when it produces not only "women's consciousness" but a "gendered episteme" (mechanics of the construction of objects of knowledge together with validity-criteria for statements of knowledge). You do not have to "read verbal texts" here. It is something comparable to Gramsci's "inventory without traces" (Antonio Gramsci, *Selections from the Prison Notebooks*, tr. Quintin Hoare and Geoffrey Nowell Smith [New York: International Publishers, 1971], p. 324). Like Mani (p. 125, n. 90), I too wish to "add" to Kosambi's "strategies." To the "supplement[ation of the linguistic study of problems of ancient Indian culture] by intelligent use of archaeology, anthropology, sociology and a suitable historical perspective" (Kosambi, "Combined Methods in Indology," *Indo-Iranian Journal* 6 [1963]: 177), I would add the insights of psychoanalysis, though not the regulative psychobiography of its choice. Alas, in spite of our factualist fetish, "facts" alone may account for women's oppression, but they will never allow us to approach gendering, a net where we ourselves are enmeshed, as we decide what (the) facts are. Because of epistemic prejudice, Kosambi's bold and plain speech can and has been misunderstood; but

his word "live" can take on board a more complex notion of the mental theater as Mani cannot: "Indian peasants in villages far from any city *live* in a manner closer to the days when the Purānas were written than do the descendants of the brahmins who wrote the Purānas" (emphasis mine). Precisely. The self-representation in gendering is regulated by the Puranic psychobiography, with the Brahmin as the model. In the last chapter I will consider what Kosambi mentions in the next sentence: "A stage further back are the pitiful fragments of tribal groups, usually sunk to the level of marginal castes; they rely heavily upon food-gathering and have the corresponding mentality." Kosambi's somewhat doctrinaire Marxism would not allow him to think of the tribal episteme as anything but only backward, of course. After the *sati* of Rup Kanwar in September 1987, a body of literature on the contemporary situation has emerged. That requires quite a different engagement (see Radha Kumar, "Agitation Against Sati 1987–88," in *The History of Doing* [Delhi: Kāli for Women, 1993], pp. 172–181.)

64 See Kumari Jayawardena, *The White Woman's Other Burden: Western Women and South Asia During British Colonial Rule* (New York: Routledge, 1995). Envy, backlash, reaction-formation; these are the routes by which such efforts may, in the absence of ethical responsibility, lead to opposite results. I have repeatedly invoked Melanie Klein and Assia Djebar in this context. See also Spivak, "Psychoanalysis in Left Field," pp. 66–69.

65 The examples of female ventriloquist complicity, quoted by Lata Mani in her brilliant article "Production of An Official Discourse on *Sati* in Early Nineteenth Century Bengal," *Economic and Political Weekly* 21.17 (26 Apr. 1986), p. WS-36, proves my point. The point is not that a refusal would not be ventriloquism for Women's Rights. One is not suggesting that only the latter is correct free will. One is suggesting that the freedom of the will is negotiable, and it is not on the grounds of a disinterested free will that we will be able to justify an action, in this case against the burning of widows, to the adequate satisfaction of all. The ethical aporia is not negotiable. We must act in view of this.

66 J. D. M. Derrett, *Hindu Law Past and Present: Being and Account of the Controversy Which Preceded the Enactment of the Hindu Code, and Text of the Code as Enacted, and Some Comments Thereon* (Calcutta: A. Mukherjee, 1957), p. 46.

67 Kosambi comments on such shifts as a matter of course. Of the much admired widow remarriage reform, e.g., he writes: "[t]hat he [R.G. Bh nd rkar] spoke for a very narrow class in the attempt to speak for the whole of India never struck him, nor for that matter other contemporary 'reformers.' Still, *the silent change of emphasis from caste to class was a necessary advance*" (D. D. Kosambi, *Myth and Reality: Studies in the Formation of Indian Culture* [Bombay: Popular Prakashan, 1962], p. 38, n. 2; emphasis mine). We would say "shift" rather than "advance"; for it is this silent century-old epistemic shift that allows today's Hindu nationalism to proclaim itself anti-casteist, nationalist—even "secular." Incidentally, to confine the construction of *Sati* to colonial negotiations, and finally to the Ram Mohun Roy-Lord William Bentinck exchange, is also to avoid the question of "subaltern consciousness." For further commentary on the differences between

Mani and Spivak, see Sumit Sarkar, "Orientalism Revisited: Saidian Frameworks in the Writing of Modern Indian History," *Oxford Literary Review* 16 (1994): 223. I remain grateful to Professor Sarkar for noticing that "Mani's article stands in marked contrast to the much more substantive discussion of pre-colonial and colonial discourses on sati in Spivak, 'Can the Subaltern Speak?'" To claim that caste or clitoridectomy is no more than a colonial construction advances nothing today. Romila Thapar tells me that the seventh-century historian Bānabhatta objected to *Sati*. There may be something Eurocentric about assuming that imperialism began with Europe.

68 Today, interference in women's cultural privacy remains a project of making rural women available for micro-enterprise in the economic sphere, and a project of bettering women's lives in the political. Demands for a more responsible tempo—woman's time—so that the violence of the change does not scar the episteme, are often impatiently rejected as cultural conservatism.

69 Ashis Nandy, "Sati: A Nineteenth Century Tale of Women, Violence and Protest," *Rammohun Roy and the Process of Modernization in India*, ed. V. C. Joshi (Delhi: Vikas Publishing House, 1975), p. 68.

70 Marx, *Capital* 3:958–959.

71 Spivak, "Diasporas," p. 248.

72 In "The Supplement of Copula: Philosophy Before Linguistics," (*Margins*, pp. 175–205), Derrida argues that every copula is a supplement. In his own work, he has reopened the copula by working on the ethical. The copula in this sentence may mean that the relationship between men and women is patriarchal until rationalized. Not very far from either consciousness-raising or classical Marxism. These suggestions call for a mourning-work hinted at in "Foucault and Najibullah."

73 I am using "Envy" in the sense established by Melanie Klein in "Envy and Gratitude," in *Envy and Gratitude and Other Works* (New York: Free Press, 1975), pp. 176–235.

74 Klein, "The Early Development of Conscience in the Child," *Love, Guilt and Reparation and Other Works (1921–1945)*, p. 257.

75 It is in this spirit that Assia Djebar asked the help of an Arabic scholar to allow her to read certain Arabic chronicles imaginatively in order to write *Far From Medina*, tr. Dorothy Blair (London: Quartet, 1994). I have been energized by Peter van de Veer's approbation in "Sati and Sanskrit: The Move from Orientalism to Hinduism," in Mieke Bal and Inge E. Boer, eds., *The Point of Theory: Practices of Cultural Analysis* (New York: Continuum, 1994), pp. 251–259.

76 Since I am no expert, the following account leans heavily on Pandurang Vaman Kane, *History of the Dharmasastra* (Poona: Bhandarkar Oriental Institute, 1963) (hereafter cited as *HD*, with volume, part, and page numbers).

77 Upendra Thakur, *The History of Suicide in India: An Introduction* (Delhi: Munshi Ram Manohar Lal, 1963), p. 9, has a useful list of Sanskrit primary sources on sacred places. This laboriously decent book betrays all the signs of the schizo-

phrenia of the colonial subject, such as bourgeois nationalism, patriarchal communalism, and an "enlightened reasonableness."

78 Nandy, "Sati."

79 Jean-François Lyotard, *The Differend: Phrases in Dispute*, tr. Georges Van Den Abbeele (Minneapolis: Univ. of Minnesota Press, 1988), p. xi.

80 Ibid., p. 13.

81 *HD*, II.2, p. 633. There are suggestions that this "prescribed penance" was far exceeded by social practice. In the passage below, published in 1938, notice the Hindu patristic assumptions about the freedom of female will at work in phrases like "courage" and "strength of character." The unexamined presuppositions of the passage might be that the complete objectification of the widow-concubine was just punishment for abdication of the right to courage, signifying subject status: "Some widows, however, had not the courage to go through the fiery ordeal; nor had they sufficient strength of mind and character to live up to the high ascetic ideal prescribed for them [*brahmacarya*]. It is sad to record that they were driven to lead the life of a concubine or *avaruddha stri* [incarcerated wife]." A. S. Altekar, *The Position of Women in Hindu Civilization: From Prehistoric Times to the Present Day* (Delhi: Motilal Banarsidass, 1938), p. 156.

82 Quoted in Dineshchandra Sen, *Brhat-Banga* (Calcutta: Univ. of Calcutta Press), 2:913–914.

83 In *The Gift of Death*, Derrida has suggested how an Abrahamic sacrifice today would be docketed as crime (pp. 85–86).

84 Thompson, *Suttee*, p. 132.

85 Here, as well as for the Brahman debate over *sati*, see Mani, "Production," pp. 71f.

86 We are speaking here of the regulative norms of Brahmanism, rather than "things as they were." See Robert Lingat, *The Classical Law of India*, trans. J. D. M. Derrett (Berkeley: University of California Press, 1973), p. 46.

87 Both the vestigial possibility of widow remarriage in ancient India and the legal institution of widow remarriage in 1856 are transactions among men. Widow remarriage is very much an exception, perhaps because it left the program of subject-formation untouched. In all the "lore" of widow remarriage, it is the father and the husband who are applauded for their reformist courage and selflessness. As Kosambi would remind us, we are only considering caste-Hindu India here.

88 Middle-class Bengali children of my generation received this indoctrination through Abanindranath Tagore, *Raj-Kahini* (Calcutta: Signet,1968), a lovely imaginative reconstruction of the famous *Annals and Antiquities of Rajasthan* (London: Oxford University Press, 1920) by James Tod (1782–1835).

89 Biju Mathews et al., "Vasudhaiva Kutumbakam."

90 Sir Monier Monier-Williams, *Sanskrit-English Dictionary* (Oxford: Clarendon Press, 1989), p. 552. Historians are often impatient if modernists seem to be attempting to import "feministic" judgments into ancient patriarchies. The real question is, of course, why structures of patriarchal domination should be un-

questioningly recorded. Historical sanctions for collective action toward social justice can only be developed if people outside of the discipline question standards of "objectivity" preserved as such by the hegemonic tradition. It does not seem inappropriate to notice that so "objective" an instrument as a dictionary can use the deeply sexist-partisan explanatory expression: "raise up issue to a deceased husband"!

91 Sunderlal T. Desai, *Mulla: Principles of Hindu Law* (Bombay: N. M. Tripathi, 1982), p. 184.

92 I am grateful to Professor Alison Finley of Trinity College (Hartford, Conn.) for discussing the passage with me. Professor Finley is an expert on the *Rg-Veda*. I hasten to add that she would find my readings as irresponsibly "literary-critical" as the ancient historian would find it "modernist"

93 Martin Heidegger, *An Introduction to Metaphysics*, tr. Ralph Mannheim (New York: Doubleday Anchor, 1961), p. 58.

94 Thompson, *Suttee*, p. 37.

95 Thompson, *Suttee*, p. 15. For the status of the proper name as "mark," see Derrida, "My Chances/*Mes Chances*: A Rendezvous with Some Epicurean Stereophonies," in Joseph H. Smith and William Kerrigan, eds., *Taking Chances: Derrida, Psychoanalysis, and Literature*, (Baltimore: Johns Hopkins Univ. Press, 1984), p. 1–32.

96 Thompson, *Suttee*, p. 137.

97 Michel Foucault, *History of Sexuality*, 1:4.

98 The European context is different here. In the monotheist tradition, as it has been argued by Derrida in his discussions specifically of Kierkegaard in *The Gift of Death*, the moment of sacrifice—Abraham ready to kill his son—turns love into hate and displaces the ethical. What is it to introduce woman into this narrative, Derrida has asked, and John Caputo has attempted to construct a benevolent American-feminist answer by speaking in various voices, as provided by the historically male imagining of women; he has even attempted to acknowledge "[t]he name of Sarah . . . [as] the name of violence. In order to protect the heritage of her son, Isaac, Sarah had Abraham take Hagar, Abraham's concubine and the Egyptian slave of Sarah, and Ishmael, the illegitimate son of Abraham and Hagar, out to the desert and abandon them. The descendants of Ishmael, the 'Ishmaelites,' became a wandering tribe of nomads, the outcasts . . . " (John Caputo, *Against Ethics: Contributions to a Poetics of Obligation With Constant Reference to Deconstruction* [Bloomington: Indiana Univ. Press, 1993], pp. 145–146). But if, for the sake of time, we remember no more than Freud's intuition, the maternal sacrifice must perhaps invoke, not merely the peoples of the Book, but the pre- and para-monotheistic world (Freud, "Moses and Monotheism," *SE* 22:83). It is not only Abraham who can be imagined—as he is by Caputo's "Johanna de Silentio" (feminine of Kierkegaard's Johannes)—"in a world without others, a world without the law" (Caputo, *Against Ethics*, p. 141). In *Beloved* Toni Morrison gives us maternal sacrifice, Sethe, the slave about to be freed (neither African nor American), historically in that world without the law. History asks for the maternal

sacrifice on the impossible passage, and does not stay the mother's hand. The ring of the covenant—the brand on Sethe's nameless mother's breast—does not ensure continuity. Historiality is not changed into genealogy. The matrilineality of slavery is ruptured on the underground railroad. Sethe does not understand her mother's tongue. On the cusp of the violent change from animisim to dehegemonised Christianity is the maternal sacrifice. It marks an obstinate refusal to rational allegorization. It is only after this shedding of blood that the first African-American is born—Denver, named after the white woman who assisted at her birth. U.S. civil society (and, of course, culture—Morrison's next book is *Jazz*) has domesticated the cusp. And *Beloved* remains a story not to pass on, the beloved ghost laid to rest. In spite of the Latin American Indian (what a multiple errant history in that naming) topos of claiming secrecy in the face of the conquistador, I remain somewhat persuaded by Doris Sommers's placing of the theme of secrecy in Morrison and Menchú together (Doris Sommers, "No Secrets," in Georg M. Gugelberger, ed., *The Real Thing: Testimonial Discourse and Latin America* [Durham: Duke Univ. Press, 1996], pp. 130–157).

99 The fact that the word was also used as a form of address for a well-born woman ("lady") complicates matters.

100 It should be remembered that this account does not exhaust her many manifestations within the pantheon.

101 I have taken this question further, in an analysis of metropolitan multiculturalism, in "Devi," essay for an exhibition on the Great Goddess at the Arthur M. Sackler gallery at the Smithsonian. See *"Moving Devi,"* in Vidya Dehejia, ed., *Devi: The Great Goddess*, pp. 181–200. Washington, DC: Smithsonian Institute, 1999.

102 A position against nostalgia as a basis of counterhegemonic ideological production does not endorse its negative use. Within the complexity of contemporary political economy, it would, for example, be highly questionable to urge that the current Indian working-class crime of burning brides who bring insufficient dowries and of subsequently disguising the murder as suicide is either a *use* or *abuse* of the tradition of *sati*-suicide. The most that can be claimed is that it is a displacement on a chain of semiosis with the female subject as signifier, which would lead us back into the narrative we have been unraveling. Clearly, one must work to stop the crime of bride burning *in every way*. If, however, that work is accomplished by unexamined nostalgia or its opposite, it will assist actively in the substitution of race/ethnos or sheer genitalism as a signifier in the place of the female subject.

103 Abena Busia, "Silencing Sycorax: On African Colonial Discourse and the Unvoiced Female," *Cultural Critique* 14 (Winter 1989–90): 81–104. Leerom Medovoi et al., "Can the Subaltern Vote?" *Socialist Review* 20.3 (July-Sept. 1990): 133–149.

104 Busia, "Silencing," p. 102.

105 V. I. Lenin, *Imperialism: The Highest Stage of Capitalism: A Popular Outline* (London: Pluto Press, 1996), pp.15, 17.

PART TWO

CONTEXTS AND TRAJECTORIES

Partha Chatterjee

REFLECTIONS ON "CAN THE SUBALTERN SPEAK?"

SUBALTERN STUDIES AFTER SPIVAK

It was terribly disappointing for me not to be present at this remarkable occasion at Columbia to reflect upon and evaluate Gayatri Spivak's essay "Can the Subaltern Speak?" twenty years after it was first presented at the University of Illinois at Urbana-Champagne in the summer of 1983. Rosalind Morris pointed out to me that since the essay was at least partially provoked by the work of the subaltern studies group, the discussions at the conference would have been incomplete without a statement from someone associated with the group. I could not presume to speak on behalf of the entire subaltern studies collective—a diverse and constantly changing community of engaged scholars, variously situated in relation to the Indian political and intellectual scene as well as the American academy. But the conference permitted me to assess and reflect on the impact of Spivak's essay on the subaltern studies project over the years since the essay's first publication.

Working in India, we did not become aware of Spivak's essay until 1985. I first met Gayatri Spivak in Oxford in the summer of 1982 at a conference organized by the British historical journal *Past and Present*. Gyan Pandey, Shahid Amin, and I were presenting papers at the conference and the first volume of *Subaltern Studies* had just appeared. We had, of course, heard of Gayatri Chakravorty Spivak as a major literary scholar. But, concerned as we then were with agrarian history and peasant movements, we did not imagine that Jacques Derrida, despite his Algerian roots, could have anything remotely to do with Indian peasants. (The French writers dear to our hearts then were Emmanuel Le Roy Ladurie and Georges Duby or, for those more theoretically inclined, Louis Althusser.) I remember the three of us ardent subalternists sitting outside an Oxford pub talking to Gayatri about our new collective project. We were to discover much later that she was beginning to make entirely unsuspected connections between her literary and philosophical interests and our historical work.

I first read "Can the Subaltern Speak?" along with a draft of her essay "Subaltern Studies: Deconstructing Historiography" sometime in early 1985. The initial reaction was bewilderment. The breathtaking range of themes, arguments and references in "Can the Subaltern Speak?" was more than I could absorb. The task was made easier by the more focused engagement with our work in the other essay. Although I have read "Can the Subaltern Speak?" perhaps a dozen times or more (most recently about three weeks ago for a cultural studies workshop for graduate students in Bangalore where it was an assigned reading), my understanding of the essay remains conditioned by the simultaneous reading of "Subaltern Studies: Deconstructing Historiography," published in *Subaltern Studies* 4 (1985) and as the introduction to *Selected Subaltern Studies* (1987).

It is difficult for me to trace the exact course through which the impact of Spivak's critique of the early *Subaltern Studies* filtered through our work and changed the contents and direction of our project. It was certainly influenced by her participation in the second subaltern studies conference in Calcutta in 1986 and in several subsequent meetings of the group and her induction into the editorial collective in 1993. I will never forget the tension and thrill of the Calcutta conference of 1986, held in an atmosphere in which our work was regarded with suspicion and hostility by the academic establishment. We had no funding or sponsorship and were holding the conference out of the accumulated royalties of the first three volumes of *Subaltern Studies*. But we discovered that we were beginning to attract our own audience, because the auditorium was packed, with people sitting in the aisles and hanging from the windows. Spivak's presentation of her analysis of the Mahasweta Devi story "The Breast-giver" was followed, I remember, by the unexpected appearance of Mahasweta Devi herself in the audience. Responding to demands that the author say something about the critic's analysis of her story, Mahasweta made a surprisingly self-disparaging and somewhat hackneyed statement of her intentions in writing the story. Many in that audience took the author's own statement as having trumped the critic's reading. For some of us, however, the event came as a dramatic reminder of the fundamental problem that Spivak had raised on the question of representing the subaltern.

Much has been written over the years on the so-called two phases of *Subaltern Studies*, not all of it with sympathy or approval. Many who had denounced the allegedly ultraradical politics of the early phase later turned coat and claimed to prefer the naively political early *Subaltern Studies* in comparison with what it became after the postmodern linguistic turn. I tried to make what I thought was an uninvolved and dispassionate assessment of the impact in my introduction to the Bengali selections from *Subaltern Studies* published in 1998. Here is how I described it:

> Research into subaltern history had shown that the subaltern was both outside and inside the domains of colonial governance and nationalist politics. To the extent that it was outside, it had retained its autonomy. But it had also entered those domains, participated in their processes and institutions and thereby transformed itself. Every bit of historical evidence was pointing to the fact that the subaltern was "a deviation from the ideal." Why then the search for a "pure structure" of subaltern consciousness? Moreover, argued Gayatri Spivak in two influential articles, subaltern history had successfully shown that the "man" or "citizen" who was the sovereign subject of bourgeois history-writing was in truth only the elite. Why was it necessary now to clothe the subaltern in the costume of the sovereign subject and put him on stage as the maker of history? Subaltern historiography had in fact challenged the very idea that there had to be a sovereign subject of history possessing an integral consciousness. Why bring back the same idea into subaltern history? It was only a myth that the subaltern could directly speak through the writings of the historian. In fact, the historian was only representing the subaltern on the pages of history. The subaltern, announced Spivak, cannot speak.

The new turn in *Subaltern Studies* began more or less from the fifth and sixth volumes published in 1989–90. It was now acknowledged, with much greater seriousness than before, that subaltern histories were fragmentary, disconnected, incomplete, that subaltern consciousness was split within itself, that it was constituted by elements drawn from the experiences of both dominant and subordinate classes. Alongside the evidence of autonomy displayed by subalterns at moments of rebellion, the forms of subaltern consciousness undergoing the everyday experience of subordination now became the subject of inquiry. Once these questions entered the agenda, subaltern history could no longer be restricted to the study of peasant revolts. Now the question was not "What is the true form of the subaltern?" The question had become "How is the subaltern represented?" Represent here meant both "present again" and "stand in place of." Both the subjects and the methods of research underwent a change.

Contrary to some commentators, I do not think we were so naive then as to believe that by digging afresh into the archives we would be able to somehow recuperate the authentic voice of the subaltern. For one thing, there were not many new "subaltern texts" found. Our labor was mostly spent in reading from a fresh standpoint certain known texts from the colonial and nationalist archives. But our reading was guided by a search for a distinctive structure of subaltern consciousness, for which we took the consciousness of the insurgent peasant as paradigmatic. The most authoritative statement of our method was laid out in Ranajit Guha's *Elementary Aspects of Peasant Insurgency in Colonial India* (1983). It was like finding the key to a new language; if we could find the grammar and dictionary of the rebel subaltern's language, we thought, we could "present again" in the academic language of historians his claim to be the subject of history (and I unhesitatingly confess that we took the rebel subaltern to be male). There was a politics here, of course. We wanted to gain historical access to the sources of peasant mobilization against the postcolonial nation-state that, in the heyday of Indira Gandhi's rule, we regarded as authoritarian and undemocratic.

I now think that Spivak's essay came to us as the poststructuralist moment in *Subaltern Studies*. More than the question of how the third world subject is represented within Western discourse, or the arguments about strategic essentialism (on which practice Spivak herself would vacillate), or the relative merits of the philosophical insights of Deleuze, Foucault, and Derrida, it is the difficult and laborious shift to a consciously poststructural method that was facilitated by Spivak's intervention. It is specious to call this a mere aping of the change in French intellectual fashions. Had there not been significant changes in the political and social context in which we worked in India, I doubt if *Subaltern Studies* would have moved the way it did from the late 1980s onward. To put it briefly, what changed before our eyes was the rapid incorporation of subaltern populations into the web of governmentality. As urban elites turned away from organized politics and forced the developmental state to retreat from its economic and social roles, the subaltern classes increasingly clamored for and inserted themselves into the spaces of electoral politics and governmental welfare to make claims on the state. It was not possible for the subalternist scholar to insist any more that the postcolonial nation-state was something "essentially" external to subaltern consciousness. Spivak's essay, I now believe, enabled us to devise methodological strategies to deal with the new set of research problems engendered by these developments.

The change was signaled as early as Ranajit Guha's remarkable essay "Chandra's Death" published in *Subaltern Studies* 5 (cf. Sunder Rajan's essay, this volume). Once the question of the "representation of the subaltern" came to the fore, the entire field of the spread of modern institutions and knowledges in colonial India was opened up for subaltern history.

Much-studied subjects such as the expansion of colonial governance, English education, movements of religious and social reform, the rise of nationalism—all these were opened to new lines of questioning by the historians of *Subaltern Studies*. Institutions such as schools and universities, newspapers and publishing houses, hospitals, doctors, medical systems, censuses, registration bureaus, the industrial labor process, scientific institutions—all became subjects of subaltern history writing. Most significantly, the themes of gender, religion, and caste were opened up for discussion with reference to the subaltern standpoint (which is not yet to say that subaltern histories were being written from a subaltern point of view or in a subaltern voice), raising many politically uncomfortable questions and complicating the received certainties of progressive politics in India. These discussions, building upon the idea of "representing the subaltern," are by no means confined to the *Subaltern Studies* volumes themselves. They have now spilled over into a much larger public arena of political debate and conflict over which the original architects of the *Subaltern Studies* project have neither influence nor control.

I have spoken here only of the impact of Spivak's two essays on the *Subaltern Studies* project as it has evolved in the intellectual and political context of India. I am aware of their other life in what is known as postcolonial studies in the Anglo-American academy. Indeed, it is largely through those two essays that the work of the subaltern studies group became known in North American universities. I have often been surprised and puzzled by the very different receptions of our work in the two contexts. It is understandable, I suppose, that the question that dominates postcolonial studies is, as Spivak proposed in 1983, "how the third-world subject is represented in Western discourse." But there is a bewildering range of answers that have been offered as the solution—from nostalgic investments in postcolonial authenticity to affirmations of postcolonial hybridity, from postcolonial multiculturalism to a postcolonial moral imperialism and even, I sometimes think, a postcolonial neo-Orientalism.

Spivak herself has traveled far from "Can the Subaltern Speak?" to *The Critique of Postcolonial Reason* (1999) in which she distanced herself from many trends in postcolonial studies that have claimed their origin in her 1983 essay. I must confess that I have never felt myself a part of those debates. It would be a foolish exaggeration to suggest that all these developments in the intellectual traditions of continents are to be attributed to one essay. But whether one takes a historical or a genealogical view of the transformation of concepts and ideas, some contributions do become landmarks. There can be no doubt that "Can the Subaltern Speak?" is one such landmark, signposting the ways to several destinations. What is remarkable is that the author herself has not stood in the same place. In the subaltern studies conference in Delhi in January 2008, someone pointed out that our group, which was once associated with the Marxist far left, was now collaborating with former Gandhians and socialists. To this fact Shahid Amin replied that heterodoxies always found a way of meeting each other; it is only orthodoxy that stands still. I don't know if Gayatri Spivak's work has produced any orthodoxies in the last two and a half decades. What I do know is that she herself remains incorrigibly heterodox, unafraid to face the unfamiliar, ever ready to grapple with new problems. *Subaltern Studies* has been deeply enriched by her intellectual comradeship.

Ritu Birla

POSTCOLONIAL
STUDIES

NOW THAT'S HISTORY

To reflect on the history of "Can the Subaltern Speak" as an idea, we are called to reflect on the idea of history as the practice of historicizing and as the narrative of subject-formation. We are also called to reflect upon the irreducible difference of historicity. Bringing these multiple meanings into play, and with unrelenting feminist praxis, "Can the Subaltern Speak?" confronts the production of subject-as-agent and the concomitant mechanics of its representation.[1] These problems also render it a formative text of postcolonial studies. Rereading it now, we are reminded that postcolonial critique should never be reducible to identity politics, nativism, or unexamined multiculturalism. It is exactly this reduction that Spivak bemoaned in the mid-1990s, when she stated in an interview that the term "post-colonial" has "bitten the dust."[2] Why? As *postcolonial* becomes a mere label in the representational politics of institutions (in academia and, more broadly, in the globalized space of nongovernmental and corporate elites), colonialism becomes a thing of the past, an unproblematized past that grounds a homogeneous "postcolonial" identity and identitarianism. This version of colonialism, and, indeed, history, remains in stark contrast to the impetus of postcolonial criticism, attentive to present and ongoing colonial formations, to the failure of decolonization, and the uncanny reincarnations of colonial relations alongside new transnational flows of humans and capital. Haunted by this task, Spivak's *A Critique of Postcolonial Reason*, for example, deconstructs the "Native Informant" in and across disciplines, charting a genealogy of the colonial, postcolonial, and then global subject.[3] In *Critique of Postcolonial Reason* the weaving of a revised version of "Can the Subaltern

Speak?" into the chapter on "History" appropriately stages this haunting, historicizing the much-cited essay in order to revitalize its contemporary concerns. In this spirit I revisit "Can the Subaltern Speak?" here not as a lost origin of postcolonial studies but as a medium for thinking the concerns of critical historical study as they are motivated, to use Spivak's subtitle from *A Critique of Postcolonial Reason*, by the vanishing present. To do so, I will follow one important thread in the essay, the problem of othering, addressed through a meticulous unraveling of subjectivity and agency as well as an ethically charged analysis of the double bind of representation.

It is perhaps the rigorous attention to varying processes of othering that best marks "Can the Subaltern Speak?" as a feminist and postcolonial text. An abstract of the major moves of the essay through this lens can serve as a roadmap to guide our future reading trajectory: Deploying the idea of subalternity as identity-in-difference, it charts two distinct but related problems of othering, the first concerning narratives and politics of identity and the second contemplating an ethics of alterity. First, the essay addresses the formation of the Other of Europe, which involves the making of a European Self, as well as that of the colonial subject as Other. This is the field in which the "Native Informant" is made—an instrument of colonial authority who speaks for "the native" in service of efficient governing. Here, the analysis draws attention to the nearly infinite ways in which what has been cast as Other can become a "Self," by appropriating otherness as the basis of an identity and by postulating a unitary subject with agency in the place of the other. The exemplary instance here is that of anticolonial nationalism, where an investment in all that is "native" and "authentic" serves to reproduce colonial logics of othering even as the emergent nation-state claims liberation.[4] But the mirroring of a European Subject of History through the affirmation of the native is not celebrated as a liberatory move by Spivak. She is not content with a politics of identity and recognition. Thus, the essay also confronts the call of the "quite-other," or the problem of alterity, that is, that which escapes consolidation into narrative and identity. Here, alterity is investigated through the question of female subaltern speech. The double meaning of other—as that which is contained within the logic of the production of the European Self and its Other *and* as that which exists outside it, as more radical alterity, drives Spivak's careful reading of the double meanings of subject, agent, and representation. In this double reading, she makes a signature critical intervention—by insisting on the discontinuity between subjectivity and agency.

The figure of woman as subaltern, as elaborated in the discussion of the discourse on widow immolation, is the obvious example of this discontinuity: Here the very subjectivity of the female emerges in a process of dissimulation. She appears in this discourse as the subject of choice, a free-willing agent who chooses submission and death. To expose this dissimulation, Spivak charts the ways in which the "voice" of the female is constructed as instrument, either for indigenous male authority or colonial patriarchy. The subjectivity of the woman here is not only read as the violent and unstable effect of an agency not her own, but she is revealed to us as an instrument of that agency. Indeed, her very instrumentality can be traced to the dissimulations entailed by the idea of her "choice."

These moves, cited in innumerable contexts from feminist theory to critical legal studies to development policy, have also posed several important questions concerning the role and force of history: as narrative for the production of identity (both individual and collective), as political practice, and as empirical ground (on which basis the former processes are frequently said to be rooted). Such a set of related questions might be formulated as

1 How can we think about history not as a narrative of identity, but as a problem of alterity?
2 How can we write a history of colonialism that does not presuppose a constant, undifferentiated, and/or homogenous postcolonial victim, while still accounting for the violent transformations and the effectivity of colonialism?
3 How can we engage the particularity, specificity, and historicity of temporal and spatial contexts, without, at the same time, reproducing discourses of native authenticity?

These questions direct us to a general tension between history as narrative, which assumes a unitary subject with agency, and the critical impetus of historical thinking, attentive to historicity and the situated complexities of subject-production.

Rereading "Can the Subaltern Speak" on the occasion of the conference, it became clear to me that one could teach a course based on this text alone. Thinking of it as a pedagogical tool serves to map its turns of supplementation, its intersectional analysis and interdisciplinary method. Thinking pedagogically, then, let us examine the trajectory of the article in its four sections, to engage especially four themes that speak to the questions at hand: the problem of the subject as philosophical and historical agent, the politics of representation in processes of subject-formation, the play of identity and alterity, and the problem of particularity, historicity, and authenticity. The text opens with the question of subject-formation, as European Self, the politics of representation, and the role of the intellectual in radical politics. The second section supplements by turning to the unnamed Other of radical European intellectual practice. We then move in this section to the production of the Other, as elaborated in the epistemic violence of the codification of Hindu law, and then outside this logic, to the idea of subalternity. The third section fine-tunes by hearing Derrida's call to the "quite-other," that is, the question of alterity as posed against authenticity, as method for attending to the politics and heterogeneous "mechanics of the constitution of the Other" (294/265). Finally, we move to the social text of sati-suicide, the violent production of the female subject, the discontinuity of subjectivity and agency, and a call to the ethics of responsibility.

Section 1 speaks to the politics of historical representation by exposing and engaging double meanings for the words *subject* and *representation,* often collapsed in philosophical and historical narrative. It offers a critique of the question of the subject as posed in a conversation between Foucault and Deleuze by engaging two senses of the word *subject*: first, as philosophical/ethical Subject (with a capital *S*) and, second, as subject of politics (with a small *s*), as in a subject of political authority, "the king's subjects." The essay thus insists that any analysis of subjectivity must be attentive to the politics of subject-formation and subjectification as well as subjection. At the same time, we are warned that attention to the politics of subject-formation does not necessarily do away with the historical-philosophical Subject: the discourse of Power in Foucault, an ostensibly "parasubjective matrix," Spivak asserts, presupposes and so "ushers in the unnamed" philosophical Subject of Power (274/241). That is, *Power* as a principle in Foucauldian analyses tends quietly to operate as a Subject with philosophical, historical, and political agency, even as such analyses ostensibly direct themselves to the located micropolitics of subject-effects.

Spivak then emphasizes how this conversation between radical philosophers also produces an "unquestioned valorization of the oppressed as subject" (274/241). It is "unquestioned' because such a valorization asserts that the oppressed subject, embedded within politics and relations of power, can speak, without mediation and messiness, as a Self (a Subject with agency). That is, it is exactly because Foucault and Deleuze make the radical claim that theory is practice that they elide the problems of representation that should burden intellectual work. Indeed, in order to assert that "'there is no more representation; there's nothing but action,'" (i.e., theory is practice), these thinkers also invest in the "reality" of the experience of the oppressed (274–275/241–242). With both moves, Foucault and Deleuze resist "speaking for" the oppressed, but their very presumptions coincide with both a positivist-essentialist assumption of "real experience" as well as a turning away from the dynamics of representation that must inform the intellectual's "difficult task of counter-hegemonic ideological production" (275/242). The emphasis on ideology here highlights a key concern of the essay, that is, to consider the mechanics of agency in the production of subjects. In ideology the vast and shifting flows of what we call power are locatable in complicated processes of subject-formation, to which the essay now turns.[5]

The critique of Foucault and Deleuze's retreat from representation is furthered by a close reading of the double meaning of representation in Marx, especially as it appears in *The Eighteenth Brumaire of Louis Bonaparte*. The attention to Marx exposes the problem of agency that remains vague in Foucault's metaphorics of power: Marx, elaborating the agency of Capital, speaks of the collective subject (in the formation of a class) that is, precisely, not the historical-philosophical agent. Spivak elaborates the problem of a subject that is not an agent for itself through the double meaning of representation in Marx. Marx speaks of representation as *vertretung*, that is, political representation, the representation of the proxy, or of "speaking for"; and representation as *darstellung*, also translated as re-presentation, as in art, as in the portrait, as in staging. (It is this double meaning that is collapsed in Deleuze's pronouncement that "'there is no more representation; there's nothing but action'" (275/242). Spivak's analysis of *The Eighteenth Brumaire* asserts that theories of ideology must engage rigorously with this twofold play of representation, the first in the philosophical staging of the subject, and the second within the state and law: "They [theories of ideology] must note how the staging of the world in representation—its scene of writing, its *Darstellung*, dissimulates the choice of and need for . . . paternal proxies, agents of power, *Vertretung*" (279/247). Bringing this play of representation to the problem of subject-formation, the text then moves to the question of othering, highlighting the fact that Foucault's analysis remains within Europe, within "the exploiter's side of the international division of labor" (280/248). Between the two processes of representation, the problem of the subaltern comes into view.

Section 2 supplements the critique of Foucault and Deleuze, then, by turning to what Spivak calls the "epistemic violence" of othering and to the other side of the international division of labor (280/248). Here, two processes are introduced. First, the constitution of the Other of Europe; this is the process of the formation of the colonial subject, that figure that is written into hegemony, that is produced within and by the logic of colonial discourses. To illuminate this phenomenon, Spivak gives the example of the production of the colonial subject in the codification of Hindu law. Then, turning to Gramsci, the reader is introduced to the problem of the subal-

tern and thus to the problem of alterity—of other spaces that exist outside
or beyond and at the limit of the logic of hegemonic formations. Significantly, the text highlights Gramsci's concern with "the intellectual's role in
the subaltern's cultural and political movement into hegemony" (283/252).
Here, Spivak returns to the question of intellectual responsibility: if Foucault and Deleuze resist "speaking for" and so retreat before the messiness
of the politics of representation, the historians of the subaltern studies
collective (here she is speaking of the collective's early work through the
mid-1980s), true to Gramsci, must ask: can the subaltern speak? Historical
analyses of the colonial formation (in India) demand that one reconsider
and even reject the assumption that the oppressed can speak, or cannot be
muted, asserting rather that muted voices are embedded deep within the
colonial archive. The historical project of subaltern studies in this period
therefore understood itself to be the recovery of the subjugated subject's
historical agency. In seeking to excavate a suppressed agency, it manifested
the exact inversion of Foucault and Deleuze's resistance to representing
the oppressed, ironically assuming the burden of representation. For Spivak, grappling with dilemmas of gender in postcoloniality, the postcolonial
context incited an even more complex interrogation of the problematics of
representation (cf. Chatterjee, this volume).

"Can the Subaltern Speak?" proceeds by theorizing subaltern space as
identity-in-difference through a reading of Ranajit Guha's inaugural text of
the collective in volume 1 of *Subaltern Studies*.[6] If, for Guha, subalternity
is a definitive location in relation to power, it is for Spivak both inside and
outside: a limit, a space at once outside and autonomous from hegemony,
but simultaneously inside as its condition of possibility. Despite the new
research enabled by subaltern studies approaches, Spivak argues that the
female subaltern remains "deeply in shadow" (288/258). Posing the question of gender extends the analysis of subalternity but also transforms it:
even within the analytics of subalternity we find the question of alterity.
This feminist intervention takes the educated reader to the limits of her
knowledge, to all those whom she cannot know. Here the text addresses
those outside, radically outside, by offering a very different politics of representation: "To confront them [that is, 'the subsistence farmers, unorganized peasant labor, the tribals, and the communities of zero workers in
the street or in the countryside'] is not to represent (*vertreten*) them but to
learn to re-present ourselves (*darstellen*)" (288–289/259). The point here
is not that subalterns do not know how to speak for themselves—an utter
misreading of the project and indeed of the story of Bhubaneswari Bhaduri.
Rather, the claim on the part of the intellectual that subalterns can and do

speak for themselves stands in for not doing anything about the problems of oppression. At the same time, the claim to do something about the problem, as simply speaking "for" the subaltern, also furthers the problem and the civilizing mission of benevolence while occluding the question of audibility. In asking us to re-present ourselves, Spivak asks us to supplement the benevolent intention of "speaking for" with an ethics of responsibility—in the sense of cultivating a capacity to respond to and be responsive to the other, without demanding resemblance as the basis of recognition. In Spivak's more recent work, this argument has been furthered to entail the demand for a supplementation of rights discourses. In essays such as "Righting Wrongs" she suggests that the necessary call to securing rights and the promise of "giving voice" are discontinuous, as are law and justice. And both impulses, well-intentioned though they might be, demand something else, namely, a reflection on the problem of othering in the project of making all commensurate. In Spivak's critical embrace of rights discourses and international civil society, privileged metropolitan subjects are awakened to processes of othering (in which they are constantly engaged) as necessarily constitutive of politics and ethics, to be consistently grappled with via the problem of representation.[7]

The call to the "quite-other" is further elaborated in section 3, on Derrida, which speaks particularly to the critique of imperialism. Spivak is concerned in this section of the essay to avoid reproducing the terms of a naive binary between Europe and its Other; she is not repudiating European philosophy in the interest of something that would be more transparently reflective of a subaltern position. Deleuze and Foucault do not stand for all of the European intellectual tradition. Rather, they represent a particular failure, within a particularly promising trajectory. Defending Derrida's concern with the production of the ethnocentric Self and its Other in writing, Spivak explains that attention to alterity enables an elaboration of the variegated processes by which the Other is constituted: "What I find useful [in Derrida] is the sustained and developing work on the mechanics of the constitution of the Other; we can use it to much greater analytic and interventionist advantage than in the invocations of the *authenticity* of the Other" (294/265).

The final section of "Can the Subaltern Speak?" thus opens with the title question followed by a warning call: "What must the elite do to watch out for the continuing construction of the subaltern?" (294/266). Here the historical project of subaltern studies—to recover the subjectivity of the subaltern by attributing to it historical agency—is supplemented with words of caution. We are warned that discourses of authenticity, dissimulating themselves as the recovery of a subaltern voice, construct the subaltern within the logic of Self and Other as a unitary subject with agency and, indeed, as the Other who has become a Self. Such moves threaten to foreclose the critical and political force of the very idea of subalternity, a force that derives at least in part from its relationship to the question of alterity. To illustrate this, Spivak's text turns to the "immense problem of the consciousness of woman as subaltern" (296/268). The close reading of the social text of sati-suicide, operating through an analogy to Freud's interest in recovering the voice of the hysteric, exposes the construction of female free will in two patriarchal discourses: the nativist, which codedwidow-immolation as ancient and sacred ritual, and the colonialist, which institutionalizedit as crime. The nativist reading, rooting itself in the texts of the *Rg-Veda* and *Dharmaśāstra*, stated (in paraphrase) that "the women actually wanted to die;" while the colonialist countered with a claim to defend women's truer desire by asserting the authority of the state to protect women and so recover their free will (297/247). As I mentioned earlier, here the analysis illuminates the dissimulation of woman's choice: in both cases, the woman's so-called free will is exactly not that; her subjectivity is only constructed as an instrument of patriarchial agency. -In this instance, we are thinking the figure of woman *as* subaltern, using gender as a tool to deconstruct subjects constituted as voice for hegemonic agency (that is, as one who can speak, but only by being ventriloquized). The empirical question of subaltern women, of the domains and possibilities of their ethico-political agency, is yet another deferral into alterity, a question again addressed by Spivak's recent work on the question of worlding, rights, and responsibility. In recent essays she has returned to the problems posed in "Can the Subaltern Speak?" to remark how much more accessible the life-worlds of subaltern women are to those who would represent them and speak on their behalf; at the same time, she notes that the possibilities for subaltern women to achieve (violently empowering) upward mobility have actually diminished. Exactly because of the proliferation of proxies to speak for her in international civil society, the subaltern woman is in fact more restricted, more muted today than she even was in an earlier moment of capital's globalization.[8] The mechanics of othering elaborated in "Can the Subaltern Speak?"—the warning about the ways in which the Other of Europe consolidates itself *as Other* through discourses of authenticity and so silences—informed major themes in the next phase of subaltern studies. An increasing attention to the study of women and postcolonial citizenship/governmentality, feminism and law, and indeed the very question of articulating the problem of historical difference has marked the movement since the publication and reception of the essay, though the empirical questions remain and the theoretical problems along with them.

"Can the Subaltern Speak?" demands that we do the rigorous work of locating processes of subject-formation while attending to the situatedness of agency.[9] It calls for the study of the particularities, the contextual specificities of the mechanics of othering, while also insisting on the interruption of the "quite-other." Both projects—those that would engage in historicizing by locating specific events and processes in time and those that would make the present vulnerable to the particular contexts and social texts of another time—have implications for the critical practice of writing history, demanding that it be informed and invigorated by a recognition of the limits of giving and taking voice. In this vein, it is useful to remember an important but often overlooked claim in "Can the Subaltern Speak?" In introducing the discussion on epistemic violence, Spivak tells us that "the clearest available example of such epistemic violence is the remotely orchestrated, far-flung, heterogeneous project to constitute the colonial subject as Other" (280–281/248–250). To illustrate, the text then turns to the British codification of Hindu law. But, before charting details, Spivak interrupts with a disclaimer: "the Indian case cannot be taken as representative of all countries, nations, cultures, and the like that may be invoked as the Other of Europe as Self" (281/250). The example of India then, is exactly not about claiming identity, that is, historicizing in service of personal nostalgia. Rather, one could say that the Indian case cannot represent—*vertreten*—it cannot speak for all cases of Othering. The attention to this specific case is a call to elaborate different stagings (re-presentations) of Othering. The claim here is to offer a particular example knowing its limits. The gesture is informed by a notion of particularity, of specificity *as* sheer difference itself, which is the logical ground of historicity. There can be no collapse into claims of authenticity.

This question of particularity—how to address the particular situation and relations that inform and constitute the basis for any study concerned with culture, political economy, history—is an interdisciplinary problem that structures how the study of "others" is institutionalized in the North American academy. Attentive to the tension between narratives of identity/authenticity and the historicity that resists it, "Can the Subaltern Speak?" gives us the tools to think about the often unexamined relationship between the celebrated rigor of studying specificity of context and the pitfalls of performing authenticity. By way of example, and considering the present relevance of the essay's postcolonial critical practice, let me offer some brief thoughts on this relationship within area studies, understood here as a project that seeks to study and validate "others" within the parameters and structures of interest that have governed intellectual production since the Second World War.

The making of area studies as an intellectual formation in the US academy has been the topic of much recent study and, indeed, of pressing geopolitics.[10] I will not rehearse the critique of area studies here, but rather consider the position of a scholar of an "area" located within a discipline. The study of "areas" emphasizes the particularity of the histories and "cultural values" of geopolitically worlded space. At the same time, disciplines in the humanities and social sciences remain dominated by studies of North America and Europe, which, however attentive to the specificities of their contexts, open up into putatively universal questions about the nation-state, capital, modernity, democracy, justice. In contrast, scholars of "areas," of the South especially, are called to provide local expertise and especially to attend to the particularities of areas. This is of course an important, absolutely necessary project, one that at its logical ground at least seeks to resist the production of universal templates for economy, history, and civilization. But what does it mean to be enabled *only* to speak for the particular? To have voice *only* as an expert of an area? This circumscribed institutional voice giving occurs when rigorous attention to the particularities of "areas" serve discourses of authenticity. Here the radicalizing claims of fragmenting master narratives with information about how things are done differently in different places loses its force, and we approach the all too ubiquitous, unquestioned valorization of the Other in the name of "cultural values." In this way, attention to the particulars and specificities of "others" evades the problem of alterity. When attention to othering serves only to consolidate the Other as native, area studies becomes identity politics. It is a process that postcolonial critique can contest but that the identitarianism of "postcolonials" cannot.

This is an important lesson for the practice of history, the critical impetus of which would recognize historicity as its epistemological ground. The concerns of "Can the Subaltern Speak?" remind us of the difference between historicity on the one hand and the call to elaborating specificity of context on the other. Commitment to historicity requires that we be attentive to the politics of representation when we narrate, exactly because the specificity of any given moment or fact is irreducibly different from the next. Being attuned to radical difference at the very ground of the empirical is different from celebrating the careful recounting of particulars in a project of giving voice. "Can the Subaltern Speak?" opened the distinction, with a critical method that took seriously the hegemonies that constitute and legitimate themselves in the process of consolidating the Other as subject, attributing to it "authenticity" and giving it voice. As such, it offered tools for the exercise of history as critical practice that challenged the more prominent role of history as narrative for identity.

Just as problems of historical representation informed "Can the Subaltern Speak?" the history and politics of globalization infuse Spivak's recent work. Since she wrote *The Critique of Postcolonial Reason,* Spivak has deployed a post-Heideggerian concept of "worlding" to theorize responsibility-based ethics, extending the arguments about the distinction between othering and alterity to a global frame. In early essays such as "The Rani of Sirmur: An Essay in Reading the Archives," and also in *The Critique,* the term *worlding,* for example, indicated the violent making of a world; one that "generates the force to make the 'native' see himself as 'other.'" Recent work has addressed worlding by moving from the mechanics of othering to the possibilities of alterity. Thus, *Death of a Discipline* has posed *the planet* as a name for an alterity that we inhabit, a way of being in the world that requires the imagination of what we cannot know, the universe, from a perspective that cannot produce mastery through mirroring. The planet, unlike the world, is a conceptual metaphor infused with the possibility of seeing from outside, of seeing from the perspective of the alien, and not merely of apprehending the unified sphere that is familiar to us from prominent discourses of absolute oversight. *The planet* is presented as replacement for *the globe,* a term that is has been newly charged by contemporary capitalism, its logic of commensurability, and the extended grasp of its new financial networks.[11] Similarly, Spivak has engaged the concept of the "quite-other," via Derrida and Levinas, to theorize the ethics of responsibility. Responsibility, engaged as attention to the call of the other, has, as I mentioned earlier, been presented as a supplement to global human rights discourses. If the "human" in human rights begins with the understanding that everyone is the same, and therefore that rights can be dispensed universally, the concept of responsibility is grounded in an understanding of the human as being in an ethical relation with the other. While rights-based discourses seek a common ground to make all differences commensurate, Spivak contemplates a limit, an unknowable alterity, an excess, which elides comparison and exchange but to which equality must extend. Spivak is concerned with how we learn to conceive of this alterity in order to respond, and here the function of literature appears as the strange institution in which imagination is trained:

> *Radical alterity—the wholly other—must be thought through imagining. To be born human is to be born angled toward an other and others. To account for this, the human being presupposes the quite-other. This is the bottom line*

*of being-human as being-in-the-ethical relation. By definition we cannot—
no self can—reach the quite-other. . . . This is the founding gap in all act or
talk, most especially in acts or talk that we understand to be closest to the
ethical—the historical and political. We must somehow attempt to supplement the gap.*[12]

"Can the Subaltern Speak?" was a vanguard attempt to supplement the
gap between the necessities of historical and political representation and the
ways of being that exceed institutional channels of voice giving. The theme
remains relevant in Spivak's recent writing and activist practice, where the
concepts of worlding and responsibility open onto the ethics and politics of
imagination. *Imagination* here is not a code word for *escape*. It is a faculty,
one that confronts and engages difference. Thus training in the humanities,
where the practice of imagining brings one into relation with other selves
and ways of being, supplements expertise in the social sciences directed at
managing or resolving difference through value-systems grounded in logics
of commensurability. If "Can the Subaltern Speak?" unpacked the politics
of representation, training in the imagination opens new ways to negotiate those politics, to engage with the other, "not to transcode," as Spivak
puts it, but to "draw a response."[13] It is also where one learns to respond,
responsibly.

NOTES

1   Spivak, "Can the Subaltern Speak?" Reference to this article will hereafter be
found in parethentical citation within the text.
2   Spivak, "Setting to Work," p. 167.
3   Spivak, *A Critique of Postcolonial Reason.*
4   For the definitive analysis of this process and its subtleties, see Chatterjee, *Nationalist Thought and the Colonial World* and *The Nation and Its Fragments.*
5   For an elaboration of the problem of power in Foucault, see Spivak, "More on
Power/Knowledge."
6   See Guha, "On Some Aspects."
7   For an elaboration of this argument, see Spivak, "Righting Wrongs." For the
idea of responsibility in the context of deconstructive ethics, see Spivak,
"Responsibility."
8   See Spivak, "Righting Wrongs." A recent interview articulates a new definition of
the subaltern as political and empirical subject. See Spivak, "Mapping the Present." In it she explains: "The subaltern is now altogether permeable, rather unlike the definition of subalternity in an earlier conjuncture by the South Asian
historian's group where the subaltern is precisely the person outside the circuit
of mobility. I have therefore formulated a new notion of restricted permeability.

The bottom is altogether permeable from above. The academic woman with cell phone. But the permeability from below up into the area of the dominant is not only as restricted as, but more restricted than it was before." Spivak, "Mapping the Present," p. 11.

9   As put in a recent discussion of democracy: "My understanding is that the complexities of subject production give us a sense of the limits of agency. This does not make agency inadequate or 'the subject' impotent." See Spivak, "A Dialogue on Democracy," p. 214.

10 See for example Spivak, *Death of a Discipline,* especially chapter 1; Spivak, "Deconstruction and Cultural Studies"; Spivak, Miyoshi, and Harootunian, *Learning Places*; Gulbenkian Commission, *Open the Social Sciences*. Recent debates about the funding of the U.S. area studies centers under Title 6 of the National Defense Education Act of 1958 affirm the necessity for such discussion.

11 On worlding, see *A Critique of Postcolonial Reason*, p. 212, and chapter 3, as well as "The Rani of Sirmur," and *Death of a Discipline,* pp. 70–73.

12 See Spivak, "A Moral Dilemma," citation from pp. 215–216. See also Spivak, "Responsibility," and "Righting Wrongs."

13 For a discussion of the call of the other in the context of *poesis* or imaginative making, policy making, and the problem of interdisciplinarity, see *Death of a Discipline*. Here the concern is to harness the "role of teaching literature as training the imagination" in "preparation for patient and provisional forever deferred arrival into the performative of the other, in order not to transcode but to draw a response." Spivak, *Death of a Discipline*, pp. 12–13.

Drucilla Cornell

THE ETHICAL AFFIRMATION OF HUMAN RIGHTS

GAYATRI SPIVAK'S INTERVENTION

Why have I written largely of women to launch the question of the recognition of ceaselessly shifting collectivities in our disciplinary practice? Because women are not a special case, but can represent the human, with the asymmetries attendant upon any such representation. As simple as that.

GAYATRI CHAKRAVORTY SPIVAK

How are we to combine Gayatri Chakravorty Spivak's insightful analysis into the complexities of political and aesthetic representation with her recent work on human rights? How does her lifelong engagement with deconstruction inform both her conceptualization and representation and the legal and moral entitlement in human rights discourse? This essay attempts to draw connections between Spivak's relentless antipositivist critique in "Can the Subaltern Speak?" with her insistence that we must suture human rights discourse to an ethic of responsibility if we are to avoid the pitfalls of Social Darwinist liberalism. This ethic is in turn analyzed in terms of Spivak's commitment to feminist practices on the ground, as these inform her own political engagement. She has sometimes been accused of reproducing a split between theoretical and practical labor or of engaging in a kind of writing and reading that either defers or annuls the possibility for engagement with political actuality. Ultimately, as we shall see, she accomplishes the opposite. She undermines theoretical license for political paralysis, thereby freeing herself to claim her continuing commitment to the big political dream of the struggle against what she refers to as worldwide class apartheid.[1] For Spivak, an ethics of responsibility begins with the acknowledgment that political contest and struggle always have to confront their own representations as these inevitably risk recapturing the subaltern in negative idealizations of it. Ethics does not replace politics, not at all. But Spivak's contribution is to show us that once we come to terms with the inevitability of representation, both in terms of ideals and people involved in political struggle, then we must, and the *must* here is the ethical moment, confront how we are shaping others through those representations so as to reinforce the images and fantasies of the colonial as well as the not-yet-decolonized imaginary.

Gayatri Spivak has always dared to be a feminist. In her first critical engagements with the historical writing of the subaltern studies group, she insisted that the inclusion of the gendered subaltern in the work of the project would not simply be a neat politically correct addition, but was itself crucial to the stated ethical purpose of the project. Dipesh Chakrabarty summarizes that ethical ambition as an aim "to be possessed of an openness so radical that I can only express it in Heideggerian terms: the capacity to hear that which one does not already understand."[2] But the dream of unlimited receptivity needs to account for gender—so as to grasp the fact that there is not a single subject whose as yet illegible speech can be listened to. In her early interventions into the subaltern studies project, Spivak powerfully argues that engagement with the gendered subaltern will inevitably do for the category of the subaltern what "woman" does to humanity, that is, mark the asymmetries attendant upon any representation of it as a concept. In her essay on human rights the subaltern, even when it is represented as a ceaselessly shifting collectivity, still is inadequate before the asymmetries that Spivak shows us to be attendant even upon representations that seek fidelity to this subaltern's ungraspability within radical theories attempting to bring it into history. Spivak's point is that any representation of the subaltern, even one that attempts to rewrite history from the perspective of the subaltern as the subject of her own history, will take us into the deepest philosophical questions of cognition and representation. The seemingly pessimistic conclusion of her rightfully famous essay "Can the Subaltern Speak?" that the subaltern cannot speak, can also be read through Spivak's radical antipositivism, which insists that there is no existing representational space in which the gendered subaltern can make itself heard; as a result, the noting of the failure of representation itself becomes a form of listening.

The feminist community that could *heed*, and I'm choosing that word carefully, the subaltern is always "to come," as we struggle to achieve fidelity to the radical openness to which Heidegger calls us. Ultimately, for Heidegger, this openness involves us in patience, for we can only wait and be open to what might be the advent of a new beginning. This advent cannot be predicted or calculated. It will arise beyond what Heidegger has called the mathematical, the scientization of all knowledge—including, we might add, the knowledge of Marxist reformists. But for Spivak our responsibility goes beyond patience. For, positioned as we are in a thoroughly unjust world, we are inevitably called by the other to act; we cannot escape the fact that we are always already involved in representational systems that place us in both an asymmetrical and a hierarchical relationship to the poorest women in the South.

Spivak returns to the limit of representation as both a political and ethical lesson in her recent work on human rights, highlighting the way in which we are already ensnared in a world picture that divides our globe into first, second, and third. Here she advocates the practice of an ethics that begins in what she calls the "unlearning of our privilege," which paradoxically is always also our entitlement to speak, write, and represent in the first place. It is the adherence to this entitlement that not only needs first to be noted before it can be unlearned, but that Spivak discloses at the base of those systems of representation that go unacknowledged in positivist appeals to direct experience as the basis for political activism. In this essay I hope to draw connections between Spivak's feminism, her relentless antipositivism, and her crucial rethinking of human rights advocacy.

In her essay "Can the Subaltern Speak?" Spivak takes Michel Foucault, Gilles Deleuze, and Felix Guattari to task for precisely their failure to grasp their own enablement as subjects who, despite all claims to the contrary, indeed are representing the working class in their claims about them, even though those claims are reduced to the status of mere presentations of the workers' voices. Spivak painstakingly shows that the supposed refusal of representation in the name of a direct experience of the masses who speak in and for themselves falls into the kind of positivism that Marx himself devoted a lifetime to critiquing in his own conception of class consciousness. For Marx, as Spivak reminds us, "In so far as millions of families live under economic conditions of existence that separate their mode of life . . . *they form a class*. In so far as . . . the identity of their interests fails to produce a feeling of community . . . *they do not form a class*."[3] In what I consider to be a correct interpretation of his writings, Spivak says that, for Marx, the struggle of a class—and it is a struggle—to become a class for itself always proceeds through at least two kinds of representation. Spivak distinguishes between *Vertreten* and *Darstellen* to point to how Marx plays with what we think of as representation of economic interests and the re-representation of these interests as they become part of the struggle by which the working class comes to consciousness as a class for itself and, indeed, as the bearer of the emancipatory project of freeing humanity from the chains of exploitation—appropriating for itself the function of the Subject, which is otherwise occupied by Capital. We can understand Spivak's distinction as she reads it through her engagement with Marx's own text in the simple example of workers forming themselves into a union. There is a difference for Marx between two kinds of economic or union struggles. The first is when workers merely join a union that is already established as a corporate entity that both *represents them and seeks to act as a proxy in their place*. In the first type of union, it is the union, and not the workers, that purports to bear the collective interest of the working class in the limited economic program of reform. The second kind of union struggle takes place when workers represent themselves as *in union*, as a class whose interests shatter the idea of economic reform within capitalism. What it means to be *in union*, then, becomes part of the struggle over the terms of the representation of the working class's emancipatory project. At times, in Marx's more programmatic work, this union can be seen to form the ultimate basis of a different form of social order altogether: first in socialism, then in communism.

Spivak's preliminary point in this essay is that the erasure of their own enablement to represent the workers through an appeal to the direct experience of that class actually involves all three thinkers, Deleuze, Guattari, and Foucault, in the constitution of the other as an idealized self-shadow. The shadow is both erased and idealized in that the resisting other becomes what the intellectual desires to be himself but is unable to achieve because of his very enablement as one who represents and therefore is unable to simply "join the masses"; the shadow of the intellectual as he might be, using that word deliberately, if he were not caught up in what Spivak calls, "the asymmetrical obliteration of the trace of that Other in its precarious Subject-ivity."[4] These three thinkers, at least in Spivak's critique, can avoid their ethical responsibility for their representations only by imagining a kind of direct action that is almost a pure activity, pure in the sense that it is not contaminated by imposed representations of any kind. Spivak's point of course is that the direct action of the working class, as imagined by intellectuals in its purity from tired reformist ideals, is itself a representation, and one that dangerously erases the representer and with it his role in the very definition of direct action. Spivak contrasts this almost willed naïveté that she associates with Deleuze and Guattari, and at times Foucault, with the painstaking deconstructions of Jacques Derrida, which always take place, and indeed can only take place, by acknowledging their dependence on representational schemas and their linguistic underpinnings.

It is this act of reflecting on the dependency and force of representation, its inescapability, that Spivak reads as an ethical moment in deconstruction. Derrida has been crucial to Spivak's work since the very beginning, and the place of deconstruction in her work only begins with what she sees as Derrida's rejection of any notion of politics as a kind of action without representational formations. Rather, Spivak focuses us on that dimension of Derrida's work that interrogates how the European subject and its own philosophical projection of the subject of man is consolidated by an outside that is both erased and yet assimilated to the constitution of its claim to entitlement through subjectivity. In other words, the other that we hear because he or she speaks to us in our language and through our forms of representation has already been assimilated, and thus appropriated, by the subject who represents him or her. If that representing subject is in the entitled position that this other is denied, then the representation will always be contaminated by that very entitlement. It is this entitlement that needs to be both noted and deconstructed if we are to engage she who is other to our current understandings, an other who calls us out of our enclosure in our accepted systems of knowledge, including historical knowledge. Thus Spivak reminds us that there are no "masses" simply "out there" with their experience, but that we—and all of us who are enabled to represent the others in any of our given fields in the university are included in this we—have to confront the representational field in which both we and the others we study are made up so as to ultimately eclipse contested representations of what might have been the gendered subaltern in history. To quote Spivak, "Between patriarchy and imperialism, subject-constitution and object-formation, the figure of the woman disappears, not into a pristine nothingness, but into a violent shuttling which is the displaced figuration of the 'third-world woman' caught between tradition and modernization. These considerations would revise every detail of judgments that seem valid for a history of sexuality in the West."[5] The radicality of Spivak's feminism asserts itself here. The implications are profound, for if we were to attend to the asymmetries attendant upon all those representations of the human that woman evokes, we would be confronted with having to revise some of our most basic presuppositions, not only about sexuality and sexual difference but also about what is human and, indeed, about what we could mean by the ideal of humanity itself.

This kind of radical revision of our judgments about the human is what Spivak calls us to in her rethinking of human rights. For Spivak here shows us the practical importance of calling us to attention so that we acknowledge who is entitled to be the representer in human rights discourse and, more specifically, who is positioned as the enforcer of human rights mandates. She is attentive to the history in which human rights (the distribution, conferral, and defense of human rights) becomes an alibi for the often violent demand that others conform to ideals and norms of Western economic subjectivity. However, it is important to note that Spivak is not against human rights. She recognizes in it the structure of a double bind. She argues instead that we must "suture" human rights discourse to a notion of responsibility, one that turns us to what is seemingly outside the self. To make the point (and every essay is also an act of pedagogy through example), Spivak uses the example that we always come into the world as creatures born into a language that we cannot own. The foreignness of this language can appear to be an oppressive exteriority. Yet, in its very otherness to us, an otherness that enables us to be at all, this language into which we are inserted through the process of learning its rules and ideal forms also points us to at least a narrow sense of obligation to the outside world. "Just as I cannot play with my own genes or access the entire linguisticity of my mother-tongue, so 'is' the presumed alterity radical in the general sense. Of course it bleeds into the narrow sense of 'accountability to the outside world,' but its anchor is in that imagined alterity that is inaccessible, often transcendentalized and formalized (as indeed is natural freedom in the rights camp)."[6] Spivak is calling us to what I have described as the ethical moment in deconstruction, which always reminds us of the ungraspable otherness that remains beyond our reach and yet in the deepest sense also constitutes who we are, the otherness in relation to which we are both indebted and unable to know the full extent of our accountability.

What I want to emphasize for our purposes here is that Spivak shows us how it is precisely that our representation of ourselves as subjects of rights, indeed our enablement to represent ourselves as such, is inseparable from the way in which the question of human nature is often "begged" in human rights discourse. How is the question begged? It is begged through an unacknowledged assumption that those who are engaged in human rights advocacy are the ones called to "do the right thing" by and for others. They are, in other words, from a certain point of view, responding to the call of the others and thus exercising their responsibility. What many human rights advocates do not note, however, is that their definition of the wrongs they are "righting" carries with it an ethically dangerous representation of those others for whom they seek to do the right thing. In Spivak's analysis, all too often, the sincere and deep desire to right wrongs is integrally bound up with Social Darwinist assumptions about what it means to help and about those who are represented as forever "in need" of our help. Of course Social Darwinist discourse is only one of many teleologies that end up privileging the West as the most progressive formation of humanity's being. But I think Spivak rightfully identifies and emphasizes Social Darwinism as the telos that inheres at the core of a certain human rights discourse. There are two reasons that the critique of such dangerous Social Darwinism seems appropriate here. First, as Michel Foucault has shown us, modern scientific knowledge often is characterized by classifications of natural kinds, and this classification takes place through purportedly transparent (but historically constituted and politically interested) descriptions of a hierarchically ordered natural reality.[7] Second, as many postcolonial and anthropological thinkers have shown us, this classification of things and types was racialized in colonialist discourse. To quote V. Y. Mundimbe:

> Although generalizations are of course dangerous, *colonialism* and *colonialization* basically mean organization, arrangement. The two words derive from the latin word *colĕre*, meaning to cultivate or to design. Indeed, the historical colonial experience does not and obviously cannot reflect the peaceful connotations of these words. But it can be admitted that the colonists (those settling a region), as well as the colonialists (those exploiting a territory by dominating a local majority) have all tended to organize and transform non-European areas into fundamentally European constructs.[8]

As Mudimbe reminds us, one crucial aspect of colonialist discourse is to transform those who are subjected—through forms of labor, systems of law, institutions of education, and the codification of everything from language to religion—through the constructs emanating from and structuring the worldviews of the colonizers. The colonialists have the task of constructing a new world and thus of extending their own; as such they inevitably impose their own world with its attendant social practices and systems of belief on those they colonize. The colonized must be subjected and ultimately transformed to become eligible for their so-called entry into the "civilized" world. For, colonialism holds out the promise that the "other" world, now conquered, will also be admitted *into* the world that colonialism is making. This promise, which is also a deferral, legitimates itself through the attribution of categorical difference and the ideology of progress. The racialization of the colonized, then, becomes a way of naturalizing the purported inferiority of their systems of belief. In this way the evolutionary goal of the colonizer for the colonized becomes naturalized, as the colonized are grasped as a "type" that is inherently inferior and in need of aid. It is the naturalization of this evolutionary schema inherent in justifications of colonization that Spivak identifies as Social Darwinist, meaning that it sustains the illusion that Western Man, using that phrase deliberately, is the most evolved form of the species, and hence that his recognition of others' rights is a form of beneficence, which is, of course, a sign of his own goodness and superiority. Human rights in this context becomes that which the colonizer distributes to protect the colonized from themselves.

Human rights, thus understood, can then become a form of pressure from above and below, which, in the most dangerous cases, for example, as we have recently seen in the case of Iraq, justifies full-scale war against leaders and peoples who supposedly do not live up to the human rights agenda. An ethics of responsibility then, takes us back to her earlier essay in which we grapple with how our entitlement to represent affects the space of representation including how we see and justify human rights. For Spivak, anything less than this suturing of an ethics of responsibility, an ethics that explicitly questions who and how wrongs are righted, to human rights discourse will lead us to justifications of human rights founded upon some avatar or another of Social Darwinism

In view of Spivak's critique of Darwinian liberalism, let us review briefly Martha Nussbaum's attempt to name basic human capabilities—a forthright attempt to solve the dilemma of how natural rights conceived precisely as human rights could manage to trump civil rights and indeed justify overriding the sovereignty of nation-states. Although Nussbaum wishes to leave space for a cultural interpretation of basic human capabilities, she believes it is possible to describe in normative terms the proper contents and functions of these capabilities and therefore what it means to be a full human being. Nussbaum is an example for Spivak of someone where benevolence toward others turns on her putatively prior knowing of what to do, prior here meaning before her engagement on the ground with the gendered subaltern. Spivak reminds us again and again that feminist advocates of rights, particularly human rights, have often gloried in recent representations of themselves as rights dispensers at the expense of coming to terms with the ethical hubris associated with their own representation of feminism and indeed freedom for women. If there was to be such a thing as "women's freedom," it would always have to evoke Spivak's community "to come," because it is just such freedom that can never be given a last word or positive description. We do not yet know what it could entail. It is only once feminist human rights advocates confront the manner in which entitlement to represent actually affects the way we understand human rights that we can begin to undertake the project of "suturing" to which Spivak calls us. Let us be

clear. Spivak is asking feminists who are serious about on-the-ground work
with and not for the gendered subaltern

> to shift their perception from the anthropological to the historico-polit-
> ical and see the same knit text-ile as a torn cultural fabric in terms of its
> removal from the dominant loom in a historical moment. That is what it
> means to be a subaltern. . . . these cultural scripts have not been allowed to
> work except as a delegitimized form forcibly out of touch with the domi-
> nant through a history that has taken capital and empire as a telos. My
> generalization is therefore precarious, though demonstrable if the effort I
> go on to describe is shared. These concept-metaphors, of suturing a torn
> fabric, of recoding a delegitimized cultural formation, are crucial to the
> entire second half of my argument.[9]

It has become commonplace to say that women's rights are human rights.
Spivak's own insistence that we confront the begged questions of human
nature and responsibility allows us to give a much more radical reading to
that well-coined phrase. That reading, again to quote Spivak, begins with
"because women are not a special case, but can represent the human," but
now, and this is her addition, "only with the asymmetries attendant upon
such a representation." This attention to the asymmetries attendant upon
such a representation of the human in human rights forces us to confront
visions of human sameness and who does the tallying of human character-
istics understood to be the basis of human rights. Thus it is not simply a
matter of adding women's rights to a list of rights, but instead it is a matter
of grappling with the way in which women's rights put awry facile descriptions of human nature. The gendered subaltern, by remaining what those of
us enabled to represent cannot represent precisely because of our enablement, forces us to see the limits of our definition of the human and, with the
asymmetries, our view of the inequalities that also make us see the subaltern
as in need of us to right wrongs, as we are the ones who grasp the meaning
of those wrongs. Who, in other words, is the "we" in this representation of
how they have been wronged?

I want to further suggest that this irreducible asymmetry of the gendered subaltern to pregiven systems of representation, including freedom
and so-called definitions of "livable" inequality, pushes us to confront the
worldwide class apartheid in which lives are actually lived, precisely at the
moment when assimilation fails and the other we are seeking to help remains both beyond our help and beyond our reach. We should not confuse
this asymmetry with a positive description or declaration that what is other
is simply other, and, therefore, not only can we not know anything about it,

but that we are off the hook in terms of having to confront our own rating systems of who counts and who does not count as human. This is why I wrote, in *Philosophy of the Limit*,[10] that what calls us to our responsibility is not only compatible with the acknowledgment of the phenomenological symmetry of the other, but demands its postulation. The other in her being as other presupposes respect for exactly this being of her otherness. I am referencing Derrida's scrupulous deconstruction of Levinas's rejection of Heidegger's ontology in ethics. Derrida carefully demonstrates that Levinas, despite himself, must reinscribe phenomenological symmetry if he is to remain true to the ethical asymmetry in which the other remains as other. We are returned to Heidegger's basic insight, referenced by Chakrabarty; the ethical openness demanded is precisely to the beings we cannot understand in advance—that which "is" other and yet "is." And it is this phenomenological symmetry that forms the basis of an ethics of asymmetry that breaks up preconceived systems of representation denying the other its otherness, which also renders deprivation, starvation, degradation, and subordination as something that confronts us not simply as an abstraction foreign to us, but one that pulls us toward the other in the face of her being.

Spivak is absolutely unequivocal in how she names this ethic of responsibility. She calls it an "ethics of class-culture difference, then: relating remotely, in view of a future 'to come,' the dispensers of rights with the victims of wrongs."[11] Her unrelenting commitment to this ethic, with its implied freedom to redistribute after the revolution, has to turn on this strange relationship between a phenomenological symmetry and an ethical asymmetry that is irreducible to existing hierarchies. That is Derrida's fundamental reminder—the ethical asymmetry that structures any relationship with the other derives from the fact that other is never mine, i.e., is other. Even a transcendental ethic that seeks to justify equality—or what Spivak calls the freedom to distribute after the revolution—has to turn on this strange combination of ethical asymmetry and phenomenological symmetry. The Derridean reminder takes us all the way back to human rights, because it is through this postulation of phenomenological symmetry that we can begin the education to which Spivak calls us by deconstructing our own hierarchical sense of entitlement. We seek to separate it from some core notion of being human, to liberate it from that complex but also violent naming of attributes that otherwise goes beyond the postulation of phenomenological symmetry.

Spivak's own words are helpful at this point:

> Human rights activists in both the North and the South have to be educated in their responsibility by making visible the significance of the begging

of the questions between natural rights and civil rights and the assumption of the representation of themselves as the dispensers of human rights, as the "fittest of the fit." All that seems possible to surmise is that the redressing work of human rights must be supplemented by an education that can continue to make unstable the presupposition that the reasonable righting of wrongs is inevitably the manifest destiny of groups—unevenly class-divided, embracing North and South—that remain poised to right them; and that, among the receiving groups, wrongs will inevitable proliferate with unsurprising regularity. Consequently, the groups that are the dispensers of human rights must realize that, just as the natural Rights of Man were contingent upon the historical French Revolution, and the Universal Declaration upon the historical events that led to the Second World War, so also the current emergence, of the human rights model as the global dominant, contingent upon the turbulence in the wake of the dissolution of imperial formations and global economic restructuring. The task of making visible the begged question grounding the political manipulation of a civil society forged on globally defined natural rights is just as urgent; and not simply by way of *cultural* relativism. (178)

We begin to unlearn our entitlement as dispensers of human rights by assuming responsibility to what Spivak calls subordinate cultures, "subordinate" in the sense that they are not assimilable into the assumptions of modern capitalism. To be part of a subordinate culture, to be deemed unproductive according to the dictates of advanced capitalism, is indeed part of what marks the subaltern as subaltern. It is what legitimates the transformative interventionism of those who can only recognize the human rights of the other by rendering her in the image of one who is productive for late capitalism. As Spivak succinctly puts it, "Indeed, this absence of redress without remote mediation is what makes the subaltern subaltern" (202). In her essay "Righting Wrongs," Spivak offers this amongst several other related definitions of the subaltern. As she puts it simply and elegantly, "by 'subaltern' I mean those removed from lines of social mobility" (180).

For Spivak, the role of the humanities can be crucial in helping us to negotiate the double binds entailed by this reading of human rights and to pursue freedom *with* the subaltern, transforming ourselves and not just demanding change of the other, to the degree that it seeks to achieve the uncoerced transformation of desires and social meanings. Spivak's important addition here is that uncoerced transformation demands that we rethink the notion of the agency of responsibility. To quote Spivak, "Subordinate cultures of responsibility, as I have argued, base the agency of responsibility in that outside of the self that is also in the self, half-archived and therefore not directly accessible" (199). To put it bluntly, Spivak argues that solidarity must lie with the alterity of the other and that even the suturing to which she calls us cannot escape being an enabling violation. The hard work of repair to which she calls us, which must as an ethical mandate take place within the subaltern's "own" language, cannot erase, to use Spivak's terms, "[the subaltern's] removal from the dominant loom in a historical moment" (199). Even a practice that takes place in the language of the subaltern cannot avoid confronting that the very mother language still contains the otherness inscribed by confrontation with dominant languages and discourses. It is only through a radically transformed archival practice that the endless process of suturing a torn fabric, to use Spivak's metaphor, and with it emerges the possibility of "recording a deligitimized cultural formation," can be attempted (199).

Nothing less than a new pedagogy will allow us to work with the gendered subaltern in and through her delegitimated cultures of subordination. Spivak, for a number of years now, has run a series of schools, first for children in rural India and now in China, that would seek to take on what she sees as the task of this fundamental teaching, a teaching, as she puts it, that demands that she learn from her students. She gives an example of what this learning means. In one of her schools, several of her students were removed from the school to "go east" with their parents. To "go east" meant not simply to take children out of school for months; "going east" meant migrating labor and keeping the family together. Spivak points to the uselessness of long drawn-out discussions of the value of education in a context where oral tradition is often found to be the basis of real wisdom. She had to discern what "going east" meant in all its complexity before she could even begin to think about whether or not she should attempt to keep any of these students in school. To quote Spivak:

> By what absurd logic would they graduate instantly into a middle-class understanding of something so counter-intuitive as "the value of education"? Such lectures produce the kind of quick-fix "legal awareness"-style lectures whose effects are at best superficial, but satisfying for the activists, until the jerrybuilt edifice falls down. When the community was addressed with sympathy, with the explicit understanding that behind this removal of the students from school lay love and responsibility, some children were allowed to stay behind next year. When I spoke of this way of dealing with absenteeism to the one hundred so-called rural teachers (stupid statistics) subsidized by the central government, one of the prejudice-ridden rural Hindu unemployed, who had suddenly become a "teacher," advised me—not knowing that this elite city person knew what

she was talking about—that the extended aboriginal community would object to the expenditure of feeding these children. Nonsense, of course, and prejudice, not unknown in the native informant. (215)

Since, for Spivak, humanities education and particularly comparative literature justifies itself as the basis of an "uncoercive rearrangement of our desires," I would argue, and I believe Spivak would agree with me, that this uncoercive rearrangement of our desires would always take place within a reenvisoning of who we are and the reimagining of the world in which we live. Our desires change as we see ourselves differently. Spivak's reader comes "with imagination ready for the effort of othering, however imperfectly, as an end in itself."[12] For Spivak, in other words, we read not to transcode, we teach not to deliver lessons, but ultimately to draw a response that allows the text itself to be endlessly subjected to the translations and readings of those who engage it outside of a simple identificatory structure. It is not a coincidence then, for Spivak, that the humanities are under attack, because they demand the patience of this slowed-down reading, and that this is exactly not the time frame of the quick-fix of the human rights watch. In this way Spivak understands her work that she does as a humanities professor at Columbia University and her work in schools in rural India as part of one project, even though, superficially, they might seem worlds apart. For those who work in universities, and in the humanities, the project of unlearning cultural relativism as cultural absolutism proceeds through the endless deconstruction of accepted views of positive reality, particularly ethical and political reality, such as certain brands of rational choice that claim to give us the last word on how we are as human and how our future is already premised in our past. Spivak's program for the educational supplement to human rights discourse is succinctly described by her and then connected to her ethics of responsibility:

> Without venturing up to that perilous necessity, I will simply recapitulate: First, the culture of responsibility is corrupted. The effort is to learn it with patience from below and to keep trying to suture it to the imagined felicitous subject of universal human rights. Second, the education system is a corrupt ruin of the colonial model. The effort is persistently to undo it, to teach the habit of democratic civility. Third, to teach these habits, with responsibility to the corrupted culture, is different from children's indoctrination into nationalism, resistance-talk, identitarianism. (226)

Can the gendered subaltern speak? Spivak's answer now, in 2004, is yes, if a complicated yes, if we seek to speak to and not merely represent them through our pregiven cognitive schemes. For we can only speak to, and with, the subaltern, if we dare the education to which Spivak calls us, and if we do so by beginning with the difficult work of reenvisioning ourselves as other than those entitled to help.

Can we dare to join with Spivak in her call for an ethics of class-culture difference? I think we must, in the name of the hope that we can still transform our world beyond the laws and mandates of neo-liberalism and global capitalism. In an important aside in the lecture "Righting Wrongs," Spivak remarks, "What follows must remain hortatory—an appeal to your imagination until we meet in the field of specific practice, here or there. Of course, we all know, with appropriate cynicism, that this probably will not be. But a ceremonial lecture allows you to tilt at windmills, to insist that such practice is the only way that one can hope to supplement the work of human rights litigation in order to produce cultural entry into modernity" (221).

At the conference for which this essay was written, we were all called to meet in a field of specific practice, to discuss Gayatri Spivak's work. The philosopher Theodor Adorno once wrote, "cynicism is the ideology of advanced capitalism." In her brave work over three decades, Spivak has fearlessly dared to "tilt at windmills" and to insist that if we give up on the struggle to change the world, with all the ethical demands this struggle places on us, we do so as a matter of our lack of ethics, not of fate. Deconstruction reminds us that we cannot know what is impossible because of the very impossibility of any full rationalization of our notions of reason.[13] Famously, Jacques Lacan gave a psychoanalytic twist to any conceptualization of the limits of reason by arguing that we can know what is impossible through the demarking of an inevitable and yet unconscious barrier between feminine sexual difference and the symbolic reality in which we live, since that reality is always marked by a phallicized system of difference.[14]

By her insistence that we be unafraid to "tilt at windmills," she refuses the confines of political realism. In this she returns to her earlier work on what is important in French feminist theory, which for Spivak is the anti-positivism that refuses to base feminism in descriptions of who we are as women, but instead on the failure of such positive descriptions to ever capture who we may dare to be as feminist activists. But if it is impossible to fully know who and how women can be represented, then we can return Derrida's insistence on the impossibility of knowing the impossible as an answer to Lacan and why such a deconstructive intervention is an important ally for Spivak. We cannot know that it is crazy to dream the big dreams including the dream that the struggles of the gendered subaltern, as they endlessly challenge our current spaces of political and aesthetic representation, may take us to a world beyond the class apartheid that Spivak consistently demands we, as feminists and human rights activists, both confront and take upon ourselves responsibility for perpetuating.

NOTES

1   Spivak, "Righting Wrongs," p. 176.

2   Chakrabarty, *Provincializing Europe*, p. 36.

3   Spivak, "Can the Subaltern Speak?" pp. 277/244–245, italics added.

4   Ibid., p. 281/249.

5   Ibid., p. 306/280.

6   Spivak, "Righting Wrongs," p. 201.

7   Foucault, *The Order of Things*.

8   Mudimbe, *The Invention of Africa*, p. 1.

9   Spivak, "Righting Wrongs," p. 199.

10   Cornell, *The Philosophy of the Limit*.

11   Spivak, "Righting Wrongs," p. 202.

12   Spivak, *Death of a Discipline*, p. 13.

13   Cornell, *The Philosophy of the Limit*, chapter 1.

14   Cornell, "Rethinking the Beyond of the Real."

PART THREE

SPEAKING OF (NOT) HEARING

Rajeswari Sunder Rajan

DEATH AND
THE SUBALTERN

It is in the context of a renewed and pervasive connection between death and being in our times that I propose to go back to an earlier theoretical intervention that named the subject in terms of a different set of attributes, those deriving from consciousness, speech and agency.[1] These criteria have defined the project of subaltern historiography,[2] whose most famous theoretical elaboration is to be found in Gayatri Chakravorty Spivak's essay "Can the Subaltern Speak?"[3] True, Spivak's most dramatic early historical example of the colonial subject who was subaltern (that is, not elite) is the sati, the Hindu woman who dies on her husband's funeral pyre. But, although it is this subject, dead and female, who gives rise to the speculations that constitute Spivak's essay, in her work and in subaltern historical and feminist inquiry more broadly it is the sati's volition, desire, and state of being immediately *preceding* such a death that structure her subjectivity.

While the death of the subaltern is significant, it is not subject-constitutive. Death surely, if anywhere, is where we might expect subalternity to come undone. But the questions posed by the subaltern's death contradict the belief in death as the great leveler. Spivak's essay explores in what ways a woman's gendered subalternity is connected to her dying, or her death to her gendered subaltern condition. Subaltern death, or the dead subaltern, poses questions about the manner of death but also about the meaning of death, a particular death, in a postmortem communication that traverses the boundary between the living and the dead. This is not merely a question of causality (what are the causes of death?) or even of visibility (what are the conditions that make the death of a subaltern woman available for accounting in the archive?); it is a question of the historian's dependency on the subaltern woman's death and on death being made to appear as the condition of possibility of the subaltern woman's emergence into historical discourse. Spivak's essay forces us to confront both disciplinary subaltern history and contemporary Euro-American biopolitical theory in different ways.

As a foil to Spivak's work, and as representative of a more conventional subaltern history, I draw into the discussion Ranajit Guha's essay, "Chandra's Death," which appeared in the fifth volume of *Subaltern Studies*, in 1987.[4] The comparison is prompted by the fact that the subaltern subject of "Chandra's Death" is also a woman who dies. For Guha, the subaltern historian, the death of the female subaltern poses and exemplifies a problematic of historiography and its method, which becomes inextricable from a problem of ethics. It is my hope that the juxtaposition will help us to perceive the rigors and extended implications of Spivak's essay more clearly. Because Spivak approaches the writing of history as a self-avowed "deconstructionist-Marxist-feminist," there are interesting contradictions that surface in the project of the recovery of subaltern consciousness that become particularly and, we may deduce, deliberately foregrounded in her essay.[5] Here I offer a reading of "Can the Subaltern Speak?" that highlights these points of productive crisis.

"CAN THE SUBALTERN SPEAK?"

In the discussion of Spivak's essay that follows, I shall focus on the suicide of Bhubaneswari Bhaduri, which comes at the essay's very end in the form of an illustrative anecdote. I shall begin with a sequence of distinct but related observations drawn from Spivak's reading of Bhubaneswari's suicide, which will allow us to take forward the connections between death and the subaltern about which her work is so richly suggestive.

Spivak offers a succinct description of her essay's trajectory, as follows: beginning with a "critique of current Western efforts to problematize the subject," "Can the Subaltern Speak?" is interested in showing how the "third-world subject is represented within Western discourse." The critique is centered on a conversation between Foucault and Deleuze in the form of an accusation that "Western intellectual production is, in many ways, complicit with Western international economic interests." These radical theorists' valorization of the oppressed as subject leads them to speak for an "essentialist, utopian politics" (*CSS* 276/244). An important appraisal of Marx's "decentering of the subject" in "The Eighteenth Brumaire," alongside Derrida's, constitutes one of the most celebrated sections of the essay. It is here that the question of *representation*, in its two senses, "a speaking for as in politics," and "'re-presentation' as in art or philosophy," (*vertreten* and *darstellen*), or picture and proxy (*CSS* 275/242), is centrally engaged.

Spivak's own intervention takes the form of what she describes as "an alternative analysis of the relations between the discourses of the West and the possibility of speaking of (or for) the subaltern woman." Here her example is the British abolition of sati (widow immolation) in early nineteenth-century India (*CSS* 271/238). Imperialism's constitution of the Hindu woman as a colonial subject needing saving from Hindu men is consolidated on the other side by an indigenous patriarchy that claimed that the sati "wanted to die." The sati is left with no space in which to speak her consciousness. The anecdote about Bhubaneswari, a female ancestor, brings the essay to a conclusion with the assertion, famously controversial, that "the subaltern cannot speak" (*CSS* 308/282–283).

This is Bhubaneswari Bhaduri's story, as relayed in Spivak's text. A young woman of sixteen or seventeen, she hanged herself in her father's house in Calcutta, in 1926. She was menstruating at the time, which would indicate that she was not pregnant (contradicting the usual assumption of "illicit love" as the cause of a young woman's suicide). Despite this sign, "illicit love" was how her death continued to be understood (when it was spoken of at all). Years later it emerged that she had killed herself because she had been unable to carry out a mission for a revolutionary group of which she was a member. Yet the "message" self-inscribed on her body was not read. "She 'spoke,' but women did not, do not, 'hear' her" (*CPR* 247/22).

My inquiry begins with speculation about what it means that the subaltern, in this instance, *dies*, and it ends with an alternative scenario of her *living on*. The question I pose is one about *exemplarity*, followed by an inquiry into the fact of her death as *suicide*. I am interested as well in the implications and consequences of her insertion into a psychobiographic narrative, which in my reading will serve as a framing for issues of violence against women that feminist scholars in India have been grappling with in many contexts. The illegibility or limits of legibility of her death within the structures of history, literature, and regulative psychobiography lead me into remarking upon the affective and ethical responses that the representation of the subaltern's death demands. In a speculative coda I invoke the figure of a woman, a character in Amitav Ghosh's novel *Shadow Lines,* whose life is uncannily similar to Bhubaneswari's—except for the circumstances of her dying. The comparison allows me to offer some connections between death and the gendered subaltern in conclusion.

Exemplarity

Let me begin by suggesting that Bhubaneswari dies because it is only this which makes her subaltern. The "subaltern cannot speak" is spoken in excess of and athwart the example of Bhubaneswari's death for at least two reasons. One, Bhubaneswari *is not* subaltern, if by subaltern we mean a determinate class position. This point is conceded several times in *A Critique of Postcolonial Reason* (Spivak's 1999 book, in which a revised version of the essay is included as part of the chapter on history). "Can the Subaltern Speak?" has been a controversial work, as we know, provoking a number of rebuttals on the lines of "the subaltern can and does speak," and other criticism, of which the status of the *example* has been a prominent point of questioning.[6] Therefore the changes, omissions, additions, and clarifications that Spivak introduces in the version in the book several years following the first publication are of interest as an implicit (and in many places explicit) reaction to the critical responses the essay has called forth. Referring to Bhubaneswari, Spivak cautions in advance: "The woman of whom I will speak . . . was not a 'true' subaltern, but a metropolitan middle-class girl" (*CPR* 273/40); and elsewhere: "It is to this intermediate group [the elite at the regional or local levels] that the second woman in this chapter belongs" (*CPR* 272/39). She goes as far as to "insist" that Bhubaneswari "was not a true subaltern" (*CPR* 308/64). She has repudiated any feelings of "romantic attachment to pure subalternity as such" as the justification for "not choosing a distinctly subaltern person" in this instance.[7] Though Spivak takes recourse to Ranajit Guha's definition of subalternity as an "identity-in-differential" rather than identitarian essence (*CPR* 271/38) as a general rule for identifying the subaltern, the more persuasive contention is that it is Bhubaneswari's identity as female (i.e., her gender) as opposed to her class position that determines her subordination (*CPR* 272/39). The vulnerability of women lies in their relative disempowerment even when they enjoy class or racial privileges, an important premise of feminist analyses of women's historical subordination. As women, the claims of Bhubaneswari or the Rani of Sirmur to subalternity can therefore "be staked out across strict lines of definition by virtue of their muting by heterogeneous circumstances" (*CPR* 308/64).

Second, "the subaltern cannot speak" is a conclusion that flies in the face of the actual instances of this subaltern's fulsome and meaningful speech/writing. Despite the failure of communication, there is no noticeable absence of or incapacity for speech on Bhubaneswari's part. Nor does her death pass unnoticed. Rather than silence and mystery around its causes, there appear to be a surplus of reasons advanced for her suicide, known and guessed at—illegitimate passion, in addition to a presumption of depression caused by her unmarried condition, as well as of course the discovery of her letter, many years later, which gives the true reason for her suicide. (This slight but significant information about Bhubaneswari's suicide note is to be found in *A Critique of Postcolonial Reason* and is missing from the earlier versions of "Can the Subaltern Speak?").[8]

No doubt suicide *in general* poses itself as enigma or mystery (words Spivak uses several times when referring to Bhubaneswari's death in *A Critique of Postcolonial Reason*) and as such might be thought to possess the power of resistance. It is significant, however, that the example she turns to for *willed* enigmatic silence is not this female ancestor. The successful (subalternized, slave) figure of silence is found elsewhere in the book, in the Friday of Coetzee's *Foe*, who resists every attempt at decipherment of his "writing." Friday, "the native," Spivak argues in this instance, "is not only a victim, but also an agent" because of his successful withholding of his secret (a "secret that may not even be a secret") (*CPR* 190).[9] It is possible no doubt to argue that both of them represent identical enigmas. But there is this notable difference: in the place of Friday's refusal to be "deciphered," we encounter Bhubaneswari's conscientious effort to explain not only the reason she kills herself but also to insist on what is *not* the reason for her action. Bhubaneswari, Spivak writes, "*intended* to be retrieved, wrote with her body . . . attempted to 'speak' across death, by rendering her body graphematic" (*CPR* 246/22; emphasis mine). And, as we know, she famously met only with failure. If I mark the distinction between Bhubaneswari and Friday, it is because I find it revealing that it is the former and not the latter that Spivak invokes in the context of subaltern speech. The differences between the two examples will help us understand why.

The incompatibility of the two figures in this comparison lies precisely in the grounds of their (failed) speech. For Spivak nowhere identifies Friday (Crusoe's or Coetzee's) as the "subaltern," but only, variously, as the "marginalized," the "native" or the "other." Why does Friday not qualify as the "subaltern"—despite his entirely disenfranchised status as slave? Spivak's more recent clarification of her particular trajectory toward subaltern theory, via her reading of Marx's "The Eighteenth Brumaire," underscores the close imbrication of subalternity with the *failure* of speech or, as she puts it, the "non-recognition of agency."[10] Friday may be the *literal* example of the subaltern who cannot—but also will not—speak (his tongue, after all, has been cut out). Bhubaneswari on the other hand serves as the *figural* example of the subaltern who cannot—but, in fact, does—speak. "Cannot" in this context signifies not speech's absence but its failure. While Friday's silence may be read as resistance (as willed refusal or simply the lack of the desire to communicate), her speech serves as an instance of failure, at the site of a strenuous attempt to communicate. In literal terms, then, Bhubaneswari's story is an imperfect example of "the subaltern cannot speak." If the intention was only to illustrate the *subaltern's* inability to speak, or the subaltern's *inability to speak,* we might ask Spivak, with her friend the Sanskritist, "why, [when there are so many other examples to hand], are you interested in the hapless Bhubaneswari?" (*CSS* 308/282).

Let me pause here to baldly state the general point I am driving at, lest my ventriloquization of the opposition's position be misunderstood as my own. I seek to rescue Spivak's argument from a common misreading by probing her choice of example. Spivak's choice of the "imperfect" in preference to the "perfect" example—her resistance to literalism—is central to an understanding of the (im)possibility of subaltern speech. In other words, and more generally, "the locution 'can the subaltern speak?' is an invitation to rethink the relation between the figural and the literal, a suggestion that no figural unit can find a proper, adequate literal referent, that the relation between the figural and the literal will always remain a differential relation, not something to be decided on the basis of the classical norm of adequation."[11]

My point will be made clearer by taking recourse to a counterexample: in my own work I have grappled with the victimage of mentally retarded women in state-run institutions in India and of female infants killed at birth.[12] These are contexts in which to raise the question of speech and intention would have been a mockery. In my analyses therefore I have moved without further ado into the issues that lie beyond *their* subjectivity, to the politics of the custodianship, advocacy, and intervention of those proximate to them. My "good" examples of the gendered subaltern—the female infant, the mentally retarded woman—are situated at the limit where it would make it redundant to say "the subaltern cannot speak," and so I refrained.

A passage from Derrida will throw some further justificatory light on what Spivak elsewhere refers to as the "aporia of exemplarity."[13] Derrida demands that a thing (text, person) be regarded as "more than a paradigm and something other than a symbol." "An example always carries beyond itself; it thereby opens up a testamentary dimension. The example is first of all for others, and beyond the self. . . . The example thus disjoined separates enough from itself or from whoever gives it so as to be no longer or not yet example *for itself*."[14] The example that is not an example is thereby enabled to retain its singularity.[15] But through its particulars it connects with—though at one point only, as the tangent touches the circle[16]—the generalization that is at stake and contributes to it, which is how it performs its exemplary function. In order not to be tautologous then, point and exemplum must be discontinuous with each other. Spivak's "radical heterology" is an attempt to break free of a circularity that, in effect, would otherwise merely pronounce "the subaltern is subaltern."[17]

Let me clarify, however: while the nonidentity of Bhubaneswari as subaltern might remain the case at the level of the *individual* or historical anecdote, there is no mystification in Spivak's reading of this figure at the *structural* level. Here Bhubaneswari's subalternity is produced as an instance of the general argument that "women outside of the mode of production narrative mark the points of fadeout in the writing of disciplinary history" and that they are "insufficiently represented or representable in that narration" (*CPR* 244/21).

Suicide

From marking the death of the subaltern who "is" not subaltern, I move on to ask what it means that Bhubaneswari's death is a death by *suicide*. The modality of death by suicide too might be regarded as untypical of the subaltern subject. If we apply the classical norms of characterization, Bhubaneswari's two definitive actions are marks of a highly developed, class-marked feminist individualism: first to join a terrorist group and then to commit suicide are successive marks of free will and independence for anyone anywhere, but particularly for a Hindu middle-class woman in the 1920s in India. Spivak describes it as a "frightening, solitary, and 'Clytemnestra-like' project for a woman."[18]

It will immediately be objected that the terms *free will* and *independence* are loaded terms, questionable when invoked in the context of a culture that arguably has no epistemic space for such categories. And no doubt for this reason, Spivak inserts Bhubaneswari's suicide within a different framework, that of a Hindu psychobiographic narrative of *sanctioned suicide*. But even in this context Bhubaneswari's suicide is a transgressive act, not only because it goes against the general religious or secular legal prohibition against suicide, but because it operates within the specific contours of a discourse of sanctioned suicide that is linked to a Hindu regulative psychobiography in which such a death is permitted only to men—with the exception of sati. And, by timing her death to coincide with the onset of menstruation, Bhubaneswari "reverses the interdict [in the *Dharmaśāstra*] against a menstruating widow's right to immolate herself." Spivak reads this act therefore as "an ad hoc, subaltern rewriting of the text of sati-suicide." It was not understood as such, however, in a society that popularly contested the image of the sacrificial sati by invoking a different source, the "hegemonic account of the blazing, fighting familial Durga" (*CSS* 308/282).

When young women kill themselves, no one, it seems, looks beyond illicit love as the reason for their action. In a recent essay Spivak observes that the "new subalterns," the rural, indigenous women who "make it" in a globalized economy, do not escape this fate either. They may enter UN statistics as "women entering politics," but, when they do, "the aporia of exemplarity is rather brutally crossed." Spivak returns several times to the example of Chuni Kotwal, the only woman belonging to the Lodha tribe who went to college. When she hanged herself under mysterious circumstances, "various rumours about illicit love affairs circulated" with dreary inevitability (even as, Spivak adds bitterly, "self-styled subalterns and oral history investigators assure each other in print that the subaltern can, indeed, speak").[19]

Suicide has another contemporary reference, in so-called terrorism. If we turn to the "true" cause of Bhubaneswari's action, we find that she was involved in the anticolonial Indian nationalist movement, which, in Bengal in the 1920s, followed the route of political violence. Looking ahead of her time to the time of the present, how can we understand her action alongside that of suicide bombers in Palestine, Sri Lanka, or New York? While suicidal resistance of presumably any kind may be read as "a message inscribed in the body when no other means will get through," Spivak reads the codeath of killer and victim in suicide bombing in particular as "both execution and mourning, for both self and other, where you die with me for the same cause, no matter which side you are on, with the implication that there is no dishonor in such shared death."[20] (Suicide bombing has this in common with sati that the victims are joined in death, so that something of Spivak's analysis of sati is echoed in her reading of terror.) Recall that Bhubaneswari could not bring herself to perform the political assassination with which she had been entrusted as a member of a "terrorist" cell (though whether from cowardice or principled revulsion we don't know). In contrast to the suicide bomber therefore, she spares the other and kills (only) herself. It is tempting to read this as the other's death *displaced* upon the self, either from remorse or as self-punishment. Spivak's speech on terror, "after 9/11," became controversial because of the call she issued to imaginatively enter into the mind of the suicide bombers. In the published version, which appeared in 2004, she admits to a contradiction between this ethical effort and the ineffability of such a death: "Even though I am trying to imagine suicide bombing without closing it off with the catch-all word 'terror,' the real lesson for the young potential suicide bombers may be that *their message will never be heard.* . . . Suicide is always an exceptional death—an impossible phrase. The most pathetic and most powerful thing about suicide bombing is that, like the ghost dance, its success is that it cannot succeed . . . it is not worth the risk" ("T" 97; my emphasis).

What emerges from these contemporary examples (which, though not related to Bhubaneshwari's death, I offer as relevant to its meaning) is the moral that suicide is constitutively indecipherable; its motives are multiple and inchoate even to the suicide herself; no clear will is operative but only its dubious substitutes, desperation, imitation, or indoctrination. What makes Bhubaneshwari's suicide a case of *subaltern* death cannot therefore be these truisms about *suicide* as such. It is rather the foreclosure of meaning: for young women, "it was a case of illicit love," for the suicide-bombers "terrorism."

Gender, Sexuality, Violence, Feminism

Bhubaneswari's subalternity is constitutively, or at any rate greatly more than incidentally, a gendered condition, specifically marked as that of the *sexed female body*.[21] Her menstruating condition at the time of death marks the "excess of the sexuate," which, Spivak maintains, escapes the codings of various systems such as nationalism, capitalism, and "the psychocultural system of sati" (*CPR* 247/67n4). Parts of women's sexed body—Bhubaneswari's menstruation, Jashoda's lactation, Douloti's prostitute body are invoked at various points in Spivak's work in this synecdochic fashion—are invested with such destabilizing potential, even when they may not always be "heard or read."[22]

Women's sexed bodies are also, of course, the site and object of violence. What leads Spivak to read the message of Bhubaneswari's menstruating body to mean the denial of illicit pregnancy and, moreover, to give priority to *this* message over the expressed and explicit reason for her death (i.e., remorse over failure to carry out an assassination)? The answer must be sought not in the literary critic's characterological analysis (that is, in terms of Bhubaneswari's motivation, intention, or interiority) but rather in the feminist historian's legitimate habit of reading gendered behavior in terms of its social conditioning. That Bhubaneswari found it insufficient to declare the true cause of her death via a suicide note but sought to convey, *in addition*, a coded message via her body, solely in order to remove any misunderstanding about an illicit pregnancy: *this* is the sign of her gendered subalternity. Whatever the transgressive potential of the sexuate body's excess (here its menstruating, unclean condition in death), it is canceled in this instance by the woman's submission to the violence of a social system's insistent demand to be satisfied about a female subject's chastity—even in death.[23] So strong, however, is the social presumption of female unchastity in death-by-suicide that she fails even in this attempt: a failure that becomes, in Spivak's reading, the fullest measure of her gendered condition, the veritable "proof" of the subaltern's inability to speak.

A qualification may be in order here nevertheless. I discern in Spivak's feminism a reluctance to treat the signs of a routine and banal "violence against women" as a sufficient diagnosis of their subaltern condition. I shall undertake a slight detour through her discussion of sati in the earlier part of the argument to highlight her search, consequently, for the roots of this violence deep in the sociocultural soil of an ethos. She expresses dissatisfaction with reading sati as *only violence* if it hides the broader question centered on the "constitution of the sexed subject" (*CPR* 300/59). In the interests of exploring the Hindu widow's sexual subalternity she therefore suggests that ascetic widowhood be viewed as a form of regression to celibacy within the regulative psychobiography. While "the *exceptional* prescription of self-immolation was so actively contested," she asks, why was *asceticism* by contrast accepted without demur as the fate of all widows? If woman is effectively defined as "the object of *one* husband," sati itself is no more than the "extreme case of the general law rather than the exception to it" (*CPR* 299/58).

The limning of a Hindu regulative psychobiography and its invocation as a text of sati's precolonial history, though an unfinished project, remains for me one of the great contributions of this essay. The general valuable point that Spivak makes (in the context of the work of the Marxist historian D. D. Kosambi) is that the study of ancient Indian culture must be aided by the insights of psychoanalysis ("though not the regulative psychobiography of its choice") because, while "facts alone may account for women's oppression, they will never allow us to approach *gendering*" (*CPR* 286/73–74, n63). It is the perception that sati-suicide must be understood within a system of "gendering" rather than only as women's oppression that impels Spivak toward the construction of (the hypothesis of) a "Hindu regulative psychobiography" in its service. To understand violence against women within the problematic of gendering, as such, rather than as evidence only of crime or male pathology required the effort of creating a broader historical framework of inquiry (precolonial, *śastric*) as well as access to a narrative inflected by a psychocultural idiom. Such a framework also permitted the elements of female transgression to be recovered and spoken.

It is this model that Spivak has provided for contemporary gender work, especially in the context of India. It is the radical thinking through of this question that was the urgent need of Indian feminist work, which, at least through the 1980s, was deeply preoccupied with the phenomenon of endemic violence against women. However, feminist activism tended to be limited to the more or less specific agenda of drawing public attention to violence against women, leading protests, and inciting the state to punish it through legislation and executive means. Spivak, operating outside this frame, was the major figure able to address the problem simultaneously at several other levels. I shall not spell out the overdeterminations of this analysis here, but limit myself to expressing the conviction that such an expansive project was needed to provide an understanding of the phenomenon of violence against women at a time when the phrase tended to suffice both to define and explain the problem. More recent works of Indian feminist historical scholarship—which have also been the most productive forms of feminist intervention—have begun to explore questions of conjugality, widowhood, sexual labor, and nationalism, which take us to the roots of cultural gendering.[24]

Representation, Ethical Responsibility, and the Function of the Imagination

To allow the suicide to remain mysterious is to return indifference to death. If we only returned the answer "Who knows?" to the question "Why did she die?" we would be enacting a dismissal analogous to the rhetorical question that is uttered by the cook, a "noncharacter" in Mahashweta Devi's story "Stanadayini," after her fling with the master's son: "What is there to tell?" "What, indeed, is there to tell?" agrees Spivak the reader. But Mahashweta the writer, she points out, thinks otherwise. It is as if the story of Jashoda itself came about as "the result of an obstinate misunderstanding of the rhetorical question that transforms the condition of the (im)-possibility of answering—of telling the story—into the condition of its possibility."[25]

"Every production of experience," she goes on to reflect, "thought, knowledge, all humanistic disciplinary production, perhaps especially the representation of the subaltern in history or literature, has this double bind at its origin."[26] In particular, the singularity of death demands from us an effort of understanding and the gesture of mourning, even as we know that as historical subject the gendered subaltern will resist such recuperation.

If the imperfect example strategically prevents analysis and explanation as such from foreclosing on *affect*, the double bind at the origin points to the *ethical* effort that is involved in the task of representation. "Can the Subaltern Speak?" had, even on first reading, seemed to me to be driven by the motor of a powerful partisanship in seeking to produce the effects of classical tragic catharsis, pity and fear. That Bhubaneswari should die *despite* the protection of her class standing, that the meaning of her suicide should be misunderstood *in spite of* her "most tremendous effort to speak": it is this that the lament "the subaltern cannot speak" insisted upon, leaving it to sound, in the absence of explanation, as a plangent cry upon the air. In *A Critique of Postcolonial Reason* Spivak provides the retrospective analysis of this rhetorical aberration (of academic-speak): "in the first version . . . I wrote in the accents of passionate lament: the subaltern cannot speak!" (*CPR* 308/63). Her "anguish" bears the mark of something like fatalism—the very opposite of the mode in which the sentence has been rhetorically recuperated in some quarters, as a sentence announcing that the "subaltern *shall* not speak!"[27]

The movement from affect to ethical response is a necessary one on the way to responsibility. We might speak of the *labor of affect* in its two senses—as consequential, but also as expenditure of effort.[28] In this case adequate knowledge or representation, even if it only can be through tragic and retroactive figuration, is the promised outcome.[29] The effort is reflected in the essay's depth and breadth that function in vigorous contradiction to the pessimism of its conclusion in the declaration "the subaltern cannot speak." There is, I think, more to be granted to Abena Busia's argument—that since, after all, she, Spivak, was able to read Bhubaneswari's case, she *has* spoken in some way[30]—than Spivak's retort suggests: "Yet the moot decipherment by another in an academic institution (willy-nilly a knowledge-production factory) many years later must not be too quickly identified with the 'speaking' of the subaltern" (*CPR* 309).[31] As a general argument for the retrievability of subaltern speech, Busia's argument is justly repudiated: turning the example into a counterexample is not a productive move. But the affective labor of the historian's discourse of representation that is *also* at stake here must not be dismissed as useless.

Living On

By way of concluding this reading of "Can the Subaltern Speak?" I shall move into imagining a life for Bhubaneswari. For this, I will turn to a modern Indian literary text, Amitava Ghosh's novel *Shadow Lines* (also published, though no doubt only coincidentally, in 1988).[32]

There is a moment in the narrative that resonates uncannily with the crisis-producing event of Bhubaneswari's story. It occurs early in the novel in the form of an autobiographical fragment related to the narrator (at the time a little boy) by his grandmother. (Both grandmother and narrator remain unnamed in the novel.) She had gone to college in Dhaka in the 1920s, she tells him, living through turbulent times. One day a party of policemen led by an English officer arrived at the college and led away one of her classmates. It turned out that he had been a member of a secret revolutionary party for many years and, just as he was about to carry out his mission of assassinating an English magistrate, he was discovered and arrested. The grandmother has dreamed about him for years since then, she says; "if only she had known, she would have gone to Khulna with him, stood by his side, with a pistol in her hands, waiting for that English magistrate. . . . I would have been frightened . . . But, yes, I would have killed him." Because, she adds, "It was for our freedom: I would have done anything to be free" (*SL* 37–39). She is equally fanatical when India is attacked by China in the 1965 war, giving away her gold chain for the war cause: "for your sake; for your freedom. We have to kill them before they kill us; we have to wipe them out" (237); and her admiration for the English lies in her belief that they are a nation who "have drawn their borders with blood." Her sister's granddaughter Ila, who lives in London, consequently dismisses her as a "warmongering fascist." Her grandson the narrator, however, disagrees: "she was not a fascist, she was only a modern middle-class woman . . . believing in the unity of nationhood and territory, of self-respect and national power; a modern middle-class life that history had denied her in its fullness and for which she could not forgive it" (*SL* 78).

Is it her dying then that saves Bhubaneswari from becoming a "fascistic warmonger" like (Ila's figuring of) the grandmother in *Shadow Lines* or from becoming a simple modern middle-class woman (as in her grandson's more charitable response): in either case forever living with and made mad by the dream of a revolutionary cause in which she did not get a chance to participate, for the "nation's freedom"? They must have been almost exact contemporaries, this grandmother and Bhubaneswari, growing up in similar middle-class families in Calcutta and Dhaka.[33] Where Bhubaneswari's death simulated sati, this other woman chose the Hindu widow's only other option, ascetic widowhood, her life marked by the severe discipline and hard work prescribed for widows who do not die.

But powerful and articulate though this woman is, we can also mark in her various displacements the traces of the subaltern. As refugee, as widow, as not-quite-not middle class ("she would not permit herself the self-deceptions that make up the fantasy world of that kind of person"), her world and times are out of joint. Most important, like Bhubaneswari she too leaves a postmortem letter. Hers is a vengeful one written to the college principal that accuses her grandson of visiting prostitutes and seeking to get him dismissed from college on that count. And although her accusation is uncannily right—uncannily, for she could have had no way of knowing about his college life—no credence is given to her letter. We are led to wonder if failure of this kind does not disclose subalternity in irrefutable ways.

Let me try to spell out why I have called upon this example from Ghosh's novel, outside the frame of reference of a theoretical excursus. I am aware that to imagine an alternative to Bhubaneswari's death—especially via a fictional example, lit upon by chance—cannot be made to prove or disprove anything. To follow the trajectory of such questioning is a species of literalism, and one cannot confound a deconstructive argument by insisting on the probabilities of plot as I have done. My intention in drawing this comparison was not, either, in some fashion to prophesy Bhubaneswari's irresistible development, on the model of the grandmother, into a "fascist warmonger" had she lived,[34] although such a turn remains, I suppose, within the realm of possibility.[35] I have resisted a tendentious reading of this kind by drawing attention to Spivak's empathy with Bhubaneswari (even though I may have at the same time marked the affective relationship as a site of tension). I have also noted Bhubaneswari's ultimate, and fatal, "inability to kill." In *Shadow Lines* itself the characterization of the grandmother as a "fascist warmonger" is attributed to Ila, who is shown to be ungenerous and biased in this judgment (as in many of her views). In drawing attention to the parallels, my intention has been primarily to situate the predicament and subject-formation of the middle-class Bengali woman caught up in the nationalist movement in the early decades of this century. By no means are these two women typical figures—and yet in both the historical records and fictional narratives the female revolutionary was prominent.[36] In a retrospective reflection on the piece, Spivak grants that Bhubaneswari's story "deserves notice also as an intervention in the field of gender and nationalism," although at the time of its writing she had "only looked at it in terms of *sati*."[37]

It is my hope that the detour through this counterexample can be made to yield a couple of points. One is to note that Spivak's example of Bhubaneswari is constructed as a *narrative*: so that death can (and, I believe, does) function in it as a kind of closure, even as an inevitability. I have tried to destabilize this closure by invoking a parallel narrative of prolonged life, of not-dying, beyond the crisis-producing event. And, second, while all of Spivak's subaltern examples do die—in addition to Bhubaneswari, there are also Jashoda, Douloti, the Rani of Sirmur, as mentioned—death is not the *sign* of subalternity. There is no necessary syllogism here: x, y, and z die; they are all (produced as) subaltern; therefore subalterns (must) die. I grant that something of this logic is implied in and by Spivak's work. I have sought to go against the grain of such implication by identifying "traces" of the subaltern in the powerful living grandmother of *Shadow Lines.*

But let us also note, at the same time, that while these endeavors are directed toward exploring the necessary connections between death and subalternity, it is in *the failure of her postmortem message* that the grandmother's impotence is finally and most fully revealed. The limits of speech, and the fact of her female gender as its most likely cause, emerge as the relevant point that her death discloses. In other words, death functions as *disclosure* rather than as attribute in and for subalternity, and it still remains the necessary condition for such disclosure of subaltern identity. The key point is this: "Indeed, it is only in their death that they [gendered subalterns] enter a narrative *for us,* they become figurable" (*CPR* 245/21–22).

CHANDRA'S DEATH

No Alternative But a Conclusion

Ranajit Guha's "Chandra's Death," a classic of subaltern studies scholarship, appeared in volume 5 of the *Subaltern Studies* in 1987. It is, as has been widely noted, the first essay that centrally tackled the female subaltern and the role of gender in the constitution of subalternity by someone in the Subaltern Studies collective other than Spivak herself. Guha rescues an obscure document, a set of legal records relating to the death of Chandra, a young Bengali low-caste woman who died some time in the middle of the nineteenth century as a result of a botched abortion. Chandra was a young widow who had become pregnant by her brother-in-law. He promptly ordered her to have an abortion, failing which he would put her in *bhek* (i.e., have her excommunicated). It is as a result of this ultimatum that her family and kin attempt the ill-fated abortion, only to find themselves indicted of the crime of murder by the colonial penal system. These fragments of legal testimony (*ekrars* or evidence) offered by the accused in the case, her sister, her mother, and the man who provided the drug to induce the abortion, have been preserved in a collection of such documents for their "sociological interest." Going against the grain of their provenance as legal and scholarly material, Guha explicitly proposes to "reclaim the document for history" (135).

This is the avowed project of subaltern history (Guha prefers to name it "critical historiography" in this essay). That project is described as a commitment to examine the "small drama and fine detail of social existence, especially at its lower depths," ignoring traditional historiography's "big events and institutions." How is this to be achieved? Guha answers: "by bending closer to the ground in order to pick up the traces of a subaltern life in its passage through time" (138). The impediment to this reconstruction is of course the inherent problem of subaltern history: the paucity of evidence, the "fragmentation" of the archive, the story that has come to us simply as "the residuum of a dismembered past" (138–139).

Guha is candid about the "urge for plenitude" that drives historical research, now frustrated by insufficient material, the absence of documentation, and the law's structuring of such material as exists into a "case." His historian's task in this essay is not so much to restore voice to the subaltern—Chandra's is irretrievably lost, those of her sister and mother are available only as legal testimony—but to provide the contextualization, the thick detail, of the event. If the law that provides the dry bones of the "facts" is the "emissary of the state," then the historian will be the recorder of the complex practices and beliefs of the community (society/*samaj*). This is the disciplinary challenge, the programmatic agenda of a revisionist historiography, which is also coded as an ethical commitment, as I began by saying; in Guha's case it is an attempt to elevate the narrative to tragedy. Significantly, Guha's analysis is declared to be explicitly feminist, aimed at exposing the operations of patriarchy and the contrasting role of female solidarity and resistance to be found in Chandra's death.

It will be immediately apparent where such a project differs from Spivak's in "Can the Subaltern Speak?" and where the two works are united in the project of identifying death and the subaltern.[38] I shall note some of these in summary form:

- Spivak provides no contextualization of the kind that Guha so fulsomely does in "Chandra's Death." I have on occasion alluded to Bhubaneswari's story as an "anecdote"—it is a notably sketchy account. So where Guha offers an elaborate context as a compensation for the slim pickings from records of the historical event, Spivak withholds such a compensatory account.
- Chandra "is" subaltern, without any further need to establish her subalternity—a member of the Bagdi caste, among the poorest and lowest of castes, and vulnerable as a widowed female. On the other hand, it is through Bhubaneswari's nonidentity as subaltern that Spivak seeks to explore the condition of gendered subalternity.
- Both women die: with the difference that Chandra is unequivocally a victim (as Spivak has herself noted), whereas Bhubaneswari's suicide has more contradictory implications for subaltern subject-constitution.

- Chandra is the widow who transgresses; Bhubaneswari is single and chaste. Yet both are prey to the same rigid patriarchal sexual norms of their society, if at different periods and at different class levels. For Guha the representatives of patriarchy are male, both individually (the lover who abandons and threatens Chandra and is himself free of any of the consequences of adultery) as well as collectively (the *samaj* that would ostracize the fallen woman). Patriarchy for Spivak, as we saw, is contained in the larger narrative of psychobiography.

- The cause of Chandra's dilemma is transparent: abortion or *bhek*, death or dishonor, imposed on her from the outside. Bhubaneswari, in contrast, internalizes these options.

- The female sexuate body bears the burden of genderedness, and both Guha and Spivak stress its potential for destabilizing norms. The difference is that Guha's writing on pregnancy as "the domain of the female body" (*CD* 162) is heavily invested in the mystique of female otherness. In his reading, following Simone de Beauvoir in *The Second Sex*, pregnancy excludes men since it is then that a woman "asserts control over her own body," when she knows that "'her body is at last her own, since it exists for the child who belongs to her'" (*CD* 163). Spivak's reading of Bhubaneswari's bodily condition is offered, by contrast, in terms of a demystified, straightforward decoding: menstruation is the sign, the simple "proof," of female nonpregnancy.

- Guha's moral in the story is female *solidarity*, transcending "kin and kutumb"; Spivak concludes by positing female *betrayal*.

- Both essays are written in an affective register marked by pathos and authorial partisanship. The male-gendered author's partisanship with suffering womanhood tends toward chivalry, I would suggest (sometimes even heightened by eroticism, as in the well-known literary example of Thomas Hardy and his female protagonist in *Tess of the d'Urbervilles*); the female-gendered author/critic turns empathy more successfully into a political act of solidarity, as in Spivak's case.

- Chandra is caught between law and society (*samaj*); Bhubaneswari/the sati between imperialism and patriarchy. These institutions are closely interlinked, of course; colonial law is the product of imperialism, and *samaj* is patriarchal. Nevertheless the terms carry a difference of emphasis that is not negligible.

Can *Guha's* subaltern speak? Chandra's silence in the records cannot be missed, especially when compared to the powerful words pronounced by Magaram. His is the "voice of an unseen but pervasive authority," even when it is only reported in the testimony of Chandra's mother (154). Chandra's silence is naturalized: what could she have to say? Her sister Brinda's speech (via her testimony), by contrast—"I administered the medicine in the belief that it would terminate her pregnancy and did not realize that it would kill her"—is subjected to repeated scrutiny by Guha. Guha steps in to read the statement thus: "she identifies herself no longer as a defendant speaking of a crime but as a person speaking of her sister and as a woman speaking of another woman . . . an utterance which defies the ruse of the law and confers on this text the dignity of a tragic discourse" (161). The authorial voice, exceeding the historian's caution, exercises the prerogative to read in this bleak defense the ringing tones of heroism and tragedy.

In the end, Guha's effort to recuperate the subaltern woman's story by representing it for us only underscores the force and truth of Spivak's analysis. There remain in his story silences that beg our question and call forth her early lament. For what we never learn (because either the record or Guha withholds it from us) is the outcome of the trial. We do not know whether Brinda and her mother are sentenced to die for their "crime." The vanishing of their death is, of course, also their death. The subaltern cannot speak.

NOTES

I am profoundly indebted to the criticism, correction, suggestions and arguments of friends who have read this paper through several drafts: I thank Dan Moshenberg, You-me Park, Venkat Rao, Anupama Rao, and Kaushik Sunder Rajan fervently for their generosity and guidance. I am grateful also to audiences at various forums where I have presented versions of this paper, starting with Columbia University, and then Oxford, Iowa, and Urbana-Champaign. I wrote this paper in the first instance at the request of Rosalind Morris and Gayatri Spivak, who honored me by asking me to participate in the 2002 conference where this volume had its beginnings. Gayatri Spivak's "Can the Subaltern Speak?" has of course spawned this as well as a thousand other responses to it. I am beholden to her scholarship, her theoretical insights, and her political integrity for the constant inspiration they have provided.

1   Subjectivity in our times—we cannot escape the observation—is coming to be defined by death rather than by the ways of living. The connection between death and the subject arises in part at least from the perception of a contemporary mode of sovereignty described as a necropolitics. Achilles Mbembe, who coined the term, traces a longstanding preoccupation with exploring the continuities between death and subjecthood in Western philosophical thought, from Hegel, via Heidegger, to the late Foucault of biopolitics, and from him to the contemporary Italian philosopher Giorgio Agamben. In the twentieth century the most intense application of such ideas was found in the colony and the plantation, Mbembe has suggested, followed by the two world wars and the Holocaust, and

in the present in the phenomena of wars on terror and the forcible occupation of territories. Mbembe, "Necropolitics."

2   The project of (especially the early) subaltern studies was one of "bringing subalternity to crisis" by using examples of subaltern insurgency. These subjects of a revisonary subaltern history "burst their bonds [of subalternity] into resistance." The project of subaltern historiography sought thereby to "hegemonise the subaltern." See Spivak, "Scattered Speculations," especially pp. 476, 477.

3   The essay first appeared in the journal *Wedge* ("Can the Subaltern Speak? Speculations on Widow Sacrifice" and in expanded form in Nelson and Grossberg, *Marxism and the Interpretation of Culture*, henceforward CSS; and is included in the chapter on history in *Critique of Postcolonial Reason*, henceforward *CPR*.

4   Guha, "Chandra's Death," henceforth *CD*.

5   In "Subaltern Studies: Deconstructing Historiography," Spivak analyses these collisions of methodological assumptions in the subaltern historiographical project as a whole.

6   Some of Spivak's other examples of subalterns who are similarly "not subaltern" are a queen (the Rani of Sirmur, who was "not a subaltern at all," *CPR*, 208), and Jashoda, the wet-nurse, a character in Mahasweta Devi's story "Stanadayini" (translated by Spivak as "The Breast-Giver"), who is a Brahman, i.e., upper-caste woman. Mahasweta Devi, "The Breast-Giver," in Spivak, *In Other Worlds*, pp. 222–240.

7   "This woman was middle class." See the interview "Subaltern Talk," especially p. 289.

8   *CPR* 307/63.

9   The Friday essay, "Theory in the Margin," appeared originally in Arac and Johnson, *Consequences of Theory*, and in *A Critique of Postcolonial Reason* it appears in the chapter on "Literature." In Coetzee's novel, *Foe*, the play of power between Susan Barton and Friday is quite explicitly raced and gendered. Susan seeks to elicit Friday's secret by teaching him many varied means of communication (speech, writing, drawing, mime), but to no avail. Coetzee himself, like Foe in the novel, exercises a scrupulous authorial reticence about not "telling" Friday's secret. There is no access to his interiority.

10 "Scattered Speculations," p. 477.

11 I am grateful to Venkat Rao for this elaboration; personal communication.

12 Sunder Rajan, *The Scandal of the State*.

13 Spivak, *A Critique of Postcolonial Reason*, p. 430.

14 Derrida, *Specters of Marx*, p. 34.

15 On "singularity," Spivak's "Scattered Speculations" is illuminating. Bhubaneswari's story (as oral history) resembles the literary text by representing itself as singular, "not as an example of a universal but as an instance of a collection of repetitions": "Singularity is life as pure immanence, what will be, of this life, as life" (475).

16 This trope is a deliberate echo of Benjamin's argument about translation: "Just as a tangent touches a circle lightly at but one point—establishing, with this touch rather than with the point, the law according to which it is to continue on its straight path to infinity—a translation touches the original lightly and only at the infinitely small point of the sense." See Benjamin, "The Task of the Translator," p. 261.

17 The phrase "radical heterology" is to be found in a different context in Derrida, *Gift of Death*, p. 83.

18 See Spivak, "Scattered Speculations," p. 481. The middle-class woman at this particular historical conjuncture (the Swadeshi movement), was "metaleptically substituting effect for cause and producing an idea of national liberation by her suicide," through her involvement in "so-called terrorist movements," Spivak writes, citing the historian Partha Chatterjee's observations on Bhubaneswari (ibid.).

19 Spivak, "Discussion," p. 328.

20 Spivak, "Terror," p. 96; henceforth "T."

21 The genderedness of these figures lies in the specific attributes *and* deployment of their sexed bodies, not in a generalized condition of being female. Spivak is emphatic that, unlike the Bhubaneswari Devi, who "used her gendered body to inscribe an unheard message," the bomber who died with Rajiv Gandhi, "also a woman, did not" ("T" 97). The female suicide bomber does not make a "gendered point," being only a victim of indoctrination (96).

22 In Spivak, "Translator's Preface," p. xxvii.

23 Orhan Pamuk's novel *Snow* bears this out with a situation of uncanny similarity. Pamuk shows that illicit love is the community's preferred explanation for the spate of suicides by young Muslim women in the Turkish town of Kars—this despite its being known that they were largely provoked by the young women's frustration over being forbidden by state regulation from wearing the veil to school. The novel's protagonist, Ka, a journalist, meets with a general reluctance among the townspeople to talk to him about the suicides. Only the parents of one young woman are forthcoming. By exposing the teacher who started the "malicious lie" that she had been pregnant, they hope to dispel the "baseless rumour about their child's chastity." Her autopsy, they tell Ka, revealed that she had been a virgin (16).

24 Notably Sarkar's *Hindu Wife, Hindu Nation*.

25 Spivak, *In Other Worlds*, p. 263.

26 Ibid.

27 *Anguish* is the word she uses in "Subaltern Talk," p. 292. The partisanship is expressed more openly in a recent autobiographical piece, "If only."

28 When struggling to write about female infanticide in contemporary India, I encountered something more than a methodological impasse. I found that, even in the reformist discourse of feminism, "empathy and pity for the human 'matter' of death" seemed to find no expression. In large part this was attributable to a

contamination of the language of sympathy. Tracking the instrumental rationality of female infanticide in the discourses of state and society, I was unnerved by its terrible logic. I was pushed into prescribing the creation of "a climate of ethical sensibility about human life and death by means of literary affect" in order to counter the logic of "explanations" such as the social devaluation of women and its causes (*The Scandal of the State*, 208). The problem of prescription remains intractable.

29 Spivak, "Scattered Speculations" engages the question of the historian's partisanship as a "performativity." In contrast to the merely "constative" function of some subaltern historiography, Spivak seeks out the more interventionist role of the Gramscian intellectual in politics. The example of Bhubaneswari had early filled her with the intention of "saving the singular oppositional" (479).

30 Busia, "Silencing Sycorax."

31 Donna Landry returns to this question in her interview with Spivak, "Subaltern Talk," in *The Spivak Reader*: doesn't the fact of Spivak's reading of Bhubaneswari's suicide indicate that "the subaltern *can* be read and represented by the attentive, complicitous critic"? And further: "Would this turn then be the final flourish of the essay's critique of Foucault and Deleuze for disingenuously claiming that because the oppressed can represent themselves, they, as intellectuals, need not represent oppressed (subaltern) groups but simply let them 'speak for themselves'?" On this occasion, Spivak is content to agree that "it does have that kind of implication," although still wishing to emphasize Bhubaneswari's effort instead: "Bhubaneswari had tried *damned* hard to represent herself" (306).

32 Ghosh's *Shadow Lines* was first published in 1988, but references here are to the student edition (1995); henceforth *SL*.

33 There are other similarities we may note: significantly both women had grand-nieces whose lives in diaspora could be read as a betrayal of their female ancestors' patriotism. The person for whom the grandmother in *Shadow Lines* develops a virulent hatred is the cosmopolitan Ila, who longs for "freedom," but for freedom of a personal kind that to the grandmother appears selfishly immoral. Compare the great-grandniece of Bhubaneswari who makes her appearance in *A Critique of Postcolonial Reason* as a "new U.S. immigrant" and an employee of a U.S. multinational. "Bhubaneswari had fought for national liberation. Her great-grandniece works for the New Empire" (CPR 311/65).

34 See Spivak, "If Only." In this piece she repeats the disagreement with this suggestion that she had first expressed at the conference at Columbia University where this essay was originally presented as a paper.

35 Foucault is alert to the dangers of this predicament: "How does one keep from being a fascist, even (especially) when one believes oneself to be a revolutionary militant?" (He is referring to Deleuze and Guattari's concern, post-1968, with opposing every manifestation of fascism). See Foucault, "Preface," in Deleuze and Guattari, *Anti-Oedipus*, pp. xi–xvi, especially xv.

36 See, for instance, Tagore's last novel, *Char Adhyay*, and note 18, this chapter.

37 Spivak, "Subaltern Talk," p. 306.

38 Spivak makes a succinct comparison between the two works herself in "Scat-
    tered Speculations": In "Chandra's Death" as in Bhubaneswari's story, she notes,
    "the dead woman remained singular. There too the theme is reproduction." But
    in Guha's essay "the woman is a victim, without even the minimal activity of sui-
    cide" (478).

Abdul JanMohamed

BETWEEN SPEAKING
AND DYING

SOME IMPERATIVES IN THE
EMERGENCE OF THE SUBALTERN IN
THE CONTEXT OF U.S. SLAVERY

Gayatri Spivak's groundbreaking and widely influential essay, "Can the Subaltern Speak?" has powerfully enabled postcolonial and minority discourses by clearing a theoretical minefield that lay buried beneath certain Eurocentric discourses as well as beneath the phallocentric appropriation of certain traditional Vedic formulations. The hidden assumptions of these discourses, had they remained buried, would have repeatedly detonated and hence derailed many critical projects designed to excavate subaltern consciousnesses. This essay, however, will not contribute to the further clearing of specific minefields, important and necessary though it may be; instead, I will take up the spirit of her essay, or at least one of its spirits: namely, "the work of the negative."[1] Though Spivak invokes Hegel only once, briefly and in passing, it is clear that her critiques of Foucault, Deleuze, and the British and Indian masculinist discourses around sati are powerful instances of the work of the negative. Even the more "positive" valorization of certain Derridean reading strategies comprises a part of this spirit to the extent that deconstruction is also inherently a work of the negative.

I would like to extend this work of the negative by examining Frederick Douglass's 1845 autobiography in light of two questions raised by Spivak's article. The first, of course, is the one that subtends the entire article: what are the varied and complex conditions of possibility that attend the production of the subaltern's speech? Yet it seems to me that this fundamental question implicitly begs another question that is equally important from historical as well as epistemological viewpoints: what are the conditions of possibility that attend the "audibility" of that speech? If, or rather when, the subaltern speaks, what needs to be the nature of our receptivity, defined ideologically and epistemologically, such that we can hear and understand some of the fundamental concerns being articulated. It seems to me heuristically important to distinguish between the conditions that attend production of the subaltern's speech, on the one hand, from those that attend its reception, on the other hand, because the former are historically unalterable whereas the latter, to the extent that they are our current critical, epistemological, and, above all, political circumstances, are amenable to change upon subjection to adequate scrutiny. I would like to focus on this question since it seems to me that, while we have valorized, amply (and rightly in some ways), the "rebellions" and "resistances" of slaves in the Western hemisphere, we have done so in a rather positivistic manner, that is, without adequate appreciation for the profound acts of repeated negation or the sustained negativity that are, it seems to me, the preconditions for these positive acts of rebellion and resistance. The second question from Spivak's essay that I would like to address is raised at the end of her essay: what are the conditions that attend the possibility of suicide as an act of potential resistance. The slave's "willingness" to face his death in the act of rebellion is quasi-suicidal; it marks a moment of profound "negativity" regarding the conditions of possibility that define the slave's "life," a life that I have explored elsewhere as being that of a "death-bound-subject."[2]

I should hasten to add that I am not interested in examining the conditions of possibility, those attending either the slave's speech/audibility or her struggle with life/death, on the purely ontological or the purely epistemological register. Rather I am concerned with them on the political register, a register in which all ontological, epistemological, ethical, aesthetic, and other considerations, however germane, are nonetheless subordinated to the question of how these registers are rearticulated by a political economy determined, in the final instance, by relations of social and psychic domination. To put it more directly, the political register is one in which the capacity to speak and to die is always already deeply coded by a complex dialectical relation between the use, exchange, and surplus values that attend the acts of speaking and listening, living and dying.[3]

In "Can the Subaltern Speak?" Spivak articulates in a fascinating way what she calls the first category of "sanctioned suicide" in Vedic texts (in the *Dharmaśāstra* and *Rg-Veda*). "The first category of suicide arises out of tattvajnāna, or the knowledge of truth. Here the knowing subject comprehends the insubstantiality or the mere phenomenality (which may be the same thing as nonphenomenality) of its identity." Because that identity is considered to be nonphenomenal, the enlightened self's "demolition of that identity is not considered *ātmaghāta* (a killing of the self). The paradox of knowing of the limits of knowledge is that the strongest assertion of agency, to negate the possibility of agency, cannot be an example of itself."[4]

I would like to concentrate, for the moment, on two aspects of this formulation. First, I think it important to emphasize that the designation of "life" or "identity" as "nonphenomenal," within the Vedic regime of truth, is a fundamentally necessary step in the process of decathecting life/identity so that its final and total negation in the act of suicide seems less of a contradiction and a paradox. That is, the epistemological paradox is in effect an existential ruse, or, to put it differently, it is already an epistemological suicide that precedes, and hence makes possible, the subsequent existential suicide: the designation of life/identity as "insubstantial" or "nonphenomenal" is a fundamental form of decathexis, which then permits the subsequent and total form of decathexis of the suicide "itself." The second act of decathexis would be impossible without the first; hence, the first is as much a suicide as is the second. Closer examination of life's "suicidal" attempt to decathect from itself may well reveal that such attempts always involve a complex chain of preceding "suicides," usually articulated on nonexistential but contiguous registers. In what follows, I will argue that all the various forms of decathexes involved in this moment are all forms of "suicide/death" and that it is the empowering negativity involved in these forms that we need to appreciate better in the acts of slave rebellion. Second, I will argue, in partial agreement with Spivak's essay but against the Heideggerian position,[5] that the possibility of suicide, as the negation of the possibility of agency, grounds, under certain specific circumstances, not only the strongest assertion of agency but can also define the capacity to know the limits of knowledge, a capacity that, from the moment of almost total negation, retroactively casts its shadow backward and permits the subaltern or the slave subject to rearticulate or reconceptualize the moment of its own "origin" and hence assert greater control over her processes of identification and sociopolitical investments.

Now, in the context of slavery, there is no question of searching for some external, moral-cum-legal/epistemological authority that would sanction suicide or articulate quasi-suicidal preconditions that permit the necessary decathexis from life/identity. However, the apparent paradoxes are quite similar in both cases. In both instances, there is a powerful stress on the work of negation in the formulation and effective control of agency. The implication is that the supreme moment of the affirmation of subjective agency consists in coming as close as possible to negating totally such agency, that final control of agency is born out of the willingness to embrace the death of this agency, and that the differential relation between the embrace of death and the rebirth of a transformed subject is always a dialectic relationship located on an asymptotic curve—the cycle of reincarnation can be an infinite process. In both contexts, the Vedic and the slave society, the recuperation of agency is predicated on a prior and almost total decathexis, a total negation of life and identity.

I

Frederick Douglass's *Narrative of the Life of Frederick Douglass: An American Slave* provides a cogent and complex articulation of this paradox via his prolonged and tenacious cathexis to negation, via, that is, a cathexis to death-as-total-decathexis.[6] In exploring that paradox here, I am following in the footsteps of Paul Gilroy's cogent and very illuminating examination of Douglass's anti-Hegelian appropriation and articulation of the instrumental function of death in the processes of enslavement. As Gilroy argues, Douglass's appropriation of the possibility of his death becomes the ground for a rearticulation of his masculinity and his agency as a subject. Gilroy simultaneously sees the appropriation as a negative and positive act, and in what follows I would like to articulate more precisely the complex relations between negativity and positivity in the refunctioning of agency.[7]

Quite early in his life, when he witnesses an other, Demby, being shot for refusing to come out of a stream so that he can be whipped by the overseer, Douglass is introduced to the status of the slave as "bare life," as life that can be killed without that murder being definable as either homicide or sacrilege. Yet this object lesson—that he and all slaves "live" confined, implicitly or explicitly, within the structure of "social death," a confinement made possible by the threat of "actual death," by the mercurial possibility that the commuted death sentence under which slaves "live" can be revoked at the master's whim—horrifying and terrorizing as it is, remains relatively abstract. Not until his rebelliousness results in his master renting him out to the slave breaker Edward Covey does Douglass begin to experience his own potential death as the fundamental negativity that constantly and totally defines his life. For the first six months on Covey's farm, Douglass "instinctively" refuses to recognize fully the immanence of his death, turning to other possibilities, even though he is repeatedly faced with the threat of death. Only when he finally refuses to turn away from his own impending death is he able to appropriate the negativity of his potential death and transform it into the basis of his freedom: only by embracing the negativity of his death is he able to recuperate his agency for his own welfare rather than for that of his master. Though the fight between Covey and Douglass and the scenes leading up to it have been examined countless times by critics, I believe that a detailed scrutiny can still yield further insights regarding the role of negativity in configuring individual agency and personal freedom.

Douglass's induction into the dialectic of death begins with the weekly whippings (provoked by his passive resistance, what he calls his "non-compliance"), which first introduces him to his condition as "bare life," a "man transformed into a brute," sunk in a melancholy stupor (58). To the extent that his bare life is defined by his "killability," he contemplates embracing his condition: "I was sometimes prompted to take my life, and that of Covey." But the possibility of such an embrace being productive is premature since he is still prevented from binding to his own death by "a combination of hope and fear," which continues his cathexis to his (bare) life (59). This attachment to bare life is slowly eroded by relentless exposures to the proximate possibility of actual-death: first, by the possibility that after Covey has split his head he may bleed to death; then, by his fear that if he returns to Covey's farm the latter will kill him; finally, by his realization that his fundamental choice consists of selecting between different modes of death ("I had spent that day mostly in the woods, having the alternative before me,—to go home and be whipped to death, or stay in the woods and be starved to death" [61–63]). The ubiquitous presence of death gradually loosens his bond to his meager life and permits him to contemplate binding with his potential death. This paradoxical turn, whereby the energies of eros, characterized according to Freud by their tendency to bind objects, are turned around entirely so that they now "bind" to thanatos, which is the process of "unbinding," is quite subtle, almost unnoticeable, in Douglass's narrative.

As he contemplates running away, he has to acknowledge that there is an equally strong possibility of being killed in the process as there is in being killed if he "succumbs." The latter consists of either his social- or actual-death: "I had as well die with ague as the fever. I have only one life to lose. I had as well be killed running as die standing" (59). "Running" here must be understood as a metonymy for all forms of avoidance and denial through which one "normally" reacts to the possibility of actual-death; by contrast, "standing" must be understood not only as a banishment of "fear," which had earlier bound him to life, but also as signifying a kind of "acceptance" of that possibility. This interpretation is bolstered by Douglass's use of the passive and active forms of the verb to designate the process of death. The possibility of "*being* killed" while running implies an avoidance and a passivity in the face of one's fate; the agent of the act of death here is the master and not the slave. By contrast, "dying" while standing and facing death implies an active appropriation, almost an embrace of one's own death: it is the slave who is here in charge of the decision to die.[8] By thus unconditionally embracing the foundational negativity that is responsible for his condition as a slave (i.e., threat of death), Douglass comes to the point where he actively appropriates the possibility of his own death and eventually realizes that his actual-death, though deeply coded as a fundamental form of negativity, can have use-value only for him, that it is a form of value the master can never appropriate. As I have argued elsewhere, the master profits enormously by wielding the *threat* of death, bolstered by occasional (if unacceptably frequent) executions, because that threat procures the slave's labor, which in turn produces, as Douglass amply testifies, enormous exchange- and surplus-value for the master. However, the actual-death of a slave holds no use- or exchange-value for the master, except in its capacity as an example for other slaves.[9]

The threat of death and the structures it puts into place, like the slave's conditionally commuted death sentence, are designed precisely to curtail drastically the agency of the slave (which would normally be bound to his own needs) and to redirect it to the needs and desires of the master. Thus the struggle to the death between master and slave is precisely a struggle over the control of the latter's agency. And the slave's fear of death or his desire to avoid it "at all costs" produces his condition as a slave. Thus a return to the scene of the death struggle permits the slave to attempt to recover his agency. This is, as is so well known, precisely what happens in the two-hour-long fight between Covey and Douglass, which the latter "wins." The resultant transformation of Douglass, his well-known "resurrection," has also been thoroughly explored. However, it may be useful to reexamine this scene for what it can reveal with regard to relations between agency and negativity within the context of slavery. First, it must be noted that the resurrection marks a completion of the dialectic of death. That is, by facing the possibility of his "actual-death" (and surviving), Douglass undoes his "social-death." He might, he says, "remain a slave in form, but the day had passed forever when I could be a slave in fact," and he thus attains his "symbolic-death." The rhetoric of resurrection implies that he has died and been reborn, that the subject-position he occupied as slave within the structure of social-death has been killed and he has survived the potential of his actual-death, thus permitting him to be reborn in a new subject-position. This is straightforward enough. However, the second, and more important point that needs to be emphasized is that this resurrection, while a profoundly positive development, is only made possible and maintained in place throughout the rest of Douglass's days in slavery by a profound negativity; the birth of his new life and his quest for freedom are nourished and sustained by a deep binding with the negativity of death, with the principle of unbinding.

Douglass is aware of this paradox, but can't fully account for it prior to or during the prolonged fight with Covey, though the resolutions regarding his potential agency in the future, which he makes after winning the fight, demonstrate that he has clearly grasped the import and necessity of the aporetic relation between life and death. Having lulled Douglass into letting his guard down, Covey attacks Douglass: "Mr. Covey seemed now to think he had me, and could do what he pleased; but at this moment—*from whence came the spirit I don't know*—I resolved to fight" (64; emphasis added). Precisely at the moment of apparent failure of strength and resistence, a substantive surplus of energy wells up from an unidentifiable source. In *The Death-Bound-Subject,* I have argued that the "embrace" of death is, under these kinds of conditions, the necessary precursor to "symbolic-death," i.e., to the annihilation of the old subject-position of the slave and the rebirth of the "same" subject in a more liberated subject-position. However, the concept of embrace remained relatively undertheorized in that text. Douglass's articulation of this moment allows us to theorize it further.

Douglass decides to fight for life *after* effectively having resigned himself to the probability of dying, that is, after having decided that the only significant freedom of choice available to him was to choose his mode of death. To the extent that a substantive cathexis to this choice implicitly entails a decathexis from "life," this choice is itself a form of death that precedes the possibility of a final death in the struggle; to bind oneself to the modes of one's potential death necessarily entails unbinding oneself from "life" or eros, which is itself fundamentally nothing more than a continuous process of binding. It is important to add that the decision to choose between different forms of death cannot be an effective transformational moment if it remains confined to the epistemological realm, but if it crosses over to the existential realm in the form of an "illocutionary utterance," that is to say, as a "symbolic act," then the choosing itself becomes a form of death. As a symbolic act, this choice constitutes an "embracing" of the possibility of death that precedes that possibility itself. There are two theoretical consequences to this formulation. The first consists of the further paradox that the implicit decathexis from "life" frees up erotic energies that then immediately return in the form of liberated, if highly "negative," cathectic energies that can "bind" first to death and then, in somewhat modified form, to "life." And this return is what Douglass marvels at in his remark about the mysterious surge of his "spirit." Second, the opening up of the space between what we might call the illocutionary-death and the existential actual-death permits us to rearticulate the notion of symbolic-death as a dynamic transformational engagement that begins with the illocutionary-death, which liberates and reconfigures cathectic energies, and ends, for the slave who survives the struggle to the death, with the moment of rebirth, thereby permitting the liberated cathectic energies to begin a new process of binding: the two moments together span and constitute the structure of what Douglass and other slaves called resurrection.

Because "normal" attitudes to death are usually grounded in denial and avoidance,[10] there are several features of the aporetic entanglement of eros and thantos, of life and death in this struggle between the master and slave that need further elaboration. First, Douglass's account, which is profoundly anti-Hegelian in so many respects, does indeed confirm Hegel's insistence that the combatant who is not willing to decathect from life will end up losing the struggle. Clearly, as Douglass points out, Covey is loath to call for help from the constabulary authorities who underwrite the institution of slavery because he is afraid that to do so will hurt his reputation as a slave breaker, which in turn will have an impact on his economic wealth. Thus it is his "attachments" to and "investments" in his "life" as a slave owner and slave breaker that force him to retreat from the battle without having won it. Douglass, on the other hand, has nothing to lose except his "bare life," which is predicated on his "social-death." Second and far more important is that success in resisting the threat of death, which, we must remember, is under these circumstances never temporary or inadvertent, depends on a deeply committed and sustained binding to the negativity of the illocutionary commitment. Douglass is fully cognizant of this when he insists, after having won the fight with Covey and been resurrected, that "I did not hesitate to let it be known of me, that the white man who expected to succeed in whipping me, must also succeed in killing me." He goes on, "From this time I was never again what might be called fairly whipped, though I remained a slave four years afterwards. I had several fights, but was never whipped" (65).

This formulation repeats in a minor key the structure of the opposition between the "passivity" of "being killed" and the "active" stance of "dying." Allowing oneself to be whipped implies the abrogation of agency; it implies a "willing" subordination of self, at however "minimal" or "reluctant" a level; by contrast, "fighting" implies a control of agency, a determination to respond to violence in kind, and a willingness to die, if necessary, in the process of fighting.[11] In both instances, that of dying and fighting, Douglass takes an active as opposed to a passive stance, and what then becomes perfectly clear is that the appropriation and assertion of "agency" results from an amalgamation of the active stance with a total commitment to a negative and negating attitude. And the rest of Douglass's narrative abounds with instances that verify his resolve as well as his decision to conjoin the active stance and negativity. In short, Douglass not only risks his life in the fight with Covey but he continues to do so in a *sustained* manner during his life as a slave. It is important to understand, from phenomenological and political viewpoints, that the illocutionary moment must be accompanied by a highly charged decathexis from life and that that charge must be sustained over a long period in order for the slave to attain his or her freedom. What I am suggesting, along with, but on a different register than the one on which Douglass articulates himself, is that the slave's quest for freedom requires a sustained commitment to the work of the negative.

II

Our access to Douglass's story and his meditations on the efficacy of the work of the negative, to the extent that they are constituted as and by processes of knowledge, is predicated, of course, on his capacity to speak or, to be more specific, on his capacity to write. We can only speculate on how many other slaves engaged in this classic version of the struggle to the death, more or less like Douglass, how many of them died in the process, how many succeeded in escaping to freedom, and so on. There were perhaps many who succeeded and many whose insights about various aspects of slavery were perhaps more insightful than those of individuals like Douglass and Harriet Jacobs. However, we have no access to these insights unless these slaves managed to become literate, like Douglass and Jacobs. Without their capacities to speak and, specifically, to write, their insights would be lost to us. Hence what I am suggesting is that Douglass's imperative commitment to the work of the negative, if it is as sustained and total as I am arguing, should manifest itself equally in the mastery of literacy and its political deployment. He is so incredibly clear, emphatic, and eloquent about the "negative" value of and "negative" motivation for mastering literacy that it is perhaps worth citing at some length his well-known remarks once again.

> The very decided manner with which he [his master] spoke, and strove to impress his wife with the evil consequences of giving me instruction, served to convince me that he was deeply sensible of the truths he was uttering. It gave me the best assurance that I might rely with the utmost confidence on the results which, he said, would follow from teaching me to read. What he most dreaded, that I most desired. What he most loved, that I most hated. That which to him was a great evil, to be carefully

shunned, was to me a great good, to be diligently sought; and the argument which he so warmly urged, against my learning to read, only served to inspire me with the desire and determination to learn. *In learning to read, I owe almost as much to the bitter opposition of my master, as to the kindly aid of my mistress. I acknowledge the benefit of both.* (38; emphasis added)

The rhetorical stylization and the repetition in parallel structure of the need to negate the master's intentions, desires, plans, etc., clearly outline the same kind of sustained and tenacious negativity here as in the struggle to the death. It may be impossible to determine to what extent the absolute nature of this need to negate the master is a product of the mature, free Douglass's confidence, which is being retroactively projected on to the immature, as yet illiterate young man, or to what extent it is an accurate index of that young man's clarity of understanding, audacity of ambition (under the circumstances), and intuitive grasp of the political value of literacy. Nevertheless, the tenacity of purpose that the young Douglass subsequently demonstrates in mastering literacy, despite the odds that he faces, incontrovertibly testifies to his sustained commitment to mastering literacy in spite/because of the negativity of the prohibition. Moreover, Douglass also demonstrates here, in acknowledging the "benefit" of both the mistress's encouragement of literacy and the master's prohibition of it, an astute appreciation of the dialectical relations of positive and negative values. And literacy, to the extent that it is crucial to the worlding of a world, involves the epistemological binding and unbinding, creating and killing of the world. Douglass is perfectly well aware of the political value of this epistemological technology, for he ascribes to it entirely "the white man's power to enslave the black man" (37).

Without theorizing it systematically, Douglass intuits (and his actions and commitments clearly demonstrate the power of this intuition) that the relations between the work of the negative in the realm of literacy and knowledge, on the one hand, and in the realm of life and death, on the other, are profoundly symbiotic. Without the acquisition of literacy via adamant negation, Douglass could never have written about the sublation of social- and actual-deaths that allowed him to be resurrected; conversely, without having first destroyed the subject-position of the slave (and subsequently having escaped physically from the realm of slavery), via equally adamant negation, he could never have survived to write about it. The two types of negations are linked more deeply, I think, than has generally been appreciated.

However, before examining the quintessential manifestation of this symbiotic relationship, we need to note that literacy permits him access to books and magazines, which in turn allows him to educate himself about the nature of slavery and freedom, and that knowledge consequently results in a burden of deep negativity produced by his inability to overcome his condition. His greater understanding of his confinement brings him, in his despondency, even closer to the possibility of his death than had the whipping and the cruel treatment by Covey: "I often found myself regretting my own existence, and wishing myself dead; and but for the hope of being free, I have no doubt but that I should have killed myself, or done something for which I should have been killed" (43).

The possibility of quasi suicide here has a function that is almost identical to the illocutionary, epistemological/affective death that precedes the possibility of actual, existential death. However, unlike that illocutionary decathexis, literacy permits Douglass to insert in this circuit a crucial moment of the most profound, almost totally unalloyed, form of erotic binding that exists in his autobiography. The erotic bonding takes place as a result of his risky decision to open what he calls the Sabbath school, where he teaches other slaves how to read and write. He teaches every Sunday, on three additional days a week in the winter, and accommodates up to forty students at one point. "We were linked and interlinked with each other," he says of his relationships with these fellows slave-students: "I loved them with a love stronger than anything I have experienced since." In effect, these individuals apparently become bound together and form a single collective subject: "We never undertook to do any thing, of any importance, without a mutual consultation. We never moved separately. We were one" (72). Yet this most positive of bonds is formed, it is important to note, under the shadow of thanatos, for even the strength of that bond is expressed in terms of death: "I believe we would have died for each other," adds Douglass. It is no accident that the slave's deepest form of commitment articulates itself in terms of his willingness to die for that attachment. Similarly, his decision to urge some of his fellow slaves to escape with him is characterized by Douglass as "my life-giving determination" (73). And, as they proceed with their plans to escape, Douglass makes it perfectly clear that they are fully aware of the high probability that they will all be killed in the attempt; however, they are equally resolved to try and to die together in the process if necessary. Thus the most substantive social and political union in the autobiography, made possible by the bonding that takes place in the Sabbath school, is itself hemmed in or "bound" by the threat of death, by the threat of total unbinding. Nevertheless, Douglass embraces this negative possibility again as he has done earlier and will not let himself be diverted from his purpose by his fear of death. Writing thus comes to perform the same kind of illocutionary function as did his "speaking," that is, his decision to let it be known that he was willing to die instead of letting himself be whipped. In Douglass's auto-biographies the work of life, of binding, is done constantly and deliberately against the work of the negative, of the unbinding power of the threat of death, and the most remarkable feature of his endeavor is that the former always draws a good part of its sustenance from the latter.

III

Douglass's reliance on the sustenance of the death-work becomes so fundamental that he draws on it not only when directly engaged in personal life-death struggles and in sociopolitical organization such as the Sabbath school but also in the *formal* structuration of his narrative: the negativity of the death-work is so powerful that Douglass appropriates and utilizes it to fascinating effect in the rhetorical organization of the knowledge that he wishes to communicate as well as in the affective structuration of that knowledge.

The affective form that Douglass's *Narrative* takes, I would like to suggest, is loosely that of a "blues." The fact that blues should provide the form as well as the substance of his narrative and that both are grounded in the death works is not surprising since, as Adam Gussow has argued, the blues originates partly in response to the phenomena of lynching.[12] Early in his narration Douglass invokes the power of the blues and ascribes to it a central role in his eventual understanding of the horror and the power of slavery. The structures and functions of the "wild songs" that he hears as a child, I would like to suggest, can be seen as the model for his narrative. First, these songs are "a tale of woe . . . [breathing] the prayer and complaints of souls boiling over with the bitterest of anguish"; they move him to tears when he first hears them and when he writes about them (24). At the most basic level, Douglass's *Narrative* is, surely, as powerful a tale of woe as any blues song. Second, like all blues, these songs combine apparently incongruous elements: "revealing at once the highest joy and the deepest sadness; [t]hey would sometimes sing the most pathetic sentiment in the most rapturous tone, and the most rapturous sentiment in the most pathetic tone" (23). At the stylistic level, Douglass's narrative also consists of a very eloquent articulation of the deeply horrifying events and experiences, the most renowned being the whipping of his aunt Hester, the horrifying description of which betrays, according to some critics, Douglass's vicarious pleasure and participation in the whipping. In spite, or perhaps because, of this "incongruity," of this joyful rendition of sorrow or the eloquent articulation of horror and the negativity of total abjection, both the blues and Douglass's story have deeply cathartic effects, relieving pain "only as an aching heart is relieved by its tears" (24).

More important, however, there are two other features of the blues that deeply inform the epistemological function of Douglass's *Narrative*. First, the blues and the narrative preserve and communicate a knowledge of the slave's sociopolitical condition; they store rudimentary knowledge for future reconsideration: "To those songs," says Douglass, "I trace my first glimmering conception of the dehumanizing character of slavery." As he writes about his past experience of these songs, he is now clearly able to articulate the meaning of "those rude and apparently incoherent songs." Most important of all, however, Douglass rightly insists that these songs contain a knowledge of slavery that is superior to other forms of knowledge about the same subject: "I have sometimes thought that the mere hearing of those songs would do more to impress some minds with the horrible character of slavery, than the reading of whole volumes of philosophy on the subject can do" (23–24). As I have been implying throughout this essay, Douglass's narrative, like the blues, encodes a more astute and complex understanding of the deathwork that structures slave society than does the theorization of philosophers such as Hegel and Kojève. And the key to that encoding is, I believe, Douglass's tenacious adherence to the deconstructive, unbinding power of negativity.

The fundamental paradox structuring the death work that fuels slave societies is that the negating, unbinding power of the threat of death is used by the master to bind the slave to the master's material and symbolic needs and desires. If the slave is impossibly bound as an unbound subject, then the impossible negativity of his subject-position can become a powerful tool for asserting his agency and potential freedom if he can learn to harness that negativity. This essay has been mapping the diverse ways in which Douglass does manage to bind to that negativity and channel it in order to resist the master's attempt to break and control him. I would like to close this examination of his endeavors by exploring in some detail one final instance of how Douglass negates the master's negation. Appropriately enough, that instance is to be found at the very beginning of the autobiography, at the point where Douglass is obliged to trace his genealogy and identify his "origin," which is to say, at the point where, as a writer, he has to "produce" himself as the subject of his autobiography. Thus precisely at the point of his symbolic-death, at the crucial reflexive moment in which he has to give (literary) birth to himself, he begins by brilliantly negating the master's attempt to negate him. Douglass's empowering cathexis of negation, born from the struggle to the death, permeates, it seems to me, all the capillary structures of his narrative, and it manifests itself at the beginning of his narrative at the microscopic level of the political economy of his syntax.

The opening sentences of *Narrative* are well enough known, but they bear repeating here:

"I was born in Tuckahoe, near Hillsborough, and about twelve miles from Easton, in Talbot County, Maryland. I have no accurate knowledge of my age, never having seen any authentic record containing it. By far the larger part of the slaves know as little of their ages as horses know of theirs, and it is the wish of most masters within my knowledge to keep their slaves thus ignorant" (15). The first sentence unhesitatingly and precisely fixes his identity in *spatial* terms; indeed, the repetition of geographic coordinates, radiating out concentrically from a single point, signals an anxiety, or at least a strong need, to anchor identity in some permanent fashion. By contrast, the second and third sentences, designed to mark the *temporal* coordinates of his identity, devolve into a complex maneuver that negotiates the politics of knowledge and, by implication, the negating power of literacy. It is, of course, fitting that the temporal register be amenable to such maneuver since it is on this register that what Lacan calls the "retroversion effect" takes place; in other words, it is only at the register on which the subject can reconstruct himself that the value of negating the negation plays the most crucial role. Thus in the very first chance that Douglass gets to meditate on his own (re) construction, he indirectly demonstrates the necessity of the work of the negative in the epistemological realms of self-knowledge, self-representation, and self-articulation. The second and third, apparently innocuous, sentences also construct a series of concentric circles designed to contain and negate knowledge. At the center lies a circle of nonknowledge—Douglass's lack of accurate knowledge of his age (second sentence) and, more generally, the notion that slaves are as ignorant as horses. Whereas the horse's capacities are innate, those of the slave have been artificially and forcefully limited by the master; in other words, the nonknowledge of the slave has been deliberately produced, contained, indeed "bound," by the circle of the master's knowledge, through which he has formulated the hegemonic and violent apparatuses designed to contain and negate the humanity of the slave. However, the third and final circle ("the wish of most masters *within my knowledge*") defines Douglass's knowledge of the political purposes of the master's knowledge; in other words, Douglass's knowledge contains and negates the master's knowledge, which was designed to contain and negate the possibility of Douglass's knowledge. The negative battle over epistemological binding and unbinding that "inaugurates" the *Narrative* also permeates its entire form and content, as I have tried to demonstrate.

The slave's need to negate the master's attempt to negate him turns out to be as crucial for the slave's ability to "speak" or "write" as it is for his ability to overcome the threat and fear of actual-death; in both cases, the work of the negative is fundamental to the possibility of a more liberated reconstitution of subjectivity or of rebirth. And, of course, it is no coincidence that the struggle over epistemological negation should find one of its clearest manifestations precisely at the point where Douglass needs to define his "identity." Douglass's engagement in "negative dialectics" is apposite at this point because, as Theodor Adorno puts it so cogently, "Dialectics is the *consistent* sense of nonidentity," or, we might say, of the infinite presence of contradiction.[13] The slave's "identity" is constituted precisely by the ever present threat of "nonidentity," of total negation via death; the slave is forced to occupy an impossible, aporetic subject-position, a subject-position that relentlessly contradicts her desire to *be* a subject. To the extent that a slave is the epitome of the subject as a contradiction of itself, he is constituted fundamentally by negativity, and when he turns on that negativity and appropriates its power, negative dialectics becomes his royal road to freedom.

The preceding analysis of Douglass's capacity to "bind" with the "unbinding" negativity that defines the political condition of his life as a death-bound subject and to channel that negativity toward his struggle to write and speak can be easily extended, with appropriate modifications, to the battles fought by Harriet Jacobs. While I cannot enter here into an extended discussion of her struggles, it should be pointed out that her decision to sequester herself, for seven years, in her grandmother's garret—a space roughly twice the size of a coffin—constitutes an "embrace" of death that is as tenacious and courageous as that of Douglass, if not more so. This garret, in which she is confined as a "socially dead" subject, in which she almost dies several times, and which she yet slyly calls her "loophole of retreat," is also the space from which she speaks, effectively enough to secure her freedom and eventually to tell her own story by brilliantly appropriating to her own ends the prevailing modes of sentimental, domestic fiction. I am invoking her example ever so briefly here in order to emphasize that my analysis of Douglass should not be seen as the articulation of an exclusively "masculinist" struggle. While gender positions may well substantively modify the kind of productive adherence to negativity that I have articulated,[14] I do not believe that they significantly determine either the *structure* of negativity that is produced by the slave's conditionally commuted death sentence or the inherent power that is available to the slave who dares to appropriate the negativity of her own constitution as a death-bound subject. While neither gender differences nor those that might distinguish the subject-position of the slave from that of the subaltern can be taken up here, I would like to close by agreeing with Gayatri Spivak that we must "acknowledge our complicity in the muting" of both subalterns and slaves.[15] And because a vast proportion of our tendency to mute the struggles of slaves and subalterns is determined by our unconscious needs and investments, and precisely because our unconscious "investment" in life blinds us to the determining and liberating power of death, I have argued that we need to draw on our "negative capability," or what I have defined in *The Death-Bound-Subject* as the capacity for "intransitive identification," to appreciate the value and power of negative dialectics (implicitly called forth by the threat of death) for various modes of resistance—for the willingness to fight to the death or for the (political) capacity to speak.

NOTES

1   Spivak, "Can the Subaltern Speak?" p. 277/244.

2   For a definition and discussion of the following concepts and terms—"death-bound-subject," "dialectics of death," "social-death," "actual-death," "symbolic-death," "death-works," and "bare life"—please see my recent book, JanMohamed, *The Death-Bound-Subject*.

3   These are also the twin imperatives that motivate Richard Wright's protagonist in *Native Son*, Bigger Thomas. When facing his death at the end of the novel, he feels "he had to die and he had to talk [about his death]." See Wright, *Early Works*, p. 845.

4   Spivak, "Can the Subaltern Speak?" p. 299/272.

5   Heidegger tenaciously adheres to Dasein's apprehension of the "possibility" of his death and strenuously argues against any form of "actualizing" that possibility, hence precluding suicide as the actualizing of the possibility of one's death. See Heidegger, *Being and Time*. For a further discussion of this opposition, see final chapter of JanMohamed, *The Death-Bound-Subject*.

6   Douglass, *Autobiographies*.

7   On the one hand, Gilroy claims that Douglass's and Margaret Garner's *"positive* preference for death rather than continued servitude can be read as a contribution towards slave discourse on the nature of freedom itself"; on the other hand, he also argues that the "repeated choice of death rather than bondage articulates *a principle of negativity* that is opposed to the formal logic and rational calculation characteristic of modern western thinking and expressed in the Hegelian slave's preference for bondage rather than death." See Gilroy, *The Black Atlantic*, p. 68 (emphasis added). I think both statements are true, and in what follows I want to tease out the specificity of a positive preference for a principle of negativity.

8   One of Wright's characters, about to be killed, articulates his agential control over his death in the following formulation: *"He* would die before he would let *them* kill him" ("Down by the River Side," p. 326; emphasis added).

9   The only exception to this formulation is, of course, that the master will derive some "exchange-value" from the execution/lynching of a slave to the extent that it is designed to ensure the compliance of other slaves. To be sure, such coercion will in turn lead to the production of further exchange-value via the labor of other slaves. However, the master will not be able to extract any further exchange-value from the labor of the slave who is killed or who kills himself.

10 This denial is what Heidegger calls the "inauthentic" attitude to death. Yet it seems to me that the jargon of authenticity masks rather than illuminates the underlying structure of the attitudes and attachments in question.

11 While it is unclear whether or not Steve Biko was influenced by Douglass, it is remarkable that he enunciates, in his interview before his murder by the apartheid regime, an identical stance in almost identical language. See his essay "On Death."

12 Gussow, *Seems Like Murder Here.*

13 Adorno, *Negative Dialectics*, p. 5 (emphasis added).

14 And indeed it does in the instances just mentioned. Jacobs is quite clear that her (aka Linda Brent's) life is so miserable that she would prefer to die were it not for her concern about the fate of her children after her death.

15 Spivak, *A Critique of Postcolonial Reason*, p. 309.

Michèle Barrett

SUBALTERNS
AT WAR

FIRST WORLD WAR COLONIAL
FORCES AND THE POLITICS OF THE
IMPERIAL WAR GRAVES COMMISSION

The First World War is currently being interpreted in a postcolonial context. The traditional focus on the trench warfare of the Western Front, with perhaps a nod toward the war at sea and the casualties on the Eastern Front, is giving way to a less Eurocentric perspective.[1] The role played by colonial soldiers, in the British case particularly the Indian Army, is attracting renewed attention.[2] A glance at one of the popular atlases of the war is enough to indicate just how much the war (which was being fought by the imperial powers for imperial motives) involved military action in the colonies themselves, as well as in Europe. In the autumn of 1914 alone, there were battles in Togoland, Cameroon, German East Africa and German Samoa; there were landings in the Solomon, Marshall and Falkland Islands, as well as the beginning of the campaign in Mesopotamia.[3] The Imperial War Museum in London was originally to be a "National" museum, but by the time it opened in 1920 the name Imperial was used explicitly to acknowledge the contribution of colonial troops to the war effort. It has long been recognized that the wartime experiences of troops from the British "Dominions," such as the Australian and New Zealand forces at Gallipoli, or the Canadians at Vimy Ridge in France, were important catalysts of solidarity and national identity. These military experiences were connected to the development of political autonomy and national independence after the war, and the memorials at these First World War sites reflect their importance in terms of national affect. The political history of commemorations of this complex colonial war is necessarily a complicated one. In Ireland, for instance, the men who fought in the British Army were often regarded as traitors to the cause of Irish independence, the Easter Rising of 1916 taking place shortly before the battle of the Somme. Consequently, the history of the official memorial in Dublin is a vexed one.[4] To mark the eightieth anniversary of the Armistice in 1998, the then president of Ireland inaugurated a particularly carefully planned memorial: the "Island of Ireland" park near Messines in Belgium, a place where troops from both sides of the present border had fought side by side in the war of 1914–18.

Commemoration of the part played by British colonial forces in the war has been the responsibility of the Imperial (and since 1960 the Commonwealth) War Graves Commission. The commission's public profile relies on a constant reiteration of the then controversial fundamental principles that were established by its founder, Sir Fabian Ware, in 1920. "The Commission's Principles," as they appear on the "Who We Are" page of their current Web site (www.cwgc.org.uk) are listed as follows:

> Each of the dead should be commemorated by name on the grave or memorial.
> Headstones and memorials should be permanent.
> Headstones should be uniform.
> There should be no distinction made on account of military or civil rank, race or creed.

The IWGC's early decisions about commemoration were contentious. They saw themselves as pioneers in creating a new respect for the common soldier—after all, merely a century before, after the battle at Waterloo, men and animals of both sides had been interred in common pits. The IWGC wanted to break down the distinction between officers and men and let them all be buried where they had fallen. Their decision not to allow the repatriation of bodies to the UK, not to differentiate soldiers by military rank or social class, and not to allow cruciform headstones on graves, all generated significant political debate and highly emotional discussion. Families who could afford it wanted to bring their bodies back for burial at home, and many were appalled that the Christian cross was not to be erected (as the French were doing) on the graves. It can now be seen that the commission's founding egalitarian resolve has resulted in cemeteries, on the Western Front and elsewhere, that are widely regarded by their many visitors as appropriate, eloquent, and dignified. They have permanence, they have consistency and they have equal treatment in terms of rank and class.

The commission also claims, however, that there should be no distinctions made according to "race and creed," a principle that is repeated everywhere in its materials. It is this element of the commission's principles that I investigate in this paper.[5] I begin with a discussion of the memorial that was erected in France in the late 1920s, marking the deaths on the Western Front of soldiers and laborers from the Indian Corps—the Neuve Chapelle memorial. The corps, dating from before the partition of India in 1947, formed part of the "Armies of Undivided India." Here we see a first, and rather dramatic, erasure of history: in the 1960s the Pakistan government, wanting to retrospectively redesignate Neuve Chapelle as an "Indo-Pakistan" memorial, persuaded the War Graves Commission simply to try to erase the word *Indian* from the memorial registers. Like all such erasures, this one carries the traces of its history. The losses of the Indian Corps on the Western Front were small compared to their losses in Mesopotamia, which are recorded on a memorial in Basra. Comparing the two monuments, using the CWGC's archives, produced a distinctive finding: the "principle" that each of the dead should be commemorated by name only held within Europe. The memorial in Basra does not list the individual names of the Indian rank and file, a policy spelled out in internal correspondence. Much has been made, by scholars of commemoration, of what Thomas Laqueur calls the "hyper-nominalism"—the endless listing of the names of the missing—of the First World War monuments.[6] But it turns out that outside Europe, numbers were sufficient, rather than names. Turning to the files on Africa, the "principle" of equal treatment was flouted consistently in the distinction that was made between what IWGC officials called "white graves" and those of the African "natives." The latter were usually not maintained. This is perhaps not surprising, especially to students of colonial history. But what is surprising is the continued effort that the War Graves Commission, and its historians and journalists, make to insist that "equal treatment" is the watchword. Ignoring the evidence, in their own files, of just how very unequal their treatment of whites and Africans was, they continue to erase the memory of the two hundred thousand and more Africans who died during the First World War.

"COMMEMORATIVE HYPER-NOMINALISM" AND THE POLITICS OF NAMING

Rudyard Kipling's inscription for a First World War memorial to troops and carriers in East Africa includes the lines "If you fight for your Country, even if you die, your sons will remember your name." As Kipling knew, the names of these particular dead fathers would not be inscribed on the memorial itself, which collectively and anonymously honors approximately fifty thousand Africans who died—fighting for and supporting the British—in the war there. No afterlife of these names is secured by the public memorial. In contrast, the perceived necessity for naming the war dead individually on the Western Front has been emphasized by Thomas Laqueur. Laqueur sees the major monuments in France and Belgium as "little more than venues for names," and discusses the design problems their architects faced in maximizing the wall space to accommodate so many names.[7] Laqueur interprets the necessity of naming every common soldier as a response to the absence of any agreed resonant imagery or ideal. This "resort to a sort of commemorative hyper-nominalism"[8] is evident on the Western Front, at Gallipoli, and elsewhere.

Thomas Laqueur sites his account in the historical context of the importance of a "name." He points out that, referring to battle casualties, Shakespeare speaks of "none else of name" in *Henry V* and "none of name" in *Much Ado About Nothing*. The name does not belong to the individual in the early modern period, rather it belongs to the lineage; naming the individual common soldier is a specifically modern development. In medieval and early modern tombs, representation of a knight could take a doubled form—on top an effigy of the "genealogical body," a body located through heraldry in its kinship systems, and below an anonymous corpse, "food for worms."[9] This image illuminates a point that Laqueur makes about the war dead: on the one hand the names of the "missing" were separated from their bodies, on the other an anonymous body (the unknown soldier) stands in for all bodies. As such, the unknown soldier is compelled to be universal, is required to be, in Laqueur's words, "bones that represent any and all bones equally well or badly."[10] This argument has some relevance for interpreting the differential treatment of colonial troops. Daniel Sherman, noting the seventy thousand deaths among the French colonial troops, explains the unwillingness to recognize them publicly: "too much recognition of colonial troops as a distinct category . . . risked raising uncomfortable questions about their subordinate status within the French empire; in this respect unitary narratives, such as those incarnated in the unknown soldier, clearly had their advantages."[11]

In Africa, where it is estimated that upwards of two hundred thousand people died, the Imperial War Graves Commission developed a policy of conserving what it called the "white graves," whilst allowing "native" graves to revert to nature. The occupants of the latter were commemorated on memorials rather than given headstones. In an eloquent phrase, employing the commission's own key difference between an identified grave and a name to be included on a memorial, the natives were described as "sent Missing." A significant distinction was made, early on, between policy in Europe, and elsewhere in the world. This can be seen by comparing two of the memorials of the soldiers serving in the Indian Army (as it then was). The memorial at Neuve Chappelle in France identifies approximately five thousand soldiers of all ranks, by individual name. In Basra, where the bulk of the thirty-five thousand Indians who died in Mesopotamia are commemorated, a different policy applied: Lord Arthur Browne, principal assistant secretary of the Imperial War Graves Commission, explained in 1924 that "outside Europe" the memorials would contain the names of the British and Indian officers, but only the total numbers of native noncommissioned officers and men, under the name of their regiment. The same policy for the Basra memorial, applied to men from the Nigeria Regiment and the West African Frontier Force. Their names, we are told, "like those of the Indians, will appear only in the Register," and not on the memorial itself. Before focusing my argument on the Imperial War Graves Commission practices in East and West Africa, I look more generally at the case of the Indian Army, as this enables us to compare practice on the Western Front with what was thought appropriate in Mesopotamia.

THE "ARMIES OF UNDIVIDED INDIA"

Gayatri Chakravorty Spivak's influential paper "Can the Subaltern Speak?" (1988) has given the idea of the subaltern general currency in literary studies, but the word has a very specific history in relation to the British Army, where it denoted an officer below the rank of Captain. In the First World War the subaltern officers were typically Second Lieutenants, in charge of a platoon of twenty men. Many of the well-known "war poets" were, or started off as, Second Lieutenants, as this was the standard junior rank: Rupert Brooke, Wilfred Owen, Siegfried Sassoon, Robert Graves, Edmund Blunden, and Edward Thomas, for example. These men were "subalterns" in army speak, rather than in Spivak speak: many were from a class background of considerable wealth and power, educated at the major private schools, then at Oxford or Cambridge.

Rather, it is the Indian Army that provides an encounter between Spivakian subalternity as a form of subordination that denies voice and agency and the definition in terms of British officer ranks. The army of prepartition India, its soldiers were later referred to as "the Armies of Undivided India." At the outbreak of the war in 1914 the various regiments of the Indian Army were organized along ethnic and caste lines, but this structure was overridden by a different hierarchy: all officers were Europeans. Sepoys could not go beyond the role of platoon commander, and commissioned officer status was simply not available. As historians have noted, it was only at the end of the war, and in response to India's contribution to it, that this changed.[12] In 1917 it was agreed in principle to grant "King's Commissions" to Indian Officers, but in practice "these men lacked the education and social graces required"—after the war they were put through the military schools and the "Indianization" of the officer corps made a reality.[13]

In September 1914 the king-emperor sent a message to the "Princes and Peoples of My Indian Empire." He declared that "nothing has moved Me more than the passionate devotion to My Throne expressed both by My Indian subjects, and by the Feudatory Princes and the Ruling Chiefs of India, and their prodigal offers of their lives and resources in the cause of the Realm."[14] The Indian Corps, a fighting force as well as labor support, arrived in Marseilles in the autumn of 1914 to join the battles on the Western Front. This experience has been documented in various military memoirs and histories, including Willcocks's *With the Indians in France* (1920),[15] Merewether and Smith's *The Indian Corps in France* (1919),[16] Heathcote's *The Indian Army* (1974),[17] and more recently Corrigan's *Sepoys in the Trenches* (1999). Experiences on the Western Front were powerfully reworked in a literary register in Mulk Raj Anand's *Across the Black Waters: a novel* (1940),[18] and fascinating personal material collected, from letters written home by Indian soldiers, as part of the censor system, has now been published.[19] The tour of duty of the Indian Corps in France lasted for fifteen months, in the course of which they notably recaptured the village of Neuve Chapelle, which the British had lost.[20] On their departure, another word came from the king: of those who had died, he said "Let it be your consolation, as it was their pride, that they gave their lives in a just cause for the honour of their sovereign and the safety of my Empire."

A memorial at Neuve Chapelle lists the names of over five thousand Indian soldiers. It was designed in 1923 by Herbert Baker, the coworker of Edwin Lutyens on the plans for New Delhi. The design of the memorial took place in a conflicted religious context: Muslims, Hindus, and Sikhs all wanted separate monuments, but it was decided to have a single memorial to all the Indians who had died in France, with inscriptions appropriate to the three main creeds.[21] In 1927 the Neuve Chapelle Indian memorial was inaugurated.

> The memorial is a sanctuary enclosed within a circular wall, the front of which is pierced and carved with Indian symbols, after the manner of the enclosing railings of the early Indian shrines. The centre of this railing is solid and on it stands a monolithic column reminiscent of the famous inscribed columns which the Emperor Asoka erected throughout India.

The column is surmounted with a Lotus capital, the Imperial crown and the Star of India. On either side of the column are carved two tigers guarding the temple of the dead. On the lower part of the column is inscribed in English "God is One, His is the Victory" with similar texts in Arabic, Hindi and Gurmukhi. The base of the column bears the inscription "India, 1914–1918."[22]

Echoing the evocation of patriotic belonging through sacrifice made famous in Rupert Brooke's "The Soldier," the recorder then speculates on a "corner of a foreign field / That is for ever England": "might we not also look upon this inscription as marking the place where we leave France and enter upon that tiny plot of French ground that is forever India?"[23]

The memorial in its final form was the end product of considerable debate. The Commonwealth War Graves Commission archives show that every aspect of the design was fully discussed between the commission and the India Office in London. One thorny issue was the presence of a cross in the design of the imperial crown. Mr. Baker was reported as saying that "he is using crowns freely in Delhi and sees no objection to there being a crown on the memorial." The India Office disagreed, General Cobbe saying from the start, in 1925, that "if the Imperial Crown designed to top the Memorial must have a Maltese cross on the top of it, I agree that it had better be left out of the design altogether." The inscriptions for the column were to say "God is One, His is the Victory," but in what languages? "Is it necessary to have anything more than English, and one Indian language?" asked the IWGC. General Cobbe of the India Office thought on balance that "if it was convenient to include a native language, it should be Urdu." Herbert Baker as architect was insistent on the four languages of English, Hindi, Urdu, and Gurmukhi. In the end they consulted Sir Frederick Kenyon, director of the British Museum, who had resolved earlier conflicts for the commission, about such inscriptions. In 1926 he cautiously replied: "I am not Orientalist enough to form an opinion. Surely it is a case for inviting native opinion. . . . We ought not to put up anything which may offend the sentiments of any large section of the population of India without being able to say that we took the best native opinion open to us."

In 1927 the king had hoped that the memorial would "be the means of bringing to their kin in India—most of whom can never visit the far distant scene of battle—vivid realization of the loving care and profound homage with which all parts of my Empire have combined to perpetuate the memory of the Indian fallen." The visitors' book at the memorial, however, now shows that cheaper international travel, and the desire to settle imperial accounts, has motivated many residents of India to make the trip to northern France.

The title page of the official register at the site has the word *Indian* deleted, in several dark blue biro lines. Erasure of the word *Indian* is reiterated, in black felt tip pen, on every single page of the register. These changes look almost like graffiti, but they are official. An amendment to the register, in 1966, announced that "it has been decided that the 1914/18 Memorial at Neuve Chapelle, formerly known as 'The Neuve Chapelle Indian Memorial' upon which are commemorated fallen members of the armies of Undivided India, will in future be known only as the Neuve Chapelle Memorial." We have here the ambiguous erasure of the word *Indian* from the paperwork at a memorial which has the word *India* carved in huge letters into the stone of its plinth. In December 2001 the Commonwealth War Graves Commission answered my inquiry about the decision to erase the word *Indian* from the register: "In November 1966 the Commission's Director of External Relations and Records decided after discussions with the representative of Pakistan to change the title of the memorial formerly known as "The Neuve Chapelle Indian Memorial" upon which are commemorated fallen members of the armies of undivided India to the Neuve Chapelle Memorial."

"For ever India" had lasted for forty years. There was an enormous amount of consultation about the details of the Indian Memorial in France in the 1920s; the Commonwealth War Graves Commission has files of papers on the topic in its storerooms, including drawings, artwork for the inscriptions, and so on. The cultural politics concerning religion and ethnicity were seen, then, as sensitive and important. In 1966 the word *Indian* was dropped over lunch. The two men lunching were Wynne Mason, the director of external relations of the CWGC, and Commodore M. M. Hussain, the head of the Military Mission at the High Commission for Pakistan in London. On June 28 Commodore Hussain wrote to Wynne Mason and mentioned that "we would . . . be grateful if you could be good enough to consider changing the name of Neuve Chapelle Indian War Memorial to 'Neuve Chapelle Indo-Pakistan War Memorial.' We feel that this distinction should be made as the sub-continent is now divided into independent states of Pakistan and India. This distinction will bring out the services rendered by people who came from the areas now constituting Pakistan."

Wynne Mason replied: "I should be delighted if you would accept an invitation to lunch with me, when we could have ample time to talk over all aspects of the matter." This they did, in late September. Mason then wrote to "My dear Hussain," saying how much he had enjoyed "chatting together over lunch." He continued that "with regard to the 1914–1918 Memorial at Neuve Chapelle, we shall ensure that in future correspondence this is referred to as The Neuve Chapelle Memorial and that the new roadside direction signs which are to be erected will be similarly inscribed." Of this decision there is no account to be found in the copious archives of the CWGC; it does not appear to have been discussed or minuted at commission meetings. There is merely one note, item 5 in an account of a senior staff meeting on October 20. "*Neuve Chapelle Indian Memorial* DER [i.e., Mason] said that following discussions with the representative of Pakistan it had become necessary to change the title of the above Memorial, which would now be known simply as the *Neuve Chapelle Memorial*. DG [Director General] said it would be as well to circularize Heads of Divisions about this."

The CWGC would never have agreed to "Indo-Pakistan"; they did not believe in retrospective redesignations of that kind. Nor was the motive obviously financial. Following the partition of India, in 1947, the contribution to the maintenance of CWGC operations was split 2:1 between India and Pakistan. The sum involved had also been substantially reduced, in recognition of the fact that so many men of the Indian Army were recorded as names on memorials rather than as graves requiring expensive maintenance. Pakistan left the CWGC when it left the commonwealth, in the 1970s, but was on good terms at this point. It seems most likely, according to current information staff at the commission, that Mason accepted the force of Hussain's political argument. No request was made to change the names of other Indian cemeteries and memorials, which retain the word *Indian* to this day. Neuve Chapelle was different in that it was not only a monument to the missing, it was a national "Indian" battle exploit memorial and as such the key site for renegotiation. Recognition of Pakistan was most easily done, it seems, by attempting to erase the word *Indian* from the memorial—a gesture laden with some irony in the context of commemorative "nominalism." The erasure has had limited success, both at the site itself and on paper. The CWGC files contain a number of testy memos, years afterward, ticking off staff for continuing to refer to the "Indian" memorial.

THE POLITICS OF NAMING "INDIANS"

However complex the subsequent political history of the "Indian" memorial at Neuve Chapelle, it certainly, however, followed the general practice of the IWGC in recording the Missing by name. From the Indian Army on the Western Front 176 officers died, more than 5,000 "other ranks," and more than 2,000 "followers" or laborers. The Indian Army was also deployed in Egypt, in East Africa, and at Gallipoli, but the bulk of the Indian casualties, of the entire war, were in Mesopotamia, where 364 officers and more than 35,000 other ranks and 17,000 followers died. The recent and ongoing war in Iraq has focused attention on the area that, during the First World War, was Mesopotamia. What was at stake then? According to Charles Chevenix Trench, author of *The Indian Army and the King's Enemies,* "the object was simple and sensible: to safeguard the Anglo-Persian Oil Company's installations at Mohammerah and on Abadan Island, without which the British Empire could not have continued the war for a week." The robust Trench continued, "twenty miles above Abadan, was the fly-blown, pestilential port of Basra, modest in its facilities but the only one in Mesopotamia."[24] This is where the Indian corps was sent. In addition to Trench's pertinent point about securing oil supplies, the campaign in Mesopotamia specifically sought to "balance the loss in prestige of failure in Gallipoli."[25] An official account, edited for the Royal Colonial Institute and published soon after the war, describes the impetus for taking risks, in Mesopotamia in the autumn of 1915, in the following terms: "The Home Government were impressed with the great political and military advantages of an occupation of Baghdad. Prospects in Gallipoli were uncertain, and it seemed likely that the Germans would break through to Constantinople. Government had need therefore of a great and striking success in the East."[26]

The Indian Army was largely responsible for the campaign in Mesopotamia, and took heavy casualties there—in excess of fifty thousand deaths. In all, over seventy-four thousand men from the Indian Army were killed in the war, a figure that exceeds the deaths of Canadians or Australians. The contrast with these (white) Dominions is instructive in another way: put very roughly, around twice as many Canadians and Australians have identified graves as are recorded on memorials to the missing. In the case of the Indian Army, less than 10 percent have identified burial places. Is this, as can plausibly be argued, the effect of Hindu and Sikh religious customs, or is there another factor in play—a lesser value attached to the lives of Indian soldiers and laborers?

This question can be explored further by comparing Neuve Chapelle with the equivalent monument in Mesopotamia. In March 1929 the "Memorial to the Missing of the Mesopotamia Expeditionary Force" was unveiled, in Basra, by the British High Commissioner to Iraq, Sir Gilbert Clayton. The ceremony itself, possibly even outdoing the opening of Neuve Chapelle in 1927, had all the imperial trappings, including a nineteen-gun salute from HMS *Lupin,* moored nearby. All the same, Sir Gilbert had anxieties about protocol and "native opinion." He went to the trouble of having a telegraph from Baghdad put into code form when he asked the Commission for advice: "Basra war memorial to missing will be unveiled by me on 27th March. As the missing includes Christians Moslems and Hindus I am doubting whether the prayers by British Chaplain would be appropriate. Can you quote precedent?" Indeed they could: "At Unveiling Indian Memorial France on which names of British officers and Indian all ranks engraved no religious ceremonial took place. Suggest same at Basra." Similarly to Neuve Chapelle, the Basra memorial had been the subject of much comment in terms of the design; there was the need to represent the three main faiths of India, but they were worried about the danger of communal conflict. The India Office ruled that a closed building was not suitable, as "a Mahomedan for instance entering such a building might very easily do something to offend the religious susceptibilities of a Hindu, and vice-versa." Early efforts by the architect had been rejected for this reason, and an open design, based around a colonnade and an obelisk, had been favored.

Despite the force of precedent, there is, however, one startling difference between these two memorials. At Neuve Chapelle every individual is recorded by name; in Basra they are not. The policy was explained in 1924 by Arthur Browne of the IWGC: "bearing in mind that the memorials themselves will in all probability not be seen by any of the relatives of the rank and file, the memorials in question outside Europe will contain only the names of the regiments concerned, followed in each case by the names of the British officers (and non-commissioned officers if any), the names of the Indian officers and the number of the native non-commissioned officers and men." On the other hand, "In Europe, where the memorials will be seen by many visitors, and where the numbers of Indian names concerned are not so great, the British and Indian officers and the Indian rank and file will be commemorated by name." Following this decision, the Indian troops would generally be recorded, not by individual name, but as a number from a particular regiment, in IWGC memorials outside Europe.

"RACE AND CREED" POLITICS

When it came to refining the details of the Basra memorial, in May 1926, we see that differentiation by the race/rank nexus was not directed exclusively at Indians. Returning the Nominal Roll, the director of records pointed out that "these men of the Native African Units should be commemorated numerically like the Indians, but if they were to find any Native officers among them they should be commemorated by name." The campaign in Mesopotamia provides a rich quarry of information about attitudes within the military and more generally at this time. Let me take one small example, from a description of the unsuccessful advance toward Baghdad in the autumn of 1915. This is a Major Dawson, crossing the River Tigris at the

Shumran Bend with the Eighty-second Punjabis. The attack was "the most magnificent thing I have ever seen. We went through three belts [of machine gun fire]. Whole platoons dropped, but we went on steadily. . . . I am awfully proud of my company. . . . My greatcoat changed hands four times. My orderly was carrying it first. He was hit and threw it to another man and so on. My Mahommedans made it a point of honour that my greatcoat must get in."[27]

What is the value of the lives of "his Mahommedans" to this Major Dawson? Judith Butler has asked, in the context of contemporary global violence: "who counts as human? Whose lives count as lives?"[28] In particular, she asks how Islamic lives, and Arab lives, are dehumanized. "To what extent have Arab peoples, predominantly practitioners of Islam, fallen outside the 'human' as it has been naturalised in its 'Western' mold by the contemporary workings of humanism?"[29] The contemporary question has a classical pedigree, as Butler's references back to Creon and Antigone usefully indicate.[30] In Mesopotamia, however, colonial power is the salient issue, rather than philosophical humanism. Plainly, the lives and deaths of the "native troops" in the First World War were not regarded as of the same value as the lives of the British. In Butler's terms, these people were outside the "exclusionary conceptions of who is normatively human": they did not count as having "a livable life and a grievable death."[31] The advance on Baghdad failed, which resulted in a retreat to the garrison at Kut-el-Amara. The spring of 1916 saw the disastrous siege of Kut, which finally surrendered in April—though not before many Indian soldiers had starved when the garrison was put onto horse and mule meat, refusing to subordinate caste eating rules to the advice of their military commanders.

The subalternity in play was that of the Indian army hierarchy, with its long tradition of a restricted cadre of white British officers, but the subsequent decisions of the IWGC also enact the erasures and silencings identified so eloquently in Spivak's account of the colonial subaltern. The official briefing notes prepared by the Imperial War Graves Commission for Sir Gilbert's unveiling ceremony at Basra stated very clearly something that was factually wrong (as Indian officers were recorded by name there), but which tells us everything about the underlying meaning of the policy. "The white officers and men are recorded by name on the Memorial, but the names of the Indian soldiers do not appear on it and will be contained only in the Register which will be published later. In addition there are certain men of the Nigeria Regiment and the West African Frontier Force who served in the Inland Water Transport and whose names, like those of the Indians, will appear only in the Register."

THE IMPERIAL WAR GRAVES COMMISSION IN AFRICA

This slip of a reference to "white" officers and men opens up a vocabulary that comes fully into play in the IWGC's work in Africa, where the distinction between "white" and "native" had far-reaching consequences. The commission's archives provide a detailed account of their work on the graves that resulted from campaigns all around the world during the 1914–18 war. The files reveal departures—particularly in Africa—from egalitarian principles which have been ignored by the various historians of the commission, most importantly Philip Longworth, whose *The Unending Vigil*, has recently been reprinted.[32] One statement of policy in West Africa was seen to be sufficiently important as a guide to practice that it has been copied and filed in the slim file of general policy "Rulings." Here is to be found a formal statement of Arthur Browne's policy. This document is a memo from Browne to the director of records at the IWGC, dated 24/11/1925 and headed "Cemetery Memorial Registers for Natives." It starts by stating that "it has always been the view of the Vice-Chairman [Fabian Ware] that identical treatment should be accorded to British and native troops so far as circumstances permit." "Therefore," said Browne, "registers should be compiled to include the names of all native soldiers who died in the war and also of native followers." Browne then notes that "if a native soldier's or follower's name is on a headstone it will of course appear in the cemetery register." Browne next takes the category of natives who have a registered grave or are known to be buried in the cemetery, but do not have individual memorials (i.e., headstones). These names, he says, should not appear on the cemetery register. They should be put in the registers of the appropriate memorial. The reason for this is that "if we were to include all the names of the latter class in the cemetery register I think we should be unnecessarily drawing attention to the fact that we have neglected to commemorate by a headstone."

This indicates that Browne, at least, was well aware that a departure from the commission's principles was occurring in Africa, and was at pains to distract attention from it. In practice, no expense of time or money was spared when tracking down the individual European or "white graves," in East and West Africa, while the known and identified graves of many Africans were abandoned and the names reclassified as "missing." Hew Strachan suggests, following Melvin Page, that "somewhere over 2 million Africans served in the First World War as soldiers or laborers, and upwards of 200,000 of them died or were killed in action."[33] The death rate among the carriers was much higher than it was for soldiers. Geoffrey Hodges puts it at over 20 percent for Nigerian carriers, which can be compared with an average death rate among the military of 7 percent.[34]

EAST AFRICA: DISTINCTIONS OF RACE AND CREED

The Imperial War Graves Commission developed a general strategy on the commemoration of African natives in their work in East Africa. In the course of 1918 there was some correspondence between the graves registration staff and the army, which included a cable from Lieutenant Colonel Stobart to the commanding officer of the East Africa Expeditionary Force stating that permanent memorials would have to wait until after the war and requesting the military authorities to "make the best local arrangements possible for ensuring the identification of these graves in the meantime." Major George Evans was the officer in charge of the registration of graves. His report estimated that there were four thousand soldiers and fifty thousand laborers to record the deaths of in East Africa, and he considered that the erection of individual headstones would be "a waste of public money." Evans proposed that native soldiers who had been buried in the bush and the porters (including those elsewhere referred to as laborers and followers) be commemorated on public statues in the principal towns of the region. Arthur Browne echoed many of these points in his recommendations for East Africa.

Fabian Ware himself, in February 1920, said that he regarded monuments to natives as a "political question" on which the IWGC would have to consult the Colonial and Foreign Office and their local representatives. The IWGC kept records of such consultations, including a meeting with the governor of Tanganyika Territory in Dar Es Salaam in December 1922. The governor "considered that the vast Carrier Corps Cemeteries at Dar-es-Salaam and elsewhere should be allowed to revert to nature as speedily as possible & did not care to contemplate the statistics of the native African lives lost."

An area of general controversy, in East Africa as elsewhere, was the policy of "concentration": this involved the exhumation of bodies and their reburial in centralized cemeteries. In the process of concentration, distinctions of race and creed appear to have been thought extremely significant. In 1922–23 a member of the IWGC's UK staff, H. Milner, clerk of works, was working in Kenya Colony attempting to identify the remains of men killed at Salaita Hill. His report includes the following observations:

> Amongst these remains were one skull with top set of false teeth, one skull with gold stoppings in 3 back teeth of lower jaw, and two skulls had each one gold tooth in the front of the upper jaws, 6 skulls had very low foreheads, apparently of a different race from the remainder but quite un-

like African Native skulls. I feel sure that at least 14 of these remains are those of European soldiers.

Milner presumed that the other six were Indians and had the twenty reburied in a common grave in Taveta Cemetery. The need to distinguish between these different, raced, remains was not, or certainly not only, so that they could be disposed of in ways that were culturally appropriate, it was so that distinctions of relative importance, and therefore entitlements to commemoration, could be established in the disposition.

One account shows this clearly operating in relation not to the distinction of "race" but to those of what the IWGC usually referred to as "creed," namely, religious belief. Also in Kenya Colony, the year before, the deputy director of works surveyed how many headstones would be needed for the cemetery at Voi. He reported that there were ninety-nine graves requiring headstones. However, he then added that "only 9 of the Native graves are specifically mentioned as being Christians but as these men have been buried in the Christian Cemetery and accorded special consideration compared with the numerous other natives who died in the vicinity, the inference I draw is, that they may be regarded as Christians and worthy of commemoration by the standard type of Headstone." He was quite clear that their Christianity could overrule their African "native" status and make them "worthy" of a headstone, which would mean that they would be entered on the cemetery register.

WEST AFRICA AND THE CIVILIZATION ARGUMENT

When it came to their work in West Africa, the IWGC was able to articulate what had already happened in East Africa as the precedent to be followed. On April 12, 1923, Browne wrote to the governor of Nigeria setting out the situation and asking for his opinion.

> According to our records there are in Nigeria some 37 graves of European and 292 of native soldiers. It is proposed that the graves of European officers and men should be treated on the usual lines as far as local conditions permit. As regards natives, conditions are somewhat different. In Kenya Tanganyikaland etc. African natives are not being individually commemorated by headstones on their graves, chiefly owing to the fact that no proper records were kept of their places of burial but also because it was realized that the stage of civilization reached by most of the East African tribes was not such as would enable them to appreciate commemoration in this manner. It has therefore been decided to commemorate the native

troops and followers in East Africa by central memorials of a general kind with suitable inscriptions.

Browne pointed out that in the case of Nigeria "the individual graves appear to be known in every case" and that the alternative to individual headstones would be "to abandon the native graves" with no identifying memorial on them. The reply came back that memorials were being created for the Nigeria Regiment, which would name those who had died and "for this reason and for those set out in paragraph 3 of your letter [the civilization argument] the erection of individual memorials to African soldiers is unnecessary."

Earlier in 1923 Browne had had a similar conversation with the governor of the Gold Coast territories (now Ghana) at a meeting in London. The record of the meeting shows that the IWGC's principles, compromised as they undoubtedly were by what they were doing in Africa, were nonetheless on the liberal side compared with the views of the colonial administrators. Sir Frederick Guggisberg thought that "the average native of the Gold Coast would not understand or appreciate a headstone" and that a central statue was a "more reasonable" idea. Lord Arthur put a sophisticated point in response: "I mentioned that in perhaps two or three hundred years' time, when the native population had reached a higher stage of civilization, they might then be glad to see that headstones had been erected on the native graves and that the native soldiers had received precisely the same treatment as their white comrades." In practice, the native graves were largely abandoned and the names of their occupants included on memorials to the missing.

In late 1928 Browne prepared a summary of the West African colonies for the IWGC. There were approximately forty-five hundred casualties to commemorate. In Sierra Leone the West African Regiment was in 1927 commanded by an officer with a different attitude. He wanted a memorial with native names individually inscribed. Browne's response was, "I do not see the necessity for it myself." Major Chettle, the director of records, gave a grudging tribute: "I suppose we had better try to have the native names engraved. These men were definitely soldiers of a rather high quality and with a military organization apparently as good as our own." The difference in practice between the "white graves" and the "natives" is shown up very clearly in the vexed history of the Cameroons. There were 63 "white graves," and the policy was to concentrate them in the cemetery in Duala. In 1933 the British vice-consul sent a report describing how, after 4 sets of remains had been exhumed and transported to Duala, they were ceremonially reburied "with full military honours." The native graves were another matter. In this instance there were 401 of them, of which only 11 were unidentified. These 390 known and named graves were given the now usual treatment and "with the concurrence of the West African governments, it is not proposed to maintain the native graves."

In May 1929 Major Chettle was asked about the position of the native graves in West Africa generally, and "if the Commission have decided to maintain the cemeteries concerned or abandon them." Captain Miskin, the registrar, noted that "for the Natives I should imagine that most of them are already commemorated on memorials, and apart from exceptional cases that will be considered adequate." Chettle added that for native burials, "permanent marking of the graves will be carried out only exceptionally if at all." Miskin concluded that, as had also been ruled in similar cases in Palestine and Iraq, "burials relating to Cemeteries for which it is unlikely that a Cemetery Register will be published shall be sent 'Missing.'"

INTERPRETATION

The treatment of the colonial troops, in the official commemorative activities of the IWGC, raises awkward questions, since the commission has, contrary to its own principles, made many distinctions on the basis of "race or creed" outside Europe. An obvious interpretation of this is the question of cost. A typical IWGC grave with headstone cost £10 and would incur maintenance costs in perpetuity. Sending the natives "missing" had a material advantage—the far cheaper option of putting a name on a memorial. Chettle noted in 1932, considering the funding of a memorial in Accra as well as the one at Kumasi, that "we have, in fact, disposed of our liabilities in the Gold Coast at an extremely cheap rate, and the expenditure of £75 on a memorial at Accra would still leave our average expenditure very low." Chasing up the sixty-three white graves in Cameroon was, on the other hand, worth considerable expenditure. At one point Browne even proposed sending an official from London specifically to oversee their fate, even though this would have raised the cost per grave from the budgeted £10 to an exorbitant £30. (This option was rejected and eventually these graves were marked with the smaller Gallipoli-style stone.) In Sierra Leone Browne drew the line at naming the carriers on a memorial, writing to Fabian Ware (from whom came the pressure for equal treatment) that "I am not including the names of the Carriers, as I do not know how far they are sufficiently civilized to justify the inclusion of their names," adding that "it would greatly increase the cost of the Memorial to include their names." This was true—there were a lot of them: 795, as against 59 dead soldiers. In the event, the names of the soldiers were recorded while the men of the Carrier Corps were "honoured" collectively.

What stances did the men working at the IWGC take on these issues? Fabian Ware (vice chairman) was pushing for equal treatment, where possible, but was actually presiding over some striking inequalities. Browne, the principal assistant secretary, was a key figure, in practice laying down policy and freely airing his views—which were typical for this period. Captain Miskin, the registrar, was a Brownite in temperament. Major Chettle, the director of records, was more cautious, tending to ask for rulings on obviously sensitive issues. It is surprising, however, that the official historians of the IWGC and CWGC have so completely "whitewashed" the issue of differential treatment by both race and creed in the practice of the organization. Fabian Ware's *The Immortal Heritage* (1937) can perhaps most readily be forgiven by the modern reader. His take on the issue of "race" was to argue that the cemetery gardeners should be British rather than Belgian.[35] Philip Longworth's *The Unending Vigil*, first published to mark fifty years' work of the commission in 1967, revised in 1985, and reprinted in 2003, is more of a challenge. He examined the archives, presumably taking in the general "Rulings" file, yet he simply slides over the many ways in which the commission did not practice the very principles he has laid out in the discussion of "the forging of principles" earlier in his book. In his discussion of "the global task," Longworth notes that there were "departures from the standards of the Western Front," particularly in Palestine, but that these were "dictated by necessity, not by disagreement with the Commission's principles."[36] Across the world, he insisted, some countries had thousands of graves, others only one: "But the single grave isolated in a wilderness was counted as important as any in a cemetery with ten thousand graves. There was no withdrawal from responsibility."[37] This same egalitarian rhetoric recurs in a recent book of photographs published to celebrate the ninetieth anniversary of the commission: it includes a picture of an isolated grave in Canada, which is "as reverently cared for as any other Commission grave."[38] There is no mention of the decision not to maintain the graves of Africans. Photographs of the African native memorials exist, but they are rarely seen in CWGC materials. In Longworth's recent history of the commission there is a photograph of the native memorial in Lagos, Nigeria, showing its sculptures of a Nigerian soldier and a carrier. No one seems to have noticed that it has been positioned and printed so as to cut off the top of the head of one of the two men.

Edwin Gibson and G. Kingsley Ward, in *Courage Remembered* (1989), piously enjoin their readers to be instructed by the commission's principles of uniformity of sacrifice.[39] They provide, unintentionally, an interesting example of unequal treatment in their reference to an exception that was made to the rule that a cemetery needed to have forty graves in it to merit the installation of a Cross of Sacrifice. One such cross was shipped out to the Falkland Islands between the wars, to honor the twenty-one graves in San Carlos cemetery.[40] These are graves to which British imperial sentiment attaches. After the defeat of the British squadron at Coronel in 1914, two "Dreadnought" battle cruisers were sent out from the UK to the Falklands and the Germans were routed by massively superior speed and firepower, causing Admiral Graf von Spee and his crews to perish there.[41] These battles were the last display of gallant and honorable naval warfare in the outer seas before the era of the perfidious submarine. Winston Churchill cabled from the admiralty that rescued German officers were entitled to the honors of war and would be permitted to retain their swords.[42] The Falkland Islands cemetery is thus a marker of a significant point in the imperial naval narrative and a marker of heightened imperial affect. No wonder the rule was broken for its commemoration. The contrast between the cemetery there and the graves of Africans, long since reverted to nature, is the "instructive" one.

Why then does the CWGC so persistently claim that equality of treatment is a principle that is applied to race and creed? A possible answer to that question would focus on the key debate in the House of Commons in 1920. The commission's principles were under real threat, and its work was in danger of being seriously disrupted, if repatriation and private memorials on the battlefields were allowed and the principle of equality defeated. The commission's principles of equal treatment had been framed by Fabian Ware in terms of social class and military rank and were indeed extremely progressive. As they were approved in 1918, they did not, according to Ware's account in 1937, emphasize the race and creed dimension. Ware refers to "three general principles": permanence, uniformity, and no distinction of "military or civil rank."[43] Similarly, the Kenyon Report of 1918, also a founding document of the commission, discusses equality of treatment in terms of "military rank and position in civil life."[44] There had obviously always been, by definition, an imperial dimension to the IWGC, and this was written into its Royal Charter in terms of a desire to "strengthen the bonds of union between all classes and races in Our Dominions" and to "promote a feeling of common citizenship and loyalty to Us and to the Empire of which they are subjects."[45] In the battle in parliament to defend the principle of equality of treatment, Westminster MP William Burdett-Coutts and Winston Churchill cast the issue in terms of the empire rather than the nation. They were building memorials to commemorate the sacrifice of an empire's soldiers, they said, and Burdett-Coutts referred to the war as having "fused and welded into one, without distinction of race, colour or creed, men from all over the Empire."[46] This claim won the debate for the IWGC and secured their position; they even published the speech as a pamphlet (CWGC Add 1/1/10). But unity across the empire was scarcely likely to imply equality of treatment. This meant that the line between a principle guiding practice and an ideal to be strived for was blurred from the beginning. Perhaps unsurprisingly, subaltern colonial troops were not commemorated equally, but the history of these decisions has not been fully acknowledged. In this way a further silencing of the subaltern takes place: not only are these lives not commemorated, the acts of exclusion are themselves erased.

NOTES

I am grateful to Gayatri Spivak, and to Rosalind Morris, for inviting me to participate in the original conference, "Can the Subaltern Speak: Reflections on the History of an Idea," and for their interesting comments on this material in its early form. I am also very grateful to Alison Donnell and Robert Young, at *Interventions*, the venue in which this essay originally appeared. For comments and advice as this paper developed, my thanks to Duncan Barrett, Santanu Das, Tracey Loughran, Keith McClelland, Nirmal Puwer, Peter Stallybrass, and to colleagues at the Imperial War Museum "materialities" seminar, run by Paul Cornish and Nicholas Saunders.

1 Morrow, *The Great War*; Strachan, *The First World War*.
2 Corrigan, *Sepoys in the Trenches*; Das, "'Indian Sisters!'"
3 Livesey, *The Viking Atlas of World War I*.
4 Jeffery, *Ireland and the Great War*.
5 A catalogue of the archive of the Commonwealth War Graves Commission, which is held at its headquarters in Maidenhead, UK, is available at the British Library and other sources. It was published by the CWGC in 1977, and compiled by Alex King. The materials cited in this paper can principally be found in the archive as follows: Rulings, WG 290; Neuve Chapelle and Basra, under the files for the memorials themselves; East and West Africa, file numbers WG 122 (1–2), WG 243 (1–4). I am very grateful to Maria Choules, at the archive, for her help.
6 Laqueur, "Memory and Naming."
7 Ibid., p.163.
8 Ibid., p. 160.
9 Jones and Stallybrass, *Renaissance Clothing*, p. 250.
10 Laqueur, "Memory and Naming," p. 158.
11 Sherman, *The Construction of Memory*, p. 101.
12 Visram, *Ayahs, Lascars, and Princes*, p. 114.
13 Ellinwood and Pradhan, *India and World War 1*, pp. 199–200.
14 Lucas, *The Empire at War*, 1:301–302.
15 Willcocks, *With the Indians in France*.
16 Merewether and Smith, *The Indian Corps in France*.

17 Heathcote, *The Indian Army.*

18 Anand, *Across the Black Waters.*

19 Omissi, *Indian Voices of the Great War.*

20 Corrigan, *Sepoys in the Trenches*, p. 247.

21 Longworth, *The Unending Vigil*, p. 37.

22 Rice, *Neuve Chapelle.*

23 Ibid.

24 Trench, *The Indian Army*, p. 75

25 Ibid., p. 76.

26 Lucas, *The Empire at War*, 5:288.

27 Trench, *The Indian Army*, p. 85

28 Butler, *Precarious Life*, p. 20.

29 Ibid., p. 32.

30 Ibid., p. 36; also see Butler, *Antigone's Claim.*

31 Butler, *Precarious Life*, p. xv.

32 Longworth, *The Unending Vigil*, 2003.

33 Strachan, *The First World War*, p. 497; Page, *Africa and the First World War*, p. 14.

34 Hodges, "Military Labour in East Africa," p. 143.

35 Ware, *The Immortal Heritage*, p. 56.

36 Longworth, *The Unending Vigil*, p. 117.

37 Ibid., p. 123.

38 Summers, *Remembered*, p. 157.

39 Gibson and Ward, *Courage Remembered*, p. 71.

40 Ibid., p. 53.

41 Corbett, *Official History of the Great War*; Irving, *Coronel and the Falklands.*

42 Churchill, *The World Crisis*, p. 434.

43 Ware, *The Immortal Heritage*, p. 30.

44 Kenyon, *War Graves*, p. 6.

45 Longworth, *The Unending Vigil*, p. 28.

46 Ibid., p. 52.

PART FOUR

CONTEMPORANEITIES AND POSSIBLE FUTURES

(NOT) SPEAKING AND HEARING

Pheng Cheah

BIOPOWER AND THE NEW INTERNATIONAL DIVISION OF REPRODUCTIVE LABOR

The signal contribution of Gayatri Chakravorty Spivak's essay, "Can the Subaltern Speak?" to contemporary critical theory is its immanent critique of theory's material embeddedness in global capitalism. What struck me when I first read the essay, and what still impresses me today, is the sharp manner in which Spivak exposed the myriad ways in which Michel Foucault's and Gilles Deleuze's accounts of power were ideologically blind to the international division of labor (IDL). Spivak's essay thus follows a classical gesture of one of Marx's own practices of ideology-critique: the critique of forms of knowledge such as Hegelian idealism and British political economy that returns them to the various formations of capital from whence they sprung by showing that their very intellectual coherence and truth-content were premised upon the distortion or mystification of the fundamental material circumstances that were their historical conditions of possibility.

There is, however, an additional twist when Spivak makes a similar critique of post-Marxists like Foucault. For, as is well known, Foucault questions the explanatory usefulness of the concept of ideology itself for understanding the reproduction of social and political relations. This move of Foucault's, Spivak suggests, is itself an ideological symptom of the fact that his theory is made in socialized capital on the dominant (i.e., Western) side of the IDL.[1] Spivak thus enjoins us to consider the IDL's infrastructural status and its complex implications for understanding the role of representation in political activism. This essay attempts to reopen Spivak's critique of Foucault, to read Foucault's analytics of biopower after Spivak, using the provocations of her essay to think about how biopower operates in the new international division of labor. Spivak foregrounds the importance of ideology in the making of the third world subject. She suggests that insofar as Foucault's theory of power is animated by a polemical rejection of the Marxist concept of ideology, it cannot help us understand the constitution of the colonized or neocolonized, although it remains valuable for understanding the constitution of the colonizer. This article poses two questions. First, what is the relationship between Foucault's analytics of power and the Marxist concept of ideology? Second, if we accept Foucault's "sanctioned ignorance" of the IDL, does biopower nevertheless have a more fundamental role in the fabrication of subjects on the other side of the IDL than Spivak allows? I will explore the second issue by considering the transnational traffic in domestic labor in hyperdeveloping Southeast Asia.

BIOPOWER, IDEOLOGY, INTEREST

Spivak's critique of Foucault has two main limbs. First, she argues that Foucault's rejection of the concept of ideology is based on a simplistic understanding of the concept that is not cognizant of its complexity in the writings of Marx and the Marxist tradition. Consequently, Foucault does not have a theory of interests and subscribes to a representationalist realism that is continuous with positivist empiricism, and this leads to a naive valorization of the concrete experience of the oppressed. Second, Foucault's theory of power, which is problematic enough in socialized capital, actually helps to consolidate advanced capitalist neocolonialism when situated in a global frame. Global capitalist exploitation is consolidated by the elaborate ideological construction of a subject of the third world or postcolonial South, whose concrete experience, as expressed in a voice consciousness retrieved through fieldwork and other forms of data gathering, gives irrefutable confirmation that capitalist modernization and development within the framework of global capitalist accumulation benefits peoples in the peripheries. Because Foucault dismisses the concept of ideology, and because he believes that the oppressed can know and express the nature of their exploitation, Foucault is complicit with the continuing ideological construction of the third world subject and, therefore, can be said to repeat the imperialist project in its current forms.

The problematic of the subaltern is broached in this context. In Spivak's view, the third world subject constructed as Europe's self-consolidating Other obscures the true heterogeneity of decolonized/postcolonial space: the superexploited under the global capitalism. Within the circuit of the

IDL, this heterogeneity encompasses the female urban subproletariat. But, outside this circuit, there are "subsistence farmers, unorganized peasant labor, the tribals, and the communities of zero workers on the street or in the countryside."[2] This is the subaltern, the name for a consciousness that exceeds and cannot be comprehended within the enclosure of disciplinary knowledge-production and intellectual activism because the traces of such a subject have been obliterated by the epistemic violence of colonial subject making through the codification of indigenous law and education. Today, the data gatherer or activist who zealously desires access to a subject of development or oppression likewise pays no attention to the complex social relations—patriarchy, polytheism, divisions of class, caste, and tribe—that constitute subaltern space and block access to it.

Indeed, for Spivak, both the clamor for and claim to have retrieved the true voice consciousness of the subaltern and the claim to *be* the subaltern are deeply complicit with the continuing development of capital through the IDL. Such claims continue the epistemic violence of colonialism. They are part of a vast array of ideologically fabricated subjects that serve as proxies expressing the subaltern's true voice and interests. If we take into account the revisions in *A Critique of Postcolonial Reason*, these proxies include the national subject of the global South, the rural woman who is the consensual recipient of microcredit, woman as subject of development in UN Plans of Action, the postcolonial/third world subject as native informant who comes from the ranks of the formerly colonial subject/the indigenous elite, and, last but not least, the "postmodern postcolonialist" who engages in "hybridist postnational talk, celebrating globalization as Americanization."[3] "It is," Spivak writes poignantly, "in the shadow of this unfortunate marionette that the history of the unheeded subaltern must unfold."[4] In her view, Foucault's account of power unwittingly facilitates the muting of the subaltern precisely because, by ignoring the functioning of ideology, he forecloses the need for counterhegemonic ideological production that would contest these proxies that efface the subaltern.

I am persuaded that Foucault is ignorant of the IDL and am especially moved by Spivak's sharp diagnosis of the continued ventriloquism and muting of the subaltern. What puzzles me, however, is the following observation in "Can the Subaltern Speak?"

> what remains useful in Foucault is the mechanics of disciplinarization and institutionalization, the constitution, as it were, of the colonizer. Foucault does not relate it to any version, early or late, proto- or post-, of imperialism. They are of great usefulness to intellectuals concerned with the decay

of the West. Their seduction for them, and fearfulness for us, is that they might allow the complicity of the investigating subject . . . to disguise itself in transparency.[5]

By noting that Foucault's analytics of power contributes little to an understanding of the constitution of subjects in peripheral space, Spivak suggests that power operates in a different manner on the other side of the IDL. Hence, she claims to offer an alternative mapping or cartography of power, one that is more adequate and, indeed, responsive to an understanding of how power actually functions in global capitalism.

As far as I can tell, Spivak's cartography makes two correctives to Foucault. First, she suggests that in European territorial imperialism and its gradual displacement into the centralization of strategic military power by the U.S.A., the sovereign modality of power remains dominant, as evidenced by the reliance on outwardly directed violence and military coercion.[6] Second, she argues that the model of economic development that flourishes in the postcolonial peripheries under this framework of the American informal empire does not involve a productive form of power that enhances the lives and capacities of workers.[7] The productive form of power Foucault focuses on is coextensive with training into consumerism, which is crucial to the historical formation of civil society and, hence, an emergent political will of the people in the hegemonic West. Because Foucault takes the European state as the tacit setting and the point of the genesis of this new form of power, he fails to consider the importance of nineteenth-century territorial imperialism as a fundamental material condition in the making of industrial Europe. If this is taken into account, Spivak argues, it will be evident that power does not function productively in the peripheries of the capitalist world-system. The goal of the contemporary IDL, which Spivak regards as "a displacement of the divided field of nineteenth-century territorial imperialism," is not to enhance the capacities of nonelite subjects as labor power or human capital.[8] Postfordism and export-oriented international subcontracting are premised on maintaining the supply of cheap labor in the peripheries. This is ensured by "an absence of labor laws (or a discriminatory enforcement of them), a totalitarian state (often entailed by development and modernization in the periphery), and minimal subsistence requirements on the part of the worker" as well as by impeding the rise of consumerism, which would lead to higher wages, labor activism, and coalition politics resistant to capital.[9]

Global capitalism, therefore, involves two macroscopic forms of power, that of state formations and political economic systems as they are constituted and interact in a global theater. Such power is both sovereign and repressive. An account of capillary power by itself, Spivak suggests, cannot explain the tenacious reproduction of exploitative capitalist relations on a global scale. Drawing on Adorno's terminology, she argues that the *macrological* formations of global capital and international geopolitics manage to exert a hold on the unpredictable *micrological* functioning of power through the ideological formation of subjects.[10] Ideology is therefore a third modality of power that mediates between and connects macrological and micrological forms of power. It is the medium and means by which class interests, as a form of socioeconomic agency, can influence and control the erratic technologies of power exerted upon individual bodies. In other words, the ideological constitution of subjects gathers these bodily forces together so that they can be harnessed and deployed to further the smooth functioning of political and economic structures of domination and exploitation. More specifically, in Spivak's view, the functioning of global capitalism involves two forms of ideological subject-constitution: "the subject-production of the worker and unemployed within nation-state ideologies in [the] Center" and the construction of a third world or postcolonial national subject as the self-consolidating Other of the hegemonic West or North that facilitates "the increasing subtraction of the working class in the Periphery from the realization of surplus value and thus from 'humanistic' training into consumerism" and obscures "the large-scale presence of paracapitalist labor as well as the heterogeneous structural status of agriculture in the Periphery."[11] Precisely because Foucault rejects the concept of ideology and the sophisticated understanding of the agency of interests it implies, his analytics of power, Spivak argues, forecloses the possibility of resisting this fundamental modality of power in global capitalism.

We do not need to be card-carrying Foucauldians (and I am not one) to observe that it is not entirely accurate to say that Foucault does not have a complex theory of interests and that he always privileges the concrete experience of the oppressed. Perhaps because Spivak's ideology-critique relies so heavily on the symptomatic reading of a marginal text in Foucault's corpus, she pushes Foucault's deep polemical engagement with Marx into the background, even suggesting at times that his analytics of power fails to adequately engage with the irreducibility of economic exploitation.[12] Consequently, Foucault's critique of the explanatory limitations of a sovereign model of power and the theory of ideology tends to be equated with a dismissal of the continuing existence and efficacy of these phenomena. In fact, however, Foucault's critique derives from an alternative understanding of how capitalism functions. In Marxist theory the demystification of the distortive or obfuscatory nature of ideology involves the reembedding of such ideational forms and their material effects within the material conditions of their genesis and production. Hence the ultimate falsity of ideology stems from the exploitative character of these underlying economic conditions, which are the *real* or *empirical* basis of ideology, and the proper object of study of Marxist thought qua science. As Foucault puts it, "in traditional Marxist analyses, ideology is a sort of negative element through which the fact is conveyed that the subject's relation to truth, or simply the knowledge relation, is clouded, obscured, violated by conditions of existence, social relations, or the political forms imposed on the subject of knowledge from the outside. Ideology is the mark, the stigma of these political or economic conditions of existence on a subject of knowledge who rightfully should be open to truth."[13] Accordingly, "ideology stands in a secondary position relative to something that functions as its infrastructure, as its material, economic determinant, and so on."[14] Indeed, ideology is doubly secondary because it is a superstructure of the political superstructure of the state viewed as a repressive apparatus of the bourgeoisie.

For Foucault, however, the rise of industrial capitalism is made possible by a new form of power that is neither ideological nor repressive. This form of power does not negate its targets, either through ideational distortion or physical violence, but actually positively shapes and produces its objects through discourses of truth. In his words,

> This political investment of the body is bound up, in accordance with complex reciprocal relations, with its economic use; it is largely as a force of production that the body is invested with relations of power and domination; but, on the other hand, its constitution as labour power is possible only if it is caught up in a system of subjection (in which need is also a political instrument meticulously prepared, calculated and used); the body becomes a useful force only if it is both a productive body and a subjected body. This subjection is not only obtained by the instruments of violence or ideology; it can also be direct, physical, pitting force against force, bearing on material elements, and yet without involving violence; it may be calculated, organized, technically thought out; make use neither of weapons nor of terror and yet remain of a physical order. That is to say, there may be a "knowledge" of the body that is not exactly the science of its functioning, and mastery of its forces that is more than the ability to conquer them: this knowledge and this mastery constitute what might be called the political technology of the body.[15]

This kind of knowledge is not ideological. It is coterminous with power and operates at the physical level of bodies. It cannot be considered superstructural because it constitutes the economic infrastructure of capitalism. By the same token, this mode of power does not issue from the political superstructure. Such power-knowledge is infrastructural because it fabricates the economic basis of capitalism, namely, the very capacity of the laboring body as a useful productive force. This mode of power does not maintain social relations through coercion or dissimulation, i.e., through the political superstructure of the state and its legal instruments or through ideology, but operates within the social body and the sphere of economic processes as their indispensable *constitutive* force. In Foucault's view, the human capacity for labor does not have the primary or a priori status Marx attributed to it. It is a product-effect of an infrastructural power, which Foucault calls infrapower:

> Capitalism penetrates much more deeply into our existence. That system, as it was established in the nineteenth century, was obliged to elaborate a set of political techniques, techniques of power, by which man was tied to something like labor—a set of techniques by which people's bodies and their time would become labor power and labor time so as to be effectively used and thereby transformed into hyperprofit. But in order for there to be hyperprofit, there had to be an infrapower [*sous-pouvoir*]. A web of microscopic, capillary political power had to be established at the level of man's very existence, attaching men to the production apparatus, while making them into agents of production, into workers. This binding of man to labor was synthetic, political; it was a linkage brought about by power. There is no hyperprofit without infrapower.... I'm referring not to a state apparatus, or to the class in power, but to the whole set of little powers, of little institutions situated at the lowest level. What I meant to do was analyze this infrapower as a condition of possibility of hyperprofit.[16]

As we can see from his comment that human needs themselves are political instruments that are fabricated by calculation, Foucault's account of infrapower contains a theory of interests and needs. But it is emphatically non-Marxist. For, like the concept of ideology, the Marxist concept of human needs refers back to an originary human subject, a subject capable of origination, albeit through the dialectical work of negativity. In Marxist theory, human needs are basic social needs that arise directly from consumption, but, more importantly, from the production process. Broadly speaking, interests are the set of social conditions that the life-activity and objective social position of a class creates (in an unconscious latent form) in its members that allows or prevents the satisfaction of basic needs.[17] In the scenario where the interests of the dominant class are particularistic and cannot fulfill the needs of society as a whole, i.e., all history, these class interests are able to sway and organize society through the ideological constitution of subjects. This hegemony is most thorough under capitalism.[18] Marxist theory, therefore, always distinguishes interests from needs, which are fundamental and basic, pertain to the whole of society, and whose development serves as the foundation of social revolution.

In contradistinction, Foucault situates needs and interests within the domain of power. Government, the second pole of biopower, involves the regulation of the life of the population understood as a system of living beings with biological traits (such as propagation, births and deaths, the level of health and life expectancy) that can be analyzed and known through specific scientific knowledges and rational technologies.[19] As such, the population can be modified, altered, and managed through policy interventions that aim to increase the state's economic resources and forces.[20] Now power is productive because it increases the capacities and aptitudes of individual bodies through investment and valorization and enhances the quality of the population as an efficient economic resource. But what is less obvious is that power also produces the subject of basic human needs. Industrial society presupposes that the individual body is the repository of labor power as a commodity that is freely and willingly exchanged for a wage to fulfill the individual's *human needs*. Insofar as welfare policies shape the population by affecting birthrates, health, and distribution, governmental technologies thoroughly invest human life and shape its basic needs. As Foucault puts it,

> the population is the subject of needs, of aspirations, but it is also the object in the hands of the government, aware, vis-à-vis the government, of what it wants, but ignorant of what is being done to it. *Interest as the consciousness of each individual who makes up the population, and interest considered as the interest of the population as a whole regardless of what the particular interests and aspirations may be of the individuals who compose it*: this is the new target and the fundamental instrument of the government of population.[21]

What is important for us is that when Foucault speaks of the interests of the population, he does not follow the Marxist distinction between interests and needs. Instead, he suggests that needs themselves are always already shaped through governmental technologies. This means that the manipulation of subjects by the shaping of interests does not occur in the first instance at the level of socioeconomic class and through ideology. Manipulation and calculation already takes place at the physical level of the fabrication of needs themselves. Foucault's cartography of power therefore works in a different way from the Marxist model Spivak sketches. It is not the making of subjects through ideology that mediates between the macrological structures of state institutions and political economy, but a subtending infrastructure of biopolitical techniques that articulate the political, legal, and ideological superstructures and the economic infrastructure into a seamless web or network. This does not mean that ideology has been rendered irrelevant. Class ideologies exist and are continually generated. However, instead of attributing a primary formative power to them, it is a matter of inscribing the processes of ideological subject-formation within the field of biopolitical techniques that sustain them. These techniques guarantee relations of domination and effects of hegemony by functioning "as factors of segregation and social hierarchization."[22]

THE NEW INTERNATIONAL DIVISION OF REPRODUCTIVE LABOR

I have argued that Foucault has a more complex account of needs and interests than Spivak allows and that his analytics of power does not sidestep the economic but seeks instead to resituate it within an infrastructural form of power. Although Spivak has subsequently qualified her initial reading of Foucault's theory of power, she has not engaged in a sustained manner with his concept of biopower.[23] Of greater significance for present purposes, she has repeated her earlier argument that Foucault's analytics of power is only pertinent to understanding the production of the colonial subject and its contemporary relays in postcoloniality.[24] Such a focus, she suggests, can only serve to block out of view the repeated effacement of the subaltern, the denial of their access to any public voice or political space in which the subaltern can attempt to regulate distribution of resources or resist the depredations of global capital in postcolonial space. The subaltern's voice is rendered inaccessible because the space of subalternity is blocked out by the dominant epistemes of decolonization and postcoloniality as the result of the subaltern's exclusion from the project of making the colonial subject and, subsequently, the project of making the postcolonial national subject or the people.

> The political goals of the new nation are supposedly determined by a regulative logic derived from the old colony, with its interest reversed: secularism, democracy, socialism, national identity and capitalist development. . . . There is always a space in the new nation that cannot share in the energy of this new reversal. This space has no established agency of traffic with the culture of imperialism. Paradoxically, this space is also

outside of organized labor, below the attempted reversals of capital logic. Conventionally, this space is described as the habitat of the *subproletariat* or the *subaltern*.[25]

The lesson of "Can the Subaltern Speak?" concerning European critical theory's sanctioned ignorance of the IDL remains as urgent today as twenty-five years ago when the essay was first written. But the question that must be posed is whether power in contemporary globalization operates according to the same regulative logic established under colonialism. We can call this the colonial paradigm of power, where the exercise of power is typified by exclusion and forcible repression. Or does power today operate in relation to the oppressed inhabitants of the postcolonial world in such a manner that the purchase of a Foucauldian analytics of power is actually expanded? Seeking to extend Spivak's valuable critical gesture, I now take my turn and ask: how does infrastructural power operate in the contemporary IDL? How have these technologies of biopower been globalized and how do they sustain projects of national economic development in the current dispensation of flexible global capitalist accumulation? Conversely, what are the modes of resistance that are opened up by these technologies?

In the spirit of being spectralized by Spivak's lesson, let us remark on a curious feature of her essay. When she elaborates on the obliteration of the trace of the subaltern woman as subject, Spivak does not actually linger in the scene of contemporary global capitalism.[26] Instead, she turns back to the epistemic violence of colonialism, which she connects, echoing Lenin's definition of imperialism, to the contemporary IDL through the center-periphery model of dependency theory. The essay repeatedly uses the word *comprador* and points to the fact that formal decolonization made little difference in terms of exploiting peoples in the former colonies as cheap labor power. Indeed, things were worse in one respect. Since the former colonizers could now continue exploiting the periphery without formally administering it, the one productive aspect of colonialism, education, is no longer necessary, and this further impedes any emergence of consumerism in the periphery. Although the essay refers to international subcontracting, and the book version drops *comprador* and updates the structures of global capitalism in terms of postfordism, fiscalization, and the implosion of the Soviet Union, the recurrent themes are the rigidity of the center-periphery divide and the lack of consumerism and development of human resources in the periphery.[27] Spivak thus gives the impression that the IDL does not allow for much mobility of countries within its hierarchy and that states of formerly colonized countries do not aggressively attempt to move up this hierarchy. If, however, we turn to the impact of what Folker Fröbel and his coauthors termed "the New International Division of Labor" (NIDL) on the hyperdeveloping Southeast Asia of the three decades before the 1997 Asian financial crisis, we get a picture of global capitalism that is different from the rigid center-periphery binarism and more compatible with Foucault's cartography of infrastructural power.[28] One of its primary traits is the establishment of an international division of reproductive labor through the traffic in foreign women who engage in domestic work, where impoverished women from the rural peripheries are integrated into the IDL as temporary migrant workers through the biopolitical crafting of their interests as subjects of needs, by weaving their very needs in the fabric of global capitalism rather than just by obscuring their voices through ideological subject-formation.

The NIDL is the result of the relocation or "outsourcing" of production processes in the textiles, consumer electronics, and semiconductor industries to developing countries with lower labor costs either through foreign direct investment or international subcontracting, while research and development and technical and managerial control remained in the center. Various East and Southeast Asian countries responded positively to this tendency. (Today outsourcing has, of course, expanded beyond manufacturing to high-tech, software, and service sector jobs such as data processing and analysis and stock market research.) They used their comparative advantage—a large and cheap labor force or skills, technical abilities, infrastructure and low taxes—to carve out a niche in this new international division of labor, basing their development on "outward looking, export-oriented industrialisation strategies."[29] The impact of these largely state-sponsored strategies of development through globalization on East and Southeast Asian growth was dramatic. They created the pre-1997 "economic miracle" of the East Asian newly industrialized economies of South Korea, Taiwan, Hong Kong, and Singapore.[30] The pattern was repeated again and again, and hyperdevelopment quickly spread to the tiger economies of Southeast Asia, which were recipients of U.S. money and Japanese, South Korean, and other intra-Asian capital flows.

What we witness here is a mobility from periphery to semiperiphery and center within the NIDL, a mobility that is premised not on keeping labor "cheap," but on the upgrading and enhancement of human resources through state policies with the objective of developing consumerism and raising standards of living. Indeed, in 1979 Singapore realized the disadvantages of industrialization through cheap labor. It sought to maintain its economic growth by actively moving away from labor-intensive production and upgrading to higher value-added forms of production based on sophisticated scientific technology, skills, and knowledge, thereby taking it beyond competition with neighboring countries with lower wages.[31] The city-state's continuing drive to maintain its competitive edge at the global level informs an ensemble of state initiatives that range from becoming a major center of research and development in high technology, becoming a cosmopolitan global city that can attract and mobilize human talent from around the globe, and, most important, fostering Singapore-based multinationals that can take their turn playing the outsourcing game and taking advantage of lower labor costs elsewhere. These state strategies were also accompanied by a set of biopolitical technologies at the level of social reproduction aimed at cultivating human capital.

On the other hand, low growth countries that had unsuccessfully adopted the path of export-oriented industrialization under the neoliberal policies of the World Bank and IMF and had to rely on the export of commodities, were economically crippled by low commodity prices, high balance of payment deficits, large foreign debt, and massive unemployment. Unlike high-growth countries that had graduated to the project of enhancing human capital, impoverished countries resorted to the active exportation of workers overseas to manage unemployment and balance-of-payment deficits. Hence a regional division of labor was created within Southeast Asia, a sharp testament to the brutally competitive character of capitalist development. The success or failure of each case of development through economic globalization appears disconnected because it is rooted in historical, economic, sociological, and political factors specific to each country. However, as far as labor power was concerned, the structural change in the logic of capital accumulation joined various countries in the region as moments within the same dynamic. For, as countries such as Singapore and Malaysia undergo a transformation in their workforce as a result of rapid industrialization, they experience a shortage of low-skilled manual labor. Because it is economically sounder for them to turn elsewhere for cheap sources of lower-end industrial and domestic labor, they begin to import migrant labor from their less developed neighbors to perform what are sometimes called 3D jobs, "dirty, dangerous and demanding." On the other hand, countries such as the Philippines, Indonesia, and Sri Lanka actively export workers overseas because of the inability of their economies to absorb the labor of their citizens. Hence, for each case of successful development through state-sponsored globalization, there seems to be another case of state-driven exportation of labor, as if this interconnection is an outcome dictated by an unseen law of the global economy. The traffic in migrant labor is, of course, not necessary to development in any absolute sense. But it was encouraged

by many states as a means of development and contributed to the economies within its circuits.

What is striking here is the systematic link between labor emigration and
development and its aggressive institutionalization through national state
policy with the sanction of international bodies. The World Bank's *World
Development Report 1991* observed that labor migration could aid in curbing
unemployment and reducing the worldwide disparity in income. Migrants
returning from more advanced countries also contributed to the diffusion
of technology.[32] The 1995 report, entitled *Workers in an Integrating World*,
described migration as "an important economic and social safety valve" that
allowed "labor to relocate to areas where it was more scarce" and stressed
the efficiency gains it created, particularly in the form of higher wages for
migrant workers, foreign exchange remittances to sending countries, the
possible stimulation of capital investment, and lower production costs in
receiving countries.[33] Exportation of labor, then, is also a form of biopower,
but it is the biopower of economically weak nation-states. These observations were merely a formal tabulation of assumptions already at play since
the 1970s, when less developed countries began exporting labor in response
to the massive increase in demand by the oil-rich Middle East. The minis-
tries of labor or manpower of these countries set up administrative bodies,
for example, the Philippine Overseas Employment Administration (POEA)
or the Sri Lanka Bureau of Foreign Employment (SLBFE), to promote and
regulate labor migration. The Marcos regime regarded the export of labor
as a matter of "national interest" and embarked on its aggressive labor export policy citing the alleviation of chronic unemployment and the relief of
the balance-of-payments deficit as the two key economic benefits. The Philippines is one of the world's largest labor exporters, second only to Mexico.
In 1997 the number of overseas contract workers (OCWs) from the Philippines was estimated at 6.1 million.[34] By December 2001 the estimated figure
of OCWs had risen to 7.4 million, representing close to 10 percent of the
population and 21 percent of the total labor force.[35] Their contribution to
the Philippine economy is indispensable. Remittances by OCWs totaled $7.4
billion in 2003 and amounted to slightly over 8 percent of the gross national
product and 19 percent of the overall export of goods and services.[36] Thus
what was initially a temporary measure to increase foreign exchange inflow
and reduce unemployment was now cynically represented by the Philippine
state as a long-term means for economic growth and national development.

What particularly interests us is that this accelerated transnational traffic in labor intensifies the feminization of transnational labor migration.
This in turn engenders an international division of reproductive labor as the

site where the techniques of biopower subtending the development policies of different nation-states intersect, converge, and clash around the figure of the foreign domestic worker (FDW). The FDW, I want to suggest, can be considered an emblematic bearer of the vicissitudes of postcolonial development in flexible global capitalism.

"The feminization of labor" generally refers to the entry of women into lowly paid work in multinational manufacturing production and the service sector in response to family hardship. Such labor ensures the international competitiveness of a country as a destination for foreign capital investment in low-value added manufacture. More specifically, the feminization of transnational labor migration refers to the growing migration of Asian women from the late 1970s onward in response to the increased international demand for workers to fill low-status feminized occupations—domestic helpers, helpers in restaurants and hotels, and entertainers, etc. This increased demand is generated by another gender dynamic within high-growth economies: the entry of middle-class women with sufficient training into white-collar employment at the same time that surplus young female labor that had been the traditional source of paid domestic work for middle-class households had been completely absorbed into industry and other nondomestic services. I will elaborate on this dynamic by focusing on Singapore because it is the most "developed" among Southeast Asian countries.

To augment the professional and skilled worker sector, the Singapore government encouraged educated middle-class women to join the workforce even as it sought to reverse their declining birth and marriage rates. Moreover, women in developed economies shoulder a double burden. They are expected to contribute to national economic growth but also to maintain the roles of wife and mother with the attendant responsibilities of household management ascribed by masculinist society.[37] It was therefore necessary to make accessible a pool of live-in foreign domestic helpers who could take care of household chores and child-care needs. In other words, the strategy of cultivating human capital by increasing the participation of highly educated women in professional occupations required the importation of low-skilled migrant workers. Hence what partly sustains postindustrial hyperdevelopment in Singapore as a necessary condition is the production of two different but constitutively interdependent subjects: the liberal middle-class professional woman and the docile FDW. The latter's work makes the former's employment possible. Singaporean women can only join the workforce if the burden of reproductive labor is transferred elsewhere. In order to attach educated middle-class women to the professions and high-value service industries, migrant women have to be tethered to the Singaporean home qua machine for the reproduction of society and human capital so that the forces of their bodies can be extracted as reproductive labor. This pervasive double tethering has developed into a dependency. Many middle-class working women in Singapore regard foreign maids as a necessity rather than a luxury—so much so that a 1996 academic study suggested that the dependency on foreign maids was here to stay, that "the maid culture has become a way of life in Singapore."[38] Thus if the sex/gender system, in Gayle Rubin's words, "determines that a 'wife' is among the necessities of a worker," then in the postindustrial hyperdevelopment of Singapore a foreign maid is widely viewed as one of the necessities of a wife so that she can work for the better of the country's economy.[39] In a sense these women migrant workers are made to shoulder the burden of development (or lack thereof) of their own nation-states and that of their host countries. Labor-receiving states actively displace the costs and burden of social reproduction to migrant women from poorer countries. This means that economic success within the NIDL generates and is sustained by a new international division of reproductive labor where the households of professional women in economically developed Southeast Asian countries are cared for by temporary migrant women from low-growth countries in the region.

THE BIOPOLITICS OF FOREIGN DOMESTIC WORKERS

I do not know whether such FDWs are subalterns. Certainly, some of them, especially those from Indonesia and Sri Lanka, come from impoverished rural areas. In subsequent work that addresses the new subaltern woman of contemporary globalization, Spivak emphatically points to her repeated silencing and exclusion by the various forces of global capitalism. On the one hand, the postcolonial national elite continues to construct "the people" as an alibi to justify development. On the other hand, transnational bodies, ranging from the United Nations to the international civil society of NGOs concerned with human rights, and the decimation of local cultures also construct the human being as the bearer of human rights as a form of legitimation of current global hegemony. Indeed, Spivak suggests that even transnational feminist NGOs concerned with women's rights are part of the instrumentalization of women in order to represent global unity as an alibi for the financialization of the globe. "What is left out is the poorest women of the South as self-conscious critical agents, who might be able to speak through those very nongovernmental organizations of the South that are not favoured by these object-constitution policies."[40] Although these more radical NGO workers are not themselves subaltern women, this exclusion can be regarded as a "stand in for the subaltern's inability to speak . . . by virtue of the fact that the subaltern's inability to speak is predicated upon an attempt to speak, to which no appropriate response is offered."[41]

It should be clear that Spivak extends the central argument from "Can the Subaltern Speak?" which is based on the colonial paradigm of power, to understand the relations between various transnational and postcolonial national agents and subalterns. Today, she writes, the "broad politics" of global development is "the silencing of resistance and of the subaltern as the rhetoric of their protest is constantly appropriated."[42] Consequently, subalternity as a structural space of difference that is obscured from public view by repression and representational mechanisms of object-constitution constitutes a residual space of resistance to the postcolonial national and global capitalist dominant. Spivak suggests that in the face of these different regimes of object-constitution—part of "the relay from imperialism to Development"—"the continuity of subaltern insurgency" is "a permanent parabasis," "a constant interruption for the full *telos* of Reason and capitalism."[43] In her view, responsible action towards the subaltern should first of all involve responding to the subaltern's speech (allowing the subaltern to "speak") as a potential front of resistance against the financialization of the globe so that its interruptive force can be intensified. This requires the revival of a responsibility-based ethics that will learn from and reconstellate "pre-capitalist" forms of thought with the abstract structures of democratic rights. Finally, through rural literacy and grassroots education programs, the subaltern can be educated to play a role in representative decision making.[44]

While Spivak's ethical vision is certainly inspiring, I want to suggest that, in global capitalism, power generally works by productive incorporation, rather than exclusion and repression through force or ideology, even if the forms of incorporation are coercive. Since coercion now occurs at the level of production of the material existence and corporeal needs of the oppressed, Spivak's understanding of the subaltern as a residual space of resistance that is excluded through dominant regimes of representation and, more generally, her understanding of ideological representation as a primary modality of power would be put into question. At the end of this chapter, I will offer some thoughts about resistance that resonate with Spivak.

The FDW represents a case of such coercive incorporation. Once again, I do not know if these FDWs are subalterns. Certainly, some of them, especially those from Indonesia and Sri Lanka, come from impoverished rural areas. But, as they accumulate funds to pay for the airfare, employment permit, other processing fees, and the extortive fees of labor recruiters, they are on their way to being incorporated into the IDL. They are certainly perceived by the family members and friends whom they are leaving behind as "more fortunate" because they will be in an economically stronger position in a few years. They are also on their way to being trained as consumers and will in turn train those they have left behind as consumers. Their foreign exchange remittances are largely used for the consumption of foreign luxury items such as washing machines and flat screen televisions.

How then can we characterize the production of this will to work abroad? Is this a form of subject-formation through class ideology or a form of subjectification through biopower? It can be argued that what drives the temporary emigration of FDWs is not only their ideological constitution as good wives, daughters, mothers, or sisters, although this is an important factor, but, more crucially, the crafting of their interests as subjects of needs by biopower, just as the ground for the importation of foreign workers is prepared by the crafting of their employers by similar governmental technologies. Consequently, the consolidation of the NIDL occurs not by obscuring the voice of the oppressed through ideology (as Spivak suggests in relation to the subaltern woman) but by incorporating their very needs in the fabric of global capitalism. Whatever the role of ideology in making the wills of these women migrants, they also go with the firm desire to improve their lives because this is how their needs and interests have been shaped by governmental technologies.

The problem, however, is that the cultivation of these two types of worker-subjects in this particular circuit of global capitalism by both labor-receiving and labor-sending countries has patently inhuman consequences. The situation at hand represents an important modification of Foucault's account of biopower. Biopower enables the maximization of the state's resources by organizing the population into a *bios*, a system of means and ends in which the contribution of each member is reciprocated with benefits and rewards that are not only monetary. However, when Foucault formulated the concept to explain the rise of industrial capitalism in Europe, he did not envisage that postindustrial hyperdevelopment outside the North Atlantic would require the mass deployment of human bodies that are engaged in *reproductive* labor and, more importantly, that the labor power in question would be a revolving pool of temporary labor consisting of *foreign* bodies that are emphatically barred from becoming part of the permanent population. Unlike expatriate professionals in high-value sectors such as finance and high tech whom the Singaporean state wishes to attract and retain as permanent settlers, FDWs are not recognized as "foreign talent," even though they are crucial to the sustaining of social and civil life. They are merely "foreign workers," to be used and discarded rather than integrated into the social fabric of the city-state. Such bodies do not need to be cultivated and augmented in the same way as those belonging to the permanent labor force. Their absorption into the permanent workforce is to be vigorously prohibited because it is not of any value to the receiving country. When exhausted, their forces can always be replenished through substitution by other temporary migrants.

This is, therefore, a form of labor whose constitution involves discipline and regulation, but without either increasing/enhancing their bodily forces through concerted training or any subjectification. FDWs, who can never hope to become citizens of Singapore and are not part of its *bios*, are constituted as quasi subjects to be utilized as means. Their only subjective incentive to be attached to the Singaporean economic machine is financial remuneration. Excluded from the system of means and ends that the state wishes to enhance through the integration of professional and educated migrant workers, FDWs are viewed in terms of sheer technical utility—as mere means to the ends of others, without any ends of their own that need to be taken into account in the state's calculations. Thus what we have is a form of governmental regulation without the welfare of the *bios*. Instead of being the objects of *productive* regulatory techniques, FDWs need to be policed to mitigate what the state euphemistically refers to as "social costs": the negative consequences that their presence inflicts on Singaporean society, problems ranging from congestion of public space to strained bilateral relations with labor-exporting countries over their abuse by the local population.

This biopolitical formation is the structural basis of the abuse of FDWs, two representative instances of which I will reproduce.

> "She Tortured Maid with Clothes Peg." Faridah Abdul Fatah was angry with her maid for waking up late. So she decided to teach Miss Sugiarti Sugino, 22, a lesson that the young woman would not forget in a hurry. She clipped eight clothes pegs to the maid's ears and then yanked them off one by one. She wanted to humiliate her. But that was not all that she did . . . [45]

> "Abused Maid Speaks: My Seven Months of Horror." "She told me that since I had cut the mooncake wrongly, she could not eat the mooncake and she had better eat my breast." She was cut, burned, beaten and bitten. Teenage maid suffered employer's abuse until her badly injured nipple fell out. Indonesian maid Kusmirah Mujadi knew that life with Jennicia Chow Yen Ping was going to be tough when she suffered her first beating just three days into the job. But the 19-year-old never expected to be running away seven months later with a bloody trail on her T-shirt marking

where Chow had bitten her excruciatingly hard on the nipple the night before. Miss Kusmirah also left the Woodlands Circle flat on the pre-dawn morning with angry keloid scars on her arms and a host of other permanent reminders of the cuts, burns and beatings meted out by Chow during the seven unhappy months spent in her employment.[46]

Such abuse is mainly perpetrated by female employers. What is important here are the concrete structural conditions that are inherently conducive to the widespread dehumanization of FDWs and not the personal cruelty or pathology of individual employers. The latter is merely a product-effect or extreme symptom of the former. The rationality at work in these structural conditions stretches from state administrative agencies to employment agencies and individual employers. It regards migrant workers as tools or means in the employer's quest for economic advancement and the larger project of national development.

This rationality is best indicated by the title of a popular book published in 1993 in the genre of entertaining instruction entitled, *"To Have and to Hold: How to Have a Maid and Keep Her.*[47] Without any irony about violating Kant's categorical imperative to treat every human being as an end in itself, the author announces in the preface that "this book looks at the foreign maid issue from the perspectives of viewing it lightly to seriously thinking how to maximise the use of the maid in the house" (vi). The proliferation of such how-to guides on "managing" a maid extends the rhetoric and tactics of managerial administration into the household. It indicates a certain commercialization of the home, the introduction of economic imperatives of utility and labor efficiency into its functioning. Employers are taught to reasonably expect "that all the work that needs to be done is done. In order to avoid having a situation where you feel cheated that your maid hasn't put in a day's work, here's what you can do. . . . Experience and commonsense will tell you that it is better to over-supervise or over-monitor (no matter how much a workaholic she is) than to feel short-changed later."[48] The foreign maid is thus the wife of the wife. But she is also an employee to be managed in order to increase her efficiency, just as the woman professional's efficiency in her workplace has to be increased. Most of this regulation is delegated by the state to employers, primarily through the imposition of a security bond. The bond is a $5,000 amount employers are required to pay to the state. An FDW is granted a work permit subject to various repressive conditions such as the prohibition of marriage to a Singapore citizen or permanent resident during her stay, the prohibition of pregnancy, submission to medical examinations for pregnancy and sexually transmitted diseases once every six months. Since the FDW will be repatriated and the bond forfeited if any of these conditions are violated, the bond works as an instrument for ensuring that the behavior and movement of FDWs is strictly policed and restricted by their employers during the term of their employment. It effectively transfers the monitoring of workers to the site of the household, where this monitoring can be performed most effectively and zealously by employers to prevent the possibility of any "illegitimate" activities even before FDWs enter into public space.

FDWs are therefore placed in the debased position of nonpersonhood from the start. Employers who want to maximize their economic usefulness and fear losing the bond engage in constant surveillance of maids, their working and eating habits, their social activities, and their use of the phone. Children are often the chief watchers. They are encouraged by their parents to tell tales about their maids, even rewarded for doing so. As a caregiver who may not command the respect of her wards, the FDW's work is not reciprocated by the emotional rewards and recognition that constitute the subjectivating and human-redemptive dimension of mothering. The advancement and development of the professional woman human being thus involves a certain inhumanity: bringing into the home a stranger who is dehumanized because she inherits the feminized chores of the wife and the mother without any of its human-redemptive aspects.

HUMAN FREEDOM IN A FIELD OF INSTRUMENTALITY

The technologies that craft the liberal middle-class professional woman and the docile FDW clearly have inhumane effects. They micrologically replicate the unevenness of the global capitalist system within the intimate sphere of the bourgeois conjugal family, a site that Habermas describes as the hallowed space for the cultivation of the universal ideals of humanity, which has here become the quotidian site of potential and actual violence.[49] This violent exploitation extends into civil society since the traffic in foreign domestic labor, which is an integral part of social life, factored into socioeconomic planning, is now a huge and profitable business with its own professional associations. The inhumanity of global capital thus marks from within and undermines the Singaporean state's ambitions to generate a cosmopolitan, civilized, and humane society through hyperdevelopment.

But what is most troubling about the instrumentalization of FDWs is its implications for international feminist solidarity. I have already noted how the consolidation of middle-class liberal feminism in Singapore is premised on the exploitation of FDWs. What does this mean for international feminist solidarity? Can the humanity of the FDW within postcolonial Asia be asserted through humanizing forces based on transnational feminist solidarity such as the Platform for Action of the Fourth World Conference on Women, Beijing 1995? Unfortunately not. The platform presupposes and relies on the same biopolitical technologies that have led to the dehumanization of FDWs. The scenario taking place in Singapore—the entry of women into white-collar work—is precisely the upward mobility narrative of woman in the developed or hyperdeveloping nation that the platform celebrates. The platform incorporates some of the language of the Covenant on Economic, Social and Cultural Rights and includes provisions regarding the right to work, right to earn a living, right to protection, and right to fair treatment in a workplace. It is also explicitly concerned with the elimination of violence against women migrants and the right to sustainable development. However, like other progressive projects of transnational sorority, the platform's basic vision is to rectify inequality vis-à-vis *men* and regards women's equality and right to development as a valuable human resource and target of biopolitical cultivation within the framework of the felicitous development and advancement of the *nation-state*.[50] The platform necessarily presupposes but disavows the competitive nature of development. In place of an acknowledgment of the harsh realities of global exploitation, it gestures toward a benign internationalism forged out of the enlightened, benevolent, and, hopefully, soon-to-be feminized mutual self-interest of nation-states, each striving to maximize its own well-being without encroaching on other nation-states in post–cold war globality.[51]

It has been suggested that the platform promotes "a slightly expanded identity for women that mandates the embracing of free market ideology in addition to maternity."[52] In uneven development, it is the migrant domestic worker who very obviously sustains the advancement and entrepreneurial spirit of her more privileged fellow Southeast-Asian sister. As par. 118 indicates, the platform can only understand violence against women as something perpetrated by men. It cannot explain the fact that, in Singapore, most of the abused FDWs are oppressed by women employers. The same fracture of the collectivity "women" compromises transnational sisterhood. Even though par. 154 recognizes the contribution of women migrant workers, global sorority was not strong enough to secure more support for the Philippines' call for the ratification of the 1990 convention on migrant workers' rights. Of the 132 countries participating in the Beijing conference, only five countries (Bangladesh, India, Pakistan, Sri Lanka, and Thailand) responded positively, and they were all labor-exporting countries. As Carmela Torres notes, "despite the liberalized trade among countries and moves to liberalize trade in services and movement of personnel, many of the richer countries which are expected to host migrant workers and their families tend to be protectionist in their attitude towards migrant workers."[53]

This competitiveness indicates that postcolonial economic development necessarily occurs within what I will call a mobile field of instrumentality. At the global level, the interests and ends of states, their administrative agencies, and the actions of employers and individual workers in the processes of economic development and labor migration constitute and are in turn conditioned by the larger structural mechanisms of capitalist accumulation. While these actors are free consensual agents who make conscious choices, they are placed in the position to make choices because they inhabit a dynamic field of imperatives and strategies that have as their ultimate end the articulation of a hierarchical division of economic development and labor. In the first place, export-oriented industrialization is premised on a hierarchy of capital, skills, technology, and labor. Moreover, while it is possible for a country to upgrade itself and ascend the IDL in a given sector, its success limits the opportunities for similar upgrading by other countries unless it upgrades further and vacates its slot in the hierarchy. Each state desires to ascend the hierarchy, and the success or failure of its policies determines the slot it will take up. Hence the pervasive economic vocabulary about the importance of "carving a niche." A country's position will shape its society, and this will in turn condition the actions of individual citizens such as a female worker's decision to seek employment overseas as a FDW. The crucial point here is that such imperatives and strategies are part of a global biopolitical field that fabricates the interests and needs of the individuals exploited by global capitalism, integrating them by weaving them into the very fabric of the system. However important ideology critique and the production of counterhegemonic ideologies that contest official visions of national development may be, they cannot match the global reach or the profound pervasiveness and depth of these biopolitical technologies as they subjectify the masses into regulatable individuals and governable populations who can be exploited and oppressed. *Contra* Spivak, the frightening thought here is that instead of being a way to resist global capitalism, training into consumerism in the postcolonial peripheries is part of the very problem. Since the rise of consumerism in a given postcolonial country depends on its economic development and ascension in the hierarchy of the NIDL, training into consumerism makes the superexploited more and more mired within the field of instrumentality that sustains global capitalism instead of enabling them to break with the system of exploitation through anticapitalist solidarity.

What then are possible sites of resistance in this cartography of power of global capitalism that I have sketched with the aid of Foucault's ideas about biopower? To return to the specific case at hand, how can the FDW be humanized? How can her humanity be reaffirmed in global capitalism? As is well known, the Universal Declaration of Human Rights is underwritten by a Kantian moral prohibition of the instrumentalization or technologization of human relations, the regarding of another human being as a tool or instrument to be used to pursue another end. As Kant puts it, "now I say that the human being and in general every rational being *exists* as an end in itself [*Zweck an sich selbst*], *not merely as a means* to be used by this or that will at its discretion; instead he must in all his actions, whether directed to himself or also to other rational beings, always be regarded *at the same time as an end*."[54] If another human being is treated as a means, if her ontological status as an end in itself is disregarded, human freedom is violated because our ontological constitution as ends in themselves is that which gives us the capacity for freedom, our inherent dignity, and other related traits we associate with human freedom. The fragility of this moral prohibition is clearly seen in the fact that it is impossible to avoid instrumentality in human relations altogether. In pragmatic action, which makes up the bulk of human relations, human beings are routinely treated as useful means. The purpose of human rights is the establishment of a juridical or quasi-juridical framework, backed up by sanctions, for the circumscription and regulation of human relations so that people can act according to their self-interests and freedom of choice *as long as* their actions do not deprive others of the same freedom that they ought to have because of their humanity. Simply put, human rights instruments aim to give a total rational form or human visage to pragmatic interaction. In a word, they attempt to *humanize* the field of instrumentality.

However, things become considerably more complicated if we remember that the biopolitical technologies sustaining the development and labor migration policies in Southeast Asia aim at nothing less than the cultivation of the full humanity of their citizens via national growth. Indeed, one of the justifications for exporting labor is a form of individual and national pedagogy. It is suggested that migrants will undergo a form of *Bildung* overseas. They will learn new skills, gain work experience, and return to impart this training, thereby enhancing the technological and knowledge resources of the nation and facilitating its development. Therefore, any attempt to reaffirm the humanity of these FDWs necessarily relies on the same technologies. I will end by discussing one attempt to humanize the FDW from emergent feminist civil society elements within Singapore, using this to draw some provisional theoretical conclusions about the field of instrumentality.

Feminist Singaporean NGOs have expressed concern about the dehumanization of FDWs, especially in the wake of the Flor Contemplacion affair.[55] The Association of Women for Action and Research (AWARE), the most visible and successful of these groups, has tried to extend its ongoing efforts at the elimination of violence and discrimination against women to include the abuse of FDWs. Some of its members have stressed that such abuse imparts the wrong social and ethical values to children and undermines Singapore's attempt to be "a civil, humanistic society." They are also alert to the fact that the abuse of FDWs by their female employers is a setback to the feminist cause because it contradicts the principles of egalitarianism and the empowerment of women that are fundamental to feminism.[56] These feminists situate the problem of domestic abuse within the broader hierarchical social structures, value systems, and attitudes in Singaporean culture that breed authoritarian elitism and callous treatment of the economically less fortunate in all levels of Singaporean life. They are interested in changing public consciousness and state practice through conscientious education/*Bildung* so that there will be a structural shift towards better treatment of FDWs.

In January 2003, members of AWARE and other societal elements joined forces with various church groups, and individuals interested in improving the conditions of FDWs in a broad alliance that presents itself in civil society terms. This alliance, which calls itself TWC2, is modeled after the Working Committee of Civil Society (TWC), an alliance that attempted to create a critical civil society by identifying present and future roles for societal activities. TWC2 draws on this momentum and focuses it on improving the welfare of FDWs, hoping that this issue will also serve to further consolidate and galvanize civil society. TWC2's concrete goal is for foreign workers to be regarded as people who have come to Singapore to earn a living and who should therefore be given all the benefits available to Singaporean workers and high-end foreign talent, such as expatriate professionals in the finance and high tech sector.[57] To achieve this goal, TWC2 has organized a whole range of campaigns to increase public awareness of the plight of FDWs. It has also initiated discussion with relevant state authorities about the necessity of statutory reforms that can become a legal basis for the protection of FDWs' rights.

These activities are animated by the same neo-Kantian theoretical principles that sharply oppose humanity to profit, money or capital. TWC2's governing theme, "Dignity Overdue: Respecting the Rights of Maids," suggests that household work is labor, the universal activity by which human beings achieve self-sustenance. It should not be subjected to "inhuman or degrading treatment" and should be accorded the respect due to other forms of labor because it possesses the dignity appropriate to all human endeavor. Two additional reasons are given for this specific focus on the welfare of domestic workers. First, their contributions "to the economic and social well-being of Singapore must be recognized and valued."[58] Second, in the larger campaign to eliminate violence against women, special attention must be given to the FDW because "she is the most vulnerable woman in our homes. She is a guest worker, here at our invitation, to support our families and earn an honest living for their own families."[59] By urging the public and the state to confer upon FDWs a sense of belonging that has so far been denied to them, TWC2 also attempts to subjectify FDWs through social recognition.

TWC2 clearly understands its efforts at humanizing FDWs and the Singapore nation-state in terms of an intensification of the participation of civil society forces in important socio-political issues. It is implied that the development of civil society as a space of freedom or autonomy from the state is a teleological good that comes with the global spread of modernity because strong civil society structures facilitate the achievement of humanity. It should be noted that these efforts are an expression of *national* shame by citizens who care about the image of their country and want their nation to be a responsible people. Thus, TWC2's members have stressed in the national press that "the current state of the foreign domestic worker in Singapore is a source of national embarrassment," and that "it is our national obligation to safeguard the welfare of foreign domestic workers."[60] Similarly, Constance Singam notes that "the abuses committed by some, along with the lack of policies and legislation to protect the rights of maids, do not speak well of our society and government.... The abuse of maids also affects Singapore's relationships with its ASEAN partners. It will reinforce the perception of Singaporean arrogance towards those who are different."[61]

On closer examination, however, this understanding of (national) civil society as a space of autonomy from state imperatives and an indispensable mechanism in the achievement of human freedom becomes questionable. For TWC2's claim to represent the universal interests of humanity, here exemplified by the domestic worker's humanity, is troubled by a curious tension between its various arguments. Unlike the universalistic argument from the inherent dignity of all labor qua human activity, TWC2's other two arguments—the vulnerability of maids and their contributions to the Singapore economy—are utilitarian arguments based on the particularistic interests and situation of employers in general because they have decided to import guest-workers and have benefited from their labor. This appeal to various forms of self-interest to justify better treatment of FDWs is radically at odds with the idea of the sacrosanct dignity and inherent freedom of all human labor, labor's transcendent status that elevates it above all particularistic interests, because it involves calculations about the benefits and consequences of domestic work. It is suggested that FDWs should be treated with greater consideration because they have been placed in a vulnerable position when Singaporeans choose to import them here. They should be treated better because it is a fitting return for what they have contributed to the national economy. And they should be treated better because otherwise, Singapore's international image will be tarnished and this will affect foreign business and trade relations. In all these calculations of appropriate ethical conduct, the FDW remains imbricated in a chain of technical or means-ends relationships. She remains an instrument or means in a field of generalized instrumentality.

What we see in these attempts to rehumanize the FDW is a diffusion of the same biopolitical technologies that produce the middle-class professional woman subject beyond the domain of state institutions. They extend biopolitical tactics to all levels of social life and activity. Only now, a small degree of the humanity previously accorded only to the middle-class employer as a member of the Singaporean *bios* is extended to the FDW to mitigate the inhumane effects of these technologies. The same technologies that dehumanize the FDW are now partially reversed to reaffirm her humanity. The progressive humane solutions proposed by civil society elements are thus inevitably circumscribed because they rely on the same corporatist-management techniques and administrative strategies for controlling maids. Such technologies are the fundamental rationality and underlying support of civil society. Consequently, there are fundamental points of connection and convergence between governmentality and the liberal institutions of civil society. The Singaporean state has increasingly appropriated TWC2's humanizing vocabulary for purely pragmatic reasons, for example, the replacement of the term, "maid," by the more respectable "domestic worker."

It would be comforting to view this shift as the gradual enlightenment of the state by civil society that will lead to genuine transformation. Hence, progressive Singaporean intelligentsia have repeatedly distinguished between progressive and conservative models of civil society, the former being people-oriented and motivated by a sense of humanity, whereas the latter is conducive to the pragmatic imperatives of a capitalist market economy. What this neat opposition glosses over is the fact that humanity itself is a form of capital. The state requires the participation of civil society because its successful functioning is based on human capital and civil society is precisely the domain for the articulation/formation of the people's interests through governmental technologies. What sustains state and civil society alike as their common substrate is precisely the techniques or means-ends relations that we have already detected in TWC2's utilitarian arguments. This field of instrumentality joins civil society to the state. It enables civil society interests to penetrate the state. But by the same token, it also allows the state to capture civil society initiatives for its own ends in the same way that the Singapore state has always copied strategies from outside to serve the ends of its economic development.

This confirms Foucault's counterintuitive argument that civil society, which we often celebrate as a space of autonomy from the state, is a product-effect of governmentality. This would make liberalism a modulation within governmentality, a form of government that seeks to minimize government in the name of society.[62] What we see in the Singaporean case is precisely a complex combination of two different technologies of government. The Singaporean state makes strategic nods to the liberal rhetoric of the free market. But this liberal rhetoric is also a form of social control that gives the state a rapacious capacity to absorb external criticism and to incorporate and rechannel "oppositional" humane ideas to further the pursuit of economic self-interest. In other words, because civil society is the crucible for the articulation of human interests, its initiatives are inherently undecidable and vulnerable to co-optation by the state. All the humanizing endeavors of civil society can have dehumanizing consequences. Indeed, many of the civil society arguments on behalf of FDWs have hierarchical implications from the start. FDWs, who can never become part of the Singapore *bios*, are not equal participants that belong to its civil society. At best, they can only be objects of benevolence, the mere recipients of goodwill from civil society because the purpose of their existence in Singapore is to make life easier for its citizens. The most that can be done is to safeguard their welfare during their stay and to upgrade their skills so that they can have better job opportunities when they return to their countries of origin.

Second, the justification for eliminating the employment of FDWs betrays the pride that civil society elements take in Singapore's advanced economic status and its corollary, an implied disdain for its less advanced neighbors. Since the material condition of civilizational superiority is economic competitiveness, the push to establish advanced domestic labor relations easily modulates into the position that Singaporeans must treat FDWs well so that they can continue to enjoy their superior economic status and standard of living. Thus one also finds arguments that justify decent treatment by appealing to economic interests: it is economically sound to be good to FDWs because they will repay the kindness of employers by working harder, and their continued presence will also make Singapore more attractive to high-value expatriate workers. One writer supported a gratuity scheme that would provide maids with a lump sum payment at the end of their contract because

> looking forward to a gratuity could also result in a better work attitude. . . . The scheme could, in addition, buy greater goodwill from neighbours such as the Philippines and Indonesia, where a significant part of their national earnings come from the remittances of their citizens, including maids, working abroad. Without our maids, Singapore would be less attractive to the families of foreign talent. So, it is in our own interest that we take better care of our maids and get them to continue coming here to work. . . . We have to show our neighbours we care for their citizens and not regard them as mere serfs.[63]

In this well-meaning latter-day version of the transformation of serfs into consensual wage labor, FDWs are always means or tools. They "help Singaporeans enjoy a better quality of life. They do things which most Singaporeans would squirm at or now regard with utter contempt, from looking after the elderly and the infirm to washing cars and windows."[64]

Contrary to TWC2's claims, the welfare of the FDW can never transcend the circuit of money and commodification. The brutal fact is that she is brought to Singapore because her employer's time and effort is regarded as more valuable and important than hers such that she is paid to perform tasks her employer does not wish to undertake. What is to be done to give full due to the FDW's human dignity? The only solution is for employers to desist from hiring FDWs. But the complete elimination of FDWs will lead to much higher costs in reproductive labor, a less comfortable style of life, and the dampening of economic productivity. The true crisis comes in recognizing that, regardless of the personal goodwill of the individual Singaporean feminist, one *cannot not* be imbricated within the exploitative hierarchical structure of the international division of labor and the division of reproductive labor that sustains it because they are crucial to Singapore's economic success. Given that the liberation of middle-class women in competitive postcolonial development is necessarily contaminated, the feminist effort to provide relief and protection to FDWs must be supplemented by the persistent questioning of the problematic character of the very form of development that has benefited feminism. Otherwise, all such efforts degenerate into the complacent appeased conscience of the liberal subject who can congratulate herself on being a decent employer.

From a theoretical angle, this is nothing other than the sobering admission that no effort to affirm and protect the human rights of FDWs can elevate the humanity of FDWs beyond instrumental relations. What occurs is merely the displacement of instrumentality from one site and level to another, a redistribution of the abusive consequences of treating persons as means to the ends of others so that the abuse does not become overly concentrated in a given location and cause the entire system to break down. There is no solution to the instrumentalization of human relations since this is rooted in the very nature of economic development within global capitalism. One needs to distinguish between at least three types of instrumental relations in this scenario: the means-ends relations of employers and foreign workers within the household; the more general relations of global exploitation of cheap labor within the hierarchy of the international division of labor; and the constitution, deployment, and regulation of human capital by labor-sending and labor-receiving states and other actors through techniques of biopower. The means-ends relations within the household sustain and reproduce the competitive and uneven nature of national economic development. What mediates between these two types of instrumentality as their obscured template and connecting substrate are biopolitical techniques. The unevenness of the first two types of instrumentality is merely the inequality of the technical relation projected within the household and writ even larger in a global frame.

Given the necessity and unavoidability of instrumental relations in human life, how can we respond to the moral imperative to treat human beings as ends in themselves? Faced with totalitarian bureaucratic domination and the late capitalist commodification of the cultural sphere, the Frankfurt School tried to reconcile these antithetical principles by making a distinction between instrumental and critical reason. Instrumental reason is human only insofar as artifice/*techne* requires intelligence. It is in fact inhuman because, in itself, it cannot lead to, and, indeed, is even inimical to, the achievement of what is proper to humanity: moral freedom. In contradistinction, the cultivational processes of critical reason are a special form of *techne* directed at our mental capacities. It is a self-instrumentalization that lifts us beyond the realm of mere instrumentality through the inculcation of universal values that facilitate the practice of moral freedom. But this mesmerizing motif of human transcendence loses its pertinence in the field of instrumentality I have analyzed here. The exploitation and abuse of FDWs stems from the instrumental character of their relations with states, employers, and other parties. Yet one cannot transcend this field of instrumentality because humanity itself is produced by technologies of biopower. The processes that generate the power of transcendence proper to humanity—self-cultivation, *Bildung*, and even critical reason—are part of the subjectifying or humanizing aspect of biopower. This is why the humanizing moment is necessarily circumscribed. The subjectifying process cannot be applied globally or uniformly to every person. Biopower cannot produce humanity in every person at one and the same time because the technical relation is based on inequality and the hierarchical division of means and ends. At any given point, there can only be competing attempts to generate humanity in a specific location and at a specific level within the field of technical relations. Yet, paradoxically, it is also from this field of instrumentality that a certain responsibility to the humanity of FDWs comes into presence as a result of a complex and sensitive series of negotiations between the mobile, conflicting interests of different forces.

The human rights of the female migrant worker are thus generated from mobile and shifting scales of solidarity. They are the product-effects of interminable political negotiations or, as Foucault would say, tactics. These rights are only a rationalization or ideational codification, a provisional terminal point of different force relations that are always shifting. Once they become institutionalized, they will influence or invest this field of relations as concrete ideals to be held up by civil society forces pressing against and making demands on labor-exporting and labor-importing states for legislative change. But these ideals cannot govern the mutations of this field from a transcendent position. We are speaking of an entirely provisional and contingent emergence of universal human norms from an instrumental force field. What is at work here is a form of technological production that cannot be regulated and transcended because it is the condition of possibility of humanity. It forms the concrete human being and all its capacities at the most material level. This constitutive imbrication of human rights in instrumentality does not inevitably lead to futility. Since we have never known a human condition that can fully control instrumentality, instead of seeing *technē* as the corruption of an ideal humanity, we should ask: how do the technologies sustaining global capital induce effects of humanity and how are these effects contaminated?

I have argued that it is important to be spectralized by the injunction of "Can the Subaltern Speak?" to attend to the international division of labor. In my view, however, such attention should lead us to question the understanding of subalternity as a structural space of difference that is always excluded by hegemonic regimes of representation as power precisely because power now functions through productive incorporation. The FDW is one example of productive incorporation. But even tribal minorities in the most remote villages in Yunnan, China are "willingly" incorporated by global capitalism through the global tourist industry and the herbal medicine export business. How do we know that this is not what "they really want"? I have suggested that any assertion of the human rights of FDWs must be thought as something that happens within a generalized field of instrumentality instead of the transcendence of instrumentality. I echo here Spivak's astute diagnoses of Northern "universalist" feminism and find solidarity with her claim that the relationship between capitalism and socialism is a homeopathic relation and that the need to "move capital persistently from self to other—economic growth as cancer to redistribution as medicine—*pharmakon*" must be interminable.[65]

NOTES

1 Spivak, "Can the Subaltern Speak?" p. 272/239; hereafter CSS. A revised version of the essay can be found in Spivak, *A Critique of Postcolonial Reason*; hereafter *CPR*. I will mainly be referring to the earlier essay. Where I have discussed any modifications in the later version, page numbers to the later text will be given following those of the earlier essay.

2 CSS 288/259.

3 *CPR* 255, 259, 361/27, 30.

4 Ibid., p. 259.

5 CSS 294/265–266. These lines were not included in *A Critique of Postcolonial Reason*.

6 CSS 290/260–261. Spivak cites Mike Davis on American imperialism here. These paragraphs are not present in the revised version.

7 On the American informal empire, see Maier, "The Politics of Productivity."

8 CSS 287/257.

9 CSS 288/258.

10 CSS 279/247; *CPR* 264/33.

11 CSS 272/239.

12 See CSS 280, 289–290/248–249, 259–261.

13 Foucault, "Truth and Juridical Forms," p. 15.

14 Foucault, "Truth and Power," p. 119.

15 Foucault, *Discipline and Punish*, pp. 25–26.

16 Foucault, "Truth and Juridical Forms," pp. 86–87.

17 Class consciousness is the conscious reflection of class interests and can only genuinely come about in capitalism. See Lukács, "Class Consciousness," p. 51: "Now class consciousness consists in fact of the appropriate and rational reactions 'imputed' [*zugerechnet*] to a particular typical position in the process of production. This consciousness is, therefore, neither the sum nor the average of what is thought or felt by the single individuals who make up the class. And yet the historically significant actions of the class as a whole are determined in the last resort by this consciousness and not by the thought of the individual—and these actions can be understood only by reference to this consciousness."

18 Ibid., p. 65: "The hegemony of the bourgeoisie really does embrace the whole of society; it really does attempt to organize the whole of society in its own interests (and in this it has had some success). To achieve this it was forced to develop a coherent theory of economics, politics and society (which in itself presupposes and amounts to a '*Weltanschaung*'), and also to make conscious and sustain its faith in its own mission to control and organize society."

19 My reconstruction of Foucault's account of biopower draws primarily on Foucault, *The History of Sexuality*, 1:138–145. The two basic forms of biopower are discipline and government. Although Foucault clearly states that techniques of government were formed later than those of discipline, he is not precise about when the shift from discipline to government took place other than noting that it occurs in the eighteenth century with the formulation of the concept of population. Foucault stresses that it is not a matter of replacing a society of discipline with one of government but one of a shift in dominance. See also "Governmentality," pp. 218–219.

20 See Foucault, "Security, Territory, and Population," and "The Politics of Health," pp. 95–96.

21 Foucault, "Governmentality," 217; emphasis added.

22 Foucault, *The History of Sexuality*, 1:141.

23 In "More on Power/Knowledge," Spivak suggests that Foucault's productive theory of power "is a much 'truer' view of things than most theories of ideology will produce. The notion of 'interpellation' is too deeply imbricated with psychoanalysis's involvement with the laws of motion of the mind" (35).

24 See "Foucault and Najibullah," p. 218: "But even if we give Foucault the benefit of the doubt here, the application of the analysis to colonialism would trace the production of the colonial subject, whose best examples, in the French case, would be Ho Chi Minh, Frantz Fanon, and Assia Djebar." A longer revised version of this piece appears as "1996: Foucault and Najibullah" in Spivak's recent book, *Other Asias*.

25 Spivak, "Women in Difference," pp. 77–78.

26 See CSS 287/257–258.

27 See CSS 287/257–258; CPR 274–275/41–42.

28 Fröbel, Heinrichs, and Kreye, *The New International Division of Labor*.

29 For a succinct account of this shift from import-substitution industrialization to export-oriented industrialization in Southeast Asia, see Robison, Higgott, and Hewison, "Crisis in Economic Strategy"; the quote is from p. 5.

30 For accounts of the relationship between foreign investment in the electronics industry and development in Southeast Asia, see Henderson, "The New International Division of Labour"; and Henderson, "Electronics Industries and the Developing World."

31 The desired forms of manufacture include specialty chemicals and pharmaceuticals, precision engineering equipment, and optical instruments and equipment. Rodan, "The Rise and Fall of Singapore's Second Industrial Revolution,"

p. 158. On the importance of the strong Singaporean state and its neutralization of unionized labor, see Rodan, "Industrialisation and the Singapore State"; and Henderson, "Changing International Division of Labour," pp. 109–110.

32 *World Development Report 1991*, p. 93.

33 *World Development Report 1995*, pp. 64–66.

34 From Stahl, "Trade in Labour Services," table 1, p. 564.

35 Philippine Overseas Employment Administration, http://www.poea.gov.ph/html/statistics.html, National Statistics Office, Republic of the Philippines, http://www.census.gov.ph/, and Department of Labor and Employment, Republic of the Philippines, http://www.dole.gov.ph.

36 Central Bank of the Philippines, http://www.bsp.gov.ph/statistics/spei/tab11.htm, http://www.bsp.gov.ph/statistics/spei/tab29.htm, and http://www.bsp.gov.ph/statistics/spei/tab1.htm.

37 For a fuller account from a resolutely bourgeois perspective, see Lee, Campbell, and Chia, *The 3 Paradoxes*.

38 "Maid Dependency Here to Stay."

39 Rubin, "The Traffic in Women," p. 164.

40 Spivak, "'Woman' as Theatre," p. 2.

41 Spivak, "Responsibility," p. 62.

42 Spivak, *A Critique of Postcolonial Reason*, p. 373.

43 Spivak, "Responsibility," pp. 56–57, notes 66, 55. In private correspondence, Spivak pointed out that "the subaltern is removed from or denied access even as, today (or perhaps always), s/he is used for exploitation or domination. In my understanding, parabasis is interruption, quite the opposite of withdrawal. It may be the withdrawal of the dominant, but it is the speech of the sustaining collective."

44 I am summarizing and condensing from "Responsibility," "Imperatives to Reimagine the Planet," and the revised version of "Foucault and Najibullah."

45 Alethea Lim, "She Tortured Maid with Clothes Pegs," *Straits Times*, November 7, 2000.

46 Wong She Maine, "Abused Maid Speaks: My Seven Months of Horror," *Straits Times*, March 20, 2002.

47 Kei, *To Have and to Hold*.

48 Ibid., pp. 76, 78.

49 See Habermas, *The Structural Transformation of the Public Sphere*, p. 48.

50 *Report of the Fourth World Conference on Women*, par. 159.

51 Par. 11 offers an optimistic view of post–cold war globality and par. 41 articulates the platform's benign internationalism.

52 Otto, "Holding up Half the Sky," p. 27.

53 Torres, "Asian Women in Migration," p. 188.

54 Kant, *Groundwork of the Metaphysics of Morals*, p. 79.

55 Contemplacion was a Filipina maid found guilty of the murder of her friend, Delia Maga, another Filipina maid, and a four-year-old Chinese boy who was Maga's charge. Her hanging in March 1995 provoked a great deal of popular un-

rest in the Philippines and severely strained diplomatic relations between Singapore and Manila.

56 See Fu and Singam, "The Culture of Exploitation and Abuse."

57 Interview with Braema Mathi, January 7 2004; cf. Braema Mathi, letter to the editor, *Straits Times*, November 7, 2003.

58 http://www.aware.org.sg/twc2/objectives.shtml.

59 http://www.aware.org.sg/twc2/wrc.shtml

60 Price and, Lim, "Reliance on Maids."

61 "Worker Treatment Reflects on Singapore."

62 See Foucault, "The Birth of Biopolitics," p. 75: "The idea of society enables a technology of government to be developed based on the principle that it itself is already 'too much,' 'in excess.' . . . Instead of making the distinction between state and civil society into a historical universal that allows us to examine all the concrete systems, we can try to see it as a form of schematization characteristic of a particular technology of government."

63 Raj, "Let's Give Our Maids More."

64 Ibid.

65 Spivak, *A Critique of Postcolonial Reason,* p. 402.

Jean Franco

MOVING ON FROM SUBALTERNITY

INDIGENOUS WOMEN IN GUATEMALA AND MEXICO

In 2003, Gayatri Spivak was invited by the Latin American Studies Association to give a keynote address at its conference. It is unusual for a non–Latin American specialist who is not a secretary of state or a Washington presence to be invited. Among members of the audience was the Guatemalan activist Rigoberta Menchú, around whom millions of words have been uttered, and a number of academics who had helped form a Latin American subaltern studies group, founded on the model of the Indian subaltern studies. The initiative had foundered on disagreements and on the incongruity of ostentatiously *not* representing the subaltern within the U.S. academy.

Spivak did not speak about Latin America but about the Iraq war, and a public discussion with Rigoberta Menchú did not take place, although her question, "Can the subaltern speak?" could not but have resonances in Latin America where writers and other intellectuals, as members of the literate class, had long claimed to speak for and represent the illiterate. As recently as the sixties and seventies there were countless conferences that debated the responsibility of the intellectual not to mention liberation theology's commitment to the poor and the challenge of active engagement posed by guerrilla movements that gave armed struggle precedence over intellectual work. Yet in none of the debates and discussions were there addressed the questions raised by Spivak's essay.

Where "Can the Subaltern Speak?" had most impact, however, was among Latin Americanists in the United States and especially in the controversies and arguments around one particular "subaltern," Rigoberta Menchú, whose interview and testimony, transcribed by Elizabeth Burgos-

Debray, was, soon after its publication in English in 1984, a year after it had appeared Spanish, celebrated and debated.[1] The book was dragged into the Lynn Cheney–inspired debates over the Western canon after it appeared on a Stanford University syllabus; it was invoked as a source of inspiration by guilt-tripped academics and claimed as a teaching tool in an effort to increase U.S. student awareness of other cultures, as an ethical example, and as a challenge to literary studies that had suppressed orality.[2] Menchú was also, with much publicity, condemned on the grounds that, for political reasons, she had spun her own biased version of Guatemalan insurgency. Following on the anthropologist David Stoll's claim that her testimonial was not always factually correct, hostile reporters immediately termed her a liar.[3] Yet the testimonial is also what made the subaltern Menchú a public intellectual and gave her an influence that cannot be limited to her published testimony of 1983. There are over 30,000 entries in Google under Rigoberta Menchú, she is director of a foundation, she receives delegations, participates in international forums, and wrote a public letter to President Vicente Fox of Mexico, urging him not to support the security council resolution supporting war against Iraq, and she has published a second book, *Rigoberta: La nieta de los Mayas,* describing the difficulties she has encountered in the public arena.[4] In other words, she is more of a political activist than a subaltern. She has become the name attached to all kinds of speculations around race, gender, and subalternity both here in the U.S. and in Guatemala where an estimated 100,000 members of the indigenous population were massacred in the eighties and more than 450 Maya villages destroyed.[5] In the context of this ethnocide, Rigoberta Menchú's survival is of some significance, and not only her survival, but the testimony that launched her from subalternity to becoming a public intellectual.

Since the discussion with Spivak did not take place, I would like to imagine it as a conversation in which both participants move beyond the positions into which some commentators would like to petrify them. In Spivak's case, that means taking into consideration some recent texts and, more important, the revisionary version of "Can the Subaltern Speak?" that appeared in the "History" chapter of A *Critique of Postcolonial Reason.*[6] It is a rich and complex chapter that ranges over archival material of the East Indian Company, in search of the Rani of Sirmur, while appropriating insights from many fields and in the process developing her critique of Deleuze and Guattari and Foucault among others. Both the earlier and later essay are acerbic criticisms of the "transparency" of those intellectuals who "report on the nonrepresented subject" and "the foreclosing of the necessity of the difficult task of counterhegemonic ideological production."[7] She also explores the erasures of the imperial historical record of the Rani, who was certainly not a subaltern. The history chapter also provides new definitions of subalternity both within nation building, a topic also brilliantly handled in the essay "'Draupadi' by Mahasweta Devi" in *In Other Worlds*,[8] and of the "new subaltern" brought into being by the financialization of the globe and the denial of consumption to sectors of the exploited population, particularly women. In the course of this wide-ranging discussion, Spivak describes her visits to Jaipur where she comes upon women gathering leaves and vegetation for their animals and comments, "these are the rural subaltern historically distanced from the relay between princely state and nation state." She continues, "They were the rural subaltern, the real constituency of feminism, accepting their lot as the norm, quite different both from urban female subproletariat in crisis and resistance."[9] This "unorganized landless female labor," she goes on to note, "is one of the targets of super-exploitation where local, national, and international capital intersect. . . . By that route of super-exploitation these women are brought into capital logic, into the possibility of crisis and resistance" (242–243), although, she argues, they cannot be placed in some general category such as "third world women's resistance." In the same chapter she mentions the emergence of the new subaltern in the New World Order: "This new subaltern under postfordism and international subcontracting becomes the mainstay of globalization" and is "rather different from the nationalist example" (276/42).

Thus, a distinction has now been made between subalternities and between the rural subaltern and urban subproletariat, for whom "the denial and withholding of consumerism and the structure of exploitation is compounded by patriarchal social relations" (277/43). Although I find somewhat enigmatic the proposal that "to confront this group is not only to represent them globally in the absence of infrastructural support, but also to learn to represent ourselves" (276/42), and would like her to expand on the suggestion, the conclusion of the chapter points forward. Weighing some responses to the essay, "Can the Subaltern Speak?" Spivak comments on a multiauthored article that appeared in the *Socialist Review* under the heading "Can the Subaltern Vote?" Agreeing with the authors that there is a fruitful way of extending the reading of subaltern speech into a collective arena, she writes, "Access to 'citizenship' (civil society) by becoming a voter (in the nation) is indeed the symbolic circuit of the mobilizing of subalternity into hegemony." To which she adds a parenthesis, "(Unless we want to be romantic purists or primitivists about 'preserving subalternity'—a contradiction in terms—this is absolutely to be desired)" (309–310). It is this point that I now want to follow up with reference not only to Rigoberta Menchú's own "mobilization into hegemony" but also to some contemporary indigenous women's movements in Latin America.

Spivak referred to Rigoberta Menchú's testimony in two footnotes to the "History" chapter of *A Critique of Postcolonial Reason*. In both instances what strikes her is the final sentences of the testimony in which Menchú declares that she has withheld some information from the transcriber and editor, Elizabeth Burgos-Debray, as well as from the reader:

> Of course, I'd need a lot of time to tell you about my people, because it's not easy to understand just like that. And I think I've given some idea of that in my account. Nevertheless I am still keeping my Indian identity a secret. I'm still keeping secret what I think no-one should know. Not even anthropologists or intellectuals, no matter how many books they have, can find out all our secrets.[10]

The first footnote is embedded in a discussion of her own position as "gadfly" and of those women who are in step with the mode of production narrative, "as participants/resisters/victims" (244–245/21, 66n1). The footnote recommends reading Menchú "against the grain of her necessarily identity-political idiom, borrowing from a much older collective tactic (namely secrecy) against colonial conquest." Commenting on the closing words of the testimony, Spivak writes, "The text is not in books and the secret keeps us, not the other way round" (245/66n1), by which I understand it "keeps us" in our place as the perpetually curious but experientially different metropolitan retriever of information.

A second footnote discusses Tony Morrison's *Beloved* in the context of maternal sacrifice as "on the cusp of the violent change from animism to dehegemonized Christianity." This is a story that, somewhat like Rigoberta's true indigenous identity, cannot be passed on. Spivak comments, "In spite of the Latin American Indian (what a multiple errant history in the naming) topos of claiming secrecy in the face of the conquistador, I remain somewhat persuaded by Doris Sommer's placing of the theme of secrecy in Morrison and Menchú together" (305/78n98). The Sommers article argues that "to read women's testimonials, curiously, is to mitigate the tension between a First World 'self' and a Third World 'other.' I do not mean this as a license to deny the differences, but as a suggestion that the testimonial subject may be a model for respectful, non-totalizing politics."[11] Of course, this is an unexceptional position in the U.S. academic context and certainly preferable to arrogance based on ignorance. Several academic critics in the U.S. have similarly made the shift from first world arrogance in order to sidestep the transparency that Spivak detects in Foucault and Deleuze, although their refusal to sin in the same way does not always convince, nor does it alter their own institutional embedding much less the ambiguities surrounding the "secrets."[12] For those of us who are institutionally embedded, the hope is to exercise responsibility along the guidelines that Rigoberta suggests—that is, dissemination of information about atrocities that need to be publicized and reserve when it comes to people's private lives, which, in the case of the indigenous, are also communal lives. The secret that is not to be passed on, is, in fact Rigoberta Menchú's indigenous identity, which binds her to a community that in this case forbids her to speak her true name.

There are two points to be made about this, first, the unacknowledged conflict between secrecy and the impulse to speak. The very genre of testimony has roots in the Christian public declaration of faith. In this respect, it is worth noting that Rigoberta's political consciousness was sparked by the base communities and the catechistic discussions of liberation theology that transmitted an anticapitalist ethos dating back to the seventeenth- and eighteenth-century missionaries.[13] The Spanish title of the testimony, "Me llamo Rigoberta Menchú y así nació mi conciencia" (My name is Rigoberta Menchú and thus my consciousness was born or this is how my consciousness was born), clearly associates the identity of Menchú, her personhood, with the acquisition of consciousness. The obligation to give testimony, however, does not apply to the secret identity given to her by the indigenous community even as that community is decimated and scattered by civil war. Secrecy binds a threatened community and was certainly learned from the long experience of defeat and appropriation as well from the exigencies of guerrilla warfare that thrust the woman subaltern into militancy. There are competing imperatives in Menchú's story between testifying and concealing that can only be illuminated by more recent developments.

Secrecy is a strategy of defense of community customs that seeks to make them invulnerable to outside scrutiny. Certainly, as long as that scrutiny is directed from the metropolis in the cause of some supposed universal it must fall under suspicion. But, in the years since the publication of Rigoberta's testimony, those customs have now been scrutinized in the name of rights by indigenous women who have undertaken their own way out of subalternity and into citizenship. This is a long road and has to be followed along its historical trajectory.

The "capture" of the settled population of the indigenous was a long process that in Mexico and the Andean region encouraged the notion of a primordial community, notwithstanding the fact that over four centuries communities were made and remade. After the conquest, the indigenes were reorganized first into Indian republics (the conquerors often used indigenous nobility to govern them), then later organized into Indian villages with limited powers but with communal lands. "While this fictional cultural autonomy," in the words of June Nash, "masked an exploitative relationship that tapped the communities for labor power and products in an unequal exchange that benefited the state and *ladino*-dominated towns, it nonetheless allows Indians to exercise distinctive cultural practices within their own communities."[14]

Consider the case of Mexico. In the nineteenth century liberal reform policy destroyed the legal basis for communal lands, many of which were seized by landowners. Only in the aftermath of the 1910–1917 Revolution was there a radical change in attitudes toward the indigenous, who now were promised land and access to nationhood and reimagined as part of the postrevolutionary nation. Article 4 of the 1917 constitution stated that "the Law will protect and promote the growth of their (indigenous) language, cultures, uses, customs, resources and specific forms of social organization and will guarantee to its members effective access to the jurisdiction of the states."[15] The Indian pueblos were thus "rescued and reconstituted as communities under the guardianship of the state."

Anthropologists and others often depicted indigenous communities as closed and resistant to change, and, for this reason, they were either idealized as anticapitalist enclaves or seen as impediments to modernization, an ambivalence reflected in fluctuating language polices that vacillated between teaching literacy in indigenous languages or in Spanish.[16] During its long domination, from 1929 to 2000, the institutional party of Mexico, the PRI (Partido Revolucionario Institucional), used corporatist strategies for maintaining the loyalty of indigenous communities. Community leaders were incorporated into the government party, and their inclusion perpetuated the fiction of a nation that would eventually become the amalgam of different races—a *mestizo* state. Even so, the primordial indigenous community remained a useful fiction of the state, even when it pursued development programs and assimilationist policies through literacy campaigns. The organization of indigenous groups into regions of refuge, into self-regulating municipalities, was, in fact, an effective method of paternalist control and neglect, especially when poverty forced the indigenous to do seasonal labor while remaining marginal to the state.

During the height of developmentalist policies in the 1980s, there were sporadic attempts to distribute land and make peasant farmers into something more than subsistence farmers by encouraging crops for export. In the 1990s this situation radically changed. Neoliberal economic reforms in the wake of a debt crisis and during the very corrupt government of Salinas de Cortari (1988–94) modified the agrarian reform program initiated by the Revolution and allowed the privatization of communal lands. Meanwhile the NAFTA (free trade agreement) which allowed cheap foreign imports of food and other staples destroyed the agrarian base of subsistence economies. The crisis was particularly acute in Chiapas where a boom in oil in the 1970s led to an accelerated demand for indigenous labor or at least male labor to work on dam construction and agricultural development programs.[17] Some indigenous men worked part-time in the oil industry, learned Spanish in the process, and left women behind to look after the villages. The indigenous were hit particularly hard in 1982 when oil prices fell and precipitated a debt crisis leading to devastating structural adjustments—for instance, the drying up of credit for poor farmers, which coincided with the decline in prices of coffee on the international market. There is no better illustration of this than Spivak's forceful description of the "third-world woman" disappearing "into a violent shuttling . . . caught between tradition and modernization, culturalism and development."[18]

Nevertheless, other circumstances came into play in Chiapas where the government's freeing of land in the Lacandon forest for cultivation and its colonization by landless peasants fortuitously altered the position of women. A complexity of factors brought together a few remaining leftist militants and a migrant indigenous peasantry and it was here, in the Lacandon forest, that the EZLN (Ejército de Liberación Nacional) was born and the gendered subaltern found her way out of subalternity.

Indigenous women, when isolated within their communities, usually spoke only their tribal tongue—tojobal, chamula, chole, zoque, tzeltal, tzotzil—a reminder of the divisive effects of colonialism. Thrown together during the colonization of the forest, no longer separated from other groups, they were also less subject to community practices. Some of the women joined the Zapatista army, where they were taught to bear arms, and it was these women who began to challenge the customs that had impeded their participation in community politics and prevented their education and their welfare. They insisted that the feminine article be used before the noun *insurgente* when referring to a woman rather than the "universal" masculine article, describing themselves as *insurgentas*.[19] The second decisive action they took was to draw up a declaration of women's rights that specifically challenged "bad customs" in the name of rights that included, among other demands, the right to choose their husband, the right to decide on the number of children they could have, the right to medical attention and education, and the right to participate in community decisions. When the Zapatistas emerged from the forest in January 1994 and proclaimed "the first rebellion against neoliberalism," women participated in the capture of municipalities. They are now estimated to number about 40 percent of the Zapatista army.[20]

The declaration of rights (Ley Revolucionaria de Mujeres del EZLN)[21] became the basis for discussion of women's rights at the National Indigenous Womens' meetings and was also publicized by Comandante Esther in an appearance before the Mexican Congress. Reference to women's right to participate in communities on an equal basis was included in the San Andrés Accords, which is the major policy platform of the Zapatistas and was agreed upon by government representatives, though never officially ratified. The accords also affirmed the autonomy of the indigenous communities.[22]

Spivak has warned us that appeals for human rights on an international level can be a first world political strategy of control. In her essay "Righting Wrongs," she advocates education from below as a training in rights so that they are not simply a response to pressure from the hegemonic powers. "If one engages in such empowerment at the lowest level, it is in the hope that the need for international/domestic-elite pressure on the state will not remain primary forever," she writes.[23]

In light of this, it is interesting to note that the Mexican government attempted a new kind of capture of indigenous women's rights by using them to undermine the autonomy of indigenous communities on the grounds that they subjugated women. The congress passed a new law that was intended to put the communities under the supervision of the unreformed state, a law that was indignantly rejected by most indigenous peoples and by Rigoberta Menchú and several prominent intellectuals.[24] The Zapatistas sent their members all over Mexico to address civil society on the question of indigenous rights and the projected law. In an inspired move, they sent a woman commandant, Esther, to address the national congress. In one of the most striking and unusual moments in Mexican history, Comandante Esther, wearing the trademark Zapatista ski mask to hide her face and speaking in Spanish, noted that it was not a military commander who had come to address congress but an indigenous woman and went on to say, "My name is Esther but that is not important now. I am a Zapatista but that is not important at this time. I am an indigenous woman and that is what matters now."[25] It was a bold move that at one and the same time looked forward to a country that respected differences, a country in which it was possible to be indigenous and Mexican. While she acknowledged the traditional subordination of women in indigenous communities and spoke of their oppression, she also asserted the rights of indigenous communities over their culture and of women's rights within those communities, thus implicitly rejecting the government's attempt to bring them under paternalistic state control.

Esther's performance was a spectacular example of the subaltern's passage into hegemony.

Nevertheless, one problem that surfaces in indigenous women's organizations is how to balance rights with the demands for autonomy so strongly supported by the EZLN.[26] This is a complex and intensely debated issue, but, however interpreted, the autonomy of indigenous communities in which men have always taken on political leadership would seem to conflict with individual rights.[27]

Margarita Gutiérrez, an indigenous intellectual of the Hñanu people of Hidalgo who advised the Zapatistas on the San Andrés Accords, and the Colombian activist Nellys Palomo have argued that the demands of the indigenous women posited a different relationship between individual and community, the private and the public. They quote the San Andrés Accords, which state, *"Autonomy begins in the home, at work, in the community and region. Equality between men and women must be guaranteed in the decision-making organs, seeing forms of organization and participation,"* in order to add the comment that democratization of the state "goes hand in hand with a democratisation of the home which, from a feminist viewpoint affects private life, so that the public changes will have resonance within the scope of the intimate sphere, the family, love, accompanied by processes of change at the level of the individual."[28] They then go on to argue that "the individual is able, in one form or another, to act, to be free and independent within the context of her social life, based on freedom and responsibility. This is the autonomy which indigenous women are fighting for."[29] What is interesting about this statement is that it does not dismiss individuality as a mere neoliberal concept, nor does it set individuality in opposition to community. A resignification of the individual has taken place as these women enter into citizenship on their own conditions.

What it means to be a subaltern in Spivak's terms encompasses "those removed from lines of social mobility," although she is emphatic in rejecting the suggestion that women be "left alone to flourish in some pristine tribality." In her essay on "Righting Wrongs," she notes that, while global culture permeates the world, there

> is a lack of communication between and among the immense heterogeneity of the subaltern cultures of the world. Cultural borders are easily crossed from the superficial cultural relativism of metropolitan countries, whereas, going the other way, the so-called peripheral countries encounter bureaucratic and policed frontiers. The frontiers of subaltern cultures, which developed no generative public role, have no channels of inter-penetration. Here, too, the problem is not solved in a lasting way by

the inclusion of exceptional subalterns in South-based global movements with leadership drawn from the descendants of colonial subjects, even as these networks network. These figures are no longer representative of the subaltern stratum in general.[30]

But if the actions of the Chiapas indigenous women tell us anything, it is that there are many ways of developing a "generative public role."

What Spivak advocates is a kind of secular education from below, radically different from the suspect benevolence of international organization and NGOs. In passing, she mentions Paulo Freire and his celebrated *Pedagogy of the Oppressed,* which she notes was written during the period of guerrilla warfare, but (as she does not note) has now been taken up by organizations in many parts of the world.[31] Indeed, there are many different forms of education from below—in the case of the Zapatista women, there is education through war (secular), through learning Spanish and applying it in public meetings, and, in the case of Rigoberta Menchú, an education through Catholic base communities.[32]

Spivak once described herself as a "gadfly"—and it is not a bad description.[33] Not only does she warn us against our own misguided benevolence, but she keeps us on the alert for those "disappearances" from history. In an inspired passage she refers to those anthropologists who see tribals as belonging to a "closely-knit social texture," to which she counters, "I am asking readers to shift their perception from the anthropological to the historico-political and see "the same knit text-ile as a torn cultural fabric, in terms of its removal from the dominant loom in a historical moment."[34] Let me complement this with another metaphor that suggests the repairing of that torn fabric. Every year on Women's Day, Sub-comandante Marcos celebrates the Zapatista women. This is what he said in 1996 (the year of the Beijing International Conference on Women, organized by the United Nations), invoking an anonymous woman, on the twelfth anniversary of the formation of the EZLN: "She begins to knit in silence and without pay, side by side and with other men and women, that complex dream which some call hope. Everything for everyone, nothing for ourselves. She meets March 8th with her face erased, and her name hidden." I don't think that Spivak would quarrel with this, nor with the ending of his speech: "To the rebels and uncomfortable Mexican women who are now bent over, underlying (sic) that history which, without them, is nothing more than a badly-made fable.

TOMORROW

If there is to be one, it will be made with the women, and above all, by them."[35]

NOTES

1   Burgos-Debray, *I, Rigoberta Menchú.*

2   Pratt, "I, Rigoberta Menchú and the "Culture Wars." Also included in the book is an essay by Arias, "Rigoberta Menchú's History," as well as documents and responses. See also Gugelberger, *The Real Thing.*

3   Stoll, *Rigoberta Menchú.* See also Palmieri, "Lies by the Nobel Prize Winner" and "The Pitiful Lies of Rigoberta Menchú," which appeared respectively in *El Periódico de Guatemala* and in the Spanish newspaper *El País,* reprinted in Arias, *The Rigoberta Menchú Controversy.*

4   Menchú, *La nieta de los Mayas.* For a discussion of this text, see Rodríguez, *Liberalism at Its Limits.*

5   Arias, "Rigoberta Menchú's History," pp. 4–5.

6   Spivak, *A Critique of Postcolonial Reason,* pp. 198–311.

7   Spivak, *A Critique of Postcolonial Reason,* pp. 248–266/22–35.

8   Spivak, "'Draupadi.'"

9   Spivak, *A Critique of Postcolonial Reason,* p. 242.

10 Burgos-Debray, *I, Rigoberta Menchú,* p. 247.

11 Sommers, "No Secrets," p. 137.

12 See especially Mignolo's attempt to establish an in-between position in *Local Histories.*

13 See Dussel, "Cuestión étnica."

14 Nash, *Mayan Visions,* p. 44.

15 Quoted by Nash, *Mayan Vistions,* p. 49

16 Heath, *Telling Tongues.*

17 Portillo Saldaña, *The Revolutionary Imagination,* pp. 214-215. See also Collier, with Quarantiello, *Basta!* and Nash, *Mayan Visions.*

18 Spivak, *A Critique of Postcolonial Reason,* p. 304/61.

19 "Marcos to the insurgentas: Insurgentas! (The Sea in March " on the EZLN Web page, "Writings of Sub-comandante Marcos of the EZLN (March 12, 2000). All the writings of Marcos are listed on this page. He is the spokesperson for the Zapatistas. Above him are the "commanders" who work with civil society. Marcos issues comuniqués, gives speeches, and tells stories.

20 Nash, *Mayan Visions,* p. 180.

21 Rovira, *Mujeres de Maíz,* p. 112.

22 Gutiérrez and Palomo, "A Woman's Eye View." Whilst the EZLN has supported indigenous autonomy, they have also formed pluriethnic communities.

23 Spivak, "Righting Wrongs," see especially p. 173.

24 "Con el voto." It should also be noted that this law was passed when the Zapatistas were under siege by the Mexican army, a siege that continues to the time of writing.

25 "Mensaje Central."

26 The EZLN has also organized pluriethnic communities in Chiapas.

27 On autonomy, see Stavenhagen, "Towards the Right to Autonomy"; and Hernández, "The Process of Creating a National Legislative Proposal." The scope of autonomy was debated in a series of national meetings of the Plural National Indigenous Assembly for Autonomy (ANIPA).

28 Gutiérrez and Palomo, "A Woman's Eye View," p. 79.

29 Ibid., p. 82.

30 Spivak," Righting Wrongs," pp. 194–195.

31 Ibid., p. l95. On some ongoing work, see the Paulo Freire On-Line Journal, alyjuma@ucla.edu.

32 There are still base communities despite the Vatican's suppression of liberation theology. See, for instance, several examples in Heyck, *Surviving Globalization*. On education and the Zapatistas, see Marcos, "Democratic Teachers and the Zapatista Dream."

33 Spivak, "History," p. 244.

34 Spivak, "Righting Wrongs," p. 199. Textile is an important metaphor in Gayatri's work. In the same essay, she speaks of "cultural fabric" and "suture."

35 Marcos, "Twelve Women."

PART FIVE

IN RESPONSE

IN RESPONSE

LOOKING BACK, LOOKING FORWARD

"Can the Subaltern Speak?" was delivered as "Power and Desire" at the Institute on "Marxist Interpretations of Culture: Limits, Frontiers, Boundaries," in the summer of 1983. That version was never published. It was an
exciting occasion, held in the evening. In the audience were my student
Forest Pyle, now teaching at the University of Oregon, Jenny Sharpe, now
teaching at UCLA; new friend Patricia Clough, then a student, now teaching
at CUNY; Peter Hitchcock, a cool stranger recently arrived from England,
now teaching at Baruch; Hap Veeser, whom I did not then know, but now a
good friend, then a student, now teaching at CCNY. At the end of the session, Cornel West ran down from the top of the auditorium to give me a hug
because, I think, I was womanfully and repeatedly invoking "the difference
of the third world"—a phrase still utterable in 1983—in the Q & A. My fellow
speakers were Ellen Willis and Catharine McKinnon. A Scots intellectual
whose name escapes me wrote much later in the *Village Voice* that it was
his first visit to the United States and he had heard Gayatri Spivak say that
Americans believed they could achieve freedom by rearranging furniture.

In that first version I was trying to unenthrall myself from Foucault and
Deleuze—because of the semanalyse people, turning all that into a kind of
American graffiti, I think. I had spoken of sati, under Lata Mani's influence.
But I had not yet written of Bhubaneswari's message.

It seems to have been a beginning, a turning of Derrida toward politics.
To achieve the turn, I looked toward the Bengali middle class out of which
I came. My work was French theory, my work was Yeats—I am a European-

ist—my work was Marx, but I wanted to make a change. In the first flush of this change I looked homeward; I went home to my class.

I have told this story many times. In 1981 I was asked by *Yale French Studies* to write about French feminism and by *Critical Inquiry* to write on deconstruction. I felt it was time for a change. The immediate result was "French Feminism in an International Frame" and a translation of Mahasweta Devi's "Draupadi."[1] In a profound response to that impulse for change, I was turning, then, to the Bengali middle class, Mahasweta Devi, of course, but also Bhubaneswari Bhaduri, who was my grandmother's sister. To begin with, then, an act of private piety.

The woman to whom Bhubaneswari wrote the letter that was forgotten was my mother's mother. The woman who told me the story was my mother. The woman who refused to understand what she had said was my first cousin. I was a student of English honors at the University of Calcutta, she of philosophy. She was quite like me in education, and yet it made no difference. She could not hear this woman who had tried with her suicide, using menstruation, that dirty secret, to erase the axioms that endorsed sati. Sati in the piece was *not* given as a generalizable example of the subaltern not speaking, or rather not being able to speak—trying to, but not succeeding in being heard. Lata misunderstood me. It was Bhubaneswari who could not be heard, even by her.

The point that I was trying to make was that if there was no valid institutional background for resistance, it could not be recognized. Bhubaneswari's resistance against the axioms that animated sati could not be recognized. She could not speak. Unfortunately, for sati, a caste-Hindu practice, there *was* an institutional validation, and I unraveled as much of it as I could. My point was not to say that they couldn't speak, but that, when someone did try to do something different, it could not be acknowledged because there was no institutional validation. It was not a point about satis not speaking.

The point I was making about Foucault and Deleuze was that when these great intellectuals talk to each other, just in conversation as it were, they betray certain kinds of convictions that, when they are in theoretical full dress, do not show themselves. I have said this also in response to the criticism that my treatment of Kant in *The Critique of Postcolonial Reason* is "under-demonstrated." It may indeed seem so. For I am not looking at Kant writing about perpetual peace, about the ethical state in *Religion Within the Boundaries of Mere Reason*, not when he is speaking about these issues in "What is Enlightenment?" not when he gives us *cosmopolitheia*, but rather where he is teaching us how to solve the most central problem of philosophy and in the description of philosophizing shows an extraordinary disrespect for the Fourth World, the Aboriginal.² That is the way I read as a literary critic. I look at the "marginal" moment that unravels the text; paradoxically, it gives us a sense of what is "normal" for the text, what norms the text.

I did not remain with Devi and nationalist women. Soon I realized that that was not the place to end. Those two women opened possibilities for me. I went on toward other kinds of things that I could think of as subalternity. In attempting to make her body speak, even unto death, Bhubaneswari had brought her subalternity to crisis. As I will expand below, I read her under the influence of the Marx of "The Eighteenth Brumaire" and recoded her under the influence of the *Subaltern Studies* group.³ But gradually I stepped into scenes where subalternity, oppression itself, was accepted as normality in the underside of the Bengali rural poor. I do not quite know how, but I became involved in hanging out in that subaltern space, attempting, while I was there, to think it a normal teaching scene. In this effort I learned something about teaching. All teaching attempts change, yet all teaching also assumes a shared scene.

Gradually, some schools came into being as I hung out, thanks to my dollar salary. These schools are fragile things, mired in a system of education that makes sure that the subaltern will not be heard except as beggars. How different this scene is from national liberation, from the neighborhood of Bhubaneswari, Madan Mitra Lane in old Calcutta. Eleven schools in Purulia and Birbhum, the two most backward districts of West Bengal, undertaken the year "Can the Subaltern Speak?" was first published.

It was not enough for me to have moved from my class of origin. I am a comparativist; I needed to move away from my mother tongue to be encountered by the subaltern. From 1989 to '94 I learned Moroccan Arabic from Peace Corps manuals and local tutors and worked my way, helped by socialist women, through the urban subproletariat, moving toward the Sahel inch by inch, in Algeria. I went every year, sometimes twice. I asked the women in the old socialist villages established by Ben Bella: "what is it to vote?" I sat in silence in Marabouts, in women's clinics. I did some electoral education with socialist women in low-income housing in Wahran. I monitored polling booths with them when the Islamic Salvation Front won the first round. In '94 I had to leave at the head of a curfew. The question that guided my time in Algeria seems to have been: who hears the subaltern? It has stayed with me since.

Since 2001 I have been learning Chinese—Mandarin mostly, some Cantonese. I go to three tiny remote schools in rural and mountainous Xishuangbanna. Can I hear the subaltern as China dismantles down below?

I do not know in what ways this strange adventure, parallel to the salaried work, the publication routine, and the lecture circuit, nourishes that stream, draws on it as well. I only know that it was the attempt to read Bhubaneswari that put me on this path.

I find myself saying that when I am in those schools I don't notice the poverty, just as I perhaps don't notice the opulence in New York. When you are teaching, you are teaching. Over the years I have come to realize that it is not my way to give people shelter, not even to make collectives for resistance. My work, as I have said many times, is the uncoercive rearrangement of desires, the nurturing of the intuition of the public sphere—a teacher's work. In Bangladesh in the eighties I traveled some with rural paramedics—to intervene in the subaltern's sense of normality, to foster preventive and nourishing habits; again, a teacher's work. This too may bring subalternity to crisis. This intervention in normality has brought me—city girl—into organizing ecological agriculture among the families and communities of my students. Here, too, a difference from "Can the Subaltern Speak?" must be noted. Not only that Bhubaneswari too, was a city girl; my class, as I mentioned. But also that she had already brought subalternity to crisis, she needed me only to read her, hear her, make her speak by default. (Derrida has a marvelous discussion of the pun in French *il faut*—it must be [done]; that it also carries the sense of it cracks, it defaults.[4] I am reminded of that as I think of my relationship with Bhubaneswari.)

We now live in a time of sweeping projects for the betterment of the world—poverty eradication, disease eradication, exporting democracy, exporting information and communication technology. I have my own political analysis of these projects. This is not the place to launch them. Let us assume that they are laudable. But, even so, in order for these projects to sustain themselves without top-down control—sustainability in the only sense that should matter—there must be a supplement of unglamorous, patient, hands-on work—the way we teach in our classrooms, to teach that way everywhere. In a general sense we know that every generation has to be educated. We forget this when it comes to the subaltern. "Can the Subaltern Speak?" put me on this line. I saw that, in two generations, women in the family had forgotten how to read her. That was a private narrative of the failure of education. As I moved on to the terrain of more general subaltern normality, I increasingly saw this as a public narrative. I began to realize that it is not just schoolrooms, teachers, textbooks and teachers, and the social permission for children to be at school that count, important as these things might be. Unless there is an increment—to make sure that, when the subaltern is on the path of hegemony, "they do not become suboppressors" and that we do not celebrate them simply because they have escaped subalternity; the other details are not socially productive.[5]

So this is where my turn to the Bengali middle class took me. I made mistakes in the first version. I have kept the statements that show that I was ignorant of the material of South Asia. One way out would have been to reveal that she was my grandmother's sister. But that would have been turned into a love fest, legitimizing myself because my grandmother's sister killed herself. In the event what I drew was many hostile published responses. But it was in fact an act of private piety.

As I have indicated, in my reference to "the betterment of the world," imperialism may have displaced itself all over the world. A thinker such as David Harvey says quite openly:

> I share with Marx the view that imperialism, like capitalism, can prepare the ground for human emancipation from want and need. In arenas like public health, agricultural productivity, and the application of science and technology to confront the material problems of existence (including the preservation of the environment), capitalism and imperialism have opened up potential paths to a better future. The problem is that the dominant class relations of capitalism and the institutional arrangements and knowledge structures to which these class powers give rise typically block the utilization of this potential. Furthermore, these class relations and institutional arrangements set in motion imperialist forms dedicated to the preservation or enhancement of the conditions of their own reproduction, leading to ever greater levels of social inequality and more and more predatory practices with respect to the mass of the world's population ("accumulation by dispossession," as I call it).
>
> My argument is that, at the present moment, the U.S. has no option except to engage in such practices unless there is a class movement internally that challenges existing class relations and their associated hegemonic institutions and political-economic practices. This leaves the rest of the world with the option of either resisting U.S. imperialism directly (as in the case of many developing country social movements) or seeking either to divert it or compromise with it by forming, for example, sub-imperialisms under the umbrella of U.S. power. The danger is that anti-imperialist movements may become purely and wholeheartedly anti-modernist movements rather than seeking an alternative globalization and an alternative modernity that makes full use of the potential that capitalism has spawned.[6]

Harvey is writing a displaced imperialism (i.e., addressing a late stage of imperialism characterized by the multiplication of subimperialisms?).

Lenin's argument, that communism needed to align itself with the national-liberationist progressive bourgeoisie, anticipates him, for it tacitly argues that the liberationist colonial subject has been "freed" by imperialism.[7] Harvey does not mention these earlier national liberationist movements, within which Bhubaneswari would have found her place.

I find it difficult to accept Harvey's endorsement of the burden imposed upon the United States today. My alternative is not to go back to old-fashioned nationalism. If I may quote myself: "In globalized postcoloniality, we can museumize national-liberation nationalism, good for exhibitions; we can curricularize national-liberation nationalism, good for the discipline of history. The task for the imagination is not to let the museum and the curriculum provide alibis for the new civilizing missions, make us mis-choose our allies."[8] I would rather focus on Harvey's phrase "unless there is a class movement internally that challenges class relations...."

Nice words. The lesson that Gramsci taught was that class alone cannot be the source of liberation within subalternity. And that is the lesson the subalternists taught in their first phase. The problem is that subaltern studies now seems not concerned about class as an analytical category at all. Between Harvey's Scylla and the subalternists' Charybdis lies my downwardly mobile trajectory. I think of education as a supplement—and a supplement can animate an alternative.

Joseph Stiglitz would offer a corrective to David Harvey's sense of the mission of the United States. In his *Globalization and Its Discontents* he argues again and again that the developing countries be allowed to set their own agenda over against the transnational agencies.[9] Yet in a recent presentation he was obliged to offer something like a good imperialism, the reconstruction of the world by America, in exchange for a bad imperialism—the war in Iraq—that he, of course, opposed. To bring to the floor what his text seems to ask for, we would need the project of listening to subalterns, patiently and carefully, so that we, as intellectuals committed to education, can devise an intuition of the public sphere in subalternity—a teacher's work.

If this teaching work is not performed, subalterns remain in subalternity, unable to represent themselves and therefore needing to be represented. The "wars of maneuver" signaled by Gramsci could not happen without leadership from above.

To represent "one" self collectively is to be in the public sphere. Marx had understood it in terms of class in "The Eighteenth Brumaire of Louis Bonaparte," where the famous line occurs. Gramsci had introduced hegemony—the condition into which the subaltern graduates as a result of a larger share of persuasion and, inevitably, some coercion from the organic intellectuals as well as the state. I mention this because when I gave "Power and Desire," the first version of "Can the Subaltern Speak?" I had read Gramsci's "Some Aspects of the Southern Question," but I read Ranajit Guha's "On Some Aspects of the Historiography of Colonial India" only a year later.[10]

When I read Guha's essay I was so overwhelmed by the work of the *Subaltern Studies* group, which he headed, that I pulled my piece, I pulled my act of private piety, that I had performed to get myself out of the prison house of just being a mere Europeanist, and pushed it into the subaltern enclave. I recoded the story.

I learned to say that "the subaltern is in the space of difference," following a wonderful passage in Guha. (I did not then understand that Guha's understanding of the subaltern would subsequently take onboard a much broader transformation of the Gramscian idea insofar as the subaltern, according to Guha, would call out in a collective voice.[11] I never went that way at all.) In fact what I had thought of when I gave the first version of the story was about not having an institutional structure of validation. And indeed, as can be read in the words Partha Chatterjee kindly sent to the conference, the subalternists themselves felt that it was my stuff from Marx's *The Eighteenth Brumaire*, on different kinds of representation: *Vertretung* or proxy and *Darstellung* or portrait, and also *representation*, that introduced a new twist in the understanding of the representation of the subaltern.

Right before the famous passage of "they cannot represent themselves"— the English translation of Marx says "they are therefore incapable of asserting their class interest in their own name whether through a parliament or through a convention." And although this is not a wrong translation, the German *geltend zu machen* is, literally, to "make it count," "make it hold." The French peasant proprietors who were completely emptied out in the gray transition from feudalism to one stage of capitalism, could not make their grievances count. They had no covenant, says Marx, they had no institutions through which they could make whatever they wanted to say count," "make it hold."

This is one of Marx's great journalistic pieces. There is a clear insight here that it is not so easy to write a liberation theology where reason is god. When he is overturning the public use of reason to make the subject the proletarian, he is elsewhere, in *Capital 1*, his only book—the other *Capital*s were put together by Engels after his death—an educator; he is trying to teach, trying to rearrange the feelings of the workers so they would think of themselves as agents of production. But when he is writing this journalistic description of the only revolution he ever saw, he has a long wonderful rhetorical paragraph that pleases every literary critic—where the "subject" is the proletarian revolution, called forth by existing social conditions, and, as the end of the paragraph shows, those conditions tell the proletarian revolution, don't wait for the right moment, leap here now. By implication, since the call is to the vain boaster in Aesop's fables, the claim of the proletarian revolution seems theoretically distant and practically urgent. Marx the rationalist asks for a restricted use of reason here. As is well known, the paragraph ends in a deliberate alteration of Aesop by Hegel. Marx then alters Aesop another way. Again, by implication, what he corrects is Hegel's vaulting confidence in historically determined reason in *The Philosophy of Right*: "As a work of philosophy," Hegel writes, this book

> must be poles apart from an attempt to construct the state as it ought to be. The instruction which it may contain cannot consist in teaching the state what it ought to be; it can only show how the state, the ethical [*sittlich*] universe, is to be understood. "*Idon Rhodos, idon kai to pedema. Hic Rhodus, hic saltus.*" To conceive of [*begreifen*] what is, this is the task of philosophy. . . . It is just as absurd to fancy that a philosophy can rise above [*hinaus übergehen*] its contemporary world as it is to fancy that an individual can overleap his own age, jump over Rhodes. If his theory really goes beyond the world as it is and builds an ideal one as it ought to be, that world exists indeed, but only in his opinions, a soft [*weich*] element which will let anything you please be shaped [*dem sich alles Beliebige einbilden lässt*]. With hardly an alteration, the proverb just quoted would run: "Here is the rose, dance thou here." What lies between reason as self-conscious mind and reason as reality to hand [*vorhandener Wirklichkeit*], what separates the former from the latter and prevents it from finding satisfaction in the latter, is the fetter of some abstraction or other which has not been liberated into the concept. To recognize reason as the rose in the cross of the present and thereby to enjoy the present, this is the rational insight which reconciles us to the actual, the reconciliation which philosophy affords us.[12]

The small but crucial change made by Marx is from "leap" as a noun to "leap" as an imperative. Unlike Hegel's, this is unannounced. *Hic Rhodus, hic saltus*—a literal translation of the Greek—is changed by Marx to *Hic Rhodus, hic salta!* By repeating Hegel's alteration immediately afterward, he changes the message of a mystical (Rosicrucian) acceptance of reason as a rose in the cross, which allows us to enjoy the present and see all change as a servitude to abstractions. He changes it to a message of change, a livelier acceptance of the Aesopian challenge.

When I was thinking of Bhubaneswari Bhaduri, I was full of "The Eighteenth Brumaire." It seems to me now that I inserted the singular suicide of my foremother into that gap between the reasonableness of theory and the urgency of the revolutionary moment. I felt that my task was to represent her in all of Marx's senses. But the gesture and the task could not yet emerge into considerations of collectivity and of the public sphere.

So that was in fact where the essay began. Not in understanding the subaltern as a state of difference. And it started the trajectory of the subaltern in my work in the possibility of creating an infrastructure here as there which would make the subaltern not accept subalternity as normality. I thought that Bhubaneswari as revolutionary subject, as it were, had questioned the presuppositions of sati, but could not be acknowledged. She remained singular. I was therefore unable to generalize from her. But I certainly never spoke of sati as anticolonial resistance. I thought the criminalization of sati, while it was an unquestioned good, had not engaged with the subject-formation of women; colonial education remained class fixed. I was trying to understand how it could be that women, perhaps two or three generations behind me, in my own formation, could have respected sati in its traditional meaning. To think that I could support sati is derisive. But I needed to step out of myself.

When, in 1986, Rup Kanwar had committed sati, her mother had smiled. It is that smile that I was anticipating—that was the text I was reading as I read the Scriptures—the *Dharmaśāstra*.[13] For the smile said yes to the Scripture. That desire had to be rearranged. I felt that Bhubaneswari rearranged that desire, coerced by situational imperatives.

She taught me yet another lesson: death as text. She made me read situations where no response happens. If the peace process carries no credibility, if a whole country is turned into a gated community, young people who do not yet know how to value life—and Bhubaneswari was seventeen years old—may feel that it is possible to write a response when you die with me for the same cause. Suicide bombers form a collectivity whose desires have been rearranged. The decision to die was something like that in Bhubaneswari as well. It was the gendering of the second decision, to postpone death, that made her exclusive. The idea that when you die with me for the same cause, since you will not listen to me, since I cannot speak to you, we do memorialize an accord—is action in extremis. How much do the Scriptures arbitrate desire? The question of the Koran, of the *Dharmaśāstra*.

The trajectory of "Can the Subaltern Speak?" has not yet ended for me. On the one hand, the schools. On the other, the search for a secularism as legal instrument of social justice that can accommodate the subaltern, a consuming interest only to be mentioned here.

NOTES

1   Spivak, "French Feminism," "'Draupadi' by Mahasweta Devi."
2   Spivak, *A Critique of Postcolonial Reason*, pp. 19–36.
3   Marx, "The Eighteenth Brumaire of Louis Bonaparte," p. 239.
4   Derrida, *Rogues*, p. 109.
5   The idea of the oppressed themselves becoming suboppressors without proper pedagogy comes from Freire, *The Pedagogy of the Oppressed*, pp. 29–34.
6   Agglutianations.com, November 3, 2003.
7   Indeed, as Harvey points out, the position is already present in Marx. See Karl Marx, "The British Rule in India," in *Surveys from Exile*, pp. 306–307. The questioning of the teleological view of Marxism is most strongly associated with Louis Althusser's structuralist project. The subalternist questioning, legitimizing Marx's position by reversal, can lean dangerously toward nationalism.
8   Spivak, "Nationalism and the Imagination."
9   Stiglitz, *Globalization and Its Discontents*, pp. 236–252 and *passim*.
10 Gramsci, "Some Aspects of the Southern Question"; Guha, "On Some Aspects."
11 Guha, *Domination Without Hegemony*, p. 134 and *passim*.
12 Hegel, *Philosophy of Right*, pp. 10–12 (translation modified).
13 Kane, *History of the Dharmasastra*.

Gayatri Chakravorty Spivak

APPENDIX

CAN THE SUBALTERN SPEAK ?

An understanding of contemporary relations of power; and of the Western intellectual's role within them, requires an examination of the intersection of a theory of representation and the political economy of global capitalism. A theory of representation points, on the one hand, to the domain of ideology, meaning, and subjectivity, and, on the other hand, to the domain of politics, the state, and the law.

The original title of this paper was "Power, Desire, Interest."[1] Indeed, whatever power these meditations command may have been earned by a politically interested refusal to push to the limit the founding presuppositions of my desires, as far as they are within my grasp. This vulgar three-stroke formula, applied both to the most resolutely committed and to the most ironic discourse, keeps track of what Althusser so aptly named "philosophies of denegation."[2] I have invoked my positionality in this awkward way so as to accentuate the fact that calling the place of the investigator into question remains a meaningless piety in many recent critiques of the sovereign subject. Thus, although I will attempt to foreground the precariousness of my position throughout, I know such gestures can never suffice.

This paper will move, by a necessarily circuitous route, from a critique of current Western efforts to problematize the subject to the question of how the third-world subject is represented within Western discourse. Along the way, I will have occasion to suggest that a still more radical decentering of the subject is, in fact, implicit in both Marx and Derrida. And I will have recourse, perhaps surprisingly, to an argument that Western intellectual production is, in many ways, complicit with Western international economic interests. In the end, I will offer an alternative analysis of the relations between the discourses of the West and the possibility of speaking of (or for) the subaltern woman. I will draw my specific examples from the case of India, discussing at length the extraordinarily paradoxical status of the British abolition of widow sacrifice.

I

Some of the most radical criticism coming out of the West today is the result of an interested desire to conserve the subject of the West, or the West as Subject. The theory of pluralized "subject-effects" gives an illusion of undermining subjective sovereignty while often providing a cover for this subject of knowledge. Although the history of Europe as Subject is narrativized by the law, political economy, and ideology of the West, this concealed Subject pretends it has "no geo-political determinations." The much-publicized critique of the sovereign subject thus actually inaugurates a Subject. I will argue for this conclusion by considering a text by two great practitioners of the critique: "Intellectuals and Power: A Conversation between Michel Foucault and Gilles Deleuze."[3]

I have chosen this friendly exchange between two activist philosophers of history because it undoes the opposition between authoritative theoretical production and the unguarded practice of conversation, enabling one to glimpse the track of ideology. The participants in this conversation emphasize the most important contributions of French poststructuralist theory: first, that the networks of power/desire/interest are so heterogeneous that their reduction to a coherent narrative is counterproductive—a persistent critique is needed; and second, that intellectuals must attempt to disclose and know the discourse of society's Other. Yet the two systematically ignore the question of ideology and their own implication in intellectual and economic history.

Although one of its chief presuppositions is the critique of the sovereign subject, the conversation between Foucault and Deleuze is framed by two monolithic and anonymous subjects-in-revolution: "A Maoist" (FD, 205) and "the workers' struggle" (FD, 217). Intellectuals, however, are named and differentiated; moreover, a Chinese Maoism is nowhere operative. Maoism here simply creates an aura of narrative specificity, which would be a harmless rhetorical banality were it not that the innocent appropriation of the proper name "Maoism" for the eccentric phenomenon of French intellectual "Maoism" and subsequent "New Philosophy" symptomatically renders "Asia" transparent.[4]

Deleuze's reference to the workers' struggle is equally problematic; it is obviously a genuflection: "We are unable to touch [power] in any point of its application without finding ourselves confronted by this diffuse mass, so that we are necessarily led . . . to the desire to blow it up completely. Every partial revolutionary attack or defense is linked in this way to the workers' struggle" (*FD*, 217). The apparent banality signals a disavowal. The statement ignores the international division of labor, a gesture that often marks poststructuralist political theory.[5] The invocation of the workers' struggle is baleful in its very innocence; it is incapable of dealing with global capitalism: the subject-production of worker and unemployed within nation-state ideologies in its Center; the increasing subtraction of the working class in the Periphery from the realization of surplus value and thus from "humanistic" training in consumerism; and the large-scale presence of paracapitalist labor as well as the heterogeneous structural status of agriculture in the Periphery. Ignoring the international division of labor; rendering "Asia" (and on occasion "Africa") transparent (unless the subject is ostensibly the "Third World"); reestablishing the legal subject of socialized capital—these are problems as common to much poststructuralist as to structuralist theory. Why should such occlusions be sanctioned in precisely those intellectuals who are our best prophets of heterogeneity and the Other?

The link to the workers' struggle is located in the desire to blow up power at any point of its application. This site is apparently based on a simple valorization of *any* desire destructive of *any* power. Walter Benjamin comments on Baudelaire's comparable politics by way of quotations from Marx.

> Marx continues in his description of the *conspirateurs de profession* as follows: " . . . They have no other aim but the immediate one of overthrowing the existing government, and they profoundly despise the more theoretical enlightenment of the workers as to their class interests. Thus their anger—not proletarian but plebian—at the *habits noirs* (black coats), the more or less educated people who represent [*vertreten*] that side of the movement and of whom they can never become entirely independent, as they cannot of the official representatives [*Repräsentanten*] of the party." Baudelaire's political insights do not go fundamentally beyond the insights of these professional conspirators. . . . He could perhaps have made Flaubert's statement, "Of all of politics I understand only one thing: the revolt," his own.[6]

The link to the workers' struggle is located, simply, in desire. Elsewhere, Deleuze and Guattari have attempted an alternative definition of desire, revising the one offered by psychoanalysis: "Desire does not lack anything; it does not lack its object. It is, rather, the subject that is lacking in desire, or desire that lacks a fixed subject; there is no fixed subject except by repression. Desire and its object are a unity: it is the machine, as a machine of a machine. Desire is machine, the object of desire also a connected machine, so that the product is lifted from the process of producing, and something detaches itself from producing to product and gives a leftover to the vagabond, nomad subject."[7]

This definition does not alter the specificity of the desiring subject (or leftover subject-effect) that attaches to specific instances of desire or to production of the desiring machine. Moreover, when the connection between desire and the subject is taken as irrelevant or merely reversed, the subject-effect that surreptitiously emerges is much like the generalized ideological subject of the theorist. This may be the legal subject of socialized capital, neither labor nor management, holding a "strong" passport, using a "strong" or "hard" currency, with supposedly unquestioned access to due process. It is certainly not the desiring subject as Other.

The failure of Deleuze and Guattari to consider the relations between desire, power, and subjectivity renders them incapable of articulating a theory of interests. In this context, their indifference to ideology (a theory of which is necessary for an understanding of interests) is striking but consistent. Foucault's commitment to "genealogical" speculation prevents him from locating, in "great names" like Marx and Freud, watersheds in some continuous stream of intellectual history.[8] This commitment has created an unfortunate resistance in Foucault's work to "mere" ideological critique. Western speculations on the ideological reproduction of social relations belong to that mainstream, and it is within this tradition that Althusser writes: "The reproduction of labour power requires not only a reproduction of its skills, but also at the same time, a reproduction of its submission to the ruling ideology for the workers, and a reproduction of the ability to manipulate the ruling ideology correctly for the agents of exploitation and repression, so that they, too, will provide for the domination of the ruling class 'in and by words' [par la parole]."[9]

When Foucault considers the pervasive heterogeneity of power, he does not ignore the immense institutional heterogeneity that Althusser here attempts to schematize. Similarly, in speaking of alliances and systems of signs, the state and war-machines (mille plateaux), Deleuze and Guattari are opening up that very field. Foucault cannot, however, admit that a developed theory of ideology recognizes its own material production in institutionality, as well as in the "effective instruments for the formation and accumulation of knowledge" (PK, 102). Because these philosophers seem obliged to reject all arguments naming the concept of ideology as only schematic rather than textual, they are equally obliged to produce a mechanically schematic opposition between interest and desire. Thus they align themselves with bourgeois sociologists who fill the place of ideology with a continuistic "unconscious" or a parasubjective "culture." The mechanical relation between desire and interest is clear in such sentences as: "We never desire against our interests, because interest always follows and finds itself where desire has placed it" (*FD*, 215). An undifferentiated desire is the agent, and power slips in to create the effects of desire: "power . . . produces positive effects at the level of desire—and also at the level of knowledge" (*PK*, 59).

This parasubjective matrix, cross-hatched with heterogeneity, ushers in the unnamed Subject, at least for those intellectual workers influenced by the new hegemony of desire. The race for "the last instance" is now between economics and power. Because desire is tacitly defined on an orthodox model, it is unitarily opposed to "being deceived." Ideology as "false consciousness" (being deceived) has been called into question by Althusser. Even Reich implied notions of collective will rather than a dichotomy of deception and undeceived desire: "We must accept the scream of Reich: no, the masses were not deceived; at a particular moment, they actually desired a fascist regime" (*FD*, 215).

These philosophers will not entertain the thought of constitutive contradiction—that is where they admittedly part company from the Left. In the name of desire, they reintroduce the undivided subject into the discourse of power. Foucault often seems to conflate "individual" and "subject";[10] and the impact on his own metaphors is perhaps intensified in his followers. Because of the power of the word "power," Foucault admits to using the "metaphor of the point which progressively irradiates its surroundings." Such slips become the rule rather than the exception in less careful hands. And that radiating point, animating an effectively heliocentric discourse, fills the empty place of the agent with the historical sun of theory, the Subject of Europe.[11]

Foucault articulates another corollary of the disavowal of the role of ideology in reproducing the social relations of production: an unquestioned valorization of the oppressed as subject, the "object being," as Deleuze admiringly remarks, "to establish conditions where the prisoners themselves would be able to speak." Foucault adds that "the masses *know* perfectly well, clearly"—once again the thematics of being undeceived—"they know far better than [the intellectual] and they certainly say it very well" (*FD*, 206, 207).

What happens to the critique of the sovereign subject in these pronouncements? The limits of this representationalist realism are reached with Deleuze: "Reality is what actually happens in a factory, in a school, in barracks, in a prison, in a police station" (*FD*, 212). This foreclosing of the necessity of the difficult task of counterhegemonic ideological production has not been salutary. It has helped positivist empiricism—the justifying foundation of advanced capitalist neocolonialism—to define its own arena as "concrete experience," "what actually happens." Indeed, the concrete experience that is the guarantor of the political appeal of prisoners, soldiers, and schoolchildren is disclosed through the concrete experience of the intellectual, the one who diagnoses the episteme.[12] Neither Deleuze nor Foucault seems aware that the intellectual within socialized capital, brandishing concrete experience, can help consolidate the international division of labor.

The unrecognized contradiction within a position that valorizes the concrete experience of the oppressed, while being so uncritical about the historical role of the intellectual, is maintained by a verbal slippage. Thus Deleuze makes this remarkable pronouncement: "A theory is like a box of tools. Nothing to do with the signifier" (*FD*, 208). Considering that the verbalism of the theoretical world and its access to any world defined against it as "practical" is irreducible, such a declaration helps only the intellectual anxious to prove that intellectual labor is just like manual labor. It is when signifiers are left to look after themselves that verbal slippages happen. The signifier "representation" is a case in point. In the same dismissive tone that severs theory's link to the signifier, Deleuze declares, "There is no more representation; there's nothing but action"—"action of theory and action of practice which relate to each other as relays and form networks" (*FD*, 206–7). Yet an important point is being made here: the production of theory is also a practice; the opposition between abstract "pure" theory and concrete "applied" practice is too quick and easy.[13]

If this is, indeed, Deleuze's argument, his articulation of it is problematic. Two senses of representation are being run together: representation as "speaking for," as in politics, and representation as "re-presentation," as in art or philosophy. Since theory is also only "action," the theoretician does not represent (speak for) the oppressed group. Indeed, the subject is not seen as a representative consciousness (one re-presenting reality adequately). These two senses of representation—within state formation and the law, on the one hand, and in subject-predication, on the other—are related but irreducibly discontinuous. To cover over the discontinuity with an analogy that is presented as a proof reflects again a paradoxical subject-privileging.[14] *Because* "the person who speaks and acts . . . is always a multiplicity," no "theorizing intellectual . . . [or] party or . . . union" can represent "those who act and struggle" (*FD*, 206). Are those who act and *struggle* mute, as opposed to those who act and *speak* (*FD*, 206)? These immense problems are buried in the differences between the "same" words: consciousness and conscience (both *conscience* in French), representation and re-presentation. The critique of ideological subject-constitution within state formations and systems of political economy can now be effaced, as can the active theoretical practice of the "transformation of consciousness." The banality of leftist intellectuals' lists of self-knowing, politically canny subalterns stands revealed; representing them, the intellectuals represent themselves as transparent.

If such a critique and such a project are not to be given up, the shifting distinctions between representation within the state and political economy; on the one hand, and within the theory of the Subject, on the other, must not be obliterated. Let us consider the play of *vertreten* ("represent" in the first sense) and *darstellen* ("re-present" in the second sense) in a famous passage in *The Eighteenth Brumaire of Louis Bonaparte*, where Marx touches on "class" as a descriptive and transformative concept in a manner somewhat more complex than Althusser's distinction between class instinct and class position would allow.

Marx's contention here is that the descriptive definition of a class can be a differential one—its cutting off and difference from all other classes: "in so far as millions of families live under economic conditions of existence that cut off their mode of life, their interest, and their formation from those of the other classes and place them in inimical confrontation [*feindlich gagenüberstellen*], they form a class."[15] There is no such thing as a "class instinct" at work here. In fact, the collectivity of familial existence, which might be considered the arena of "instinct," is discontinuous with, though operated by, the differential isolation of classes. In this context, one far more pertinent to the France of the 1970s than it can be to the international periphery, the formation of a class is *artificial* and economic, and the economic agency or *interest* is impersonal because it is systematic and heterogeneous. This agency or interest is tied to the Hegelian critique of the individual subject, for it marks the subject's empty place in that process without a subject which is history and political economy. Here the capitalist is defined as "the conscious bearer [*Träger*] of the limitless movement of capital."[16] My point is that Marx is not working to create an undivided subject where desire and interest coincide. Class consciousness does not operate toward that goal. Both in the economic area (capitalist) and in the political (world-historical agent), Marx is obliged to construct models of a divided and dislocated subject whose parts are not continuous or coherent with each other. A celebrated passage like the description of capital as the Faustian monster brings this home vividly.[17]

The following passage, continuing the quotation from *The Eighteenth Brumaire*, is also working on the structural principle of a dispersed and dislocated class subject: the (absent collective) consciousness of the small peasant proprietor class finds its "bearer" in a "representative" who appears to work in another's interest. The word "representative" here is not "*darstellen*"; this sharpens the contrast Foucault and Deleuze slide over, the contrast, say, between a proxy and a portrait. There is, of course, a relationship between them, one that has received political and ideological exacerbation in the European tradition at least since the poet and the sophist, the actor and the orator, have both been seen as harmful. In the guise of a post-Marxist description of the scene of power, we thus encounter a much older debate: between representation or rhetoric as tropology and as persuasion. *Darstellen* belongs to the first constellation, *vertreten*—with stronger suggestions of substitution—to the second. Again, they are related, but running them together, especially in order to say that beyond both is where oppressed subjects speak, act, and know for themselves, leads to an essentialist, utopian politics.

Here is Marx's passage, using "*vertreten*" where the English use "represent," discussing a social "subject" whose consciousness and *Vertretung* (as much a substitution as a representation) are dislocated and incoherent: The small peasant proprietors "cannot represent themselves; they must be represented. Their representative must appear simultaneously as their master, as an authority over them, as unrestricted governmental power that protects them from the other classes and sends them rain and sunshine from above. The political influence [in the place of the class interest, since there is no unified class subject] of the small peasant proprietors therefore finds its last expression [the implication of a chain of substitutions—*Vertretungen*—is strong here] in the executive force [*Exekutivgewalt*—less personal in German] subordinating society to itself."

Not only does such a model of social indirection-necessary gaps between the source of "influence" (in this case the small peasant proprietors), the "representative" (Louis Napoleon), and the historical-political phenomenon (executive control)—imply a critique of the subject as individual agent but a critique even of the subjectivity of a *collective* agency. The necessarily dislocated machine of history moves because "the identity of the interests" of these proprietors "fails to produce a feeling of community, national links, or a political organization." The event of representation as *Vertretung* (in the constellation of rhetoric-as-persuasion) behaves like a *Darstellung* (or rhetoric-as-trope), taking its place in the gap between the formation of a (descriptive) class and the nonformation of a (transformative) class: "In so far as millions of families live under economic conditions of existence that separate their mode of life . . . they form a class. In so far as . . . the identity of their interests fails to produce a feeling of community . . . they do not form a class." The complicity of *Vertreten* and *Darstellen*, their identity-in-difference as the place of practice—since this complicity is precisely what Marxists must expose, as Marx does in *The Eighteenth Brumaire*—can only be appreciated if they are not conflated by a sleight of word.

It would be merely tendentious to argue that this textualizes Marx too much, making him inaccessible to the common "man," who, a victim of common sense, is so deeply placed in a heritage of positivism that Marx's irreducible emphasis on the work of the negative, on the necessity for de-fetishizing the concrete, is persistently wrested from him by the strongest adversary, "the historical tradition" in the air.[18] I have been trying to point out that the uncommon "man," the contemporary philosopher of practice, sometimes exhibits the same positivism.

The gravity of the problem is apparent if one agrees that the development of a transformative class "consciousness" from a descriptive class "position" is not in Marx a task engaging the ground level of consciousness. Class consciousness remains with the feeling of community that belongs to national links and political organizations, not to that other feeling of community whose structural model is the family. Although not identified with nature, the family here is constellated with what Marx calls "natural exchange," which is, philosophically speaking, a "placeholder" for use value.[19] "Natural exchange" is contrasted to "intercourse with society," where the word "intercourse" (*Verkehr*) is Marx's usual word for "commerce." This "intercourse" thus holds the place of the exchange leading to the production of surplus value, and it is in the area of this intercourse that the feeling of community leading to class agency must be developed. Full class agency (if there were such a thing) is not an ideological transformation of consciousness on the ground level, a desiring identity of the agents and their interest—the identity whose absence troubles Foucault and Deleuze. It is a *contestatory* replacement as well as an *appropriation* (a *supplementation*) of something that is "artificial" to begin with—"economic conditions of existence that separate their mode of life." Marx's formulations show a cautious respect for the nascent critique of individual and collective subjective agency. The projects of class consciousness and of the transformation of consciousness are discontinuous issues for him. Conversely, contemporary invocations of "libidinal economy" and desire as the determining interest, combined with the practical politics of the oppressed (under socialized capital) "speaking for themselves," restore the category of the sovereign subject within the theory that seems most to question it.

No doubt the exclusion of the family, albeit a family belonging to a specific class formation, is part of the masculine frame within which Marxism marks its birth.[20] Historically as well as in today's global political economy, the family's role in patriarchal social relations is so heterogeneous and contested that merely replacing the family in this problematic is not going to break the frame. Nor does the solution lie in the positivist inclusion of a monolithic collectivity of "women" in the list of the oppressed whose unfractured subjectivity allows them to speak for themselves against an equally monolithic "same system."

In the context of the development of a strategic, artificial, and second-level "consciousness," Marx uses the concept of the patronymic, always within the broader concept of representation as *Vertretung*: The small peasant proprietors "are therefore incapable of making their class interest valid in their proper name [*im eigenen Namen*], whether through a parliament or through a convention." The absence of the nonfamilial artificial collective proper name is supplied by the only proper name "historical tradition" can offer—the patronymic itself—the Name of the Father: "Historical tradition produced the French peasants' belief that a miracle would occur, that a man named Napoleon would restore all their glory. And an individual turned up"—the untranslatable *"es fand sich"* (there found itself an individual?) demolishes all questions of agency or the agent's connection with his interest—"who gave himself out to be that man" (this pretense is, by contrast, his only proper agency) "because he carried [*trägt*—the word used for the capitalist's relationship to capital] the Napoleonic Code, which commands" that "inquiry into paternity is forbidden." While Marx here seems to be working within a patriarchal metaphorics, one should note the textual subtlety of the passage. It is the Law of the Father (the Napoleonic Code) that paradoxically prohibits the search for the natural father. Thus, it is according to a strict observance of the historical Law of the Father that the formed yet unformed class's faith in the natural father is gainsaid.

I have dwelt so long on this passage in Marx because it spells out the inner dynamics of *Vertretung*, or representation in the political context. Representation in the economic context is *Darstellung*, the philosophical concept of representation as staging or, indeed, signification, which relates to the divided subject in an indirect way. The most obvious passage is well known: "In the exchange relationship [*Austauschverhältnis*] of commodities their exchange-value appeared to us totally independent of their use-value. But if we subtract their use-value from the product of labour, we obtain their value, as it was just determined [*bestimmt*]. The common element which represents itself [*sich darstellt*] in the exchange relation, or the exchange value of the commodity, is thus its value."[21]

According to Marx, under capitalism, value, as produced in necessary and surplus labor, is computed as the representation/sign of objectified labor (which is rigorously distinguished from human activity). Conversely, in the absence of a theory of exploitation as the extraction (production), appropriation, and realization of (surplus) value as *representation of labor power*, capitalist exploitation must be seen as a variety of domination (the mechanics of power as such). "The thrust of Marxism," Deleuze suggests, "was to determine the problem [that power is more diffuse than the structure of exploitation and state formation] essentially in terms of interests (power is held by a ruling class defined by its interests)" (*FD*, 214).

One cannot object to this minimalist summary of Marx's project, just as one cannot ignore that, in parts of the *Anti-Oedipus*, Deleuze and Guattari build their case on a brilliant if "poetic" grasp of Marx's *theory* of the money form. Yet we might consolidate our critique in the following way: the relationship between global capitalism (exploitation in economics) and nation-state alliances (domination in geopolitics) is so macrological that it cannot account for the micrological texture of power. To move toward such an accounting one must move toward theories of ideology—of subject formations that micrologically and often erratically operate the interests that congeal the macrologies. Such theories cannot afford to overlook the category of representation in its two senses. They must note how the staging of the world in representation—its scene of writing, its *Darstellung*—dissimulates the choice of and need for "heroes," paternal proxies, agents of power—*Vertretung*.

My view is that radical practice should attend to this double session of representations rather than reintroduce the individual subject through totalizing concepts of power and desire. It is also my view that, in keeping the area of class practice on a second level of abstraction, Marx was in effect keeping open the (Kantian and) Hegelian critique of the individual subject as agent.[22] This view does not oblige me to ignore that, by implicitly defining the family and the mother tongue as the ground level where culture and convention seem nature's own way of organizing "her" own subversion, Marx himself rehearses an ancient subterfuge.[23] In the context of poststructuralist claims to critical practice, this seems more recuperable than the clandestine restoration of subjective essentialism.

The reduction of Marx to a benevolent but dated figure most often serves the interest of launching a new theory of interpretation. In the Foucault-Deleuze conversation, the issue seems to be that there is no representation, no signifier (Is it to be presumed that the signifier has already been dispatched? There is, then, no sign-structure operating experience, and thus might one lay semiotics to rest?); theory is a relay of practice (thus laying problems of theoretical practice to rest) and the oppressed can know and speak for themselves. This reintroduces the constitutive subject on at least two levels: the Subject of desire and power as an irreducible methodological presupposition; and the self-proximate, if not self-identical, subject of the oppressed. Further, the intellectuals, who are neither of these S/subjects, become transparent in the relay race, for they merely report on the non-represented subject and analyze (without analyzing) the workings of (the unnamed Subject irreducibly presupposed by) power and desire. The produced "transparency" marks the place of "interest"; it is maintained by vehement denegation: "Now this role of referee, judge, and universal witness is one which I *absolutely refuse* to adopt." One responsibility of the critic might be to read and write so that the impossibility of such interested individualistic refusals of the institutional privileges of power bestowed on the subject is taken seriously. The refusal of the sign-system blocks the way to a developed theory of ideology. Here, too, the peculiar tone of denegation is heard. To Jacques-Alain Miller's suggestion that "the institution is itself discursive," Foucault responds, "Yes, if you like, but it doesn't much matter for my notion of the apparatus to be able to say that this is discursive and that isn't . . . given that my problem isn't a linguistic one" (*PK,* 198). Why this conflation of language and discourse from the master of discourse analysis?

Edward W. Said's critique of power in Foucault as a captivating and mystifying category that allows him "to obliterate the role of classes, the role of economics, the role of insurgency and rebellion," is most pertinent here.[24] I add to Said's analysis the notion of the surreptitious subject of power and desire marked by the transparency of the intellectual. Curiously enough, Paul Bové faults Said for emphasizing the importance of the intellectual, whereas "Foucault's project essentially is a challenge to the leading role of both hegemonic and oppositional intellectuals.[25] I have suggested that this "challenge" is deceptive precisely because it ignores what Said emphasizes—the critic's institutional responsibility.

This S/subject, curiously sewn together into a transparency by denegations, belongs to the exploiters' side of the international division of labor. It is impossible for contemporary French intellectuals to imagine the kind of Power and Desire that would inhabit the unnamed subject of the Other of Europe. It is not only that everything they read, critical or uncritical, is caught within the debate of the production of that Other, supporting or critiquing the constitution of the Subject as Europe. It is also that, in the constitution of that Other of Europe, great care was taken to obliterate the textual ingredients with which such a subject could cathect, could occupy (invest?) its itinerary——not only by ideological and scientific production, but also by the institution of the law. However reductionistic an economic analysis might seem, the French intellectuals forget at their peril that this entire overdetermined enterprise was in the interest of a dynamic economic situation requiring that interests, motives (desires), and power (of knowledge) be ruthlessly dislocated. To invoke that dislocation now as a radical discovery that should make us diagnose the economic (conditions of existence that separate out "classes" descriptively) as a piece of dated analytic machinery may well be to continue the work of that dislocation and unwittingly to help in securing "a new balance of hegemonic relations."[26] I shall return to this argument shortly. In the face of the possibility that the intellectual is complicit in the persistent constitution of Other as the Self's shadow, a possibility of political practice for the intellectual would be to put the economic "under erasure," to see the economic factor as irreducible as it reinscribes the social text, even as it is erased, however imperfectly, when it claims to be the final determinant or the transcendental signified.[27]

II

The clearest available example of such epistemic violence is the remotely orchestrated, far-flung, and heterogeneous project to constitute the colonial subject as Other. This project is also the asymmetrical obliteration of the trace of that Other in its precarious Subject-ivity. It is well known that Foucault locates epistemic violence, a complete overhaul of the episteme, in the redefinition of sanity at the end of the European eighteenth century.[28] But what if that particular redefinition was only a part of the narrative of history in Europe as well as in the colonies? What if the two projects of epistemic overhaul worked as dislocated and unacknowledged parts of a vast two-handed engine? Perhaps it is no more than to ask that the subtext of the palimpsestic narrative of imperialism be recognized as "subjugated knowledge," "a whole set of knowledges that have been disqualified as inadequate to their task or insufficiently elaborated: naive knowledges, located low down on the hierarchy, beneath the required level of cognition or scientificity" (*PK*, 82).

This is not to describe "the way things really were" or to privilege the narrative of history as imperialism as the best version of history.[29] It is, rather, to offer an account of how an explanation and narrative of reality was established as the normative one. To elaborate on this, let us consider briefly the underpinnings of the British codification of Hindu Law.

First, a few disclaimers: In the United States the third-worldism currently afloat in humanistic disciplines is often openly ethnic. I was born in India and received my primary, secondary, and university education there, including two years of graduate work. My Indian example could thus be seen as a nostalgic investigation of the lost roots of my own identity. Yet even as I know that one cannot freely enter the thickets of "motivations," I would maintain that my chief project is to point out the positivist-idealist variety of such nostalgia. I turn to Indian material because, in the absence of advanced disciplinary training, that accident of birth and education has provided me with a sense of the historical canvas, a hold on some of the pertinent languages that are useful tools for a bricoleur, especially when armed with the Marxist skepticism of concrete experience as the final arbiter and a critique of disciplinary formations. Yet the Indian case cannot be taken as representative of all countries, nations, cultures, and the like that may be invoked as the Other of Europe as Self.

Here, then, is a schematic summary of the epistemic violence of the codification of Hindu Law. If it clarifies the notion of epistemic violence, my final discussion of widow-sacrifice may gain added significance.

At the end of the eighteenth century, Hindu law, insofar as it can be described as a unitary system, operated in terms of four texts that "staged" a four-part episteme defined by the subject's use of memory: *sruti* (the heard), *smriti* (the remembered), *sastra* (the learned-from-another), and *vyavahara* (the performed-in-exchange). The origins of what had been heard and what was remembered were not necessarily continuous or identical. Every invocation of *sruti* technically recited (or reopened) the event of originary "hearing" or revelation. The second two texts—the learned and the performed—were seen as dialectically continuous. Legal theorists and practitioners were not in any given case certain if this structure described the body of law or four ways of settling a dispute. The legitimation of the polymorphous structure of legal performance, "internally" noncoherent and open at both ends, through a binary vision, is the narrative of codification I offer as an example of epistemic violence.

The narrative of the stabilization and codification of Hindu law is less well known than the story of Indian education, so it might be well to start there.[30] Consider the often-quoted programmatic lines from Macaulay's infamous "Minute on Indian Education" (1835): "We must at present do our best to form a class who may be interpreters between us and the millions whom we govern; a class of persons, Indian in blood and colour, but English in taste, in opinions, in morals, and in intellect. To that class we may leave it to refine the vernacular dialects of the country, to enrich those dialects with terms of science borrowed from the Western nomenclature, and to render them by degrees fit vehicles for conveying knowledge to the great mass of the population."[31] The education of colonial subjects complements their production in law. One effect of establishing a version of the British system was the development of an uneasy separation between disciplinary formation in Sanskrit studies and the native, now alternative, tradition of Sanskrit "high culture." Within the former, the cultural explanations generated by authoritative scholars matched the epistemic violence of the legal project.

I locate here the founding of the Asiatic Society of Bengal in 1784, the Indian Institute at Oxford in 1883, and the analytic and taxonomic work of scholars like Arthur Macdonnell and Arthur Berriedale Keith, who were both colonial administrators and organizers of the matter of Sanskrit. From their confident utilitarian-hegemonic plans for students and scholars of Sanskrit, it is impossible to guess at either the aggressive repression of Sanskrit in the general educational framework or the increasing "feudalization" of the performative use of Sanskrit in the everyday life of Brahmanic-hegemonic India.[32] A version of history was gradually established in which the Brahmans were shown to have the same intentions as (thus providing the legitimation for) the codifying British: "In order to preserve Hindu society intact [the] successors [of the original Brahmans] had to reduce everything to writing and make them more and more rigid. And that is what has preserved Hindu society in spite of a succession of political upheavals and foreign invasions."[33] This is the 1925 verdict of Mahamahopadhyaya Haraprasad Shastri, learned Indian Sanskritist, a brilliant representative of the indigenous elite within colonial production, who was asked to write several chapters of a "History of Bengal" projected by the private secretary to the governor general of Bengal in 1916.[34] To signal the asymmetry in the relationship between authority and explanation (depending on the race-class of the authority), compare this 1928 remark by Edward Thompson, English intellectual: "Hinduism was what it seemed to be. . . . It was a higher civilization that won [against it], both with Akbar and the English."[35] And add this, from a letter by an English soldier-scholar in the 1890s: "The study of Sanskrit, 'the language of the gods' has afforded me intense enjoyment during the last 25 years of my life in India, but it has not, I am thankful to say, led me, *as it has some*, to give up a hearty belief in our own grand religion."[36]

These authorities are *the very best* of the sources for the nonspecialist French intellectual's entry into the civilization of the Other.[37] I am, however, not referring to intellectuals and scholars of postcolonial production, like Shastri, when I say that the Other as Subject is inaccessible to Foucault and Deleuze. I am thinking of the general nonspecialist, nonacademic population across the class spectrum, for whom the episteme operates its silent programming function. Without considering the map of exploitation, on what grid of "oppression" would they place this motley crew?

Let us now move to consider the margins (one can just as well say the silent, silenced center) of the circuit marked out by this epistemic violence, men and women among the illiterate peasantry, the tribals, the lowest strata of the urban subproletariat. According to Foucault and Deleuze (in the First World, under the standardization and regimentation of socialized capital, though they do not seem to recognize this) the oppressed, if given the chance (the problem of representation cannot be bypassed here), and on the way to solidarity through alliance politics (a Marxist thematic is at work here) *can speak and know their conditions*. We must now confront the following question: On the other side of the international division of labor from socialized capital, inside and outside the circuit of the epistemic violence of imperialist law and education supplementing an earlier economic text, *can the subaltern speak?*

Antonio Gramsci's work on the "subaltern classes" extends the class-position/class-consciousness argument isolated in *The Eighteenth Brumaire*. Perhaps because Gramsci criticizes the vanguardistic position of the Leninist intellectual, he is concerned with the intellectual's role in the subaltern's cultural and political movement into the hegemony. This movement must be made to determine the production of history as narrative (of truth). In texts such as "The Southern Question," Gramsci considers the movement of historical-political economy in Italy within what can be seen as an allegory of reading taken from or prefiguring an international division of labor.[38] Yet an account of the phased development of the subaltern is thrown out of joint when his cultural macrology is operated, however remotely, by the epistemic interference with legal and disciplinary definitions accompanying the imperialist project. When I move, at the end of this essay, to the question of woman as subaltern, I will suggest that the possibility of collectivity itself is persistently foreclosed through the manipulation of female agency.

The first part of my proposition—that the phased development of the subaltern is complicated by the imperialist project—is confronted by a collective of intellectuals who may be called the "Subaltern Studies" group.[39] They *must* ask, Can the subaltern speak? Here we are within Foucault's own discipline of history and with people who acknowledge his influence. Their project is to rethink Indian colonial historiography from the perspective of the discontinuous chain of peasant insurgencies during the colonial occupation. This is indeed the problem of "the permission to narrate" discussed by Said.[40] As Ranajit Guha argues,

> The historiography of Indian nationalism has for a long time been dominated by elitism—colonialist elitism and bourgeois-nationalist elitism
> . . . shar[ing] the prejudice that the making of the Indian nation and the

development of the consciousness—nationalism—which confirmed this process were exclusively or predominantly elite achievements. In the colonialist and neo-colonialist historiographies these achievements are credited to British colonial rulers, administrators, policies, institutions, and culture; in the nationalist and neo-nationalist writing—to Indian elite personalities, institutions, activities and ideas.[41]

Certain varieties of the Indian elite are at best native informants for first-world intellectuals interested in the voice of the Other. But one must nevertheless insist that the colonized subaltern subject is irretrievably heterogeneous.

Against the indigenous elite we may set what Guha calls "the *politics of the people*," both outside ("this was an *autonomous* domain, for it neither originated from elite politics nor did its existence depend on the latter") and inside ("it continued to operate vigorously in spite of [colonialism], adjusting itself to the conditions prevailing under the Raj and in many respects developing entirely new strains in both form and content") the circuit of colonial production.[42] I cannot entirely endorse this insistence on determinate vigor and full autonomy, for practical historiographic exigencies will not allow such endorsements to privilege subaltern consciousness. Against the possible charge that his approach is essentialist, Guha constructs a definition of the people (the place of that essence) that can be only an identity-in-differential. He proposes a dynamic stratification grid describing colonial social production at large. Even the third group on the list, the buffer group, as it were, between the people and the great macrostructural dominant groups, is itself defined as a place of in-betweenness, what Derrida has described as an "*antre*":[43]

ELITE: 1. Dominant foreign groups.

2. Dominant indigenous groups on the all-India level.

3. Dominant indigenous groups at the regional and local levels.

4. The terms "people" and "subaltern classes" have been used as synonymous throughout this note. The social groups and elements included in this category represent the demographic difference between the total Indian population and all those whom we have described as the "elite."

Consider the third item on this list—the *antre* of situational indeterminacy these careful historians presuppose as they grapple with the question, Can the subaltern speak? *"Taken as a whole and in the abstract* this . . . category . . . was *heterogeneous* in its composition and thanks to the uneven character of regional economic and social developments, *differed from area to area.* The same class or element which was dominant in one area . . . could be among the dominated in another. This could and did create many ambiguities and contradictions in attitudes and alliances, especially among the lowest strata of the rural gentry, impoverished landlords, rich peasants and upper middle class peasants all of whom belonged, *ideally speaking*, to the category of people or subaltern classes. "[44]

"The task of research" projected here is "to investigate, identify and measure the *specific* nature and degree of the *deviation* of [the] elements [constituting item 3] from the ideal and situate it historically." "Investigate, identify, and measure the specific": a program could hardly be more essentialist and taxonomic. Yet a curious methodological imperative is at work. I have argued that, in the Foucault-Deleuze conversation, a postrepresentationalist vocabulary hides an essentialist agenda. In subaltern studies, because of the violence of imperialist epistemic, social, and disciplinary inscription, a project understood in essentialist terms must traffic in a radical textual practice of differences. The object of the group's investigation, in the case not even of the people as such but of the floating buffer zone of the regional elite-subaltern, is a *deviation* from an *idea*—the people or subaltern—which is itself defined as a difference from the elite. It is toward this structure that the research is oriented, a predicament rather different from the self-diagnosed transparency of the first-world radical intellectual. What taxonomy can fix such a space? Whether or not they themselves perceive it—in fact Guha sees his definition of "the people" within the master-slave dialectic—their text articulates the difficult task of rewriting its own conditions of impossibility as the conditions of its possibility.

"At the regional and local levels [the dominant indigenous groups] . . . if belonging to social strata hierarchically inferior to those of the dominant all-Indian groups *acted in the interests of the latter and not in conformity to interests corresponding truly to their own social being.*" When these writers speak, in their essentializing language, of a gap between interest and action in the intermediate group, their conclusions are closer to Marx than to the self-conscious naivete of Deleuze's pronouncement on the issue. Guha, like Marx, speaks of interest in terms of the social rather than the libidinal being. The Name-of-the-Father imagery in *The Eighteenth Brumaire* can help to emphasize that, on the level of class or group action, "true correspondence to own being" is as artificial or social as the patronymic.

So much for the intermediate group marked in item 3. For the "true" subaltern group, whose identity is its difference, there is no unrepresentable subaltern subject that can know and speak itself; the intellectual's solution is not to abstain from representation. The problem is that the subject's itinerary has not been traced so as to offer an object of seduction to the representing intellectual. In the slightly dated language of the Indian group, the question becomes, How can we touch the consciousness of the people, even as we investigate their politics? With what voice-consciousness can the subaltern speak? Their project, after all, is to rewrite the development of the consciousness of the Indian nation. The planned discontinuity of imperialism rigorously distinguishes this project, however old-fashioned its articulation, from "rendering visible the medical and juridical mechanisms that surrounded the story [of Pierre Riviere]." Foucault is correct in suggesting that "to make visible the unseen can also mean a change of level, addressing oneself to a layer of material which had hitherto had no pertinence for history and which had not been recognized as having any moral, aesthetic or historical value." It is the slippage from rendering visible the mechanism to rendering vocal the individual, both avoiding "any kind of analysis of [the subject] whether psychological, psychoanalytical or linguistic," that is consistently troublesome (*PK*, 49–50).

The critique by Ajit K. Chaudhury, a West Bengali Marxist, of Guha's search for the subaltern consciousness can be seen as a moment of the production process that includes the subaltern. Chaudhury's perception that the Marxist view of the transformation of consciousness involves the *knowledge* of social relations seems to me, in principle, astute. Yet the heritage of the positivist ideology that has appropriated orthodox Marxism obliges him to add this rider: "This is not to belittle the importance of understanding peasants' consciousness or workers' consciousness *in its pure form*. This enriches our knowledge of the peasant and the worker and, possibly, throws light on how a particular mode takes on different forms in different regions, *which is considered a problem of second-order importance in classical Marxism*."[45]

This variety of "internationalist" Marxism, which believes in a pure, retrievable form of consciousness only to dismiss it, thus closing off what in Marx remain moments of productive bafflement, can at once be the object of Foucault's and Deleuze's rejection of Marxism and the source of the critical motivation of the Subaltern Studies group. All three are united in the assumption that there is a pure form of consciousness. On the French scene, there is a shuffling of signifiers: "the unconscious" or "the subject-in-oppression" clandestinely fills the space of "the pure form of consciousness." In orthodox "internationalist" intellectual Marxism, whether in the First World or the Third, the pure form of consciousness remains an idealistic bedrock which, dismissed as a second-order problem, often earns it the reputation of racism and sexism. In the Subaltern Studies group it needs development according to the unacknowledged terms of its own articulation.

For such an articulation, a developed theory of ideology can again be most useful. In a critique such as Chaudhury's, the association of "consciousness" with "knowledge" omits the crucial middle term of "ideological production": "Consciousness, according to Lenin, is associated with a *knowledge* of the interrelationships between different classes and groups; i.e., a knowledge of the materials that constitute society. . . . These definitions acquire a meaning only within the problematic within a definite knowledge object— to *understand* change in history, or specifically, change from one mode to another, *keeping the question of the specificity of a particular mode out of the focus*."[46]

Pierre Macherey provides the following formula for the interpretation of ideology: "What is important in a work is what it does not say. This is not the same as the careless notation 'what it refuses to say,' although that would in itself be interesting: a method might be built on it, with the task of *measuring silences*, whether acknowledged or unacknowledged. But rather this, what the work *cannot* say is important, because there the elaboration of the utterance is carried out, in a sort of journey to silence."[47] Macherey's ideas can be developed in directions he would be unlikely to follow. Even as he writes, ostensibly, of the literariness of the literature of European provenance, he articulates a method applicable to the social text of imperialism, somewhat against the grain of his own argument. Although the notion "what it refuses to say" might be careless for a literary work, something like a collective ideological *refusal* can be diagnosed for the codifying legal practice of imperialism. This would open the field for a political-economic and multidisciplinary ideological reinscription of the terrain. Because this is a "worlding of the world" on a second level of abstraction, a concept of refusal becomes plausible here. The archival, historiographic, disciplinary-critical, and, inevitably, interventionist work involved here is indeed a task of "measuring silences." This can be a description of "investigating, identifying, and measuring . . . the deviation" from an ideal that is irreducibly differential.

When we come to the concomitant question of the consciousness of the subaltern, the notion of what the work *cannot* say becomes important. In the semioses of the social text, elaborations of insurgency stand in the place of "the utterance." The sender—"the peasant"—is marked only as a pointer to an irretrievable consciousness. As for the receiver, we must ask who is "the real receiver" of an "insurgency"? The historian, transforming "insurgency" into "text for knowledge," is only one "receiver" of any collectively intended social act. With no possibility of nostalgia for that lost origin, the historian must suspend (as far as possible) the clamor of his or her own consciousness (or consciousness-effect, as operated by disciplinary training), so that the elaboration of the insurgency, packaged with an insurgent-consciousness, does not freeze into an "object of investigation," or, worse yet, a model for imitation. "The subject" implied by the texts of insurgency can only serve as a counterpossibility for the narrative sanctions granted to the colonial subject in the dominant groups. The postcolonial intellectuals learn that their privilege is their loss. In this they are a paradigm of the intellectuals.

It is well known that the notion of the feminine (rather than the subaltern of imperialism) has been used in a similar way within deconstructive criticism and within certain varieties of feminist criticism.[48] In the former case, a figure of "woman" is at issue, one whose minimal predication as indeterminate is already available to the phallocentric tradition. Subaltern historiography raises questions of method that would prevent it from using such a ruse. For the "figure" of woman, the relationship between woman and silence can be plotted by women themselves; race and class differences are subsumed under that charge. Subaltern historiography must confront the impossibility of such gestures. The narrow epistemic violence of imperialism gives us an imperfect allegory of the general violence that is the possibility of an episteme.[49]

Within the effaced itinerary of the subaltern subject, the track of sexual difference is doubly effaced. The question is not of female participation in insurgency, or the ground rules of the sexual division of labor, for both of which there is "evidence." It is, rather, that, both as object of colonialist historiography and as subject of insurgency, the ideological construction of gender keeps the male dominant. If, in the context of colonial production, the subaltern has no history and cannot speak, the subaltern as female is even more deeply in shadow.

The contemporary international division of labor is a displacement of the divided field of nineteenth-century territorial imperialism. Put simply, a group of countries, generally first-world, are in the position of investing capital; another group, generally third-world, provide the field for investment, both through the comprador indigenous capitalists and through their ill-protected and shifting labor force. In the interest of maintaining the circulation and growth of industrial capital (and of the concomitant task of administration within nineteenth-century territorial imperialism), transportation, law, and standardized education systems were developed—even as local industries were destroyed, land distribution was rearranged, and raw material was transferred to the colonizing country. With so-called decolonization, the growth of multinational capital, and the relief of the administrative charge, "development" does not now involve wholesale legislation and establishing educational *systems* in a comparable way. This impedes the growth of consumerism in the comprador countries. With modern telecommunications and the emergence of advanced capitalist economies at the two edges of Asia, maintaining the international division of labor serves to keep the supply of cheap labor in the comprador countries.

Human labor is not, of course, intrinsically "cheap" or "expensive." An absence of labor laws (or a discriminatory enforcement of them), a totalitarian state (often entailed by development and modernization in the periphery), and minimal subsistence requirements on the part of the worker will ensure it. To keep this crucial item intact, the urban proletariat in comprador countries must not be systematically trained in the ideology of consumerism (parading as the philosophy of a classless society) that, against all odds, prepares the ground for resistance through the coalition politics Foucault mentions (*FD*, 216). This separation from the ideology of consumerism is increasingly exacerbated by the proliferating phenomena of international subcontracting. "Under this strategy, manufacturers based in developed countries subcontract the most labor intensive stages of production, for example, sewing or assembly, to the Third World nations where labor is cheap. Once assembled, the multinational re-imports the goods under generous tariff exemptions—to the developed country *instead of selling them to the local market.*" Here the link to training in consumerism is almost snapped. "While global recession has markedly slowed trade and investment worldwide since 1979, international subcontracting has boomed.... In these cases, multinationals are freer to resist militant workers, revolutionary upheavals, and even economic downturns."[50]

Class mobility is increasingly lethargic in the comprador theaters. Not surprisingly, some members of *indigenous dominant* groups in comprador countries, members of the local bourgeoisie, find the language of alliance politics attractive. Identifying with forms of resistance plausible in advanced capitalist countries is often of a piece with that elitist bent of bourgeois historiography described by Ranajit Guha.

Belief in the plausibility of global alliance politics is prevalent among women of dominant social groups interested in "international feminism" in the comprador countries. At the other end of the scale, those most separated from any possibility of an alliance among "women, prisoners, conscripted soldiers, hospital patients, and homosexuals" (*FD*, 216) are the females of the urban subproletariat. In their case, the denial and withholding of consumerism and the structure of exploitation is compounded by patriarchal social relations. On the other side of the international division of labor, the subject of exploitation cannot know and speak the text of female exploitation, even if the absurdity of the nonrepresenting intellectual making space for her to speak is achieved. The woman is doubly in shadow.

Yet even this does not encompass the heterogeneous Other. Outside (though not completely so) the circuit of the *international* division of labor, there are people whose consciousness we cannot grasp if we close off our benevolence by constructing a homogeneous Other referring only to our own place in the seat of the Same or the Self. Here are subsistence farmers, unorganized peasant labor, the tribals, and the communities of zero workers on the street or in the countryside. To confront them is not to represent (*vertreten*) them but to learn to represent (*darstellen*) ourselves. This argument would take us into a critique of a disciplinary anthropology and the relationship between elementary pedagogy and disciplinary formation. It would also question the implicit demand, made by intellectuals who choose a "naturally articulate" subject of oppression, that such a subject come through history as a foreshortened mode-of-production narrative.

That Deleuze and Foucault ignore both the epistemic violence of imperialism and the international division of labor would matter less if they did not, in closing, touch on third-world issues. But in France it is impossible to ignore the problem of the *tiers monde,* the inhabitants of the erstwhile French African colonies. Deleuze limits his consideration of the Third World to these old local and regional indigenous elite who are, ideally, subaltern. In this context, references to the maintenance of the surplus army of labor fall into reverse-ethnic sentimentality. Since he is speaking of the heritage of nineteenth-century territorial imperialism, his reference is to the nation-state rather than the globalizing center: "French capitalism needs greatly a floating signifier of unemployment. In this perspective, we begin to see the unity of the forms of repression: restrictions on immigration, once it is acknowledged that the most difficult and thankless jobs go to immigrant workers; repression in the factories, because the French must reacquire the 'taste' for increasingly harder work; the struggle against youth and the repression of the educational system" (*FD,* 211–12). This is an acceptable analysis. Yet it shows again that the Third World can enter the resistance program of an alliance politics directed against a *"unified* repression" only when it is confined to the third-world groups that are directly accessible to the First World.[51] This benevolent first-world appropriation and reinscription of the Third World as an Other is the founding characteristic of much third-worldism in the U.S. human sciences today.

Foucault continues the critique of Marxism by invoking geographical discontinuity. The real mark of "geographical (geopolitical) discontinuity" is the international division of labor. But Foucault uses the term to distinguish between exploitation (extraction and appropriation of surplus value; read, the field of Marxist analysis) and domination ("power" studies) and to suggest the latter's greater potential for resistance based on alliance politics. He cannot acknowledge that such a monist and unified access to a conception of "power" (methodologically presupposing a Subject-of-power) is made possible by a certain stage in exploitation, for his vision of geographical discontinuity is geopolitically specific to the First World:

> This geographical discontinuity of which you speak might mean perhaps the following: as soon as we struggle against *exploitation*, the proletariat not only leads the struggle but also defines its targets, its methods, its places and its instruments; and to ally oneself with the proletariat is to consolidate with its positions, its ideology, it is to take up again the motives for their combat. This means total immersion [in the Marxist project]. But if it is against *power* that one struggles, then all those who acknowledge it as intolerable can begin the struggle wherever they find themselves and in terms of their own activity (or passivity). In engaging in this struggle that is *their own*, whose objectives they clearly understand and whose methods they can determine, they enter into the revolutionary process. As allies of the proletariat, to be sure, because power is exercised the way it is in order to maintain capitalist exploitation. They genuinely serve the cause of the proletariat by fighting in those places where they find themselves oppressed. Women, prisoners, conscripted soldiers, hospital patients, and homosexuals have now begun a specific struggle against the particular form of power, the constraints and controls, that are exercised over them. (*FD*, 216)

This is an admirable program of localized resistance. Where possible, this model of resistance is not an alternative to, but can complement, macrological struggles along "Marxist" lines. Yet if its situation is universalized, it accommodates unacknowledged privileging of the subject. Without a theory of ideology, it can lead to a dangerous utopianism.

Foucault is a brilliant thinker of power-in-spacing, but the awareness of the topographical reinscription of imperialism does not inform his presuppositions. He is taken in by the restricted version of the West produced by that reinscription and thus helps to consolidate its effects. Notice the omission of the fact, in the following passage, that the new mechanism of power in the seventeenth and eighteenth centuries (the extraction of surplus value without extraeconomic coercion is its Marxist description) is secured *by means of* territorial imperialism—the Earth and its products—"elsewhere." The representation of sovereignty is crucial in those theaters: "In the seventeenth and eighteenth centuries, we have the production of an important phenomenon, the emergence, or rather the invention, of a new mechanism of power possessed of highly specific procedural techniques . . . which is also, I believe, absolutely incompatible with the relations of sovereignty. This new mechanism of power is more dependent upon bodies and what they do than the Earth and its products" (*PK*, 104).

Because of a blind spot regarding the first wave of "geographical discontinuity," Foucault can remain impervious to its second wave in the middle decades of our own century, identifying it simply "with the collapse of Fascism and the decline of Stalinism" (*PK*, 87). Here is Mike Davis's alternative view: "It was rather the global logic of counter-revolutionary violence which created conditions for the peaceful economic interdependence of a chastened Atlantic imperialism under American leadership. . . . It was multi-national military integration under the slogan of collective security against the USSR which preceded and quickened the interpenetration of the major capitalist economies, making possible the new era of commercial liberalism which flowered between 1958 and 1973."[52]

It is within the emergence of this "new mechanism of power" that we must read the fixation on national scenes, the resistance to economics, and the emphasis on concepts like power and desire that privilege micrology. Davis continues: "This quasi-absolutist centralization of strategic military power by the United States was to allow an enlightened and flexible subordinancy for its principal satraps. In particular, it proved highly accommodating to the residual imperialist pretensions of the French and British . . . with each keeping up a strident ideological mobilization against communism all the while." While taking precautions against such unitary notions as "France," it must be said that such unitary notions as "*the* workers' struggle," or such unitary pronouncements as "like power, resistance is multiple and can be integrated in global strategies" (*PK*, 142), seem interpretable by way of Davis's narrative. I am not suggesting, as does Paul Bové, that "for a displaced and homeless people [the Palestinians] assaulted militarily and culturally . . . a question [such as Foucault's 'to engage in politics . . . *is* to try to know with the greatest possible honesty whether the revolution is desirable'] is a foolish luxury of Western wealth."[53] I am suggesting, rather, that to buy a self-contained version of the West is to ignore its production by the imperialist project.

Sometimes it seems as if the very brilliance of Foucault's analysis of the centuries of European imperialism produces a miniature version of that heterogeneous phenomenon: management of space—but by doctors; development of administrations—but in asylums; considerations of the periphery— but in terms of the insane, prisoners, and children. The clinic, the asylum, the prison, the university—all seem to be screen-allegories that foreclose a reading of the broader narratives of imperialism. (One could open a similar discussion of the ferocious motif of "deterritorialization" in Deleuze and Guattari.) "One can perfectly well not talk about something because one doesn't know about it," Foucault might murmur (*PK*, 66). Yet we have already spoken of the sanctioned ignorance that every critic of imperialism must chart.

III

On the general level on which U.S. academics and students take "influence" from France, one encounters the following understanding: Foucault deals with real history, real politics, and real social problems; Derrida is inaccessible, esoteric, and textualistic. The reader is probably well acquainted with this received idea. "That [Derrida's] own work," Terry Eagleton writes, "has been grossly unhistorical, politically evasive and in practice oblivious to language as 'discourse' [language in function] is not to be denied."[54] Eagleton goes on to recommend Foucault's study of "discursive practices." Perry Anderson constructs a related history: "With Derrida, the self-cancellation of structuralism latent in the recourse to music or madness in Lévi-Strauss or Foucault is consummated. With no commitment to exploration of social realities at all, Derrida had little compunction in undoing the constructions of these two, convicting them both of a 'nostalgia of origins'—Rousseauesque or pre-Socratic, respectively—and asking what right either had to assume, on their own premises, the validity of their discourses."[55]

This paper is committed to the notion that, whether in defense of Derrida or not, a nostalgia for lost origins can be detrimental to the exploration of social realities within the critique of imperialism. Indeed, the brilliance of Anderson's misreading does not prevent him from seeing precisely the problem I emphasize in Foucault: "Foucault struck the characteristically prophetic note when he declared in 1966: 'Man is in the process of perishing as the being of language continues to shine ever more brightly upon our horizon.' But who is the 'we' to perceive or possess such a horizon?" Anderson does not see the encroachment of the unacknowledged Subject of the West in the later Foucault, a Subject that presides by disavowal. He sees Foucault's attitude in the usual way, as the disappearance of the knowing Subject as such; and he further sees in Derrida the final development of that tendency: "In the hollow of the pronoun [we] lies the aporia of the programme."[56] Consider, finally, Said's plangent aphorism, which betrays a profound misapprehension of the notion of "textuality": "Derrida's criticism moves us *into* the text, Foucault's *in* and *out*."[57]

I have tried to argue that the substantive concern for the politics of the oppressed which often accounts for Foucault's appeal can hide a privileging of the intellectual and of the "concrete" subject of oppression that, in fact, compounds the appeal. Conversely, though it is not my intention here to counter the specific view of Derrida promoted by these influential writers, I will discuss a few aspects of Derrida's work that retain a long-term usefulness for people outside the First World. This is not an apology. Derrida is hard to read; his real object of investigation is classical philosophy. Yet he is less dangerous when understood than the first-world intellectual masquerading as the absent nonrepresenter who lets the oppressed speak for themselves.

I will consider a chapter that Derrida composed twenty years ago: "Of Grammatology As a Positive Science" (*OG,* 74–93). In this chapter Derrida confronts the issue of whether "deconstruction" can lead to an adequate practice, whether critical or political. The question is how to keep the ethnocentric Subject from establishing itself by selectively defining an Other. This is not a program for the Subject as such; rather, it is a program for the benevolent *Western* intellectual. For those of us who feel that the "subject" has a history and that the task of the first-world subject of knowledge in our historical moment is to resist and critique "recognition" of the Third World through "assimilation," this specificity is crucial. In order to advance a factual rather than a pathetic critique of the European intellectual's ethnocentric impulse, Derrida admits that he cannot ask the "first" questions that must be answered to establish the grounds of his argument. He does not declare that grammatology can "rise above" (Frank Lentricchia's phrase) mere empiricism; for, like empiricism, it cannot ask first questions. Derrida thus aligns "grammatological" knowledge *with the same problems* as empirical investigation. "Deconstruction" is not, therefore, a new word for "ideological demystification." Like "empirical investigation . . . tak[ing] shelter in the field of grammatological knowledge" obliges "operat[ing] through 'examples'" (*OG,* 75).

The examples Derrida lays out—to show the limits of grammatology as a positive science—come from the appropriate ideological self-justification of an imperialist project. In the European seventeenth century, he writes, there were three kinds of "prejudices" operating in histories of writing which constituted a "symptom of the crisis of European consciousness" (*OG,* 75): the "theological prejudice," the "Chinese prejudice," and the "hieroglyphist prejudice." The first can be indexed as: God wrote a primitive or natural script: Hebrew or Greek. The second: Chinese is a perfect *blueprint* for philosophical writing, but it is only a blueprint. True philosophical writing is "independen[t] with regard to history" (*OG,* 79) and will sublate Chinese into an easy-to-learn script that will supersede actual Chinese. The

third: that Egyptian script is too sublime to be deciphered. The first prejudice preserves the "actuality" of Hebrew or Greek; the last two ("rational"
and "mystical," respectively) collude to support the first, where the center
of the logos is seen as the Judaeo-Christian God (the appropriation of the
Hellenic Other through assimilation is an earlier story)—a "prejudice" still
sustained in efforts to give the cartography of the Judaeo-Christian myth
the status of geopolitical history:

> The concept of Chinese writing thus functioned as a sort of *European hal-*
> *lucination.* . . . This functioning obeyed a rigorous necessity. . . . It was not
> disturbed by the knowledge of Chinese script . . . which was then avail-
> able. . . . A *"hieroglyphist prejudice"* had produced the same effect of *in-*
> *terested blindness.* Far from proceeding . . . from ethnocentric scorn, the
> occultation takes the form of an hyperbolical admiration. We have not fin-
> ished demonstrating the necessity of this pattern. Our century is not free
> from it; each time that ethnocentrism is precipitately and ostentatiously
> reversed, some effort silently hides behind all the spectacular effects to
> *consolidate an inside* and to draw from it some domestic benefit. (*OG,* 80;
> Derrida italicizes only "hieroglyphist prejudice")

Derrida proceeds to offer two characteristic possibilities for solutions to
the problem of the European Subject, which seeks to produce an Other that
would consolidate an inside, its own subject status. What follows is an account of the complicity between writing, the opening of domestic and civil
society, and the structures of desire, power, and capitalization. Derrida then
discloses the vulnerability of his own desire to conserve something that is,
paradoxically, both ineffable and nontranscendental. In critiquing the production of the colonial subject, this ineffable, nontranscendental ("historical") place is cathected by the subaltern subject.

Derrida closes the chapter by showing again that the project of grammatology is obliged to develop *within* the discourse of presence. It is not just
a critique of presence but an awareness of the itinerary of the discourse of
presence in one's *own* critique, a vigilance precisely against too great a claim
for transparency. The word "writing" as the name of the object and model
of grammatology is a practice "only within the *historical* closure, that is to
say within the limits of science and philosophy" (*OG,* 93).

Derrida here makes Nietzschean, philosophical, and psychoanalytic,
rather than specifically political, choices to suggest a critique of European
ethnocentrism in the constitution of the Other. As a postcolonial intellectual, I am not troubled that he does not *lead* me (as Europeans inevitably seem
to do) to the specific path that such a critique makes necessary. It is more

important to me that, as a European philosopher, he articulates the *European* Subject's tendency to constitute the Other as marginal to ethnocentrism and locates *that* as the problem with all logocentric and therefore also all grammatological endeavors (since the main thesis of the chapter is the complicity between the two). *Not* a general problem, but a *European* problem. It is within the context of this ethnocentricism that he tries so desperately to demote the Subject of thinking or knowledge as to say that *"thought is . . .* the blank part of the text" (*OG,* 93); that which is thought is, if blank, still in *the text* and must be consigned to the Other of history. That inaccessible blankness circumscribed by an interpretable text is what a postcolonial critic of imperialism would like to see developed within the European enclosure as *the* place of the production of theory. The postcolonial critics and intellectuals can attempt to displace their own production only by presupposing that *text-inscribed* blankness. To render thought or the thinking subject transparent or invisible seems, by contrast, to hide the relentless recognition of the Other by assimilation. It is in the interest of such cautions that Derrida does not invoke "letting the other(s) speak for himself" but rather invokes an "appeal" to or "call" to the "quite-other" (*tout-autre* as opposed to a self-consolidating other), of "rendering *delirious* that interior voice that is the voice of the other in us."[58]

Derrida calls the ethnocentrism of the European science of writing in the late seventeenth and early eighteenth centuries a symptom of the general crisis of European consciousness. It is, of course, part of a greater symptom, or perhaps the crisis itself, the slow turn from feudalism to capitalism via the first waves of capitalist imperialism. The itinerary of recognition through assimilation of the Other can be more interestingly traced, it seems to me, in the imperialist constitution of the colonial subject than in repeated incursions into psychoanalysis or the "figure" of woman, though the importance of these two interventions *within* deconstruction should not be minimized. Derrida has not moved (or perhaps cannot move) into that arena.

Whatever the reasons for this specific absence, what I find useful is the sustained and developing work on the *mechanics* of the constitution of the Other; we can use it to much greater analytic and interventionist advantage than invocations of the *authenticity* of the Other. On this level, what remains useful in Foucault is the mechanics of disciplinarization and institutionalization, the constitution, as it were, of the colonizer. Foucault does not relate it to any version, early or late, proto- or post-, of imperialism. They are of great usefulness to intellectuals concerned with the decay of the West. Their seduction for them, and fearfulness for us, is that they might allow the complicity of the investigating subject (male or female professional) to disguise itself in transparency.

IV

Can the subaltern speak? What must the elite do to watch out for the continuing construction of the subaltern? The question of "woman" seems most problematic in this context. Clearly, if you are poor, black, and female you get it in three ways. If, however, this formulation is moved from the first-world context into the postcolonial (which is not identical with the third-world) context, the description "black" or "of color" loses persuasive significance. The necessary stratification of colonial subject-constitution in the first phase of capitalist imperialism makes "color" useless as an emancipatory signifier. Confronted by the ferocious standardizing benevolence of most U.S. and Western European human-scientific radicalism (recognition by assimilation), the progressive though heterogeneous withdrawal of consumerism in the comprador periphery, and the exclusion of the margins of even the center-periphery articulation (the "true and differential subaltern"), the analogue of class-consciousness rather than race-consciousness in this area seems historically, disciplinarily, and practically forbidden by Right and Left alike. It is not just a question of a *double* displacement, as it is not simply the problem of finding a psychoanalytic allegory that can accommodate the third-world woman with the first.

The cautions I have just expressed are valid only if we are speaking of the subaltern woman's consciousness—or, more acceptably, subject. Reporting on, or better still, participating in, antisexist work among women of color or women in class oppression in the First World or the Third World is undeniably on the agenda. We should also welcome all the information retrieval in these silenced areas that is taking place in anthropology, political science, history, and sociology. Yet the assumption and construction of a consciousness or subject sustains such work and will, in the long run, cohere with the work of imperialist subject-constitution, mingling epistemic violence with the advancement of learning and civilization. And the subaltern woman will be as mute as ever.[59]

In so fraught a field, it is not easy to ask the question of the consciousness of the subaltern woman; it is thus all the more necessary to remind pragmatic radicals that such a question is not an idealist red herring. Though all feminist or antisexist projects cannot be reduced to this one, to ignore it is an unacknowledged political gesture that has a long history and collaborates with a masculine radicalism that renders the place of the investigator transparent. In seeking to learn to speak to (rather than listen to or speak for) the historically muted subject of the subaltern woman, the postcolonial intellectual *systematically* "unlearns" female privilege. This systematic unlearning involves learning to critique postcolonial discourse with the best tools it can provide and not simply substituting the lost figure of the colonized. Thus, to question the unquestioned muting of the subaltern woman even within the anti-imperialist project of subaltern studies is not, as Jonathan Culler suggests, to "produce difference by differing" or to "appeal . . . to a sexual identity defined as essential and privilege experiences associated with that identity."[60]

Culler's version of the feminist project is possible within what Elizabeth Fox-Genovese has called "the contribution of the bourgeois-democratic revolutions to the social and political individualism of women."[61] Many of us were obliged to understand the feminist project as Culler now describes it when we were still agitating as U.S. academics.[62] It was certainly a necessary stage in my own education in "unlearning" and has consolidated the belief that the mainstream project of Western feminism both continues and displaces the battle over the right to individualism between women and men in situations of upward class mobility. One suspects that the debate between U.S. feminism and European "theory" (as theory is generally represented by women from the United States or Britain) occupies a significant corner of that very terrain. I am generally sympathetic with the call to make U.S. feminism more "theoretical." It seems, however, that the problem of the muted subject of the subaltern woman, though not solved by an "essentialist" search for lost origins, cannot be served by the call for more theory in Anglo-America either.

That call is often given in the name of a critique of "positivism," which is seen here as identical with "essentialism." Yet Hegel, the modern inaugurator of "the work of the negative," was not a stranger to the notion of essences. For Marx, the curious persistence of essentialism within the dialectic was a profound and productive problem. Thus, the stringent binary opposition between positivism/essentialism (read, U.S.) and "theory" (read, French or Franco-German via Anglo-American) may be spurious. Apart from repressing the ambiguous complicity between essentialism and critiques of positivism (acknowledged by Derrida in "Of Grammatology As a Positive Science"), it also errs by implying that positivism is not a theory. This move allows the emergence of a proper name, a positive essence, Theory. Once again, the position of the investigator remains unquestioned. And, if this territorial debate turns toward the Third World, no change in the question of method is to be discerned. This debate cannot take into account that, in the case of the woman as subaltern, no ingredients for the constitution of the itinerary of the trace of a sexed subject can be gathered to locate the possibility of dissemination.

Yet I remain generally sympathetic in aligning feminism with the critique of positivism and the defetishization of the concrete. I am also far from averse to learning from the work of Western theorists, though I have learned to insist on marking their positionality as investigating subjects. Given these conditions, and as a literary critic, I tactically confronted the immense problem of the consciousness of the woman as subaltern. I reinvented the problem in a sentence and transformed it into the object of a simple semiosis. What does this sentence mean? The analogy here is between the ideological victimization of a Freud and the positionality of the postcolonial intellectual as investigating subject.

As Sarah Kofman has shown, the deep ambiguity of Freud's use of women as a scapegoat is a reaction-formation to an initial and continuing desire to give the hysteric a voice, to transform her into the *subject* of hysteria.[63] The masculine-imperialist ideological formation that shaped that desire into "the daughter's seduction" is part of the same formation that constructs the monolithic "third-world woman." As a postcolonial intellectual, I am influenced by that formation as well. Part of our "unlearning" project is to articulate that ideological formation—by *measuring* silences, if necessary—into the *object* of investigation. Thus, when confronted with the questions, Can the subaltern speak? and Can the subaltern (as woman) speak?, our efforts to give the subaltern a voice in history will be doubly open to the dangers run by Freud's discourse. As a product of these considerations, I have put together the sentence "White men are saving brown women from brown men" in a spirit not unlike the one to be encountered in Freud's investigations of the sentence "A child is being beaten."[64]

The use of Freud here does not imply an isomorphic analogy between subject-formation and the behavior of social collectives, a frequent practice, often accompanied by a reference to Reich, in the conversation between Deleuze and Foucault. So I am not suggesting that "White men are saving brown women from brown men" is a sentence indicating a *collective* fantasy symptomatic of a *collective* itinerary of sadomasochistic repression in a *collective* imperialist enterprise. There is a satisfying symmetry in such an allegory, but I would rather invite the reader to consider it a problem in "wild psychoanalysis" than a clinching solution.[65] Just as Freud's insistence on making the woman the scapegoat in "A child is being beaten" and elsewhere discloses his political interests, however imperfectly, so my insistence on imperialist subject-production as the occasion for this sentence discloses my politics.

Further, I am attempting to borrow the general methodological aura of Freud's strategy toward the sentence he constructed *as a sentence* out of the many similar substantive accounts his patients gave him. This does not mean I will offer a case of transference-in-analysis as an isomorphic model for the transaction between reader and text (my sentence). The analogy between transference and literary criticism or historiography is no more than a productive catachresis. To say that the subject is a text does not authorize the converse pronouncement: the verbal text is a subject.

I am fascinated, rather, by how Freud predicates a *history* of repression that produces the final sentence. It is a history with a double origin, one hidden in the amnesia of the infant, the other lodged in our archaic past, assuming by implication a preoriginary space where human and animal were not yet differentiated.[66] We are driven to impose a homologue of this Freudian strategy on the Marxist narrative to explain the ideological dissimulation of imperialist political economy and outline a history of repression that produces a sentence like the one I have sketched. This history also has a double origin, one hidden in the maneuverings behind the British abolition of widow sacrifice in 1829,[67] the other lodged in the classical and Vedic past of Hindu India, the *Rg-Veda* and the *Dharmaśāstra*. No doubt there is also an undifferentiated preoriginary space that supports this history.

The sentence I have constructed is one among many displacements describing the relationship between brown and white men (sometimes brown and white women worked in). It takes its place among some sentences of "hyperbolic admiration" or of pious guilt that Derrida speaks of in connection with the "hieroglyphist prejudice." The relationship between the imperialist subject and the subject of imperialism is at least ambiguous.

The Hindu widow ascends the pyre of the dead husband and immolates herself upon it. This is widow sacrifice. (The conventional transcription of the Sanskrit word for the widow would be *sati*. The early colonial British transcribed it *suttee*.) The rite was not practiced universally and was not caste- or class-fixed. The abolition of this rite by the British has been generally understood as a case of "White men saving brown women from brown men." White women—from the nineteenth-century British Missionary Registers to Mary Daly—have not produced an alternative understanding. Against this is the Indian nativist argument, a parody of the nostalgia for lost origins: "The women actually wanted to die."

The two sentences go a long way to legitimize each other. One never encounters the testimony of the women's voice-consciousness. Such a testimony would not be ideology-transcendent or "fully" subjective, of course, but it would have constituted the ingredients for producing a countersentence.

As one goes down the grotesquely mistranscribed names of these women, the sacrificed widows, in the police reports included in the records of the East India Company, one cannot put together a "voice." The most one can sense is the immense heterogeneity breaking through even such a skeletal and ignorant account (castes, for example, are regularly described as tribes). Faced with the dialectically interlocking sentences that are constructible as "White men are saving brown women from brown men" and "The women wanted to die," the postcolonial woman intellectual asks the question of simple semiosis—What does this mean?—and begins to plot a history.

To mark the moment when not only a civil but good society is born out of domestic confusion, singular events that break the letter of the law to instill its spirit are often invoked. The protection of women by men often provides such an event. If we remember that the British boasted of their absolute equity toward and noninterference with native custom/law, an invocation of this sanctioned transgression of the letter for the sake of the spirit may be read in J. D. M. Derrett's remark: "The very first legislation upon Hindu Law was carried through without the assent of a single Hindu." The legislation is not named here. The next sentence, where the measure is named, is equally interesting if one considers the implications of the survival of a co-lonially established "good" society after decolonization: "The recurrence of *sati* in independent India is probably an obscurantist revival which cannot long survive even in a very backward part of the country."[68]

Whether this observation is correct or not, what interests me is that the protection of woman (today the "third-world woman") becomes a signifier for the establishment of a good society which must, at such inaugurative moments, transgress mere legality, or equity of legal policy. In this particular case, the process also allowed the redefinition as a crime of what had been tolerated, known, or adulated as ritual. In other words, this one item in Hindu law jumped the frontier between the private and the public domain.

Although Foucault's *historical narrative,* focusing solely on Western Europe, sees merely a tolerance for the criminal antedating the development of criminology in the late eighteenth century (*PK,* 41), his theoretical *description* of the "episteme" is pertinent here: "The *episteme is* the 'apparatus' which makes possible the separation not of the true from the false but of what may not be characterized as scientific" (*PK,* 197)—ritual as opposed to crime, the one fixed by superstition, the other by legal science.

The leap of *suttee* from private to public has a clear and complex relationship with the changeover from a mercantile and commercial to a territorial and administrative British presence; it can be followed in correspondence among the police stations, the lower and higher courts, the courts of directors, the prince regent's court, and the like. (It is interesting to note that, from the point of view of the native "colonial subject," also emergent from the feudalism-capitalism transition, *sati is* a signifier with the reverse social charge: "Groups rendered psychologically marginal by their exposure to Western impact . . . had come under pressure to demonstrate, to others as well as to themselves, their ritual purity and allegiance to traditional high culture. To many of them *sati* became an important proof of their conformity to older norms at a time when these norms had become shaky within."[69]

If this is the first historical origin of my sentence, it is evidently lost in the history of humankind as work, the story of capitalist expansion, the slow freeing of labor power as commodity, that narrative of the modes of production, the transition from feudalism via mercantilism to capitalism. Yet the precarious normativity of this narrative is sustained by the putatively changeless stopgap of the "Asiatic" mode of production, which steps in to sustain it whenever it might become apparent that the story of capital logic is the story of the West, that imperialism establishes the universality of the mode of production narrative, that to ignore the subaltern today is, willy-nilly, to continue the imperialist project. The origin of my sentence is thus lost in the shuffle between other, more powerful discourses. Given that the abolition of *sati* was in itself admirable, is it still possible to wonder if a perception of the origin of my sentence might contain interventionist possibilities?

Imperialism's image as the establisher of the good society is marked by the espousal of the woman as *object* of protection from her own kind. How should one examine the dissimulation of patriarchal strategy, which apparently grants the woman free choice as *subject?* In other words, how does one make the move from "Britain" to "Hinduism"? Even the attempt shows that imperialism is not identical with chromatism, or mere prejudice against people of color. To approach this question, I will touch briefly on the *Dharmaśāstra* (the sustaining scriptures) and the *Rg-Veda* (Praise Knowledge). They represent the archaic origin in my homology of Freud. Of course, my treatment is not exhaustive. My readings are, rather, an interested and inexpert examination, by a postcolonial woman, of the fabrication of repression, a constructed counternarrative of woman's consciousness, thus woman's being, thus woman's being good, thus the good woman's desire, thus woman's desire. Paradoxically, at the same time we witness the unfixed place of woman as a signifier in the inscription of the social individual.

The two moments in the *Dharmaśāstra* that I am interested in are the discourse on sanctioned suicides and the nature of the rites for the dead.[70] Framed in these two discourses, the self-immolation of widows seems an exception to the rule. The general scriptural doctrine is that suicide is reprehensible. Room is made, however, for certain forms of suicide which, as formulaic performance, lose the phenomenal identity of being suicide. The first category of sanctioned suicides arises out of *tatvajñāna,* or the knowledge of truth. Here the knowing subject comprehends the insubstantiality or mere phenomenality (which may be the same thing as nonphenomenality) of its identity. At a certain point in time, *tat tva* was interpreted as "that you," but even without that, *tatva is* thatness or quiddity. Thus, this enlightened self truly knows the "that"-ness of its identity. Its demolition of that identity is not *ātmaghāta* (a killing of the self). The paradox of knowing of the limits of knowledge is that the strongest assertion of agency, to negate the possibility of agency, cannot be an example of itself. Curiously enough, the *self-sacrifice* of gods is sanctioned by natural ecology, useful for the working of the economy of Nature and the Universe, rather than by self-knowledge. In this *logically* anterior stage, inhabited by gods rather than human beings, of this particular chain of displacements, suicide and sacrifice (*ātmaghāta* and *ātmadāna*) seem as little distinct as an "interior" (self-knowledge) and an "exterior" (ecology) sanction.

This philosophical space, however, does not accommodate the self-immolating woman. For her we look where room is made to sanction suicides that cannot claim truth-knowledge as a state that is, at any rate, easily verifiable and belongs in the area of *sruti* (what was heard) rather than *smirti* (what is remembered). This exception to the general rule about suicide annuls the phenomenal identity of self-immolation if performed in certain places rather than in a certain state of enlightenment. Thus, we move from an interior sanction (truth-knowledge) to an exterior one (place of pilgrimage). It is possible for a woman to perform *this* type of (non)suicide.[71]

Yet even this is not the *proper* place for the woman to annul the proper name of suicide through the destruction of her proper self. For her alone is sanctioned self-immolation on a dead spouse's pyre. (The few male examples cited in Hindu antiquity of self-immolation on another's pyre, being proofs of enthusiasm and devotion to a master or superior, reveal the structure of domination within the rite.) This suicide that is not suicide may be read as a simulacrum of both truth-knowledge and piety of place. If the former, it is as if the knowledge *in a subject* of its own insubstantiality and mere phenomenality is dramatized so that the dead husband becomes the exteriorized example and place of the extinguished subject and the widow becomes the (non)agent who "acts it out." If the latter, it is as if the metonym for all sacred places is now that burning bed of wood, constructed by elaborate ritual, where the woman's subject, legally displaced from herself, is being consumed. It is in terms of this profound ideology of the displaced place of the female subject that the paradox of free choice comes into play. For the male subject, it is the felicity of the suicide, a felicity that will annul rather than establish its status as such, that is noted. For the female subject, a sanctioned self-immolation, even as it takes away the effect of "fall" (*pātaka*) attached to an unsanctioned suicide, brings praise for the act of choice on another register. By the inexorable ideological production of the sexed subject, such a death can be understood by the female subject as an *exceptional* signifier of her own desire, exceeding the general rule for a widow's conduct.

In certain periods and areas this exceptional rule became the general rule in a class-specific way. Ashis Nandy relates its marked prevalence in eighteenth- and early nineteenth-century Bengal to factors ranging from population control to communal misogyny.[72] Certainly its prevalence there in the previous centuries was because in Bengal, unlike elsewhere in India, widows could inherit property. Thus, what the British see as poor victimized women going to the slaughter is in fact an ideological battleground. As P. V. Kane, the great historian of the *Dharmasāstra,* has correctly observed: "In Bengal, [the fact that] the widow of a sonless member even in a joint Hindu family is entitled to practically the same rights over joint family property which her deceased husband would have had . . . must have frequently induced the surviving members to get rid of the widow by appealing at a most distressing hour to her devotion to and love for her husband" (*HD* II.2, 635).

Yet benevolent and enlightened males were and are sympathetic with the "courage" of the woman's free choice in the matter. They thus accept the production of the sexed subaltern subject: "Modern India does not justify the practice of *sati,* but it is a warped mentality that rebukes modern Indians for expressing admiration and reverence for the cool and unfaltering courage of Indian women in becoming *satis* or performing the *jauhar* for cherishing their ideals of womanly conduct" (*HD* II.2, 636). What Jean-Francois Lyotard has termed the *"différend,"* the inacessibility of, or untranslatability from, one mode of discourse in a dispute to another, is vividly illustrated here.[73] As the discourse of what the British perceive as heathen ritual is sublated (but not, Lyotard would argue, translated) into what the British perceive as crime, one diagnosis of female free will is substituted for another.

Of course, the self-immolation of widows was not *invariable* ritual prescription. If, however, the widow does decide thus to exceed the letter of ritual, to turn back is a transgression for which a particular type of penance is prescribed.[74] With the local British police officer supervising the immolation, to be dissuaded after a decision was, by contrast, a mark of real free choice, a choice of freedom. The ambiguity of the position of the indigenous colonial elite is disclosed in the nationalistic romanticization of the purity, strength, and love of these self-sacrificing women. The two set pieces are Rabindranath Tagore's paean to the "self-renouncing paternal grandmothers of Bengal" and Ananda Coomaraswamy's eulogy of *suttee* as "this last proof of the perfect unity of body and soul."[75]

Obviously I am not advocating the killing of widows. I am suggesting that, within the two contending versions of freedom, the constitution of the female subject *in life is* the place of the *différend*. In the case of widow self-immolation, ritual is not being redefined as superstition but as *crime*. The gravity of *sati* was that it was ideologically cathected as "reward," just as the gravity of imperialism was that it was ideologically cathected as "social mission." Thompson's understanding of *sati* as "punishment" is thus far off the mark:

> It may seem unjust and illogical that the Moguls, who freely impaled and flayed alive, or nationals of Europe, whose countries had such ferocious penal codes and had known, scarcely a century before suttee began to shock the English conscience, orgies of witch-burning and religious persecution, should have felt as they did about suttee. But the differences seemed to them this the victims of their cruelties were tortured by a law which considered them offenders, whereas the victims of suttee were punished for no offense but the physical weakness which had placed them at man's mercy. The rite seemed to prove a depravity and arrogance such as no other human offense had brought to light.[76]

All through the mid- and late-eighteenth century, in the spirit of the codification of the law, the British in India collaborated and consulted with learned Brahmans to judge whether *suttee* was legal by their homogenized version of Hindu law. The collaboration was often idiosyncratic, as in the case of the significance of being dissuaded. Sometimes, as in the general Sastric prohibition against the immolation of widows with small children, the British collaboration seems confused,[77] In the beginning of the nineteenth century, the British authorities, and especially the British in England, repeatedly suggested that collaboration made it appear as if the British condoned this practice. When the law was finally written, the history of the long period of collaboration was effaced, and the language celebrated the noble Hindu who was against the bad Hindu, the latter given to savage atrocities:

> The practice of Suttee ... is revolting to the feeling of human nature.... In many instances, acts of atrocity have been perpetrated, which have been shocking to the Hindoos themselves. ... Actuated by these considerations

the Governor-General in Council, without intending to depart from one of the first and most important principles of the system of British Government in India that all classes of the people be secure in the observance of their religious usages, so long as that system can be adhered to without violation of the paramount dictates of justice and humanity, has deemed it right to establish the following rules. . . . (*HD* II.2, 624–25)

That this was an alternative ideology of the graded sanctioning of suicide as exception, rather than its inscription as sin, was of course not understood. Perhaps *sati* should have been read with martyrdom, with the defunct husband standing in for the transcendental One; or with war, with the husband standing in for sovereign or state, for whose sake an intoxicating ideology of self-sacrifice can be mobilized. In actuality, it was categorized with murder, infanticide, and the lethal exposure of the very old. The dubious place of the free will of the constituted sexed subject as female was successfully effaced. There is no itinerary we can retrace here. Since the other sanctioned suicides did not involve the scene of this constitution, they entered neither the ideological battleground at the archaic origin—the tradition of the *Dharmaśāstra*—nor the scene of the reinscription of ritual as crime the British abolition. The only related transformation was Mahatma Gandhi's reinscription of the notion of *satyāgraha*, or hunger strike, as resistance. But this is not the place to discuss the details of that sea-change. I would merely invite the reader to compare the auras of widow sacrifice and Gandhian resistance. The root in the first part of *satyāgraha* and sati are the same.

Since the beginning of the Puranic era (ca. a.d. 400), learned Brahmans debated the doctrinal appropriateness of *sati* as of sanctioned suicides in sacred places in general. (This debate still continues in an academic way.) Sometimes the cast provenance of the practice was in question. The general law for widows, that they should observe *brahmacarya*, was, however, hardly ever debated. It is not enough to translate *brahmacarya* as "celibacy." It should be recognized that, of the four ages of being in Hindu (or Brahmanical) *regulative* psychobiography, *brahmacarya is* the social practice anterior to the kinship inscription of marriage. The man—widower or husband—graduates through *vānaprastha* (forest life) into the mature celibacy and renunciation of samnyāsa (laying aside).[78] The woman as wife is indispensable for *gārhasthya,* or householdership, and may accompany her husband into forest life. She has no access (according to Brahmanical sanction) to the final celibacy of asceticism, or *samnyāsa*. The woman as widow, by the general law of sacred doctrine, must regress to an anteriority transformed into stasis. The institutional evils attendant upon this law are well known; I am considering its asymmetrical effect on the ideological formation of the sexed subject. It is thus of much greater significance that there was no debate on this nonexceptional fate of widows—either among Hindus or between Hindus and British—than that the *exceptional* prescription of self-immolation was actively contended.[79] Here the possibility of recovering a (sexually) subaltern subject is once again lost and overdetermined.

This legally programmed asymmetry in the status of the subject, which effectively defines the woman as object of *one* husband, obviously operates in the interest of the legally symmetrical subject-status of the male. The self-immolation of the widow thereby becomes the extreme case of the general law rather than an exception to it. It is not surprising, then, to read of heavenly rewards for the sati, where the quality of being the object of a unique possessor is emphasized by way of rivalry with other females, those ecstatic heavenly dancers, paragons of female beauty and male pleasure who sing her praise: "In heaven she, being solely devoted to her husband, and praised by groups of *apsarās* [heavenly dancers], sports with her husband as long as fourteen Indras rule" (*HD* II.2, 631).

The profound irony in locating the woman's free will in self-immolation is once again revealed in a verse accompanying the earlier passage: "As long as the woman [as wife: *strī*] does not burn herself in fire on the death of her husband, she is never released [*mucyate*] from her female body [*strisarīr*—i.e., in the cycle of births]." Even as it operates the most subtle general release from individual agency, the sanctioned suicide peculiar to woman draws its ideological strength by *identifying* individual agency with the supraindividual: kill yourself on your husband's pyre now, and you may kill your female body in the entire cycle of birth.

In a further twist of the paradox, this emphasis on free will establishes the peculiar misfortune of holding a female body. The word for the self that is actually burned is the standard word for spirit in the noblest sense (*ātman*), while the verb "release," through the root for salvation in the noblest sense (*muc* › *moksa*) is in the passive (*mocyate*), and the word for that which is annulled in the cycle of birth is the everyday word for the body. The ideological message writes itself in the benevolent twentieth-century male historian's admiration: "The *Jauhar* [group self-immolation of aristocratic Rajput war-widows or imminent war-widows] practiced by the Rajput ladies of Chitor and other places for saving themselves from unspeakable atrocities at the hands of the victorious Moslems are too well known to need any lengthy notice" (*HD* II.2, 629).

Although *jauhar* is not, strictly speaking, an act of *sati,* and although I do not wish to speak for the sanctioned sexual violence of conquering male armies, "Moslem" or otherwise, female self-immolation in the face of it is a legitimation of rape as "natural" and works, in the long run, in the interest of unique genital possession of the female. The group rape perpetrated by the conquerors is a metonymic celebration of territorial acquisition. Just as the general law for widows was unquestioned, so this act of female hero-ism persists among the patriotic tales told to children, thus operating on the crudest level of ideological reproduction. It has also played a tremendous role, precisely as an overdetermined signifier, in acting out Hindu com-munalism. Simultaneously, the broader question of the constitution of the sexed subject is hidden by foregrounding the visible violence of *sati*. The task of recovering a (sexually) subaltern subject is lost in an institutional textuality at the archaic origin.

As I mentioned above, when the status of the legal subject as property-holder could be temporarily bestowed on the *female* relict, the self-immola-tion of widows was stringently enforced. Raghunandana, the late fifteenth-/ sixteenth-century legalist whose interpretations are supposed to lend the greatest authority to such enforcement, takes as his text a curious passage from the *Ṛg-Veda*, the most ancient of the Hindu sacred texts, the first of the *Srutis*. In doing so, he is following a centuries-old tradition, commemorating a peculiar and transparent misreading at the very place of sanction. Here is the verse outlining certain steps within the rites for the dead. Even at a sim-ple reading it is clear that it is "not addressed to widows at all, but to ladies of the deceased man's household whose husbands were living." Why then was it taken as authoritative? This, the unemphatic transposition of the dead for the living husband, is a different order of mystery at the archaic origin from the ones we have been discussing: "Let these whose husbands are worthy and are living enter the house with clarified butter in their eyes. Let these wives first step into the house, tearless, healthy, and well adorned" (*HD* II.2, 634). But this crucial transposition is not the only mistake here. The author-ity is lodged in a disputed passage and an alternate reading. In the second line, here translated "Let these wives first step into the house," the word for first is *agré*. Some have read it as *agné*, "O fire." As Kane makes clear, however, "even without this change Apararka and others rely for the practice of *Sati* on this verse" (*HD* IV.2, 199). Here is another screen around one origin of the history of the subaltern female subject. Is it a historical oneirocritique that one should perform on a statement such as: "Therefore it must be admitted that either the MSS are corrupt or Raghunandana committed an innocent slip" (*HD* II.2, 634)? It should be mentioned that the rest of the poem is ei-ther about that general law of *brahmacarya*-in-stasis for widows, to which sati is an exception, or about *niyōga*—"appointing a brother or any near kins-man to raise up issue to a deceased husband by marrying his widow."[80]

If P. V. Kane is the authority on the history of the *Dharmaśāstra*, Mulla's *Principles of Hindu Law* is the practical guide. It is part of the historical text of what Freud calls "kettle logic" that we are unraveling here, that Mulla's textbook adduces, just as definitively, that the *Ṛg-Vedic* verse under consideration was proof that "remarriage of widows and divorce are recognized in some of the old texts."[81]

One cannot help but wonder about the role of the word *yonī*. In context, with the localizing adverb *agré* (in front), the word means "dwelling place." But that does not efface its primary sense of "genital" (not yet perhaps specifically *female* genital). How can we take as the authority for the choice of a widow's self-immolation a passage celebrating the entry of adorned wives into a dwelling place invoked on this occasion by its *yonī*-name, so that the extracontextual icon is almost one of entry into civic production or birth? Paradoxically, the imagic relationship of vagina and fire lends a kind of strength to the authority-claim.[82] This paradox is strengthened by Raghunandana's modification of the verse so as to read, "Let them first ascend the fluid abode (or origin, with, of course, the *yonī*-name—*a rōhantu jalayōnimagné*], O fire [or of fire]." Why should one accept that this "probably mean[s] 'may fire be to them as cool as water'" (*HD* II.2, 634)? The fluid genital of fire, a corrupt phrasing, might figure a sexual indeterminacy providing a simulacrum for the intellectual indeterminacy of *tattvajñāna* (truth-knowledge).

I have written above of a constructed counternarrative of woman's consciousness, thus woman's being, thus woman's being good, thus the good woman's desire, thus woman's desire. This slippage can be seen in the fracture inscribed in the very word *sati*, the feminine form of *sat*. *Sat* transcends any gender-specific notion of masculinity and moves up not only into human but spiritual universality. It is the present participle of the verb "to be" and as such means not only being but the True, the Good, the Right. In the sacred texts it is essence, universal spirit. Even as a prefix it indicates appropriate, felicitous, fit. It is noble enough to have entered the most privileged discourse of modern Western philosophy: Heidegger's meditation on Being.[83] *Sati*, the feminine of this word, simply means "good wife."

It is now time to disclose that *sati* or *suttee* as the proper name of the rite of widow self-immolation commemorates a grammatical error on the part of the British, quite as the nomenclature "American Indian" commemorates a factual error on the part of Columbus. The word in the various Indian languages is "the burning of the *sati*" or the good wife, who thus escapes the regressive stasis of the widow in *brahmacarya*. This exemplifies the race-class-gender overdeterminations of the situation. It can perhaps be caught even when it is flattened out: white men, seeking to save brown women from brown men, impose upon those women a greater ideological constriction by absolutely identifying, *within discursive practice,* good-wifehood with self-immolation on the husband's pyre. On the other side of thus constituting the *object,* the abolition (or removal) of which will provide the occasion for establishing a good, as distinguished from merely civil, society, is the Hindu manipulation of female *subject*-constitution which I have tried to discuss.

(I have already mentioned Edward Thompson's *Suttee,* published in 1928. I cannot do justice here to this perfect specimen of the justification of imperialism as a civilizing mission. Nowhere in his book, written by someone who avowedly "loves India," is there any questioning of the "beneficial ruthlessness" of the British in India as motivated by territorial expansionism or management of industrial capital.[84] The problem with his book is, indeed, a problem of representation, the construction of a continuous and homogeneous "India" in terms of heads of state and British administrators, from the perspective of "a man of good sense" who would be the transparent voice of reasonable humanity. "India" can then be represented, in the other sense, by its imperial masters. The reason for referring to *suttee* here is Thompson's finessing of the word *sati* as "faithful" in the very first sentence of his book, an inaccurate translation which is nonetheless an English permit for the insertion of the female subject into twentieth-century discourse.[85])

Consider Thompson's praise for General Charles Hervey's appreciation of the problem of *sati:* "Hervey has a passage which brings out the pity of a system which looked only for prettiness and constancy in woman. He obtained the names of satis who had died on the pyres of Bikanir Rajas; they were such names as: 'Ray Queen, Sun-ray, Love's Delight, Garland, Virtue Found, Echo, Soft Eye, Comfort, Moonbeam, Love-lorn, Dear Heart, Eye-play, Arbour-born, Smile, Love-bud, Glad Omen, Mist-clad, or Cloud-sprung—the last a favourite name.'" Once again, imposing the upper-class Victorian's typical demands upon "his woman" (his preferred phrase), Thompson appropriates the Hindu woman as his to save against the "system." Bikaner is in Rajasthan; and any discussion of widow-burnings of Rajasthan, especially within the ruling class, was intimately linked to the positive or negative construction of Hindu (or Aryan) communalism.

A look at the pathetically misspelled names of the *satis* of the artisanal, peasant, village-priestly, moneylender, clerical, and comparable social groups in Bengal, where *satis* were most common, would not have yielded such a harvest (Thompson's preferred adjective for Bengalis is "imbecilic"). Or perhaps it would. There is no more dangerous pastime than transposing proper names into common nouns, translating them, and using them as sociological evidence. I attempted to reconstruct the names on that list and began to feel Hervey-Thompson's arrogance. What, for instance, might "Comfort" have been? Was it "Shanti"? Readers are reminded of the last line of T. S. Eliot's Waste *Land*. There the word bears the mark of one kind of stereotyping of India—the grandeur of the ecumenical Upanishads. Or was it "Swasti"? Readers are reminded of the *swastika*, the Brahmanic ritual mark of domestic comfort (as in "God Bless Our Home") stereotyped into a criminal parody of Aryan hegemony. Between these two appropriations, where is our pretty and constant burnt widow? The aura of the names owes more to writers like Edward Fitzgerald, the "translator" of the *Rubayyat of Omar Khayyam* who helped to construct a certain picture of the Oriental woman through the supposed "objectivity" of translation, than to sociological exactitude. (Said's *Orientalism*, 1978, remains the authoritative text here.) By this sort of reckoning, the translated proper names of a random collection of contemporary French philosophers or boards of directors of prestigious southern U.S. corporations would give evidence of a ferocious investment in an archangelic and hagiocentric theocracy. Such sleights of pen can be perpetuated on "common nouns" as well, but the proper name is most susceptible to the trick. And it is the British trick with *sati* that we are discussing. After such a taming of the subject, Thompson can write, under the heading "The Psychology of the '*Sati*'," "I had intended to try to examine this; but the truth is, it has ceased to seem a puzzle to me."[86]

Between patriarchy and imperialism, subject-constitution and object-formation, the figure of the woman disappears, not into a pristine nothingness, but into a violent shuttling which is the displaced figuration of the "third-world woman" caught between tradition and modernization. These considerations would revise every detail of judgments that seem valid for a history of sexuality in the West: "Such would be the property of repression, that which distinguishes it from the prohibitions maintained by simple penal law: repression functions well as a sentence to disappear, but also as an injunction to silence, affirmation of non-existence; and consequently states that of all this there is nothing to say, to see, to know."[87] The case of *suttee* as exemplum of the woman-in-imperialism would challenge and deconstruct this opposition between subject (law) and object-of-knowledge (repression) and mark the place of "disappearance" with something other than silence and nonexistence, a violent aporia between subject and object status.

Sati as a woman's proper name is in fairly widespread use in India today. Naming a female infant "a good wife" has its own proleptic irony, and the irony is all the greater because this sense of the common noun is not the primary operator in the proper name.[88] Behind the naming of the infant is *the* Sati of Hindu mythology, Durga in her manifestation as a good wife.[89] In part of the story, Sati—she is already called that—arrives at her father's court uninvited, in the absence, even, of an invitation for her divine husband Siva. Her father starts to abuse Siva and Sati dies in pain. Siva arrives in a fury and dances over the universe with Sati's corpse on his shoulder. Visnu dismembers her body and bits are strewn over the earth. Around each such relic bit is a great place of pilgrimage.

Figures like the goddess Athena—"father's daughters self-professedly uncontaminated by the womb"—are useful for establishing women's ideological self-debasement, which is to be distinguished from a deconstructive attitude toward the essentialist subject. The story of the mythic Sati, reversing every narrateme of the rite, performs a similar function: the living husband avenges the wife's death, a transaction between great male gods fulfills the destruction of the female body and thus inscribes the earth as sacred geography. To see this as proof of the feminism of classical Hinduism or of Indian culture as goddess-centered and therefore feminist is as ideologically contaminated by nativism or reverse ethnocentrism as it was imperialist to erase the image of the luminous fighting Mother Durga and invest the proper noun Sati with no significance other than the ritual burning of the helpless widow as sacrificial offering who can then be saved. There is no space from which the sexed subaltern subject can speak.

If the oppressed under socialized capital have no necessarily unmediated access to "correct" resistance, can the ideology of *sati*, coming from the history of the periphery, be sublated into any model of interventionist practice? Since this essay operates on the notion that all such clear-cut nostalgias for lost origins are suspect, especially as grounds for counter-hegemonic ideological production, I must proceed by way of an example.[90]

(The example I offer here is not a plea for some violent Hindu sisterhood of self-destruction. The definition of the British Indian as Hindu in Hindu law is one of the marks of the ideological war of the British against the Islamic Mughal rulers of India; a significant skirmish in that as yet unfinished war was the division of the subcontinent. Moreover, in my view, individual examples of this sort are tragic failures as *models* of interventionist practice, since I question the production of models as such. On the other hand, as objects of discourse analysis for the non-self-abdicating intellectual, they can illuminate a section of the social text, in however haphazard a way.)

A young woman of sixteen or seventeen, Bhuvaneswari Bhaduri,[91] hanged heself in her father's modest apartment in North Calcutta in 1926. The suicide was a puzzle since, as Bhuvaneswari was menstruating at the time, it was clearly not a case of illicit pregnancy. Nearly a decade later, it was discovered that she was a member of one of the many groups involved in the armed struggle for Indian independence. She had finally been entrusted with a political assassination. Unable to confront the task and yet aware of the practical need for trust, she killed herself.

Bhuvaneswari had known that her death would be diagnosed as the outcome of illegitimate passion. She had therefore waited for the onset of menstruation. While waiting, Bhuvanesari, the *brahmacārini* who was no doubt looking forward to good wifehood, perhaps rewrote the social text of *sati*-suicide in an interventionist way. (One tentative explanation of her inexplicable act had been a possible melancholia brought on by her brother-in-law's repeated taunts that she was too old to be not-yet-a-wife.) She generalized the sanctioned motive for female suicide by taking immense trouble to displace (not merely deny), in the physiological inscription of her body, its imprisonment within legitimate passion by a single male. In the immediate context, her act became absurd, a case of delirium rather than sanity. The displacing gesture—waiting for menstruation—is at first a reversal of the interdict against a menstruating widow's right to immolate herself; the unclean widow must wait, publicly, until the cleansing bath of the fourth day, when she is no longer menstruating, in order to claim her dubious privilege.

In this reading, Bhuvaneswari Bhaduri's suicide is an unemphatic, ad hoc, subaltern rewriting of the social text of *sati*-suicide as much as the hegemonic account of the blazing, fighting, familial Durga. The emergent dissenting possibilities of that hegemonic account of the fighting mother are well documented and popularly well remembered through the discourse of the male leaders and participants in the independence movement. The subaltern as female cannot be heard or read.

I know of Bhuvaneswari's life and death through family connections. Before investigating them more thoroughly, I asked a Bengali woman, a philosopher and Sanskritist whose early intellectual production is almost identical to mine, to start the process. Two responses: (a) Why, when her two sisters, Saileswari and Raseswari, led such full and wonderful lives, are you interested in the hapless Bhuvaneswari? (b) I asked her nieces. It appears that it was a case of illicit love.

I have attempted to use and go beyond Derridean deconstruction, which I do not celebrate as feminism as such. However, in the context of the problematic I have addressed, I find his morphology much more painstaking and useful than Foucault's and Deleuze's immediate, substantive involvement with more "political" issues—the latter's invitation to "become woman"—which can make their influence more dangerous for the U.S. academic as enthusiastic radical. Derrida marks radical critique with the danger of appropriating the other by assimilation. He reads catachresis at the origin. He calls for a rewriting of the utopian structural impulse as "rendering delirious that interior voice that is the voice of the other in us." I must here acknowledge a long-term usefulness in Jacques Derrida which I seem no longer to find in the authors of *The History of Sexuality* and *Mille Plateaux*.[92]

The subaltern cannot speak. There is no virtue in global laundry lists with "woman" as a pious item. Representation has not withered away. The female intellectual as intellectual has a circumscribed task which she must not disown with a flourish.

NOTES

This original formulation of "Can the Subaltern Speak?" was first published in Cary Nelson and Lawrence Grossberg, eds., *Marxism and the Interpretation of Cultures* (1988), pp. 271–313.

1   I am grateful to Khachig Tololyan for a painstaking first reading of this essay.

2   Louis Althusser, *Lenin and Philosophy and Other Essays*, trans. Ben Brewster (New York: Monthly Review Press, 1971), p. 86.

3   Michel Foucault, *Language, Counter-Memory, Practice: Selected Essays and Interviews*, trans. Donald F. Bouchard and Sherry Simon (Ithaca: Cornell University Press, 1977), pp. 205–17 (hereafter cited as *FD*). I have modified the English version of this, as of other English translations, where faithfulness to the original seemed to demand it.

It is important to note that the greatest "influence" of Western European intellectuals upon U.S. professors and students happens through collections of essays rather than long books in translation. And, in those collections, it is understandably the more topical pieces that gain a greater currency. (Derrida's "Structure, Sign, and Play" is a case in point.) From the perspective of theoretical production and ideological reproduction, therefore, the conversation under consideration has not necessarily been superseded.

4   There is an implicit reference here to the post-1988 wave of Maoism in France. See Michel Foucault, "On Popular Justice: A Discussion with Maoists," *Power/Knowledge: Selected Interviews and Other Writings, 1972–77*, trans. Colin Gordon et al. (New York: Pantheon), p. 134 (hereafter cited as *PK*). Explication of the reference strengthens my point by laying bare the mechanics of appropriation. The status of China in this discussion is exemplary. If Foucault persistently clears himself by saying "I know nothing about China," his interlocutors show toward China what Derrida calls the "Chinese prejudice."

5   This is part of a much broader symptom, as Eric Wolf discusses in *Europe and the People without History* (Berkeley: University of California Press, 1982).

6   Walter Benjamin, *Charles Baudelaire: A Lyric Poet in the Era of High Capitalism,* trans. Harry Zohn (London: Verso, 1983), p. 12.

7   Gilles Deleuze and Felix Guattari, *Anti-Oedipus: Capitalism and Schizophrenia,* trans. Richard Hurley et al. (New York: Viking Press, 1977), p. 26.

8   The exchange with Jacques-Alain Miller in *PK* ("The Confession of the Flesh") is revealing in this respect.

9   Althusser, *Lenin and Philosophy,* pp. 132–33.

10 For one example among many see *PK,* p. 98.

11 It is not surprising, then, that Foucault's work, early and late, is supported by too simple a notion of repression. Here the antagonist is Freud, not Marx. "I have the impression that [the notion of repression] is wholly inadequate to the analysis of the mechanisms and effects of power that it is so pervasively used to characterize today *(PK, 92)*." The delicacy and subtlety of Freud's suggestion—that under repression the phenomenal identity of affects is indeterminate because something unpleasant can be desired as pleasure, thus radically reinscribing the relationship between desire and "interest"—seems quite deflated here. For an elaboration of this notion of repression, see Jacques Derrida, *Of Grammatology,* trans. Gayatri Chakravorty Spivak (Baltimore: Johns Hopkins University Press, 1976), p. 88f. (hereafter cited as *OG*); and Derrida, *Limited inc.: abc,* trans. Samuel Weber, Glyph 2 (1977), p. 215.

12 Althusser's version of this particular situation may be too schematic, but it nevertheless seems more careful in its program than the argument under study. "Class *instinct,*" Althusser writes, "is subjective and spontaneous. Class *position* is objective and rational. To arrive at proletarian class positions, the class instinct of proletarians only needs to be *educated;* the class instinct of the petty bourgeoisie, *and* hence of intellectuals, has, on the contrary, to be *revolutionized" (Lenin and Philosophy,* p. 13).

13 Foucault's subsequent explanation *(PK,* 145) of this Deleuzian statement comes closer to Derrida's notion that theory cannot be an exhaustive taxonomy and is always formed by practice.

14 Cf. the surprisingly uncritical notions of representation entertained in *PK,* 141, 188. My remarks concluding this paragraph, criticizing intellectuals' representations of subaltern groups, should be rigorously distinguished from a coalition politics that takes into account its framing within socialized capital and unites people not because they are oppressed but because they are exploited. This model works best within a parliamentary democracy, where representation is not only not banished but elaborately staged.

15 Karl Marx, *Surveys from Exile,* trans. David Fernbach (New York: Vintage Books, 1974), p. 239.

16 Karl Marx, *Captial. A Critique of Political Economy,* vol. 1, trans. Ben Fowkes (New York: Vantage Books, 1977), p. 254.

17 Marx, *Capital,* I, p. 302.

18 See the excellent short definition and discussion of common sense in Errol Lawrence, "Just Plain Common Sense: The 'Roots' of Racism," in Hazel V. Carby et al.,

The Empire Strikes Back: Race and Racism in 70s Britain (London: Hutchinson, 1982), p. 48.

19 "Use value" in Marx can be shown to be a "theoretical fiction"—as much of a potential oxymoron as "natural exchange." I have attempted to develop this in "Scattered Speculations on the Question of Value," a manuscript under consideration by *Diacritics*. [This manuscript was later published under that title in *Diacritics*, 15.4 (1985), pp. 73–93.—ed.]

20 Derrida's "Linguistic Circle of Geneva," especially p. 143f., can provide a method for assessing the irreducible place of the family in Marx's morphology of class formation. In *Margins of Philosophy*, trans. Alan Bass (Chicago: University of Chicago Press, 1982).

21 Marx, *Capital*, I, p. 128.

22 I am aware that the relationship between Marxism and neo-Kantianism is a politically fraught one. I do not myself see how a continuous line can be established between Marx's own texts and the Kantian ethical moment. It does seem to me, however, that Marx's questioning of the individual as agent of history should be read in the context of the breaking up of the individual subject inaugurated by Kant's critique of Descartes.

23 Karl Marx, *Grundrisse: Foundations of the Critique of Political Economy*, trans. Martin Nicolaus (New York: Viking Press, 1973), pp. 162–63.

24 Edward W. Said. *The World, the Text, the Critic* (Cambridge: Harvard University Press, 1983), p. 243.

25 Paul Bové, "Intellectuals at War: Michel Foucault and the Analysis of Power," *Sub-Stance*, 36/37 (1983), p. 44.

26 Carby, *Empire*, p. 34.

27 This argument is developed further in Spivak, "Scattered Speculations." Once again, the *Anti-Oedipus* did not ignore the economic text, although the treatment was perhaps too allegorical. In this respect, the move from schizo- to rhyzo-analysis in *Mille plateaux* (Paris: Seuil, 1980) has not been salutary.

28 See Michel Foucault, *Madness and Civilization: A History of Insanity in the Age of Reason*, trans. Richard Howard (New York: Pantheon Books, 1965), pp. 251, 262, 269.

29 Although I consider Fredric Jameson's *Political Unconscious: Narrative as a Socially Symbolic Act* (Ithaca: Cornell University Press, 1981) to be a text of great critical weight, or perhaps *because* I do so, I would like my program here to be distinguished from one of restoring the relics of a privileged narrative: "It is in detecting the traces of that uninterrupted narrative, in restoring to the surface of the text the repressed and buried reality of this fundamental history, that the doctrine of a political unconscious finds its function and its necessity" (p. 20).

30 Among many available books, I cite Bruse Tiebout McCully, *English Education and the Origins of Indian Nationalism* (New York: Columbia University Press, 1940).

31 Thomas Babington Macaulay, *Speeches by Lord Macaulay: With His Minute on Indian Education*, ed. G. M. Young (Oxford: Oxford University Press, AMS Edition, 1979), p. 359.

32 Keith, one of the compilers of the Vedic Index, author of *Sanskrit Drama in Its Origin, Development, Theory, and Practice*, and the learned editor of the *Krsnaya-jurveda* for Harvard University Press, was also the editor of four volumes of *Selected Speeches and Documents of British Colonial Policy* (1763 to 1937), of *International Affairs* (1918 to 1937), and of the *British Dominions* (1918 to 1931). He wrote books on the sovereignty of British dominions and on the theory of state succession, with special reference to English and colonial law.

33 Mahamahopadhyaya Haraprasad Shastri, *A Descriptive Catalogue of Sanskrit Manuscripts in the Government Collection under the Care of the Asiatic Society of Bengal* (Calcutta: Asiatic Society of Bengal, 1925), vol. 3, p. viii.

34 Dinesachandra Sena, *Brhat Banga* (Calcutta: Calcutta University Press, 1925), vol. 1, p. 6.

35 Edward Thompson, *Suttee: A Historical and Philosophical Enquiry into the Hindu Rite of Widow-Burning* (London: George Allen and Unwin, 1928), pp. 130, 47.

36 Holograph letter (from G. A. Jacob to an unnamed correspondent) attached to inside front cover of the Sterling Memorial Library (Yale University) copy of Colonel G. A. Jacob, ed., *The Mahanarayana-Upanishad of the Atharva-Veda with the Dipika of Narayana* (Bombay: Government Central Books Department, 1888); italics mine. The dark invocation of the dangers of this learning by way of anonymous aberrants consolidates the asymmetry.

37 I have discussed this issue in greater detail with reference to Julia Kristeva's *About Chinese Women*, trans. Anita Barrows (London: Marion Boyars, 1977), in "French Feminism in an International Frame," *Yale French Studies*, 62 (1981).

38 Antonio Gramsci, "Some Aspects of the Southern Question," in *Selections from Political Writing, 1921–1926*, trans. Quintin Hoare (New York: International Publishers, 1978). I am using "allegory of reading" in the sense developed by Paul de Man, *Allegories of Reading: Figural Language in Rousseau, Nietzsche, Rilke, and Proust* (New Haven: Yale University Press, 1979).

39 Their publications are: *Subaltern Studies I: Writings on South Asian History and Society*, ed. Ranajit Guha (Delhi: Oxford University Press, 1982); *Subaltern Studies II: Writings on South Asian History and Society*, ed. Ranajit Guha (Delhi: Oxford University Press, 1983); and Ranajit Guha, *Elementary Aspects of Peasant Insurgency in Colonial India* (Delhi: Oxford University Press, 1983).

40 Edward W. Said, "Permission to Narrate," *London Review* of *Books* (Feb. 18, 1984).

41 Guha, *Studies*, I, p. 1.

42 Guha, *Studies*, I, p. 4.

43 Jacques Derrida, "The Double Session," *Dissemination*, trans. Barbara Johnson (Chicago: University of Chicago Press, 1981).

44 Guha, *Studies*, I, p. 8 (all but the first set of italics are the author's).

45 Ajit K. Chaudhury, "New Wave Social Science," *Frontier*, 16–24 (Jan. 28. 1984), p. 10 (italics are mine).

46 Chaudhury, "New Wave Social Science," p. 10.

47 Pierre Macherey, *A Theory of Literary Production*, trans. Geoffrey Wall (London: Routledge, 1978), p. 87.

48 I have discussed this issue in "Displacement and the Discourse of Woman," in Mark Krupnick, ed., *Displacement: Derrida and After* (Bloomington: Indiana University Press, 1983), and in "Love Me, Love My Ombre, Elle: Derrida's 'La carte postale,'" *Diacritics* 14, no. 4 (1984), pp. 19–36.

49 This violence in the general sense that is the possibility of an episteme is what Derrida calls "writing" in the general sense. The relationship between writing in the general sense and writing in the narrow sense (marks upon a surface) cannot be cleanly articulated. The task of grammatology (deconstruction) is to provide a notation upon this shifting relationship. In a certain way, then, the critique of imperialism is deconstruction as such.

50 "Contracting Poverty," *Multinational Monitor*, 4, no. 8 (Aug. 1983), p. 8. This report was contributed by John Cavanagh and Joy Hackel, who work on the International Corporations Project at the Institute for Policy Studies (italics are mine).

51 The mechanics of the invention of the Third World as signifier are *susceptible* to the type of analysis directed at the constitution of race as a signifier in Carby, *Empire*.

52 Mike Davis. "The Political Economy of *Late-Imperial* America," *New Left Review*, 143 (Jan.Feb. 1984), p. 9.

53 Bové, "Intellectuals," p. 51.

54 Terry Eagleton, *Literary Theory: An Introduction* (Minneapolis: University of Minnesota Press, 1983), p. 205.

55 Perry Anderson. *In the Tracks of Historical Materialism* (London: Verso, 1983), p. 53.

56 Anderson, *In the Tracks*, p. 52.

57 Said, *The World*, p. 183.

58 Jacques Derrida, "Of an Apocalyptic Tone Recently Adapted in Philosophy," trans. John P. Leavy, Jr., in *Semia*, p. 71.

59 Even in such excellent texts of reportage and analysis as Gail Omvedt's *We Will Smash This Prison! Indian Women in Struggle* (London: Zed Press, 1980), the assumption that a group of Maharashtrian women in an urban proletarian situation, reacting to a radical white woman who had "thrown in her lot with the Indian destiny," is representative of "Indian women" or touches the question of "female consciousness in India" is not harmless when taken up within a first-world social formation where the proliferation of communication in an internationally hegemonic language makes alternative accounts and testimonies instantly accessible even to undergraduates.

Norma Chinchilla's observation, made at a panel on "Third World Feminisms: Differences in Form and Content" (UCLA. Mar. 8, 1983), that antisexist work in the Indian context is not genuinely antisexist but antifeudal, is another case in point. This permits definitions of sexism to emerge only after a society has entered the capitalist mode of production, thus making capitalism and patriarchy conveniently continuous. It also invokes the vexed question of the role of the "'Asiatic' mode of production" in sustaining the explanatory power of the normative narrativization of history through the account of modes of production, in however sophisticated a manner history is construed.

The curious role of the proper name "Asia" in this matter does not remain confined to proof or disproof of the empirical existence of the actual mode (a problem that became the object of intense maneuvering within international communism) but remains crucial even in the work of such theoretical subtlety and importance as Barry Hindess and Paul Hirst's *Pre-Capitalist Modes of Production* (London: Routledge, 1975) and Fredric Jameson's *Political Unconscious*. Especially in Jameson, where the morphology of modes of production is rescued from all suspicion of historical determinism and anchored to a poststructuralist theory of the subject, the "Asiatic" mode of production, in its guise of "oriental despotism" as the concomitant state formation, still serves. It also plays a significant role in the transmogrified mode of production narrative in Deleuze and Guattari's *Anti-Oedipus*. In the Soviet debate, at a far remove, indeed, from these contemporary theoretical projects, the doctrinal sufficiency of the "Asiatic" mode of production was most often doubted by producing for it various versions and nomenclatures of feudal, slave, and communal modes of production. (The debate is presented in detail in Stephen F. Dunn, *The Fall and Rise of the Asiatic Mode of Production* [London: Routledge, 1982].) It would be interesting to relate this to the repression of the imperialist "moment" in most debates over the transition from feudalism to capitalism that have long exercised the Western Left. What is more important here is that an observation such as Chinchilla's represents a widespread hierarchization within third-world feminism (rather than Western Marxism), which situates it within the long-standing traffic with the imperialist concept-metaphor "Asia."

I should add that I have not yet read Madhu Kishwar and Ruth Vanita, eds., *In Search of Answers: Indian Women's Voices from Manushi* (London: Zed Books, 1984).

60 Jonathan Cutler, *On Deconstruction: Theory and Criticism after Structuralism* (Ithaca: Cornell University Press, 1982), p. 48.

61 Elizabeth Fox-Genovese, "Placing Woman's History in History," *New Left Review*, 133 (May-June 1982), p. 21.

62 I have attempted to develop this idea in a somewhat autobiographical way in "Finding Feminist Readings: Dante-Yeats," in Ira Konigsberg, ed., *American Criticism in the Poststructuralist Age* (Ann Arbor: University of Michigan Press, 1981).

63 Sarah Kofman, *L'énigme de la femme: La femme dans les textes de Freud* (Paris: Galilée, 1980). [This text was translated into English as *The Enigma of Woman: Woman in Freud's Writings*, trans. Catherine Porter (Ithaca: Cornell University Press, 1985).—ed.]

64 Sigmund Freud, "'A Child Is Being Beaten': A Contribution to the Study of the Origin of Sexual Perversions," *The Standard Edition of the Complete Psychological Works of Sigmund Freud*, trans. James Strachey et al. (London: Hogarth Press, 1955), vol. 17.

65 Freud, "'Wild' Psycho-Analysis," Standard Edition, vol. 11.

66 Freud, "'A Child Is Being Beaten,'" p. 188.

67 For a brilliant account of how the "reality" of widow-sacrifice was constituted or "textualized" during the colonial period, see Lata Mani, "The Production of Colonial Discourse: Sati in Early Nineteenth Century Bengal" (Masters Thesis, University of California at Santa Cruz, 1983). I profited from discussions with Ms. Mani at the inception of this project.

68 J. D. M. Derrett, *Hindu Law Past and Present: Being an Account of the Controversy Which Preceded the Enactment of the Hindu Code, and Text of the Code as Enacted, and Some Comments Thereon* (Calcutta: A. Mukherjee and Co., 1957), p. 46.

69 Ashis Nandy, "Sati: A Nineteenth Century Tale of Women, Violence and Protest," *Rammohun Roy and the Process of Modernization in India*, ed. V. C. Joshi (Delhi: Vikas Publishing House, 1975), p. 68.

70 The following account leans heavily on Pandurang Vaman Kane, *History of the Dharmasastra* (Poona: Bhandarkar Oriental Research Institute, 1963) (hereafter cited as *HD*, with volume, part, and page numbers).

71 Upendra Thakur, *The History of Suicide in India: An Introduction* (Delhi: Munshi Ram Manohar Let, 1963), p. 9, has a useful list of Sanskrit primary sources on sacred places. This laboriously decent book betrays all the signs of the schizophrenia of the colonial subject, such as bourgeois nationalism, patriarchal communalism, and an "enlightened reasonableness."

72 Nandy, "Sati."

73 Jean-Francois Lyotard, *Le différend* (Paris: Minuit, 1984).

74 *HD*, 11.2, p. 633. There are suggestions that this "prescribed penance" was far exceeded by social practice. In the passage below, published in 1938, notice the Hindu patristic assumptions about the freedom of female will at work in phrases like "courage" and "strength of character." The unexamined presuppositions of the passage might be that the complete objectification of the widow-concubine was just punishment for abdication of the right to courage, signifying subject status: "Some widows, however, had not the courage to go through the fiery ordeal; nor had they sufficient strength of mind and character to live up to the high ascetic ideal prescribed for them by *brahmacarya*. It is sad to record that they were driven to lead the life of a concubine or *avarudda stri* [incarcerated wife]." A. S. Altekar, *The Position of Women in Hindu Civilization: From Prehistoric Times to the Present Day* (Delhi: Motilal Banarsidass, 1938), p. 156.

75 Quoted in Sena, *Brhat-Banga*, II, pp. 913–14

76 Thompson, *Suttee*, p. 132.

77 Here, as well as for the Brahman debate over *sati*, see Mani, "Production," pp. 71f.

78 We are speaking here of the regulative norms of Brahmanism, rather than "things as they were." See Robert Lingat, *The Classical Law of India*, trans. J. D. M. Derrett (Berkeley: University of California Press. 1973), p. 48.

79 Both the vestigial possibility of widow remarriage in ancient India and the legal institution of widow remarriage in 1856 are transactions among men. Widow remarriage is very much an exception, perhaps because it left the program of subject-formation untouched. In all the "lore" of widow remarriage, it is the father and the husband who are applauded for their reformist courage and selflessness.

80 Sir Monier Monier-Williams, *Sanskrit-English Dictionary* (Oxford: Clarendon Press, 1899), p. 552. Historians are often impatient if modernists seem to be attempting to import "feministic" judgments into ancient patriarchies. The real question is, of course, why structures of patriarchal domination should be unquestioningly recorded. Historical sanctions for collective action toward social justice can only be developed if people outside of the discipline question standards of "objectivity" preserved as such by the hegemonic tradition. It does not seem inappropriate to notice that so "objective" an instrument as a dictionary can use the deeply sexist-partisan explanatory expression: "raise up issue to a deceased husband"!

81 Sunderlal T. Desai, *Mulla: Principles of Hindu Law* (Bombay: N. M. Tripathi, 1982), p. 184.

82 I am grateful to Professor Alison Finley of Trinity College (Hartford, Conn.) for discussing the passage with me. Professor Finley is an expert on the *Rg-Veda*. I hasten to add that she would find my readings as irresponsibly "literary-critical" as the ancient historian would find it "modernist."

83 Martin Heidegger, *An Introduction to Metaphysics*, trans. Ralph Manheim (New York: Doubleday Anchor, 1961), p. 58.

84 Thompson, *Suttee*, p. 37.

85 Thompson, *Suttee*, p. 15. For the status of the proper name as "mark," see Derrida, "Taking Chances."

86 Thompson, *Suttee*, p. 137.

87 Michel Foucault, *The History of Sexuality*, trans. Robert Hurley (New York: Vintage Books, 1980), vol. 1, p. 4.

88 The fact that the word was also used as a form of address for a well-born woman ("lady") complicates matters.

89 It should be remembered that this account does not exhaust her many manifestations within the pantheon.

90 A position against nostalgia as a basis of counterhegemonic ideological production does not endorse its negative use. Within the complexity of contemporary political economy, it would, for example, be highly questionable to urge that the current Indian working-class crime of burning brides who bring insufficient dowries and of subsequently disguising the murder as suicide is either a use or abuse of the tradition of *sati*-suicide. The most that can be claimed is that it is a

displacement on a chain of semiosis with the female subject as signifier, which would lead us back into the narrative we have been unraveling. Clearly, one must work to stop the crime of bride burning *in every way.* If, however, that work is accomplished by unexamined nostalgia or its opposite, it will assist actively in the substitution of race/ethnos or sheer genitalism as a signifier in the place of the female subject.

91 In this first version of the essay, Spivak spells Bhuvaneswari's name with a *v,* but in *A Critique of Postcolonial Reason,* she uses a slightly different orthography, and spells the name Bhubaneswari Bhaduri. We have kept the different spellings to mark the changing conventions that were operative in the different moments of publication.—ed.

92 I had not read Peter Dews, "Power and Subjectivity in Foucault," *New Left Review,* 144 (1984), until I finished this essay. I look forward to his book on the same topic. There are many points in common between his critique and mine. However, as far as I can tell from the brief essay, he writes from a perspective uncritical of critical theory and the intersubjective norm that can all too easily exchange "individual" for "subject" in its situating of the "epistemic subject." Dews's reading of the connection between "Marxist tradition" and the "autonomous subject" is not mine. Further, his account of "the impasse of the second phase of poststructuralism as a whole" is vitiated by his nonconsideration of Derrida, who has been against the privileging of language from his earliest work, the "Introduction" in Edmund Husserl, *The Origin of Geometry,* trans. John Leavy (Stony Brook, N.Y.: Nicolas Hays, 1978). What sets his excellent analysis quite apart from my concerns is, of course, that the Subject within whose History he places Foucault's work is the Subject of the European tradition (pp. 87, 94).

BIBLIOGRAPHY

Abu-Lughod, Lila. "The Romance of Resistance: Tracing Transformations of Power Through Bedouin Women." *American Ethnologist* 17 (1990): 41–45.

Adorno, Theodor. *Negative Dialectics*. Trans. E. B. Ashton. New York: Continuum, 1997.

Ahmad, Aijaz. *In Theory: Classes, Nations, Literatures*. New York: Verso, 1992.

Altekar, A. S. *The Position of Women in Hindu Civilization: From Prehistoric Times to the Present Day*. Delhi: Motilal Banarsidass, 1938.

Althusser, Louis. *Lenin and Philosophy and Other Essays*. Trans. Ben Brewster. New York: Monthly Review Press, 1971.

Anand, Mulk Raj. *Across the Black Waters: A Novel*. London: Jonathan Cape, 1940.

Anderson, Benedict. *Imagined Communities: Reflections on the Origin and Spread of Nationalism*. London: Verso, 1983.

Anidjar, Gil. *Our Place in Al-Andalus: Kabbalah, Philosophy, Literature in Arab-Jewish Letters*. Stanford: Stanford University Press, 2002.

Apter, Emily. "French Colonial Studies and Postcolonial Theory." *Sub-Stance* 76/77 24, nos. 1–2 (1995): 169–180.

Arias, Arturo. "Rigoberta Menchú's History Within the Guatemalan Context." In Arturo Arias, ed., *The Rigoberta Menchú Controversy*, pp. 3–38. Minneapolis: University of Minnesota Press, 2001.

—— ed. *The Rigoberta Menchú Controversy*. Minneapolis: University of Minnesota Press, 2001.

Balibar, Etienne and Immanuel Wallerstein. *Race, Nation, Class: Ambiguous Identities*. Trans. Chris Turner. New York: Verso, 1991.

Benjamin, Walter. *Charles Baudelaire: A Lyric Poet in the Era of High Capitalism*. Trans. Harry Zohn. London: Verso, 1983.

—— "The Task of the Translator." In Marcus Bullock and Michael W. Jennings, eds., *Walter Benjamin: Selected Writings, Volume 1 (1913–26)*, pp. 253–263. Cambridge: Harvard University Press, 1996.

Bhabha, Homi K. "DisnemiNation." In *Nation and Narration*, pp. 291–322. New York: Routledge, 1990.

Biko, Steve. "On Death." In *I Write What I Like*, pp. 152–153. San Francisco: Harper and Row, 1986.

Boddy, Janice. *Wombs and Alien Spirits: Women, Men, and the Zār Cult in Northern Sudan*. Madison: University of Wisconsin Press, 1989.

Bolla, Peter de. "Disfiguring History." *Diacritics* 16 (Winter 1986): 49–58.

Brown, Wendy. *Regulating Aversion: Tolerance in an Age of Identity and Empire*. Princeton: Princeton University Press, 2007.

Burgos-Debray, Elizabeth, ed. *I, Rigoberta Menchú: An Indian Woman in Guatemala*. Trans. Ann Wright. London: Verso, 1984.

Busia, Abena. "Silencing Sycorax: On African Colonial Discourse and the Unvoiced Female." *Cultural Critique* 14 (Winter 1989–90): 81–104.

Butler, Judith. *Antigone's Claim: Kinship Between Life and Death*. New York: Columbia University Press, 2000.

—— *Bodies That Matter: On the Discursive Limits of "Sex."* New York: Routledge, 1993.

—— *Precarious Life: The Powers of Mourning and Violence*. London: Verso, 2000.

Butler, Judith and Gayatri Chakravorty Spivak. *Who Sings the Nation-State? Language, Politics, Belonging*. New York: Seagull, 2007.

Caputo, John. *Against Ethics: Contributions to a Poetics of Obligation with Constant Reference to Deconstruction*, pp. 145–146. Bloomington: Indiana University Press, 1993.

Cavanagh, John and Joy Hackel. "Contracting Poverty." *Multinational Monitor* 4, no. 8 (August 1983). http://multinationalmonitor.org/hyper/issues/1983/08/fuentes.html; accessed July 6, 2009.

Chakrabarty, Dipesh. *Habitations of Modernity: Essays in the Wake of Subaltern Studies*. Chicago: University of Chicago Press, 2002.

—— "Postcoloniality and the Artifice of History: Who Speaks for 'Indian' Pasts?" *Representations* 37 (Winter 1992): 1–26.

—— *Provincializing Europe*. Princeton: Princeton University Press, 2000.

Chatterjee, Partha. *Nationalist Thought and the Colonial World: A Derivative Discourse?* London: Zed, 1986.

—— *The Nation and Its Fragments*. Princeton: Princeton University Press, 1993.

Chaudhury, Ajit K. "New Wave Social Science." *Frontier* 16, no. 2 (January 28, 1984): 10–12.

Churchill, Winston. *The World Crisis, 1911–1914*. London: Thornton Butterworth, 1923.

Collier, George A., with Elizabeth Lowery Quarantiello. *Basta! Land and the Zapatista Rebellion in Chiapas.* Oakland: Food First, 1994.

Comaroff, Jean. *Body of Power, Spirit of Resistance: The Culture and History of a South African People.* Chicago: University of Chicago Press, 1985.

"Con el voto de PAN, PRI y PVEM aprueba la Cámara la ley indígena." *La Jornada,* April 29, 2001. www.jornada.unam.mx/2001/4/29/003n1pol.htm; accessed July 6, 2009.

Corbett, Julian. *Official History of the Great War, Naval Operations.* Vol. 1. London: Imperial War Museum, Battery, 1997.

Cornell, Drucilla. "Rethinking the Beyond of the Real." *Cardoza Law Review* 16, nos. 3–4 (1994/95): 729–792.

—— *The Philosophy of the Limit.* New York: Routledge, 1992.

Corrigan, Gordon. *Sepoys in the Trenches: The Indian Corps on the Western Front, 1914–1915,* Staplehurst: Spellmount, 1999.

Culler, Jonathan. *On Deconstruction: Theory and Criticism After Structuralism.* Ithaca: Cornell University Press, 1982.

Das, Santanu. "'Indian Sisters! . . . Send your husbands, brothers, sons': India, Women, and the First World War." In Alison S. Fell and Ingrid Sharp, eds., *The Women's Movement in Wartime: International Perspectives, 1914–19.* Basingstoke: Palgrave Macmillan, 2007.

Deleuze, Gilles and Felix Guattari. *Anti-Oedipus: Capitalism and Schizophrenia.* Trans. R. Hurley. London: Athlone, 1984.

—— *A Thousand Plateaus: Capitalism and Schizophrenia.* Trans. Brian Massumi. Minneapolis: University of Minnesota Press, 1987.

Derrett, J. D. M. *Hindu Law Past and Present: Being an Account of the Controversy Which Preceded the Enactment of the Hindu Code, and Text of the Code as Enacted, and Some Comments Thereon.* Calcutta: A. Mukherjee, 1957.

Derrida, Jacques. "Desistance." In Philippe Lacoue-Labarthe, ed., *Typography: Mimesis, Philosophy, Politics,* pp. 1–42. Trans. Christopher Fynsk. Cambridge: Harvard University Press, 1989.

—— *Gift of Death.* Trans. David Wills. Chicago: University of Chicago Press, 1995.

—— *Given Time: 1. Counterfeit Money.* Trans. Peggy Kamuf. Chicago: University of Chicago Press.

—— *Limited inc. abc.* Evanston: Northwestern University Press, 1988.

—— "Linguistic Circle of Geneva." In Jacques Derrida, *Margins of Philosophy,* pp. 137–154. Trans. Alan Bass. Chicago: University of Chicago Press, 1982.

—— *Margins of Philosophy.* Trans. Alan Bass. Chicago: University of Chicago Press, 1982.

—— "My Chances/*Mes Chances*: A Rendezvous with Some Epicurean Stereophonies." In Joseph H. Smith and William Kerrigan, eds., *Taking Chances: Derrida, Psychoanalysis, and Literature,* pp. 1–32. Baltimore: Johns Hopkins University Press, 1984.

—— *Of Grammatology*. Trans. Gayatri Chakravorty Spivak. Baltimore: Johns Hopkins University Press, 1976.

—— *Rogues: Two Essays on Reason*. Trans. Pascale-Anne Brault and Michael Naas. Stanford University Press, 2005.

—— "Signature Event Context." In Jacques Derrida, *Margins of Philosophy*, pp. 307–330. Trans. Alan Bass. Chicago: University of Chicago Press, 1982.

—— *Specters of Marx: The State of the Debt, the Work of Mourning, and the New International*. Trans. Peggy Kamuf. New York: Routledge, 1994.

—— "Structure, Sign, and Play in the Discourse of the Human Sciences." In Richard Macksey and Eugenio Donato, eds., *The Structuralist Controversy: The Languages of Criticism and the Sciences of Man*, pp. 247–272. Baltimore: Johns Hopkins University Press, 1972.

—— "The Supplement of Copula: Philosophy Before Linguistics." In Jacques Derrida, *Margins of Philosophy*, pp. 175–205. Trans. Alan Bass. Chicago: University of Chicago Press, 1982.

Desai, Sunderlal T. *Mulla: Principles of Hindu Law*. Bombay: N. M. Tripathi, 1982.

Devi, Mahasweta. "The Breast-Giver." In Gayatri Chakravorty Spivak, *In Other Worlds: Essays in Cultural Politics*, pp. 222–240. New York: Routledge, 1987.

Dhareshwar, Vivek. "'Our Time': History, Sovereignty, Politics." *Economic and Political Weekly*, February 11, 1995, pp. 317–324.

Djebar, Assia. *Far From Medina*. Trans. Dorothy Blair. London: Quartet, 1994.

Douglass, Frederick. *Autobiographies*. New York: Library of America, 1996.

Dussel, Enrique. "Cuestión étnica, popular en un cristianismo policéntrico." In *Teología y Liberación. Religión, cultura y ética. Ensayos en torno a la obra de Gustavo Gutiérrez*, pp. 141–155. Lima: Instituto Bartolomé de las Casas-Rimac, 1991.

Ellinwood, Dewitt C. and S. D. Pradhan, eds. *India and World War 1*, pp. 18–37. New Delhi: Manobar, 1978.

Foucault, Michel. *Discipline and Punish: The Birth of the Prison*. Trans. Alan Sheridan. Harmondsworth: Penguin, 1979.

—— "Governmentality." In James Faubion, ed., *The Essential Works of Michel Foucault*. Vol. 3: *Power*, pp. 201–222. Trans. Robert Hurley et al. New York: New Press, 2000.

—— *Language, Counter-Memory, Practice: Selected Essays and Interviews*. Trans. Donald Bouchard and Sherry Simon. Ithaca: Cornell University Press, 1977.

—— *Madness and Civilization: A History of Insanity in the Age of Reason*. Trans. Richard Howard. New York: Pantheon, 1965.

—— "On Popular Justice: A Discussion with Maoists." *Power/Knowledge: Selected Interviews and Other Writings, 1972–77*, pp. 1–36. Trans. Colin Gordon et al. New York: Pantheon.

—— "Security, Territory, and Population." In Paul Rabinow, ed., *The Essential Works of Michel Foucault*. Vol. 1: *Ethics, Subjectivity, and Truth*, pp. 68–71. Trans. Robert Hurley et al. New York: New Press, 1997.

———. "The Birth of Biopolitics." In Paul Rabinow, ed., *The Essential Works of Michel Foucault*. Vol. 1: *Ethics, Subjectivity and Truth*, pp. 73–79. Trans. Robert Hurley et al. New York: New Press, 1997.

——— *The History of Sexuality*. Vol. 1: *An Introduction*. Trans. Robert Hurley. New York: Vintage, 1980.

——— *The Order of Things: An Archaeology of Human Sciences*. New York: Vintage, 1994.

——— "The Politics of Health in the Eighteenth Century." In James Faubion, ed., *The Essential Works of Michel Foucault*. Vol. 3: *Power*, pp. 90–105. Trans. Robert Hurley et al. New York: New Press, 2000.

——— "Truth and Juridical Forms." In *The Essential Works of Foucault*. Vol. 3: *Power*, pp. 1–89. Trans. Robert Hurley et al. New York: New Press, 2000.

——— "Truth and Power." In *The Essential Works of Foucault*. Vol. 3: *Power*, pp. 111–133. Trans. Robert Hurley et al. New York: New Press, 2000.

——— "What Is Enlightenment?" In Paul Rabinow, ed., *The Foucault Reader*, pp. 32–42. New York: Pantheon, 1984.

Freire, Paolo. *The Pedagogy of the Oppressed*. Trans. Myra Bergman Ramos. New York: Herder and Herder, 1970.

Freud, Sigmund. "'A Child Is Being Beaten': A Contribution to the Study of the Origin of Sexual Perversion" (1919). In James Strachey, ed., *The Standard Edition of the Works of Sigmund Freud*, 17:175–204. London: Hogarth, 1953–1974.

——— "Moses and Monotheism" (1939). In James Strachey, ed., *The Standard Edition of the Works of Sigmund Freud*, 23:3–137. London: Hogarth, 1953–1974.

——— "'Wild' Psycho-Analysis." In James Strachey, ed., *The Standard Edition of the Works of Sigmund Freud*, 11:219–28. London: Hogarth, 1953–1974.

Fröbel, Folker, Jürgen Heinrichs, and Otto Kreye. *The New International Division of Labor. Structural Unemployment in Industrialised Countries and Industrialization in Developing Countries*. Trans. Pete Burgess. Cambridge: Cambridge University Press, 1980.

Fu, Kelly and Constance Singam. "The Culture of Exploitation and Abuse." Unpublished MS, January 5, 2003.

Gandhi, Leela. *Postcolonial Theory: A Critical Introduction*. New York: Columbia University Press, 1998.

Ghosh, Amitav. *Shadow Lines*. Delhi: Oxford University Press, 1995.

Gibson, Edwin and G. Kingsley Ward. *Courage Remembered: The Story Behind the Construction and Maintenance of the Commonwealth's Military Cemeteries and Memorials of the Wars of 1914–1918 and 1939–1945*. London: HMSO, 1989.

Gilroy, Paul. *The Black Atlantic: Modernity and Double Consciousness*. Cambridge: Harvard University Press, 1993.

Ginzburg, Carlo. *Myths, Emblems, Clues*. Trans. John and Anne C. Tedeschi, London: Hutchinson, 1990.

Gramsci, Antonio. *Selections from the Prison Notebooks*. Trans. Quintin Hoare and Geoffrey Nowell Smith. New York: International, 1971.

—— "Some Aspects of the Southern Question." In *Selections from Political Writings (1921–1926)*, pp. 421–462. Trans. Quintin Hoare. New York: International, 1978.

—— *The Southern Question.* Trans. Pasquale Verdicchio. West Lafayette, IN: Bordighera, 1995.

Gugelberger, George M. *The Real Thing: Testimonial Discourse and Latin America.* Durham: Duke University Press, 1996.

Guha, Ranajit "Chandra's Death." In *Subaltern Studies* V, pp. 135–165. New Delhi: Oxford University Press, 1987.

—— *Domination Without Hegemony: History and Power in Colonial India.* Cambridge: Harvard University Press, 1997.

—— *Elementary Aspects of Peasant Insurgency in Colonial India.* Delhi: Oxford University Press, 1983; rpr. Durham: Duke University Press, 1999.

—— "On Some Aspects of the Historiography of Colonial India." In Ranajit Guha, ed., *Subaltern Studies* 1, pp. 1–8. New Delhi: Oxford University Press, 1982.

Guha, Ranajit, ed. *Subaltern Studies* 1. New Delhi: Oxford University Press, 1982.

Guha, Ranajit and Gayatri Chakravorty Spivak, eds. *Selected Subaltern Studies.* New York: Oxford University Press, 1988.

Gulbenkian Commission. *Open the Social Sciences: Report of the Gulbenkian Commission on the Restructuring of the Social Sciences.* Stanford: Stanford University Press, 1996.

Gussow, Adam. *Seems Like Murder Here: Southern Violence and the Blues Tradition.* Chicago: University of Chicago Press, 2002.

Gutiérrez, Margarita and Nellys Palomo. "A Woman's Eye View of Autonomy." In Arecely Burguete Cal y Mayor, ed., *Indigenous Autonomy in Mexico*, pp. 53–82. Copenhagen: IWGIA, 2000.

Habermas, Jürgen. *The Structural Transformation of the Public Sphere.* Trans. Thomas Burger. Cambridge: MIT Press, 1989.

Hall, Stuart. "The Problem of Ideology—Marxism Without Guarantees." In Betty Matthews, ed., *Marx: A Hundred Years On*, pp. 57–84. London: Lawrence and Wishart, 1983.

Hardiman, David. "'Subaltern Studies' at Crossroads." *Economic and Political Weekly* 21, no. 7 (February 15, 1986): 288–290. http://www.jstor.org/stable/4375333; accessed April 5, 2009.

Heath, Shirley Brice. *Telling Tongues: Language Policy in Mexico, Colony to Nation.* New York: Teachers College Press, 1972.

Heathcote, Thomas Anthony. *The Indian Army: The Garrison of British Imperial India, 1822–1922.* Newton Abbot: David and Charles, 1974.

Hegel, G. W. F. *Philosophy of Right.* Trans. T. M. Knox. Oxford: Oxford University Press, 1967.

Heidegger, Martin. *An Introduction to Metaphysics.* Trans. Ralph Mannheim. New York: Doubleday Anchor, 1961.

——*Being and Time.* Trans. John Macquarrie and Edward Robinson. New York: Harper and Row, 1962.

Henderson, Jeffrey. "Changing International Division of Labour in the Electronics Industry." In Duncan Campbell, Aurelio Parisotto, Anil Verma and Asma Lateef, eds., *Regionalization and Labour Market Interdependence in East and Southeast Asia,* pp. 92–126. New York: St. Martin's, 1997.

——"Electronics Industries and the Developing World: Uneven Contributions and Uncertain Prospects." In Leslie Sklair, ed., *Capitalism and Development,* pp. 258–288. New York: Routledge, 1994.

——"The New International Division of Labour and American Semiconductor Production in Southeast Asia." In C. J. Dixon, D. Drakakis-Smith, and H. D. Watts, eds., *Multinational Corporations and the Third World,* , pp. 91–117. Boulder: Westview, 1986.

Hernández, Margarita Ruiz. "The Process of Creating a National Legislative Proposal for Autonomy." In Arecely Burguete Cal y Mayor, ed., *Indigenous Autonomy in Mexico,* pp. 24–52. Copenhagen: IWGIA, 2000.

Heyck, Denis Lynn Daly. *Surviving Globalization in Three Latin American Communities.* Toronto: Broadview, 2002.

Hodges, Geoffrey. "Military Labour in East Africa and Its Impact on Kenya." In Melvin Page, ed., *Africa and the First World War,* pp. 137–151. Basingstoke: Macmillan, 1987.

Huntington, Samuel P. *The Clash of Civilizations and the Remaking of World Order.* New York: Simon and Schuster, 1996.

Irigaray, Luce. "The Necessity for Sexuate Rights." In Margaret Whitford, ed., *The Irigaray Reader,* pp. 204–211. Cambridge: Blackwell, 1991.

Irving, John. *Coronel and the Falklands.* London: Philpot, 1927.

Jameson, Fredric. "Marx's Purloined Letter." *New Left Review,* no. 209 (1995): 75–109.

——*The Political Unconscious: Narrative as a Socially Symbolic Act.* Ithaca: Cornell University Press, 1981.

JanMohamed, Abdul. *The Death-Bound-Subject: Richard Wright's Archaeology of Death.* Durham: Duke University Press, 2005.

Jay, Martin. *Force Fields: Between Intellectual History and Cultural Critique.* New York: Routledge, 1993.

Jayawardena, Kumari. *The White Woman's Other Burden: Western Women and South Asia During British Colonial Rule.* New York: Routledge, 1995.

Jeffery, Keith. *Ireland and the Great War.* Cambridge: Cambridge University Press, 2000.

Jones, Ann Rosalind and Peter Stallybrass. *Renaissance Clothing and the Materials of Memory.* Cambridge: Cambridge University Press, 2000.

Kane, Pandurang Vaman. *History of the Dharmasastra.* Poona: Bhandarkar Oriental Institute, 1963.

Kant, Immanuel. *Groundwork of the Metaphysics of Morals*. In Immanuel Kant, *Practical Philosophy*. Ed. and trans. Mary J. Gregor. Cambridge: Cambridge University Press, 1996.

Kei. C. P. *To Have and to Hold*. Singapore: Armour, 1993.

Kenyon, Frederick. *War Graves: How the Cemeteries Abroad Will Be Designed*. London: HMSO, 1918.

Klein, Melanie. "Envy and Gratitude." In Melanie Klein, *Envy and Gratitude and Other Works*, pp. 176–235. New York: Free Press, 1975.

—— "The Early Development of Conscience in the Child." In Melanie Klein, *Love, Guilt and Reparation and Other Works (1921–1945)*, pp. 248–257. New York: Free Press, 1984.

Kofman, Sarah. *The Enigma of Woman: Woman in Freud's Writings*. Trans. Catherine Porter. Ithaca: Cornell University Press, 1985.

Kosambi, D. D. "Combined Methods in Indology." *Indo-Iranian Journal* 6 (1963):177–202. Rpt. in Brajadulal Chattopadhyaya, ed., *Combined Methods in Indology and Other Writings*. Delhi: Oxford, 2002.

—— *Myth and Reality: Studies in the Formation of Indian Culture*. Bombay: Popular Prakashan, 1962.

Kristeva, Julia. *About Chinese Women*. Trans. Anita Barrows. London: Marion Boyars, 1977.

Kumar, Radha. "Agitation Against Sati 1987–88." In *The History of Doing*, pp. 172–181. Delhi: Kāli for Women, 1993.

Landy, Marcia. *Film, Politics, and Gramsci*, pp. 73–98. Minneapolis: University of Minnesota Press, 1994.

Laqueur, Thomas W. "Memory and Naming in the Great War." In John R. Gillis, ed., *Commemorations: The Politics of National Identity*, pp. 150–167. Princeton: Princeton University Press, 1994.

Lawrence, Errol. "Just Plain Common Sense: The 'Roots' of Racism." In Center for Contemporary Cultural Studies, ed., *The Empire Strikes Back: Race and Racism in 70s Britain*, pp. 93–140. London: Hutchinson, 1982.

Lee, Jean, Kathleen Campbell, and Audrey Chia. *The Three Paradoxes: Working Women in Singapore*. Singapore: AWARE, 1999.

Lenin, V. I. *Imperialism, the Highest Stage of Capitalism: A Popular Outline*. Chicago: Junius, 1996.

Lingat, Robert. *The Classical Law of India*. Trans. J. D. M. Derrett. Berkeley: University of California Press, 1973.

Livesey, Anthony. *The Viking Atlas of World War I*. London: Viking, 1994.

Longworth, Philip. *The Unending Vigil: A History of the Commonwealth War Graves Commission*. London: Leo Cooper, 2003 [1967, 1985].

Lucas, Charles. *The Empire at War*. Vol. 1. London: Oxford University Press, 1921.

—— *The Empire at War*. Vol. 5. London: Oxford University Press, 1926.

Lukács, Georg. "Class Consciousness." In *History and Class Consciousness: Studies in Marxist Dialectics*, pp. 46–82. Trans. Rodney Livingstone. Cambridge: MIT Press, 1971.

Lyotard, Jean-François. *The Differend: Phrases in Dispute*. Trans. Georges Van Den Abbeele. Minneapolis: University of Minnesota Press, 1988.

Macaulay, Thomas Babington. *Speeches by Lord Macaulay: With His Minute on Indian Education*. Ed. G. M. Young. Oxford: Oxford University Press, AMS Edition, 1979.

"Maid Dependency Here to Stay, Study Finds." *Straits Times*, February 3, 1996.

Maier, Charles S. "The Politics of Productivity: Foundations of American International Economic Policy After World War II." In Peter J. Katzenstein, ed., *Between Power and Plenty: Foreign Economic Policies of Advanced Industrial States*. Madison: University of Wisconsin Press, 1978.

Mallon, Florence E. "The Promise and Dilemma of Subaltern Studies: Perspectives from Latin American History." *American Historical Review* 99, no. 5 (December 1994): 1491–1515.

Mani, Lata. "Contentious Traditions: The Debate on *Sati* in Colonial India." In Kumkum Sangari and Sudesh Vaid, eds., *Recasting Women: Essays in Colonial History*, pp. 88–126. Delhi: Kāli for Women, 1989.

—— "Production of an Official Discourse on *Sati* in Early Nineteenth-Century Bengal." *Economic and Political Weekly* 21, no. 17 (April 26, 1986): WS32–WS40.

Marcos, Sub-comandante. "Democratic Teachers and the Zapatista Dream." In Juana Ponce de León, ed., *Our Word Is Our Weapon: Selected Writings of Subcomandante Marcos*, pp. 274–277. New York: Seven Stories, 2001.

——"Twelve Women in the Twelfth Year: The Moment of War." In Juana Ponce de León, ed., *Our Word Is Our Weapon*, pp. 5–12. New York: Seven Stories, 2001.

Marks, Shula. *Not Either an Experimental Doll*. Bloomington: Indiana University, Press, 1987.

Marx, Karl. *Capital: A Critique of Political Economy*. Trans. Ben Fowkes. 3 vols. New York: Viking Penguin, 1977.

——*Grundrisse: Foundations of the Critique of Political Economy*. Trans. Martin Nicolaus. New York: Viking, 1973.

——*Surveys from Exile*. Trans. David Fernbach. New York: Penguin, 1973.

——"The British Rule in India." In Karl Marx, *Surveys from Exile*, pp.301–307. Trans. David Fernbach. New York: Penguin, 1973.

——"The Eighteenth Brumaire of Louis Bonaparte." In Karl Marx, *Surveys from Exile*, pp. 143–249. Trans. David Fernbach. New York: Penguin, 1973.

——*The Ethnological Notebooks (Studies of Morgan, Phear, Maine, Lubbock)*. Ed., with an introduction, Lawrence Krader. Assen: Van Gorcum and Comp, 1972.

—— "The Future Results of the British Rule in India." In Karl Marx, *Surveys from Exile*, pp. 319–325. Trans. David Fernbach. New York: Penguin, 1973.

Mathews, Biju, et al. "Vasudhaiva Kutumbakam: The Hindu in the World." Unpublished MS.

Mbembe, Achilles. "Necropolitics." *Public Culture* 15, no. 1 (Winter 2003): 11–40.

Medovoi, Leerom and Shankar Raman. "Can the Subaltern Vote?" *Socialist Review* 20, no. 3 (July–September 1990): 133–149.

Menchú, Rigoberta. *La nieta de los Mayas*. Mexico City: El País/Santilla, 1998.

"Mensaje Central del EZLN ante el Congreso de la Union. Miércoles, 28 de marzo de 2001. Comandante Esther." In Reinhard Krüger, ed., *Mexico Insurgent: Los Zapatistas y la marcha por la dignidad indígena, 24 Febrero–11 Marzo 2001: Los discursos en el Congreso y el regreso a Chiapas*, pp. 93–103. Berlin: Weidler, 2001.

Merewether, J. W. B. and F. Smith. *The Indian Corps in France*. London: Murray, 1919.

Mignolo, Walter. *Local Histories/Global Designs: Coloniality, Subaltern Knowledges, and Border Thinking*. Princeton: Princeton University Press, 2000.

Mohanty, Chandra Talpade. "Under Western Eyes: Feminist Scholarship and Colonial Discourses." In Chandra Talpade Mohanty, Anne Russo, and Lourdes Torres, eds., *Third World Women and the Politics of Feminism*, pp. 51–80. Bloomington: Indiana University Press, 1991.

Monier-Williams, Sir Monier. *Sanskrit-English Dictionary*. Oxford: Clarendon, 1989.

Moore, Donald S. "Subaltern Struggles and the Politics of Place: Remapping Resistance in Zimbabwe's Eastern Highlands." *Cultural Anthropology* 13, no. 3 (August 1998): 344–381.

Morrison, Toni. *Beloved*. New York: Plume 1998.

Morrow, John H. *The Great War: An Imperial History*. Abingdon: Routledge, 2004.

Morton, Stephen. *Gayatri Spivak*. New York: Routledge, 2003.

——*Gayatri Spivak: Ethics, Subalternity, and the Critique of Postcolonial Reason*. London: Polity, 2007.

Mudimbe, V. Y. *The Invention of Africa: Gnosis, Philosophy, and the Order of Knowledge*. Bloomington: Indiana University Press, 1998.

Nandy, Ashis. "Sati: A Nineteenth Century Tale of Women, Violence and Protest." In V. C. Joshi, ed., *Rammohun Roy and the Process of Modernization in India*, pp.168–194. Delhi: Vikas, 1975.

Nash, June. *Mayan Visions: The Quest for Autonomy in the Age of Globalization*. New York: Routledge, 2001.

O'Hanlon, Rosalind. "Recovering the Subject: Subaltern Studies and Histories of Resistance in Colonial South Asia." *Modern Asian Studies* 22, no. 1 (1988): 189–224.

O'Hanlon, Rosalind and D. A. Washbrook. "After Orientalism: Culture, Criticism, and Politics in the Third World." *Comparative Studies in Society and History* 34, no. 1 (January 1992): 141–167.

Omissi, David. *Indian Voices of the Great War: Soldiers Letters, 1914–18.* Basingstoke: Macmillan, 1999.

Otto, Dianne. "Holding Up Half the Sky, But for Whose Benefit? A Critical Analysis of the Fourth World Conference on Women." *Australian Feminist Law Journal* 6 (March 1996): 7–30.

Page, Melvin, ed. *Africa and the First World War.* Basingstoke: Macmillan, 1987.

Palmieri, Jorge. "Lies by the Nobel Prize Winner." In Arturo Arias, ed., *The Rigoberta Menchú Controversy,* pp. 73–75. Minneapolis: University of Minnesota Press, 2001.

—— "The Pitiful Lies of Rigoberta Menchú." In Arturo Arias, ed., *The Rigoberta Menchú Controversy,* pp. 78–81. Minneapolis: University of Minnesota Press, 2001.

Pamuk, Orhan. *Snow.* Trans. Maureen Freely. New York: Knopf, 2004.

Prakash, Gyan. "Can the 'Subaltern' Ride? A Reply to O'Hanlon and Washbrook." *Comparative Studies in Society and History* 34, no. 1 (January 1992): 168–184.

—— "Subaltern Studies as Postcolonial Criticism." *American Historical Review* 99, no. 5 (1994): 1475–1490.

Pratt, Mary Louise. "I, Rigoberta Menchú and the "Culture Wars." In Arturo Arias, ed., *The Rigoberta Menchú Controversy,* pp. 29–48. Minneapolis: University of Minnesota Press, 2001.

Price, Imran Andrew and Lim Chi-Sharn. "Reliance on Maids—Let's Have Affordable Alternatives." Letter. *Straits Times,* October 3, 2003.

Rabinow, Paul. "Anthropological Observation and Self-Formation." In João Biehl, Byron Good, and Arthur Kleinman, eds., *Subjectivity: Ethnographic Investigations,* pp. 98–118. Berkeley: University of California Press, 2007.

Raj, Conrad. "Let's Give Our Maids More." *Streats,* March 10, 2003.

Rawls, John. *Political Liberalism.* New York: Columbia University Press, 1993.

Ray, Sangeeta. *Gayatri Chakravorty Spivak: In Other Words.* London: Wiley-Blackwell, 2009.

Report of the Fourth World Conference on Women. Beijing, September 4–15, 1995, A/CONF.177/20, October 17, 1995.

Rice, Stanley. *Neuve Chapelle—India's Memorial in France, 1914–1918: An Account of the Unveiling.* London: Imperial War Graves Commission, 1928.

Robison, Richard, Richard Higgott, and Kevin Hewison. "Crisis in Economic Strategy in the 1980s: The Factors at Work." In Richard Robison, Richard Higgott, and Kevin Hewison, eds., *Southeast Asia in the 1980s: The Politics of Economic Crisis,* pp. 1–15. Sydney: Allen and Unwin, 1987.

Rodan, Garry. "Industrialisation and the Singapore State in the Context of the New International Division of Labour." In Richard Higgott and Richard Robison, eds., *Southeast Asia: Essays in the Political Economy of Structural Change,* pp. 172–194. London: Routledge and Kegan Paul, 1985.

—— "The Rise and Fall of Singapore's 'Second Industrial Revolution.'" In Richard Robison, Richard Higoott, and Kevin Hewison, eds., *Southeast Asia in the*

1980s: The Politics of Economic Crisis, pp. 149–176. Sydney: Allen and Unwin, 1987.

Rodríguez, Ileana, ed. *The Latin American Subaltern Studies Reader.* Durham: Duke University Press, 2001.

—— *Liberalism at Its Limits: Crime and Terror in the Cultural Text.* Pittsburgh: University of Pittsburgh Press, 2009.

Rovira, Guiomar. *Mujeres de Maíz.* Mexico: Era, 1997.

Rubin, Gayle. "The Traffic in Women: Notes on the 'Political Economy' of Sex." In Rayna R. Reiter, ed., *Toward an Anthropology of Women*, pp. 157–185. New York: Monthly Review Press, 1975.

Said, Edward W. "Permission to Narrate." *London Review of Books*, February 16, 1984.

—— *The World, the Text, the Critic.* Cambridge: Harvard University Press, 1983.

Saldaña Portillo, María Josefina. *The Revolutionary Imagination in the Americas and the Age of Development.* Durham: Duke University Press, 2003.

Sanders, Mark. *Gayatri Chakravorty Spivak: Live Theory.* New York: Continuum, 2006.

Sarkar, Sumit. "Orientalism Revisited: Saidian Frameworks in the Writing of Modern Indian History." *Oxford Literary Review* 16 (1994): 205–24.

—— "The Fascism of the Sangh Parivar." *Economic and Political Weekly*, January 30, 1993, pp. 163–167.

Sarkar, Tanika. *Hindu Wife, Hindu Nation.* New Delhi: Permanent Black, 2001.

Sassen, Saskia. "On Economic Citizenship." In *Losing Control? Sovereignty in an Age of Globalization*, pp. 31–58. New York: Columbia University Press, 1996.

Scott, James. *Domination and the Arts of Resistance: Hidden Transcripts.* New Haven: Yale University Press, 1990.

—— *Weapons of the Weak: Everyday forms of Peasant Resistance.* New Haven: Yale University Press, 1985.

Scott, Joan Wallach. "Experience." In Judith Butler and Joan W. Scott, eds., *Feminists Theorize the Political*, pp. 22–40. New York: Routledge, 1992.

Selden, Raman. *A Reader's Guide to Contemporary Literary Theory.* New York: Prentice-Hall, 1997.

Sherman, Daniel J. *The Construction of Memory in Interwar France.* Chicago: University of Chicago Press, 1999.

Shetty, Sandhya and Elizabeth Jane Bellamy. "Postcolonialism's Archive Fever." Review of *Archive Fever* and *Of Grammatology* by Jacques Derrida; "Can the Subaltern Speak?" by Gayatri Chakravorty Spivak. *Diacritics* 30, no. 1 (Spring 2000): 25–48.

Smith, Jay. "No More Language Games: Words, Beliefs, and the Political Culture of Early Modern France," *American Historical Review* 102, no. 5 (December 1997): 1416.

Sommer, Doris. "No Secrets." In Georg M. Gugelberger, ed., *The Real Thing: Testimonial Discourse and Latin America*, pp. 130–157. Durham: Duke University Press, 1996.

Spivak, Gayatri Chakravorty. *A Critique of Postcolonial Reason: Toward a History of the Vanishing Present*. Cambridge: Harvard University Press, 1999.

—— "A Dialogue on Democracy." Interview with David Plotke. In David Trend, ed., *Radical Democracy: Identity, Citizenship and the State*, pp. 209–222. New York: Routledge, 1995.

—— "A Moral Dilemma." In Howard Marchitello, ed., *What Happens to History: The Renewal of Ethics in Contemporary Thought*, pp. 215–236. New York: Routledge, 2001.

—— "Can the Subaltern Speak?" (1988). In Lawrence Grossberg and Cary Nelson, eds., *Marxism and the Interpretation of Culture*, pp. 271–313. Urbana: University of Illinois Press; Basingstoke: Macmillan.

—— "Can the Subaltern Speak? Speculations on Widow Sacrifice." *Wedge* 7/8 (Winter/Spring 1985): 120–130.

—— *Death of a Discipline*. New York: Columbia University Press, 2006.

—— "Deconstruction and Cultural Studies: Arguments for a Deconstructive Cultural Studies." In Nicholas Royle, ed., *Deconstructions: A User's Guide*, pp. 14–23. Oxford: Blackwell, 2000.

—— "Diasporas Old and New: Women in a Transnational World." *Textual Practice* 10, no. 2 (1996): 245–269.

—— "Discussion: An Afterword on the New Subaltern." In Partha Chatterjee and Pradeep Jeganathan, eds., *Community, Gender and Violence: Subaltern Studies XI*, pp. 305–333. Delhi: Permanent Black, 2000.

—— "'Draupadi' by Mahasweta Devi, with a Foreword by Gayatri Chakravorty Spivak." In Gayatri Chakravorty Spivak, *In Other Worlds: Essays in Cultural Politics*, pp. 179–196. New York: Routledge, 1987.

—— "Foucault and Najibullah." In Kathleen L. Komar and Ross Shideler, eds., *Lyrical Symbols and Narrative Transformations: Essays in Honor of Ralph Freedman*. Columbia, SC: Camden House, 1998.

—— "French Feminism in an International Frame." In Gayatri Chakravorty Spivak, *In Other Worlds: Essays in Cultural Politics*, pp. 136–141. New York: Routledge, 1987.

—— "Ghostwriting." *Diacritics* 25, no. 2 (Summer 1995): 65–84.

—— "If Only." *Writing a Feminist's Life: The Legacy of Carolyn G. Heilbrun. Scholar and Feminist Online* 4, no. 2 (Spring 2006). Barnard Center for Research on Women. www.barnard.edu/sfonline.

—— "Imperatives to Re-imagine the Planet." In Willi Goetschel, ed., *Imperatives to ReImagine the Planet/Imperative zur Neuerfindung des Planeten*, Vienna: Passagen, 1999. Rpt. in *Alphabet City*, no. 7 (2000): 266–279.

—— *In Other Worlds: Essays in Cultural Politics*. New York: Routledge, 1987.

—— "Mapping the Present." Interview with Meyda Yegennoglu and Mahmut Mutman. *New Formations* 45 (January 2002): 9–23.

—— "More on Power/Knowledge." In Thomas E. Wartenburg, ed., *Rethinking Power*, pp. 149–173. Albany: State University of New York Press, 1992.

—— "Nationalism and the Imagination." In C. Vijayasree, Meenakshi Mukherjee, Harish Trivedi, and Vijay Kumar, eds., *Nation in Imagination: Essays on Natinalism, Sub-Nationalisms, and Narration*, pp. 1–20. Hyderabad: Orient Longman, 2007.

—— "1996: Foucault and Najibullah." In *Other Asias*, pp. 132–160.

—— *Other Asias*. Oxford: Blackwell, 2009.

—— "Psychoanalysis in Left Field: Examples to Fit the Title." *American Imago* 51, no. 2 (1994): 161–196. Rpt. in Sonu Shamdasani and Michael Münchow, eds., "Psychoanalysis in Left Field and Fieldworking: Examples to Fit the Title." *Speculations After Freud: Psychoanalysis, Philosophy, and Culture*, pp. 41–75. London: Routledge, 1994.

—— Re-Imagining Communities." In C. Vijayasree, Meenakshi Mukherjee, Harish Trivedi, and Vijay Kumar, eds., *Nation in Imagination: Essays on Natinalism, Sub-Nationalisms, and Narration*, pp. 21–36. Hyderabad: Orient Longman, 2007.

—— "Responsibility." *boundary 2* 21, no. 3 (Fall 1994): 19–64.

—— "Righting Wrongs." *South Atlantic Quarterly* 103, nos. 2/3 (Spring/Summer 2004): 523–581.

—— "Scattered Speculations on the Subaltern and the Popular." *Postcolonial Studies* 8, no. 4 (2005): 475–486; in Gayatri Chakravorty Spivak, *In Other Worlds: Essays in Cultural Politics*, pp. 154–175. New York: Routledge, 1987.

—— "Setting to Work (Transnational Cultural Studies)." In Peter Osborne, ed., *A Critical Sense: Interviews with Intellectuals*, pp. 163–177. London: Routledge, 1996.

—— "Subaltern Studies: Deconstructing Historiography." In Ranajit Guha, ed., *Subaltern Studies IV: Writings on South Asian History and Society*, pp. 330–363. New Delhi: Oxford University Press, 1985.

—— "Subaltern Talk." Interview with Donna Landry and Gerald Maclean. In Donna Landry and Gerald Maclean, eds., *The Spivak Reader*, pp. 287–308. New York: Routledge, 1996.

—— "Teaching for the Times." In Bhikhu Parekh and Jan Nederveen Pieterse, eds., *The Decolonization of the Imagination*, pp. 177–202. London: Zed, 1995.

—— "Righting Wrongs." In Nicholas Owen, ed., *Human Rights and Human Wrongs: The Oxford Amnesty Lectures*, pp. 164–207. New York: Oxford University Press, 2003.

—— "Terror: A Speech After 9–11." *boundary 2* 31, no. 2 (Summer 2004): 81–111.

—— "Theory in the Margin: Coetzee's *Foe* Reading Defoe's *Crusoe/Roxana*." In Jonathan Arac and Barbara Johnson, eds., *Consequences of Theory: Selected*

Papers of the English Institute, 1987–88, pp. 154–180. Baltimore: Johns Hopkins University Press, 1991.

—— "The Rani of Sirmur: An Essay in Reading the Archives," *History and Theory* 3, no. 24 (1985): 247–272.

—— "Three Women's Texts and a Critique of Imperialism." *Critical Inquiry* 12, no. 1 (1985): 243–261.

—— "Translator's Preface." In Mahasweta Devi, *Imaginary Maps*, pp. xxiii–xxix. Ed. and trans. Gayatri Chakravorty Spivak. New York: Routledge, 1995.

—— "Who Claims Sexuality in the New World Order?" Conference on Culture/Sex/Economies, LaTrobe University (Melbourne), December 16–19, 1994; Conference on Silencing Women: Feminism(s), Censorship and Difference, University of California-Riverside, February 25, 1995; Commonwealth Center for Cultural and Literary Change, University of Virginia, April 19, 1995; Pembroke Center for Research on Women, Brown University, April 11, 1996.

—— "'Woman' as Theatre: United Nations Conference on Women, Beijing 1995." *Radical Philosophy* 75 (January/February 1996), 2–4.

Spivak, Gayatri Chakravorty, Miyoshi Masao, and H. D. Harootunian, eds., *Learning Places: The Afterlives of Area Studies*. Durham: Duke, 2002.

Stahl, Charles. "Trade in Labour Services and Migrant Worker Protection with Special Reference to East Asia." *International Migration* 37, no. 3 (1999): 545–568.

Stavenhagen, Rodolfo. "Towards the Right to Autonomy in Mexico." In Arecely Burguete Cal y Mayor, ed., *Indigenous Autonomy in Mexico*, pp. 10–21.

Stiglitz, Joseph. *Globalization and Its Discontents*. New York: Norton, 2003.

Stoll, David. *Rigoberta Menchú and the Story of All Poor Guatemalans*. Boulder: Westview, 1999.

Strachan, Hew. *The First World War*, vol. 1: *To Arms*. Oxford: Oxford University Press, 2001.

Summers, Julie. *Remembered: The History of the Commonwealth War Graves Commission*. London: Merrell, 2007.

Sunder Rajan, Rajeswari. *The Scandal of the State*. Durham: Duke University Press, 2003.

Tagore, Abanindranath. *Raj-Kahini*. Calcutta: Signet, 1968.

Tagore, Rabindranath. *Char Adhyay/Four Chapters*. Calcutta, 1934; English ed., New Delhi: Srishti, 2002.

Thakur, Upendra. *The History of Suicide in India: An Introduction*. Delhi: Munshi Ram Manohar Lal, 1963.

Thapar, Romila. *Asoka and the Decline of the Mauryas*. Delhi: Oxford University Press, 1961.

—— *From Lineage to State: Social Formations in the Mid-First Millennium in the Ganga Valley*. Oxford: Oxford University Press, 1984.

Thompson, Edward. *Suttee: A Historical and Philosophical Enquiry Into the Hindu Rite of Widow-Burning.* London: Allen and Unwin, 1925[28?].

Tod, James. *Annals and Antiquities of Rajasthan.* London: Oxford University Press, 1920.

Torres, Carmela. "Asian Women in Migration in the Light of the Beijing Conference." In Graziano Battistella and Anthony Paganoni, eds., *Asian Women in Migration,* pp. 183–190. Quezon City: Scalabrini Migration Center, 1996.

Trench, Charles Chevenix, *The Indian Army and the King's Enemies, 1900–1947.* London: Thames and Hudson, 1988.

Van de Veer, Peter. "Sati and Sanskrit: The Move from Orientalism to Hinduism." In Mieke Bal and Inge E. Boer, eds., *The Point of Theory: Practices of Cultural Analysis,* pp. 251–259. New York: Continuum, 1994.

Visram, Rosina. *Ayahs, Lascars, and Princes: Indians in Britain, 1700–1947.* London: Pluto, 1986.

Ware, Fabian. *The Immortal Heritage: An Account of the Work and Policy of the Imperial War Graves Commission During Twenty Years, 1917–1937.* Cambridge: Cambridge University Press, 1937.

Willcocks, James. *With the Indians in France.* London: Constable, 1920.

Wolf, Eric. *Europe and the People Without History.* Berkeley: University of California Press, 1982.

"Worker Treatment Reflects on Singapore." Letter. *Straits Times,* October 3, 2003.

World Development Report 1991. New York: Oxford University Press, 1991.

World Development Report 1995. New York: Oxford University Press, 1995.

Wright, Richard. *Early Works: Lawd Today! Uncle Tom's Children, Native Son.* New York: Library of America, 1991.

Young, Robert. *White Mythologies: Writing History and the West.* New York: Routledge, 1990.

CONTRIBUTORS

MICHÈLE BARRETT is professor of modern literary and cultural theory in the School of English and Drama at Queen Mary, University of London. Her interests include the work of Virginia Woolf, gender, and the history of social theory; for the past few years her research has focused on broader cultural legacies of the First World War. Her many publications include *Casualty Figures: How Five Men Survived the First World War* (2007), *The Great War and Post-modern Memory* (2000), *Star Trek: The Human Frontier* (2000), *Imagination in Theory: Culture, Writing, Words and Things* (1999), *The Politics of Truth: From Marx to Foucault* (1991), and *Women's Oppression Today* (1980).

RITU BIRLA is associate professor of history and faculty associate at the Centre for Ethics, University of Toronto. Her work brings histories of capitalism into conversation with research on colonial and postcolonial governmentality in India. Interested in historicizing "the market" as template for the social, her historical writing has addressed the legal fictions, social imaginaries, and cultural politics of colonial economic governance as well as the formation of colonial subject as modern capitalist. Her historiographical essays have considered transnational history as the practice of translation and the relationship of history, subjectivity, and ethics. She is the author of *Stages of Capital: Law, Culture and Market Governance in Late Colonial India* (2009).

PARTHA CHATTERJEE is professor of anthropology and Middle East and Asian languages and cultures (MEALAC) at Columbia University, and professor of political science, Centre for Studies in Social Sciences, Calcutta. A key member of the subaltern studies group, Professor Chatterjee is the author of numerous works, including *Nationalist Thought and the Colonial World* (1986), *The Nation and Its Fragments* (1993), *A Possible India* (1997),

The Present History of West Bengal (1997), *A Princely Impostor? The Strange and Universal History of the Kumar of Bhawal* (2002), and *The Politics of the Governed: Popular Politics in Most of the World* (2004).

PHENG CHEAH is professor in the Department of Rhetoric at the University of California at Berkeley. He is the author of *Spectral Nationality: Passages of Freedom from Kant to Postcolonial Literatures of Liberation* (New York: Columbia University Press, 2003), and *Inhuman Conditions: On Cosmopolitanism and Human Rights* (2006). He has coedited (with Suzanne Guerlac) *Derrida and the Time of the Political* (2009), (with Jonathan Culler) *Grounds of Comparison: Around the Work of Benedict Anderson* (2003), and (with Bruce Robbins) *Cosmopolitics: Thinking and Feeling Beyond the Nation* (1998). He is currently completing a book on reinventing world literature in an age of global financialization and another book on the concept of instrumentality.

DRUCILLA CORNELL is professor of political science at Rutgers University, a position she assumed in 1994 after having taught at the Benjamin N. Cardozo School of Law. She has written numerous articles on contemporary Continental thought, critical theory, grassroots political and legal mobilization, jurisprudence, women's literature, feminism, aesthetics, psychoanalysis, and political philosophy. Her books include *Beyond Accomodation: Ethical Feminism, Deconstruction, and the Law* (1991), *The Philosophy of the Limit* (1992), *Transformations: Recollective Imagination and Sexual Difference* (1993), *The Imaginary Domain: Abortion, Pornography, and Sexual Harrassment* (1995), *At the Heart of Freedom: Feminism, Sex, and Equality* (1998), *Just Cause: Freedom, Identity, and Rights* (2000), *Between Women and Generations: Legacies of Dignity* (2002).

JEAN FRANCO was the first professor of Latin American literature in England. She has been at Columbia University since 1982, first in the Department of Spanish and Portuguese and later in the Department of English and Comparative Literature. She is now professor emerita. Professor Franco is general editor of the Library of Latin America series, published by Oxford University Press. She has been writing on Latin American literature since the early sixties and has published numerous books and articles. Among them: *The Modern Culture of Latin America* (1967), *César Vallejo: The Dialectics of Poetry and Silence* (1976), *An Introduction to Latin American Literature* (1969), *Plotting Women: Gender and Representation in Mexico* (1989), and *Marcando diferencias: Cruzando fronteras* (1996). A selection of essays, *Critical Passions*, edited by Mary Louise Pratt and Kathleen Newman, was published in October 1999 by Duke University Press. Her book, *The Decline and Fall of the Lettered City: Latin America and the Cold War* was published by Harvard University Press in 2001 and was translated into Spanish as *Decadencia y caída de la ciudad letrada* in the collection Debates. The book was awarded the Bolton-Johnson Prize by the Conference of Latin American Historians for the best work in

English on the history of Latin America published in 2003. In 2005 she was awarded the Aguila Azteca Prize by the Mexican government, the highest honor given to non-Mexicans. At present she is at work on a new book entitled "Cruel Modernity."

ABDUL JANMOHAMMED is professor of English in the Department of English at Berkeley. Professor JanMohamed works on postcolonial fiction and theory; African American fiction; minority discourse; and critical theory. Among many articles and coedited works, he is the author of *The Death-Bound-Subject: Richard Wright's Archaeology of Death* (2005) and *Manichean Aesthetics: The Politics of Literature in Colonial Africa* (1983).

ROSALIND C. MORRIS is professor of anthropology and former associate director of the Institute of Comparative Literature and Society at Columbia University, where she has also served as director of the Institute for Research on Women and Gender. In addition to essays on the mass media and modernity, the politics of culture, visuality and representation, the signification of violence, gender and the history of social theory, her books include *New Worlds from Fragments: Film, Ethnography, and the Representation of Northwest Coast Cultures* (1994) and *In the Place of Origins: Northern Thailand and Its Mediums* (2000). Her most recent book is *Photographies East: The Camera and Its Histories in East and Southeast Asia* (2009). A collection of her essays on the American wars after 9/11 is forthcoming under the title "Wars I Have (Not) Seen." She is currently completing a book on her research in the gold mining communities of South Africa, tentatively entitled "Unstable Ground."

RAJESWARI SUNDER RAJAN is Global Distinguished Professor in the English department at New York University. Before moving to NYU in 2006, she was professorial fellow at Wolfson College and reader in the English faculty at the University of Oxford. She is the author of *Real and Imagined Women: Gender, Culture and Postcolonialism* (New York: Routledge, 1993), *The Scandal of the State: Women, Law, Citizenship in Postcolonial India* (2003), and, edited, jointly with Anuradha Needham, *The Crisis of Secularism in India* (2007).

GAYATRI CHAKRAVORTY SPIVAK is University Professor and former director of the Institute of Comparative Literature and Society at Columbia University. In addition to writing "Can the Subaltern Speak?" she has authored and translated numerous books, including *Myself Must I Remake: The Life and Poetry of W. B. Yeats* (1974), *Of Grammatology* (translation with critical introduction of Jacques Derrida, *De la grammatologie*, 1976), *In Other Worlds: Essays in Cultural Politics* (1987), *Selected Subaltern Studies* (ed., 1988), *The Post-Colonial Critic: Interviews, Strategies, Dialogues* (1990), *Thinking Academic Freedom in Gendered Post-Coloniality* (1993), *Outside in the Teaching Machine* (1993), *Imaginary Maps* (translation with critical introduction of three stories by Mahasweta Devi, 1994), *The Spivak Reader* (1995), *Breast*

Stories (translation with critical introduction of three stories by Mahasweta Devi, 1997), *Old Women* (translation with critical introduction of two stories by Mahasweta Devi, 1999), *Imperatives to Re-Imagine the Planet/Imperative zur Neuerfindung des Planeten* (ed. Willi Goetschel, 1999), *A Critique of Postcolonial Reason: Towards a History of the Vanishing Present* (1999), *Song for Kali: A Cycle* (translation with introduction of Ramproshad Sen, 2000), *Chotti Munda and His Arrow* (translation with critical introduction of a novel by Mahasweta Devi, 2002), *Death of a Discipline* (2003), *Other Asias* (2008), and "Red Thread" (forthcoming).

INDEX